Welfare Economics

Towards a More Complete Analysis

Yew-Kwang Ng
Personal Chair in Economics
Monash University
Australia

First published 2004 by
PALGRAVE MACMILLAN
Houndmills, Basingstoke, Hampshire RG21 6XS and
175 Fifth Avenue, New York, N.Y. 10010
Companies and representatives throughout the world

PALGRAVE MACMILLAN is the global academic imprint of the Palgrave Macmillan division of St. Martin's Press, LLC and of Palgrave Macmillan Ltd. Macmillan® is a registered trademark in the United States, United Kingdom and other countries. Palgrave is a registered trademark in the European Union and other countries.

ISBN 0–333–97121–3

This book is printed on paper suitable for recycling and made from fully managed and sustained forest sources.

A catalogue record for this book is available from the British Library.

Library of Congress Cataloging-in-Publication Data
Ng, Yew-Kwang.
    Welfare economics : towards a more complete analysis / Yew-Kwang Ng.
        p.   cm.
    Includes bibliographical references and index.
    ISBN 0–333–97121–3
    1. Welfare economics.   I. Title.
    HB99.3.N449 2003
    330.15′56—dc21   2003051788

10   9   8   7   6   5   4   3   2
13   12   11   10   09   08   07   06   05   04

Printed and bound in Great Britain by
Antony Rowe Ltd, Chippenham and Eastbourne

Contents

Preface

While it has been called 'welfare economics' for nearly a century, traditional welfare economics actually only analyses preferences. Recently I have been making a small effort to push the analysis to the level of real welfare, or happiness. This was the main reason for writing this book. Going deeper from the level of preference to that of welfare (that is, happiness) is necessary as preference is not our ultimate objective – happiness is. This extension can not only lead to new findings in welfare economics but also suggests a need for reformulation of the welfare foundation of public policy in general and cost–benefit analysis in particular.

In the last dozen years or so I have worked closely with my colleague Xiaokai Yang on the analysis of economies of specialisation that arise from the division of labour and the implications of these on growth, trade and the evolution of economic organisations. This analysis has included various welfare economic issues associated with increasing returns and organisational efficiency. The extension of welfare economic analysis to cover such issues is also discussed. Despite these extensions, the subtitle of this book is perhaps a little ambitious and more emphasis should be given to 'towards' than to 'complete', as it is very far from being a complete analysis.

The intended readers of this book include advanced undergraduates, graduates and specialists. The conflict that arises from the diversity of the intended readers is resolved by putting the more technical and advanced material into appendixes and by using an asterisk to denote material that the beginner can omit without losing continuity. The expert may, however, be particularly interested in this material. The same applies to the endnotes, which mostly contain bibliographical references or technical comments. Chapter sections marked with two asterisks contain new arguments. An asterisk after the title of a reference indicates that the work in question is more advanced, mathematical or touches on a technical point.

It might be thought that the diversity of the intended readers will render the book inefficient either as a basic textbook or as a treatise, but it is hoped that the following explanation will largely dispel any such apprehension. First, a textbook is read not only by students but also by lecturers. The former will benefit more from the basic discussions in this book and the latter from the more advanced parts. By getting lecturers actively interested in reading the book, more effective teaching may result when it is used as a text (lecturers do not always have the patience to read through basic textbooks). Meanwhile students who are encountering welfare economics for the first time may have the very slight inconvenience of having to skip some sections in the first reading, but will find that they are useful and provide interest for a second reading that will bring a much deeper understanding of welfare economics. Furthermore they may use this book and the many references therein as a guide to further study. By the time they reach the end they may find that the book is worth more than a basic text plus an advanced treatise (the two usually do not completely cohere with and complement each other).

Second, as a treatise it is useful for the author to explain the basic concepts and theories and his own opinions on them before he embarks on his own argumentation. In this regard experts may find that the basic discussion is worth reading. While some will find it a little too elementary, they should have little difficulty deciding which parts to skip. Similarly those readers who have some elementary training in or understanding of welfare economics and wish to advance their understanding, (for example graduate students and economists who do not specialise in welfare economics) may find it useful to review the basic concepts before going further. An explanation of the organisation of the book is provided in Section 1.5 and summaries are provided at the end of each chapter, before the appendices.

Partly because of the semitreatise nature of the book and partly because it is more efficient to deal with topics with which I am familiar, the selection of the non-basic topics is admittedly idiosyncratic. However I believe that a largely unbiased coverage has been achieved for the basic topics. Due to space limitation I have not been able to include detailed discussions of as many topics as I would have wished, but Appendix 12.1 is intended to remedy this. Moreover, due to time limitation and my other commitments I have not been able to improve the quality of the text as much as I would have liked. While the discussion may be a little terse in places and some ambiguities may be present, this has the advantage of provoking independent reasoning. In any event, if the reader has the patience to reread the unclear parts, comprehension should not be difficult to achieve. Beginners will find lecturers' instructions and seminar discussions helpful in this respect. For average beginners, therefore, the book might most profitably be used under instruction.

To make the book accessible to as large an audience as possible given the content, the discussion is mainly non-mathematical and relies heavily on simple two-dimensional illustrations. Mathematics is used only when essential and appears mainly in appendices. The conceptual discussions start from the very basic and proceed to the fairly complicated, including some new arguments. The features of the book that can be found in its previous incarnation (Ng, 1979/1983) include a methodological argument for a positive welfare economics (Chapter 1), a proposed rehabilitation of Little's welfare criterion (Sections 3.2.2 and 3.3), resolving Arrow's paradox of social choice by revealing the intensity of preferences (Section 5.4), the 'conscience effect' in externalities (Section 7.4) and above all a theory of third best (Sections 9.4 and 9.5) with an extension to the equity-efficiency consideration, reaching the remarkable conclusion that 'a dollar is a dollar to whomever it goes' (Appendix 9.1). New features include a proposed quasi-Pareto criterion that requires the potential for full compensation within each income group (Section 3.5), diamond goods (goods valued for their exchange value) and the havoc they play with the Marshallian measure of consumer surplus (Section 4.7), resolution of the paradox of interpersonal cardinal utility (Section 5.5), a reconsideration of the excess costs of financing for public spending that suggests economists grossly overestimate the costs of public spending (Section 8.2), and the argument that if economists as a group were aware of the true relationship of equality versus incentives they would be in favour of reverse distributional weighting, counting a dollar to the poor as worth less than a dollar to the rich in all specific cases (Section A9.1.4). The major new extensions are the two completely new chapters; Chapter 10, which examines welfare economic issues within the new Yang–Ng framework for economies of specialisation, and Chapter 11, which attempts to push the analysis beyond the traditional focus on preference to the ultimate level of happiness.

Happy reading!

YEW-KWANG NG

List of Abbreviations

AC	Average cost
CIC	Community indifference contour
CS	Compensating surplus
CV	Compensating variation
ES	Equivalent surplus
EV	Equivalent variation
GUFF	Grand utility feasibility frontier
IIA	Independence of irrelevant alternatives
MC	Marginal cost
MDE	Marginal dollar equivalent
MRS	Marginal rate of substitution
MRT	Marginal rate of transformation
MU	Marginal utility
MV	Marginal valuation
SWF	Social welfare function
UPC	Utility possibility curve
WMP	Weak majority preference

List of Symbols

G	Number of goods
I	Number of individuals
$x\,I^j y$	Individual J is indifferent between alternatives x and y
J, K	Our two individuals, Jan and Kevin
p	Price
$x\,P^i y$	Individual i prefers x to y
q	A given distribution of a collection (bundle) of goods
Q	A given collection of goods
xRy	xPy or xIy
U	Utility
W	Welfare
x^i_g	Amount of good g consumed by individual i
X, Y	Two representative goods

Note: Superscripts indicate different individuals, different situations or different bundles of goods; subscripts indicate different goods in the same bundle or different indifference levels for a given preference pattern (except in Chapter 7, where the individuals J and K appear in subscripts).

1
Introduction

Welfare economics is a very important branch of economic theory. It serves as a foundation for many applied (relatively speaking) branches of economics, such as public finance, cost–benefit analysis and the economics of government policy in many areas, including international trade, industry and welfare (social security and so on). The importance of welfare economics is scarcely in any doubt.

Most people would agree with Pigou (1922, who was the first to address welfare economics as an independent area of study), that 'practical usefulness, not necessarily, of course, immediate and direct, but still practical usefulness of some sort' is what we mainly look for in economic investigation. In other words, bearing fruit is more important than just shedding light. To apply economics beneficially in government policies and to solve social issues we need some guidelines or criteria. Most practical policy problems are not simple enough to allow easy answers. For example if a change will increase the national income but make it more unequally distributed, is it desirable? If a policy will make certain groups of people better off and others worse off, should it be adopted? Should government revenue be raised more by direct or by indirect taxes? Should we go for freer trade even if that will lead to the collapse of some industries? Is globalisation desirable? Should we tax or regulate pollution? To what extent should we conserve our scarce resources? Is economic growth a good thing? The study of welfare economics can help us to answer these questions, but just what is welfare economics?

(Beginners may find the methodological discussion in this chapter rather abstract. Nonetheless they are advised to read it and will come to understand it better after they have read a few more chapters. However if they cannot bear to read it, they can restrict their reading to Section 1.5 and go on to Chapter 2 without much loss of continuity. More advanced readers are advised to read the methodological discussion carefully.)

1

1.1   What is welfare economics?

Welfare economics is a branch of study that endeavours to formulate propositions that enable us to state that social welfare in one economic situation is greater or lesser than in another. This definition is not much different from the following one by Mishan (1969b, p. 13) 'Theoretical welfare economics is... that branch of study which endeavours to formulate propositions by which we may rank, on the scale of better or worse, alternative economic situations open to society.' In fact if we define social welfare as whatever is good, or whatever ought to be maximised, then the two definitions are identical. However the terms 'better' and 'worse' are explicitly normative, while 'social welfare' may be given a normative or a positive interpretation. It is true that most people tend to regard social welfare as a normative term, but there is no logical reason why we cannot adopt a positive definition of it. Two such definitions are presented below.

First, social welfare can be defined as a vector of individual welfares:

$$W = W(W^1, W^2, \ldots, W^I) \tag{1.1a}$$

where W^i is the welfare of the ith individual and I is the relevant number of individuals. Here individual welfare can be taken as an individual's well-being, or more explicitly, his or her happiness, with happiness subsuming both sensual pleasure and pain and spiritual delight and suffering. But how can individual (net) happiness be measured? One way of escaping this difficulty is to assume that individuals are the best judges of their own welfare and that they maximise this welfare. So whenever they prefer x to y they are assumed to be happier at x than at y. We can then use their utility function (which represents their preference) as an ordinal indicator of their welfare (on ordinal versus cardinal measurability, see Section 1.4). Alternatively we can define social welfare as a vector of individual (ordinal) utilities. One way or another, we have

$$W = (U^1, U^2, \ldots, U^I), \tag{1.1b}$$

where U^i is a utility function representing the ordinal preference of individual i. (We are not concerned here with the technical questions of the conditions that are necessary or sufficient for such a representation; for this see Ng, 1979/83, app. 1B.)

A vector is said to be larger than another if and only if some of its elements are larger than and none of its elements is smaller than the corresponding elements of the other vector. Thus if we define social welfare as a vector of individual welfares (or utilities), we say that social welfare increases if and only if W^i (or U^i) increases for some i and decreases for no i. If welfare increases for some individual and decreases for some other individual, the ordinal

change in social welfare (according to the vector definition) is undefined in sign and magnitude.

The vector concept of social welfare must be carefully distinguished from the concept of a Paretian social welfare function (SWF). The Pareto criterion says that social welfare increases if some individuals are made better off without any individual being made worse off, where 'better off' means 'happier' or 'in a more preferred situation'. A Paretian SWF accepts the Pareto criterion. Hence an increase in some W^i (or U^i) and a decrease in no W^i (or U^i) is a sufficient but not a necessary condition for an increase in social welfare. For example, for individuals to live in America it is sufficient that they live in New York, but it is not necessary for them to live in New York – they may instead live in Washington, which is also in America. Similarly if a change satisfies the Pareto criterion it must be regarded as a good change according to a Paretian SWF. But a change need not necessarily satisfy the Pareto criterion to be regarded as a good change. For example a change may make a few individuals marginally worse off but many individuals significantly better off, so it can be regarded as a good change by a Paretian SWF. A Paretian SWF can be written as

$$W = f(W^1, W^2, \ldots, W^I) \tag{1.2a}$$

$$\partial f / \partial W^i > 0 \text{ for all } i \tag{1.2b}$$

Equation 1.2a is an individualistic Bergson SWF (Bergson, 1938) and Equation 1.2b makes it Paretian. By the definition of a function, there exists only one value of W for each set of values of W^i, $i = 1, \ldots, I$. Thus if we have a (specific and fully defined) Paretian SWF we know that social welfare in an alternative situation is greater or lesser even if some W^i vary in opposite directions compared with the original situation. But for the vector concept of social welfare such a comparison is not available.

The vector concept of social welfare is of course of limited interest due to its avoidance of interpersonal comparisons of welfare or utility. Most people accept the Pareto criterion as a sufficient but not necessary condition for an increase in social welfare. But it is difficult to get people to agree on a specific Paretian SWF or to provide the necessary and sufficient condition for an increase in social welfare. Hence what is generally accepted is a vague, unspecified Paretian SWF in the form of Equation 1.2 but with the precise form of f unknown. Hence the vector concept of social welfare in a sense captures the 'minimum content' of this agreement. For example an analysis that deals only with the *necessary* conditions for Pareto optimality may be based on the vector concept of social welfare only. We can then say that the vector social welfare is not maximised unless such and such hold, whereupon the analysis does not have to be based even on the existence of a general unspecified form of SWF, Paretian or not, and one need not be concerned with the conditions for the existence of a mathematical function. Moreover even people who do not accept the Pareto value judgment can agree that the analysis has some objective meaning. This makes it possible to interpret welfare economics as a positive study.

Another positive definition of social welfare is the utilitarian concept of the sum total of individual happiness:

$$W = W^1 + W^2 + \ldots + W^I = \sum_{i=1}^{I} W^i \tag{1.3a}$$

or if a more objective indicator is desired, one may prefer:

$$W = U^1 + U^2 + \ldots + U^I = \sum_{i=1}^{I} U^i \tag{1.3b}$$

The advantage of adopting Equation 1.3 instead of Equation 1.1 is that with Equation 1.3 social welfare is not incomparable if some W^i increase and some decrease. A difficulty with Equation 1.3 is the problem of interpersonal comparison of welfare or utility (see Section 1.4). Since these individual welfare or utility indices are to be summed, we must be able to find a common unit. In other words the utility functions have to be unit comparable (Sen, 1970b). We shall return to this problem later. At the moment it is sufficient to note that while the problem of interpersonal comparability of utility is a tricky one, it is not insoluble in principle (see Section 5.4.1). It is conceivable that, perhaps several hundred (or a thousand) years from now, neurology may have advanced to the stage where the level of happiness can be accurately correlated to some cerebral reaction that can be measured by a 'eudaimonometer'. Hence the definition of social welfare in Equation 1.3 is an objective definition, although the objects are the subjective feelings of individuals. Deciding whether a particular dish is delicious is subjective, but the fact that a particular individual enjoys that dish is objective. However before we find a perfect 'eudaimonometer' we may disagree widely about the measurement of W^i or even U^i. But if we adopt an objective definition of individual welfare, or happiness or utility, such disagreement is a difference in the subjective judgment of fact, not a difference in basic value judgment (see Appendix 1.1 on the difference between basic value judgment and subjective judgments of fact). The question of whether we ought to pursue or maximise social welfare, as objectively defined in Equation 1.3, is a value question, but the analysis of objectively defined concepts can proceed with or without agreement on such a value question.

It is true that, unless objectively defined concepts are of some interest, analysis of them, while possible, is of little relevance. For example one may define X as the sum of the square root of the number of hairs of individuals divided by the sum of their bank account numbers, and analyse the factors that affect X. However such exercises are of little interest. Hence one would not build a welfare economics based on a definition of social welfare that appeals to no one. It will be argued in Section 5.4.1 that the concept of social welfare in Equation 1.3 is consistent with a widely acceptable set of value judgments. It is, however, unlikely that any specific concept of social welfare will find universal acceptance as the right objective to maximise. For example even the Pareto value judgment, which seems so mild and reasonable, has its vehement opponents (although it is likely that the opposition is based on a misunderstanding of the Pareto value judgment – see Section 2.1). Conversely the seemingly crazy objective of maximising the welfare of the worst off (implying a zero trade-off between the welfare of the second worst off and that of the worst off) attracts overwhelming attention and has a sizeable group of adherents. Thus what welfare economists can do is to use either a concept of social welfare that they believe to be the right objective, the one that most people or the government believe to be so, or some compromise. This is not very different from other branches of study. For example one may investigate ways to preserve 'mo-xu-you'. This line of research may prove highly useful if mo-xu-you becomes very scarce relative to demand. Even if mo-xu-you remains a free good, its study may not be of much use but it still constitutes a part of our scientific knowledge.

The advantage of adopting an objective definition of social welfare is that it enables us to regard welfare economics as a positive study. However, whether welfare economics is positive or normative is by no means widely agreed upon in the profession.

1.2 Is welfare economics a positive or normative study?

A positive study asks the question. What is? A normative study asks the question: what ought to be? According to Mill (1844, pp. 123–4), 'These two ideas differ from one another as the understanding differs from the will, or as the indicative mood in grammar differs from the imperative. The one deals in facts, the other in precepts. Science is a collection of truths; art, a body of rules, or directions for conduct.' Positive propositions can be verified or falsified, or at least are verifiable or falsifiable in principle. Normative propositions, on the other hand, cannot be true or false; they can only be persuasive or otherwise.

Now, what about welfare economics? While there is no consensus, a majority of economists seem to regard welfare economics as normative (although a minority emphasise the importance of ethics in economics – see for example Hennipman, 1995; Vickers, 1997). This seems a little curious as a majority also regard economics as a science. If economics is a science (which is positive), then welfare economics, as part of economics, should also be a positive study. But is welfare economics perhaps not part of economics? There is an apparent inconsistency here.

The answer to our question depends on our attitude towards the study of welfare economics. If we define social welfare in some positive sense and confine ourselves to studying the economic factors that affect social welfare, then it is a positive study. On the other hand, if we want to go a step further and do not confine ourselves to saying that a certain measure will increase social welfare (defined in some positive sense), but try to say that a certain measure should be adopted, then we are adopting normative language. We can, however, avoid making value judgments by instead saying, 'If the objective is such and such, then the measure should be undertaken', without committing ourselves to the value judgments behind the objective function.

One possible objection to our attempt to define the concept of social welfare in a positive sense should be considered. The term social welfare has been so widely used in the normative sense that any attempt to define it positively is more likely to cause confusion than to clarify the issue. To forestall such an objection we can refer to the vector concept of social welfare as the welfare vector and to the Benthamite (that is, utilitarian) concept of social welfare as the welfare aggregate.

Little objection can be raised against the concept of welfare vector, apart, perhaps, from its limited usefulness. The concept of welfare aggregate presents more difficulties. Before we can aggregate individual welfares we must be able to measure them and compare them. This requires us to consider the distinction between welfare and utility before considering the problem of utility measurability and interpersonal comparability.

1.3   Welfare versus utility*

It was stated above that one way to reduce the difficulty of measuring individuals' welfare is to take their preference as an indicator of their welfare, such that whenever they prefer x to y we infer that their welfare is higher in x than in y. There are, however, three reasons why this may not always be a good indicator.

First, preference may differ from welfare due to ignorance and imperfect foresight. While individuals may prefer x to y believing that they will be better off in x than in y, it may turn out to be the other way round. This is the question of *ex ante* estimate versus *ex post* welfare. (The recent distinction by Kahneman *et al.*, 1997, between decision utility and experienced utility is based on the same difference.) While the *ex ante* concept is relevant for explaining behaviour, it is the *ex post* one that is actual welfare. Thus Harsanyi (1997) emphasises that informed preferences should be used for normative purposes instead of actual preferences.

Second, the preference of individuals may be affected not only by their own welfare but also by their consideration for the welfare of others. Thus it is possible for individuals to prefer x to y and yet be less happy in x than in y because they believe that other people are happier in x than in y. While it is true that the belief that other people are happy may make them happy, this may not be strong enough to outweigh the loss they suffer from changing from y to x. For example individuals may vote for party x, even though they know that they will be better off with party y in government. The reason why they vote for x is that they believe that the majority of the people will be much better off with x. This may make them feel better (affective altruism) and is a type of external effect. Although this external benefit may not be important enough to compensate for, in terms of subjective happiness, their personal loss, say in income, under x, they may yet vote for x due to their moral concern (non-affective altruism) for the majority. To give an even more dramatic example, consider a group of individuals who expect to lead a very happy life. If their country is invaded they may volunteer for a mission that is certain to result in their death. The prospect of being citizens of a conquered country – especially when added to the guilty conscience that would come from failing to volunteer for the mission – may not be too bright, but overall they might still be fairly happy to lead such a life. Yet they choose death for the sake of their fellow countrymen. They do not maximise their own welfare. (This divergence between welfare and preference due to consideration for others is discussed in Ng, 1969b, p. 43; Ng, 1999a; Sen, 1973c.)

Some economists have difficulty seeing the distinction between preference and welfare, saying that whenever individuals prefer x to y they must be, or at least believe themselves to be, happier in x than in y. This difficulty is completely baffling. Clearly parents often sacrifice their happiness for the welfare of their children, and it is not easy to see why similar sacrifices cannot be made for a friend, relative, fellow countryman, any other human being on any sentient creature. (For interviews with real-life altruists, see Monroe, 1996, Part I. For a survey of evidence of true altruism, see Hoffman, 1981. One piece of evidence is that a person is more likely to help someone when he or she is the only other person around, contrary to the egoistic explanation that help is given merely to gain the approval of onlookers. Cf. Charness and Rabin, 2002.)

It may be doubted that the existence of true, non-affective altruism is consistent with Darwinian natural selection. However preferences are the result of both cultural and genetic inheritance, and it has been demonstrated that prosocial traits might well have evolved under the joint influence of cultural and genetic transmission (Boyd and Richerson, 1985; Sober and Wilson, 1998; Bowles, 2000).[1]

---

1. Moreover, 'highly developed human capacities for insider-outsider distinctions and cultural uniformity within communities greatly increase the likely importance of group selection of genetically transmitted traits and hence the evolutionary viability of group-beneficial traits' (Bowles and Gintis, 2000, p. 1419). On the evolutionary basis of altruism towards one's relatives, see Hamilton (1964) and Bergstrom (1996).

If some readers doubt the existence of truly non-affective altruism, they may be convinced that in fact they themselves possess some degree of non-affective altruism if they consider the following hypothetical choice. Suppose that you are asked by the Devil to press either button A or button B within two seconds. You know with certainty that one of the following will happen depending on which button you press. During the two seconds you will be so preoccupied with pressing the right button that your welfare will be zero whichever button you press. After pressing you will lose your memory of the present world and hence will feel no guilt, warm glow or the like, irrespective of which button you press.

- Button A: you will go to Bliss with a welfare level of 1 000 000 trillion units. Everyone else will go to Hell with a welfare level of minus 1 000 000 trillion units each.
- Button B: you will go to Bliss Minus with a welfare level of 999 999 trillion units. Everyone else will go Niceland with a welfare level of 999 trillion units each.
- If you press neither button within the two seconds, you and everyone else will go to Hell.

By construction, choosing A will maximize your welfare but most people will choose B out of non-affective altruism. If you still think that you will choose A, change Bliss Minus into a welfare level of 999 999.999999999 trillion units. If you still opt for A, it has to be conceded that you are not non-affectively altruistic. But how could you have the heart to condemn all others to Hell for a fractional increase in your own welfare? (In my view the existence and degree of non-affective altruism marks true morality.)

Assuming that the preference of an individual can be represented by a utility function (on which see Ng, 1979/83, app. 1B), the difference between welfare and preference discussed above may be illustrated thus. The preference of a rational individual with perfect knowledge (irrationality will be discussed below) is in general a function of the welfare of all individuals.[2] It terms of her or his utility function, we have:

---

2. While Equation 1.4 is a much more general function than the usual utility function, it still involves some simplification. Apart from its incomplete account of irrationality, it also largely ignores such factors as agency (one may prefer to be the one who helps to increase the welfare of others; see Sen, 1987), though to some extent such factors could be partially accounted for by interpreting some of the x's in Equation 1.5 as donations, activities that help others and so on (but the causal connections between such activities and the welfare of others are difficult to reflect in the simplified formulation in the text). This simplification is similar to that of the usual utility function, where only the amounts of goods consumed are important, not how they are acquired and so on.

$$U^i = U^i (W^1, W^2, \ldots, W^I) \tag{1.4}$$

In general it is not true that individual i prefers x to y if and only if $W^i(x) > W^i(y)$. This is so for the special (though it may be a very important) case of a 'self-concerned' individual (who has no non-affective altruism), where $U^i = U^i(W^i)$. Even for such a self-concerned individual, his or her welfare may still assume the following general form

$$W^i = W^i(x_1^1, \ldots, x_G^1, x_1^2, \ldots, x_G^2, \ldots, x_G^I, W^1, \ldots, W^{i-1}, W^{i+1}, \ldots, W^I)$$

$$\equiv W^i(x_{g=1,\ldots,G}^{i=1,\ldots,I}; W^{j\neq i}), \tag{1.5}$$

where x_g^j is the value of the gth variable (good, service or activity) by the jth individual, and $x_{g=1,\ldots,G}^{i=1,\ldots,I}$ is just a shorthand way of writing the I times G variables. It should be noted that $\partial w^i/\partial x_g^i$ in Equation 1.5 includes only the direct effect – for example the effect of your smoking on my health – and does not include the indirect effect through W^j, since that is included in $(\partial w^i/\partial w^j)(\partial w^j/\partial x_g^j)$, for example the effect of your smoking on your health (hence welfare), which affects my welfare if I mind about your welfare.

Self-concerned individuals must be distinguished from 'self-minded' and 'self-attending' ones. Self-concerned people have no concern for the welfare of others except insofar as their own welfare is affected. The welfare (but not necessarily also the preference) of self-minded individuals is not affected by the *welfare* of others. The welfare of self-attending individuals is not affected by the *activities* of others. Individuals who are both self-minded and self-attending can be called 'self-regarding'.

In our world of pervasive interdependence the existence of a truly self-attending person is doubtful, though for certain problems it can be assumed for analytical simplicity without much loss. Non-self-concerned (if to do with positive concern) can also be termed non-affective altruism, while non-self-minded can be called affective altruism. Self-concerned individuals are more likely to exist (it could be suggested that over 90 per cent of people are 99.9 percent self-concerned except with respect to their immediate family.) Generous people who help others a lot are not necessarily non-self-concerned since they may only be providing that help because it makes them feel happy. In other words, affective altruists are more common than non-affective altruists.

A self-centred individual is one who is both self-concerned and self-minding:

$$U^i = U^i\left(W^i[X_{g=1,\ldots,G}^{j=1,\ldots,I}]\right) = f^i\left(X_{g=1,\ldots,G}^{j=1,\ldots,I}\right). \tag{1.6}$$

If this individual is also self-regarding, he or she can be called extremely self-centred:

$$U^i = U^i\left(W^i\left[X^i_{g=1,\ldots,G}\right]\right) = f^i\left(X^i_{g=1,\ldots,G}\right). \tag{1.7}$$

It might be thought that our classification of self-concerned and so on is rather artificial and useless. However for certain problems the distinction provides insights that have policy implications. For example the presence of non-affective altruism may render the Pareto principle with respect to preference unacceptable (Ng, 2000a, app. D) and either affective and/or non-affective altruism may render the Coase Theorem invalid (see Section 7.4 below).

Third, individuals may have irrational preferences. The preference of individuals is defined as irrational if they prefer x over y despite the fact that their welfare is higher in y than in x, and their preference is unaffected by considerations of the welfare of other individuals (any sentient creature can be an individual here), or by ignorance or imperfect foresight. The definition of irrationality is such as to make the three factors discussed here exhaustive causes of divergence between preference and welfare.

While few if any individuals are perfectly ignorant and irrational, some degrees of ignorance (or imperfect information) and imperfect rationality clearly apply to most individuals (for reviews of the relevant literature in philosophy and psychology see Cohen, 1983; Evans and Over, 1996; Kahneman and Tversky, 1996; Stein, 1996), though some alleged irrationalities could be simply due to errors, computational limitations and incorrect norms by the experimenters (Stanovich and West, 2000). There are a number of causes other than ignorance and a concern for the welfare of others, that may make preferences differ from happiness and hence be irrational according to the definition here. The following two (perhaps not completely independent) causes can both be explained, or at least partly, by biological factors (on the biological basis of social behaviour see Wilson, 1975; Crawford and Kreps, 1998).

First, there is the tendency among many people to discount the future or even to ignore it completely. This tendency has been widely noted, including by economists. For example Pigou (1929, p. 25) called it the 'faulty telescopic faculty', Ramsey (1928, p. 543) called it 'weakness of imagination' about the future, and Harrod (1948, p. 40) regarded it as the 'conquest of reason by passion'. Discounting future consumption, income and any other monetary value is rational as a dollar now can be transformed into more than a dollar in the future. Discounting future utility may still be rational if realisation of the future utility is uncertain (for healthy people, this uncertainty is usually very small). Discounting the future for more than these acceptable reasons is probably irrational. A manifestation of such irrationality is insufficient savings for old age, necessitating compulsory and heavily subsidised superannuation schemes. The present author came across an extreme example of the failure to provide properly for retirement during a survey on how much more people would be willing to save if the rate of interest were higher (Ng, 1992a). The question implicitly assumed that everyone did some saving, as the answers were in terms of the extra percentage that would be saved. One subject declared that he did not save anything. He was then asked to change the answer 'saving 20 percent more' into 'saving $20 more per month' but he still said he could not be persuaded to save anything no matter what the interest rate (500 per cent was mentioned). He only conceded a willingness to save when he was asked 'What if a dollar saved now becomes a million dollars next year?' I was careful to find out that this healthy looking young man was not expecting an early death from a terminal disease or the like.

The behaviour of most other animals is largely determined by preprogrammed instincts rather than a careful calculation of present costs versus future benefits. The storing of food by ants, squirrels and so on is largely, if not completely, instinctive. If calculated choices are made by animals, they are largely confined to sizing up the current situation to decide the best move at the moment, such as fight or flight. The ability to anticipate rewards in the fairly distant future requires much more reason, imagination and 'telescopic faculty'. While we know that we are endowed with such a faculty, because it is virtually absent in most other species it is natural to conclude that it is not yet fully developed in our own, and that different members of our species will possess it to differing degrees. Moreover, as Ben-Ner and Putterman (2000, p. 95) put it, 'Given the cumulative character of biological change – that is, its tendency to build opportunistically on pre-existing structures – the evolutionary approach leads us to expect that the mind is most unlikely to be a perfect reasoning machine.'

Second, there is the excessive temptation of pleasure (especially present pleasure versus future costs, which relates this cause to the preceding one) and powerful biological drives. After the evolution of flexible species (defined as those whose behaviour was governed not only by automatic programmed responses but also by choice), natural selection ensured that choices would be consistent with fitness by endowing flexible species with a reward–penalty system. Thus eating when hungry and mating with fertile members of the opposite sex were rewarded with pleasure, and damage to the body was penalised with pain. (This meant that flexible species were also 'rational', as defined by Ng, 1996b, who shows that complex niches favoured rational species that made the environment even more complex, leading to a virtuous cycle that accelerated the rate of evolution. This partly explains the dramatic speed of evolution based mainly on random mutation and natural selection, a speed doubted by creationists.)

On top of *ex post* rewards and penalties, we are endowed with inner drives to satisfy fitness-enhancing functions such as mating. On the whole these powerful temptations and drives work in the right direction, making us do things that enhance both our biological fitness and own psychological welfare. However, since evolution is largely to do with fitness maximisation and the welfare-enhancing aspect only indirectly enhances fitness, some divergence between our behaviour and our welfare is inevitable, as our behaviour is determined not only by rational calculation but also by programmed inclinations, including drives. (See Ng, 1995, on the divergence between fitness and welfare maximisation, especially with respect to the number of offspring.) It has also been shown that 'wanting' (or preference) and 'liking' (or welfare) are mediated by different neural systems in the brain and are psychologically dissociable from each other. In other words individuals may prefer something without liking it or prefer something more strongly than can be justified by their liking for it, and *vice versa*. In particular, neural sensitisation of the brain's dopamine system by addictive drugs can create an intense want that goes far beyond that which can be explained by a mere liking of the drugs and the need to relieve withdrawal symptoms (see Berridge, 1999, for a review). As an example of powerful drives, adolescent girls and boys are often propelled by their sexual drive to engage in careless sexual acts, despite the risks to their long-term welfare, such as an unwanted pregnancy or the contracting of Aids. While this is partly due to ignorance, the power of biological drives cannot be denied.

Consider a specific example. Suppose that a man agrees that, in the case of choices that involve risks, the correct thing to do is to maximise expected welfare (assuming there are no effects on the welfare of others) and actually does so for most choices. However for choices to do with sex he chooses x over y even though his expected welfare is lower with x than with y and he knows this to be the case. Here x may involve having sex with many persons without clear knowledge of whether they have Aids (this knowledge, it is assumed, is not feasible to obtain and hence not relevant). His (expected) welfare-reducing choice of x may be due to the biological inclination to have many sexual encounters. He knows that doing so gives him a not insignificant chance of contracting Aids and hence is welfare-reducing. He has all the relevant feasible information and yet chooses (due to the powerful sex drive) x which he knows to be of lower expected welfare. (This is not really a hypothetical example. It can be confidently stated that, out of 100 average adult males, at least 10 have actually made such a choice. If one wants more solid evidence, one only has to look at the frequency of prostitution and extramarital sex.) Should we call this preference informed as the person has all the relevant feasible information, or not informed because it is not in accord with his real interests?

The above two causes of irrational preference illustrate the point that, due either to imperfections in our endowed faculties or to the biological bias in favour of reproductive fitness, we may do things that not are consistent with our welfare. The question here is, for normative purposes should we use welfare or actual preferences/behaviour? Clearly we should use welfare instead of behaviour dictated by biological fitness. According to an old Chinese dictum, 'Out of the three unfilial acts, not having offspring is the greatest'. However for the human species as a whole the population is certainly not getting smaller, and any long-term social welfare function that accounts for the welfare of future generations should account for that. If we were to go for biological fitness, we would prefer unlimited procreation to a smaller population with a higher aggregate welfare even if we would all be suffering with the former option. 'We' are the feeling selves who ultimately care about our welfare (positive minus negative affective feelings). 'We' are not 'them', the unfeeling genes that urge us to maximise our reproductive fitness. Unlike species that are almost completely controlled by their genes and the environment, we are able to change our reproductive fate by using such measures as birth control. For normative issues it is our welfare, rather than the dictates of unfeeling genes, that should count. (For a survey of different concepts of individual welfare see Ackerman *et al.*, 1997.)

In addition to the above biological causes there is another source of imperfect rationality. Individuals may stick rigidly to some habit, custom, principle or the like even if they know that this is detrimental to their present or future welfare and the welfare of others, taking account of all effects and repercussions. Customs, rules, moral principles and so on have a rational basis as they provide simple guides to behaviour that is, or at least on the whole, conducive to social welfare. It would be too cumbersome and time-consuming for individuals to weigh the potential gains and losses in terms of social welfare or their own welfare each time they had to make a decision. Hence they tend to stick to their routines, rules, principles and so on without thinking about the gains and losses. If this occasionally results in decisions that are inconsistent with their welfare and the welfare of others, it can be regarded as a cost of pursuing generally good rules. If, say, there is a change in circumstances, strict adherence to some rules may result in persistent net losses in welfare, taking everything into account. Individuals may stick to these rules without knowing that they are no longer conducive to welfare. Then the divergence between preference and welfare can be attributed to ignorance. If they know this and still stick to the rules, they are irrational.

Many readers may disagree with the definition of irrationality adopted here. For example, suppose a man sticks rigidly to the principle of honesty and would not tell a lie even if that would save his life and contribute to the welfare of others, taking everything else into account. According to our definition here, he is acting irrationally, but for those who see honesty as an ultimate good in itself, he may not be irrational. But are there not occasions when it is better to tell a lie? Should not one lie to an invading army that is known to be cruel and unscrupulous? If we were to press hard enough with such questions, it is likely that most people would ultimately rely on welfare as the justification for any moral principles such as honesty. Personally, I take the (weighted or unweighted) aggregate welfare of all sentient creatures or a part thereof as the only rational ultimate end (my basic value judgment – see Appendix 1.1), and hence define irrationality accordingly. I am aware of the controversial nature of this definition, but it is not necessary to agree with the definition of irrationality given here to agree with the arguments of this book. If preferred, the word 'irrational', as used here, could be taken as 'irrational according to the objective of welfare maximisation'.

However are moral principles really fundamental? Before the development of morality and the like, we (perhaps still in the form of apes) had no moral or other principles, no concept of commitment and justice, and so on. Self-interest dominated, although this does not preclude the existence of genetically endowed altruism for the maximisation of inclusive fitness. As we evolved and relied more and more on our higher intelligence and social interaction for survival, moral feelings also evolved and helped our survival by encouraging cooperation. This was enhanced by recognising the importance of such moral practices as honesty in aiding our struggle against nature (including wild animals) and competing human groups. No one can deny that the initial evolution/development of morality must have been purely instrumental in enhancing our welfare and/or our survival and reproductive fitness as morality had not previously existed. We then learned and taught our children to value moral principles and so on in order to increase the degree of adherence to these principles and hence improve our welfare. Eventually some if not most people came to value these principles for themselves, by learning and probably also instinctively. The evolution of such commitment-enhancing devices as blushing might have been fitness-enhancing (see Frank, 1987). Failure to see the ultimate values is a kind of illusion fostered by learning (one dare not say indoctrination) and perhaps genetics. However it is possible to have considerable respect for people with such illusions – they probably make better citizens, friends and colleagues. But illusions they are nevertheless, or at least at the analytical or critical level. While on the whole they are positive in that they help maintain moral standards, they do have a cost in that they delay the rejection of certain outdated moral principles.

One real-world example where violation of the preferences of people actually improved their welfare happened in the mid 1960s in Singapore under Lee Kuan Yew's government. Lee decided to expropriate a cemetery and use the land for public development. The human remains were exhumed and reburied elsewhere. This could be regarded as extreme violation of the sanctity of the dead and most descendants would not accept a small fortune in compensation for it. Even if the government had only to pay a small fraction of the willingness to accept, the sum would certainly have turned out to be prohibitive. However it can be argued that Lee was right to attend to the welfare of the living rather than the dead, even if this went against people's wishes, failed to pass the traditional cost–benefit test based on preferences, and failed to to pass a democratic vote (also based on preferences).

It is interesting to examine why people's preference should not prevail in this case. First, it was partly due to the external costs created by excessive respect for the sanctity of the dead. An individual who failed to show due respect would have run the risk of social censure. Due respect for the dead may have served a useful function but it had become excessive due to complex social customs, including the individually rational but socially harmful strategy of pretending to be very respectful. (If this reason can be explained by traditional analysis in terms of external costs, the next one cannot.) Second, even abstracting away the danger of social disrespect, individuals might have genuinely found it unacceptable for the remains of their relatives to be disturbed. However as the order for compulsory exhumation was made by the government they would have accepted it as unavoidable and beyond their control, and hence would have suffered little loss in welfare. It was thus more than a publicness problem. If the decision had been put to the vote, most of them would have felt compelled by respect for the dead to vote against development of the site. But as the decision had been made for them by the government their distress might not have been as great. Thus Lee's decision almost certainly increased social welfare despite being against the preferences of the people. (However this very exceptional example does not justify autocratic decisions against the will of people in general.)

An interesting question arises as to how we should classify the second aspect of the above example according to our tripartite classification (imperfect knowledge, concern for the welfare of others, and imperfect rationality). It could be thought that, provided that the dead are included under 'others', it should be classified as concern for the welfare of others. However until there is evidence to convince us otherwise, it can be said that the dead are not capable of having welfare. Hence it should be classified as imperfect rationality. According to our definition of rationality it is not (perfectly) rational to put respect for the dead over and above the welfare of the living, apart from such concerns as fear of social ostracisation.

Despite the above discussion of divergence between welfare and utility, it is convenient to ignore such divergences except when we come to discuss problems where divergence is important (such as in the case of merit goods and materialistic bias, as discussed in Section 12.3 and Chapter 11 respectively). In other words, in the absence of specific evidence/considerations to the contrary we shall assume that, as a rule, all individuals are the best judges of their own welfare and choose to maximise their welfare. Then the question of welfare measurability coincides with that of utility measurability, to which we now turn.

1.4   Utility measurability and interpersonal comparability

Many students of economics have at some stage been baffled by the controversy over whether utility is measurable or not measurable, cardinally measurable or just ordinally measurable. Ordinal measurability involves the ability to rank. One can say that utility at x is higher than that at y, but one cannot specify how much higher, or compare the differences in utility. Thus one cannot say whether utility at x is higher than that at y by an amount more or less than the amount the utility at y is higher than that at z. If utility is just ordinally measurable, the utility function is said to be unique up to a positive monotonic transformation, since any positive monotonic transformation of a function ($f = g(U)$, $g' > 0$) leaves the ranking unchanged. On the other hand the measurability of utility *differences* makes the utility function unique up to a positive affine transformation, sometimes called a linear transformation ($f = a + bU$, where a and b are constants and b is positive). This transformation leaves the proportions of utility differences unchanged. With full cardinal measurability the only permissible transformation is a positive proportionate one (*Let $f = bU$, where b is* a positive constant). One can then say how many times utility at x is equal to that at y and also know what corresponds to zero utility.

The confusion over utility measurability is partly due to the use of the term 'utility' both as a measure of subjective satisfaction and as an indicator of objective choice or preference. Another source of confusion is the insufficient distinction between measurability in principle and measurability in practice. In the case of utility as a measure of the subjective satisfaction of an individual, it seems clear that it is cardinally measurable in principle, though in practice it can be very difficult. The difficulties include inaccuracies and possible dishonesty in preference revelation. Moreover even the individual concerned may find it difficult to give a precise measure. For example I prefer grapefruit to oranges and prefer oranges to apples. If you ask me, 'Do you prefer a grapefruit to an orange more strongly than an orange to an apple? I will say, 'That depends on what kinds of fruit I have eaten recently, and on what sort of meal I am having'. If all these are known, then I will be able to give a definite answer. Thus, subject to practical difficulties, my subjective utility is cardinally measurable. If it was just ordinally measurable I would not just have difficulty answering the question, I would also dismiss it as meaningless. It seems clear that any individual will be able to compare the difference in subjective utility between having an apple and an orange and that between having an orange and a house, and be able to compare the difference in subjective disutility between the bite of an ant and the sting of a bee and that between a sting of a bee and having the right arm cut off.

It also seems meaningful to say that I was at least twice as happy in 2002 as in 1992. If I have a perfect memory, I may even be able to pin down the ratio of happiness to, say, 2.8. It also seems sensible for someone to say, 'Had I known the suffering I would undergo I would have committed suicide long ago', or 'If I had to lead such a miserable life, I would wish I had never been born'. Hence, it makes sense to speak of negative or positive utility. Somewhere in the middle there is something corresponding to zero utility. According to Armstrong (1951, p. 269),

There can be little doubt that an individual, apart from his attitude of preference or indifference to a pair of alternatives, may also desire an alternative not in the sense of preferring it to some other alternative, or may have an aversion towards it not in the sense of contra-preferring it to some other alternative. There seem to be pleasant situations that are intrinsically desirable and painful situations that are intrinsically repugnant. It does not seem unreasonable to postulate that welfare is +*ve* in the former case and −*ve* in the latter.

Hence it seems clear that utility or welfare as a subjective feeling is in principle measurable in a full cardinal sense.

On the other hand we can use a utility function purely as an objective indicator of individuals' preference ordering, such that $U(x) > U(y)$ if and only if they prefer x to y and $U(x) = U(y)$ if and only if they are indifferent; and we may not be interested in anything other than the above ordinal aspect of the utility function. Then any monotonically increasing transformation of a valid utility function is an acceptable indicator and a utility function possesses only ordinal significance. For some problems (such as the theory of consumer choice), knowledge of the preference orderings is all that is required and hence an analyst can abstract away the cardinal aspect of the utility function. This, however, does not mean that for problems where the intensity of preference is relevant (such as social choice), one cannot adopt cardinal utility functions, provided due attention is paid to the practical difficulties. To deny the use of cardinal utility is to commit what could be called the 'fallacy of misplaced abstraction'. The technical problems with the existence of a utility function that represents an individual's preference are discussed in Ng (1979/83, app. 1B). Here we shall, for the most part, take the existence of a utility function for granted. We now turn to the problem of interpersonal comparisons of utility.

Different types and degrees of comparability can be distinguished. Level comparability refers to the comparison of total utilities; it answers questions such as 'Is person *J* happier than person *K*?' Unit comparability refers to differences in utilities between situations. It answers questions such as 'Is *J* made better off by more than *K* is made worse off by moving from *x* to *y*?' Full comparability subsumes the possibility of both level comparability and unit comparability. Non-comparability excludes both. In between lies partial comparability (Sen, 1970a, p. 99, 1970b) where rough, imprecise comparisons of units or levels of utilities can be made. Different social welfare functions and different problems need different types of comparability (Sen, 1974, 1977b). For example if we are interested in maximising the sum of individual utilities given the number of individuals, then what we need is unit comparability. On the other hand, if we adopt the Rawlsian criterion of maximising the welfare of the worst-off individual, what we need is level comparability (contrary to common belief, the general possibility of level comparability implies unit comparability under fairly general conditions – see Ng, 1984c).

There is a long tradition among economists to regard statements that involve interpersonal comparisons of utility as value judgments (Robbins, 1932, 1938; Wicksteed, 1933). I have argued elsewhere (Ng, 1972b, 1997; see also Appendix 1.1) that such statements are just subjective judgments of fact. The judgment that J is happier than K and that J's gain in happiness will exceed K's loss of happiness if there is a change from x to y does not imply what ought to be done until an objective function (which necessarily involves value judgments) is specified. Thus if our objective is to maximise the sum of utilities, we choose y; if we want to maximise the utility of the worst-off individual, we choose x (assuming that K is and will remain the worst-off individual). Judgments that involve interpersonal comparisons of utility are subjective judgments of fact even though the facts are the subjective feelings of individuals. However, due to this subjective nature it is very difficult to measure individual utilities and to compare them interpersonally with any degree of precision. While such difficulties should not be underestimated, they do not make interpersonal comparisons value judgments.

1.5   The organisation of the book

The rest of this book is organised as follows. Chapter 2 is devoted to Pareto optimality and emphasises the *necessary* conditions for optimality. Chapter 3, on welfare criteria, is concerned with the *sufficient* conditions for social improvement (qualitative), and in Chapter 4 the more quantitative topic of consumer surplus is discussed. Chapters 5 and 6 address the issues of social choice and income distribution, respectively. In Chapter 7 the focus shifts to market imperfections. Perhaps the most important of these is externality (including pollution – students of mine who smoked stopped doing so after this topic had been covered). A special category of externality – public goods – is considered in Chapter 8. When discussing market imperfections the question of second best arises when some of the optimal conditions cannot be met. The theory of second best, as well as the present author's theory of third best and its application to derive a principle of treating a dollar as a dollar in specific issues, are discussed in Chapter 9. Chapter 10 discusses welfare economic issues raised by the Yang–Ng framework when analysing the division of labour and the evolution of economic organisations. Chapter 11 attempts to push welfare analysis from the level of preferences to that of happiness. Finally, Chapter 12 touches on wider welfare issues and speculates about the need for an interdisciplinary study of happiness.

As outlined in the Preface, some of the chapter sections and appendices are marked with asterisks. In the main, the ones without asterisks contain basic material that is essential for beginners. The ones with a single asterisk are a little more advanced and are likely to appeal to those who already have a basic knowledge of welfare economics. Those with two asterisks contain new arguments of interest to the expert (although beginners may attempt to read all the sections and appendices if they do not find them too demanding). The attention of experts is also drawn to the following: the methodological issues discussed in this chapter and its appendix; in Chapter 3, the assessment of Little and Mishan's argument with respect to welfare criteria (Sections 3.2.2 and 3.3), and the quasi-Pareto criterion proposed by the present author (Section 3.5); in Chapter 4, Appendix 4.2; in Chapter 8, overestimation of the costs of public spending (Section 8.2), and the Clarke–Groves incentive-compatible mechanism for preference revelation (Section 8.3); in Chapter 9, the theory of third best (Section 9.4); and the entirety of Chapters 10 and 11.

1.6 Summary

Welfare economics is a branch of study that endeavours to formulate propositions that enable us to state that social welfare in one economic situation is greater or lesser than in another. It can be regarded as a positive study if a positive definition of social welfare is adapted or if the social welfare function is taken as given. Usually, social welfare is taken as some function of individual welfares or utilities. Welfare may diverge from utility (or preference) due to a concern for the welfare of others, or to ignorance or irrationality. Subject to practical difficulties, individual utility can be cardinally measured; interpersonal comparisons of utility are not value judgments. Distinguishing basic value judgments from subjective judgments of fact enhances the role of economists in policy recommendation (Appendix 1.1).

Appendix 1.1: Basic Value Judgments and Subjective Judgments of Fact

When there is a disagreement about policy matters, about what ought to be done, it is usually said that this is a matter of different value judgments on which no objective discussion is possible. In the second section it will be shown that this is not usually true, but first we shall consider a revised (or sister) definition of Sen's concept of basic value judgment.

A1.1.1   Positive statements versus value judgments

Positive statements are concerned with what is, what was or what will be in the objective sense; normative statements (or value judgments) are concerned with what ought to be, what is morally right or wrong, good or bad. This is a sufficiently clear distinction for our purposes. It is true that the philosophical problems of metanormative theory are by no means completely settled; there is much scope for disagreement about whether the statement 'this picture is beautiful' is positive or normative. (I regard the statement as positive if it means 'this picture appears beautiful to me', as evaluative if it means 'I think this is a beautiful picture', and as normative if it means 'this picture *is* beautiful!', implying that others should accept it as beautiful.) But for the present purpose the finer distinctions between the evaluative, the ethical and the normative are not of direct importance and will therefore be disregarded. What will be emphasised is the distinction between basic and non-basic (or derived) value judgments.

A1.1.2   Basic versus non-basic value judgments*

Sen (1970a, p. 59) defines basic judgments as follows: 'A value judgment can be called "basic" to a person, if the judgment is supposed to apply under all conceivable circumstances, and it is "non-basic" otherwise.' For example individuals may judge that 'An increase in national income indicates a better situation' (judgment A). This is not a basic value judgment if they agree that an increase in the national income would not signify a better situation if the poor were made much poorer. If they were to revise their judgment and say that, 'For a poor country in which everyone had the same income, it would be a better situation, *ceteris paribus*, if everyone's income increased by the same amount' (judgment B), and they stuck to this under all circumstances, should we regard it as their basic value judgment? If we were to ask 'Why do you regard that as a better situation?' and they replied that it was because everyone would become happier, then it would be reasonable to regard judgment B as non-basic (to those individuals).

In the above example the individuals may believe that 'It is desirable to make every individual happier' (judgment C). They stick to judgment B under all circumstances because the conditions 'a poor country', 'equal income', 'equal increments', '*ceteris paribus*' and so on are sufficient (or are believed to be sufficient) to make every individual happier. Thus judgment B is derived from value judgment C and from certain factual, positive statements or judgments. We shall therefore call a value judgment basic to individuals if it is not derived from some other value judgment and they believe in it for its own ethical appeal. Whether this definition differs from Sen's depends on the interpretation of 'all conceivable circumstances' (ibid.) In the above example, the individuals' belief in judgment B is based on judgment C. If we were to ask, 'Will you stick to judgment B even if a policy based on it does not make anyone happier?', then presumably they would have to say 'No' (I owe this observation to Sen). Thus if circumstances in which acting in accordance with judgment B does not make anyone happier are regarded as conceivable circumstances despite the fact that the individuals believe that they are sufficient to make everyone happier, then Sen's definition may not be different from ours. In fact with this broad interpretation of 'conceivable circumstances' the two definitions are equivalent.

We shall first show that if a value judgment is non-basic in our sense, it is also non-basic in Sen's sense (with the broad interpretation), and then show the reverse. If judgment X is based on judgment Y and some factual knowledge or judgments, this means that, given Y, X applies in the factual domain α. X may or may not apply outside α. Let us expand α to α', within which X applies and beyond which it does not apply. This is just a conceptual expansion and no actual specification of α' is necessary. The universal domain – that is, the domain of all possible (non-zero probability) circumstances – is donated by Ω. If $\Omega - \alpha'$ is not empty, then obviously X is a non-basic judgment in Sen's sense. If α' is itself the universal domain, then $\Omega - \alpha'$ is empty. If we confine 'all conceivable circumstances' to the universal domain, X applies under all conceivable circumstances and is a basic value judgment in Sen's sense. But if we do not confine 'all conceivable circumstances' to the universal domain, then X does not apply beyond α' and is therefore a non-basic judgment in Sen's sense.

If judgment Z is not basic in Sen's sense, then it applies in some domain β but does not apply outside that domain. Suppose that judgment T applies outside domain β. It does not matter whether the individuals concerned can make up their mind in a definite way. Thus judgment T may just mean 'No opinion' or 'If..., then...; If..., then...We can then combine Z and T into a single judgment, V. This combination is always possible (on which more below) since V may just stand for 'If β, Z; if non-β, T'. Then clearly judgment Z is based on judgment V and on some factual statements or judgments that delineate β. It is therefore also non-basic in our sense.

From the above it can be said that if a value judgment is non-basic in Sen's sense it is necessarily non-basic in our sense; if it is non-basic in our sense, whether it is also necessarily non-basic in Sen's sense will depend on the interpretation of 'all conceivable circumstances'. Even if we adopt a broad interpretation such that the two definitions coincide, it may still be useful to look at it in our way. Thus in the example above we may not be able to specify a conceivable circumstance in which the individuals will relinquish judgment B until we reveal their more basic value judgment C by asking them 'Why B?'. Similarly, even if we wish to stick to our definition of basic, it may be useful to test for basicness using Sen's method. It is sometimes difficult to ascertain whether a certain value judgment is based on another just by asking 'Why?'

For example individuals may mistakenly but sincerely believe that their judgment 'No one shall kill a human being' (judgment D) is not based on another and is due purely to its ethical appeal. They may not be able to answer the question 'Why do you believe in judgment D?', or they may reply 'I believe in it because I believe in it!' It may therefore seem that judgment D is their basic value judgment. But if we introduce them to the factual circumstances of euthanasia or a fight against an invading army, they may admit that they no longer accept judgment D. Their initial belief that judgment D was basic was thus mistaken. If it had been truly basic, it could not have been shown to be inapplicable under any circumstances.

A1.1.3   Can individuals have more than one basic value judgment?

Suppose an individual has two value judgments that they regard as basic. Then either these judgments are not in conflict with each other under any circumstances or they are under some (or all) circumstances. If the latter is the case, then it is clear that the two judgments cannot both be basic. If the two never give conflicting results, then we can combine them into a single one. For example the judgments 'No female should kill a human being' and 'No male should kill a human being' are never in conflict and can be combined into one, 'No person should kill a human being. An individual may have many diverse basic value judgments that cannot be combined into a single statement and the only way to combine them is to list them exhaustively, for example. 'One should not murder; one should not...' It may then just be a semantic point whether we regard mutually non-conflicting judgments as numerous value judgments or as parts that form a single value judgment or value system. It is even possible that the individuals themselves may think that it is not possible to list all their basic value judgments exhaustively as new ones may crop up, especially with the specification of a new set of circumstances. However in such cases the numerous value judgments are likely to be non-basic. If rational people press themselves hard enough with the question 'Why do I think this is a good thing?', all their supposedly basic value judgments can probably be reduced to a few or just one principle (their basic value judgment) that gives rise to various expressions under various circumstances. Most, if not all, reasonable people will agree that, for society, our ultimate goal should be the maximisation of an increasing function of and only of individual welfare, that is:

$$W = W(W^1, W^2, \ldots, W^I), \frac{\partial W}{\partial W^i} > 0 \qquad (A1.1)$$

where W indicates social welfare, W^i the welfare of the ith member, and I the number of members concerned. (If we are not using a static analysis then we have to maximise a welfare function through time, discounted to account for the uncertainty of continuing existence. If we are, as we should be, also concerned with sentient creatures other than human beings, we have to include their welfare.)

However even if we can agree on a specific form of the function, this could hardly serve as our only guide under all circumstances. This is so because it is difficult to know whether a particular action will increase or reduce welfare due to the complexity of the real world. From experience, however, we learn that actions that are in accordance with certain principles (honesty, respecting other people's freedom and so on) usually contribute to welfare. Eventually these principles tend to be valued for their own sake. This may explain the diversity and numerousness of basic value judgments.

A1.1.4 Subjective judgments of fact

The distinction between basic and non-basic value judgments is of some importance, as noted by Sen (1970a, ch. 5). If two persons disagree over a basic value judgment, the only possible scientific (factual, logical) solution is for one to show to the other that the judgment in question is not really a basic value judgment. If it really is basic, no ground is left for scientific argument. One of them may of course try to persuade the other to change his or her basic value judgment. But this is an exercise in ethical persuasion, not scientific discussion. This does not mean that scientists should not engage in such persuasion. Scientists are human beings as much as any other person and are entitled to engage in ethical persuasion provided they do not confuse scientific discussion with ethical persuasion, or attempt to confuse their audience.

On the other hand, if the disagreement is about factual judgments or non-basic value judgments, scientific discussion alone may be sufficient to settle the dispute. However, since our scientific knowledge is never complete a final agreement may not be reached even by two logical persons with the same basic value judgments. This is due to possible differences in 'subjective judgments of fact' (Ng, 1972b). These are estimates made in the absence of definite scientific knowledge and hence may be influenced by the personal interests, values, experience and so on of the person making them. For example it has been observed that, when considering the same statistics, left-wing economists tend to infer that progressive taxation does not have a disincentive effect, while right-wing economists tend to infer that it does (Klappholz, 1964, p. 103). However disagreement about subjective judgments of fact can, or at least in principle, be subject to further discussion and scientific testing. With the advancement of science such differences may eventually disappear, though they are likely to be replaced by others (on consensus among economists, see Kearl *et al.*, 1979).

As a scientist, one has no business to make any basic value judgment, and as a citizen a scientist is no more qualified than any other citizen to make basic value judgments. But this is not so for non-basic value judgments and subjective judgments of fact. If we have any faith in the usefulness of a branch of study, we must admit that scientists in that branch are more qualified than a layperson to make subjective judgments of fact that are closely related to their field of study. For example, while an economist may be hard put to judge the effects on economic growth of two alternative balance-of-payments policies, a layperson is likely to know nothing at all about the effects. Thus the ability to distinguish subjective judgments of fact and non-basic value judgments from basic value judgments increases the role of scientists in policy recommendation. If we were to lump all three under 'value judgments' and refrain, as scientists, from making such judgments, we would have to leave all but undisputable scientific facts to the politicians.

Another source of disagreement about policy matters is differences of interest, rather than differences in values or judgments of fact. For example the leaders of a strong trade union may press for a large wage rise despite knowing that it will lead to inflation and/or unemployment. On the ethical level they may admit (although not in public) that their action is not good for society as a whole. But on the practical level they may be guided mainly by self-interest.

A1.1.5 Summary

To summarise, disagreements (especially on policy matters) may arise as a result of one or more of the following:

- Conflicts between personal or sectional interests.
- Differences in basic value judgments.
- Differences in the subjective judgment of facts.
- Differences over alleged facts or in logical analysis.

Disagreements of the fourth type can readily be resolved by objective demonstration or logical discussion. Any remaining disagreements on this score can only be ascribed to ignorance or the inability to reason. Disagreements of the first type can be resolved by a political compromise of some sort, or by the exercise or threat of force. Alternatively, especially in the long run, they may be resolved by teaching people to be more social-minded or by making their interests more compatible. Disagreements of the second type can only be resolved by ethical persuasion (however see, Piderit, 1993, for the argument that even value judgments are susceptible to rational justification). It is disagreements due to differences in subjective judgments of fact that offer the most scope for further discussion, analysis and argument. Apart from the conflict of interest, it is also, I believe, the most important source of disagreement.

Since a non-basic value judgment is based on a basic value judgment plus factual information or a subjective judgment of fact, differences in value judgments are due either to differences in basic values or to differences over subjective judgments of fact, ignoring factual and logical mistakes. The latter type of difference (over subjective judgments of fact) tends to be more prevalent and is usually regarded as a direct disagreement about value judgments on which no further argument is possible, as no distinction is made between basic value judgments and subjective judgments of fact. The above discussion sounds a warning against this confusion.

2
Pareto Optimality

The concept of Pareto optimality plays a major part in welfare economics. Many theorems and optimality conditions are formulated with reference to Pareto optimality because the Pareto principle is widely accepted as a value judgment, while judgments that involve interpersonal comparisons of utility are more controversial. However this does not mean that welfare economics has to be based only on the Pareto principle. Indeed theorems and analysis based on 'extra-Paretian' principles have been developed. Nevertheless Pareto optimality will continue to be one of the most important concepts in welfare economics, and hence it warrants careful study.

2.1 The Pareto principle

Whenever we say that one situation is better than another, or that a situation is optimal, we are basing our assessment, explicitly or implicitly, on a certain set of value judgments. A situation that is regarded as optimal according to one set of values may rank very low according to another set. For example an increase in GNP, even if it results only from the production of 'goods' and has not involved any 'bads', such as increased air pollution, may still be regarded as a bad thing by those who believe that humankind must not pursue material comfort. Thus Pareto optimality is optimal with reference to value judgments that are consistent with the Pareto principle.

According to the Pareto principle a change is desirable if it makes some individuals better off without making any others worse off. This is a value judgment, but it is a very weak one in the sense that most people will accept it, and in the sense that many other value judgments subsume the Pareto principle but also contain something more. (An assumption, whether factual or a value judgment, is said to be weak if it does not assume very much and therefore is likely to be realistic and/or acceptable. Hence if the same conclusions are derived, the weaker the assumptions used the better. For conclusions, in contrast, the stronger the better.) For example, consider the value judgment that a change is desirable if it makes N persons significantly better off and fewer than N persons insignificantly worse off. No matter what constitutes 'significantly better off', it is clear that this judgment subsumes the Pareto principle, as every change approved by the Pareto principle will also be approved by the judgment. On the other hand, not all changes approved by it will pass the test of the Pareto principle, since some of the changes may make some people worse off. Hence the judgment is stronger than the Pareto principle.

The 'better off' in the Pareto principle can be defined with respect to preference or welfare. If it is defined with respect to preference (as is usually assumed), divergences between preference (or utility) and welfare (discussed in Section 1.3 above) may make those taking welfare as more fundamental than preference to reject the Pareto principle or to reformulate the principle in terms of welfare. If we either ignore the divergences between preference and welfare or define 'better off' in accordance with preferred concept, it can probably be agreed that it takes a rather peculiar ethic to reject the Pareto principle. Since some individuals are made better off and no one is made worse off, why reject the change?

However some economists have come out strongly against the Pareto principle, although it seems that their objections to the Paretian value judgment are based on somewhat misguided interpretations of it. For example consider the following quotation: 'If we adopt a series of economic policies which make the richer group richer but have the poorer group at the same absolute level, then according to a Pareto-type social welfare function...we would be necessarily raising the level of social welfare' (Nath, 1969, p. 228). This assertion follows from Nath's rather peculiar interpretation of the Paretian value judgment: 'If any change in the allocation of resources increases the income and leisure of everyone or at least of one person (or more strictly one household) without reducing those of any other, then the change should be considered to have increased social welfare' (ibid., p. 9). The actual Paretian value judgment is that 'a change is desirable if it makes someone better off without making others worse off.'[1] This will yield Nath's interpretation only if an additional factual assumption is made: that there is no externality in consumption. (If there are external effects on consumption, individuals may be made worse off even if their income remains unchanged as they may be envious of the increased consumption enjoyed by others, find it difficult to keep up with the consumption level of their neighbours, or simply feel worse off because of the extra empty bottles disposed of by their neighbours.)

---

1. Pareto spoke of 'benefit' and 'detriment', not 'richer'. For example 'The points of the type P [that is, Pareto optimal] are such that we cannot deviate from them to the benefit or detriment of all the members of the community' (Pareto, 1935, p. 1466n).

Even if the Pareto principle is universally accepted, there will still be cases where some people are made better off and some worse off. In such cases we cannot use the Pareto principle alone to guide our decisions. However the Pareto principle is a sufficient value basis for many propositions pertaining to the allocation of resources and even to the distribution of income. For these propositions, we would naturally wish to use Ockham's razor to shave off the unnecessary assumptions, be these value judgments or factual.

2.2   The conditions for Pareto optimality

The conditions for Pareto optimality in the traditional framework of analysis can be divided into first-order necessary conditions and second-order 'sufficient' conditions. The first-order conditions have been widely discussed (see for example Little, 1957, chs 8–9; Bator, 1957; Winch, 1971, ch. 4; Boadway and Bruce, 1984). A mathematical derivation of the first-order conditions is provided in Appendix 2.1, where all the necessary conditions are derived in one maximisation problem, in contrast to the usual procedure of separately maximising productive efficiency and consumer satisfaction. The 'production of commodities by means of commodities' is also taken into account.

2.2.1   The first-order conditions

The first order or marginal conditions consist of the condition for exchange, the condition for production and the top-level condition.

To begin with the optimal condition for exchange, we shall assume for the moment that various amounts of final goods have already been produced, and hence the problem is how to allocate them among the individuals in the economy. At this stage we shall also assume divisibility (that is, the goods and factors of production are divisible to any desired amount), continuity ('nature does not jump'), the absence of transaction or allocation costs, and the absence of external effects of consumption and production. Under these assumptions the Pareto condition for exchange states that the marginal rate of substitution (MRS) between any pair of goods must be the same for all individuals who consume the two goods. This proposition is be justified by the following simple argument.

If the MRS between any pair of goods, say, X and Y, is different for any pair of individuals, J and K, it can be shown that one individual can be made better off without the other being made worse off. For example, suppose that the MRS of X for Y (MRS_{XY}) equals one for J and two for K. In other words one X is worth (in terms of utility) one Y at the margin to J, and is worth two Y to K. Thus if we take one X from J and give it to K, and take one Y from K and give it to J, K is made better off while J stays indifferent. We could have made both of them better off if we had transferred 1.5 Y instead of one Y from K to J. The possibility of making one person better off without making the other worse off means that Pareto optimality has not been attained. This possibility can be shown to exist as long as the MRS of a pair of goods is different between any pair of individuals. Hence for a Pareto optimum the MRS of any pair of goods must be the same for all individuals who consume that pair of goods.

The above argument is illustrated in Figure 2.1, which is known as the Edgeworth box. The box is formed by superimposing the inverted indifference map of K on the indifference map of J, such that the origin of K (O^K) is north-east of O^J and the axes are parallel, as shown. Moreover the width of the rectangle (O^JM = O^KN) measures the total available amount of X and the height of the rectangle (O^JN = O^KM) measures that of Y. X^J stands for the amount of X consumed by J, and so on. Any point (for example E) on the box represents a specific distribution of X and Y between J and K. For example at point E, J consumes O^JA amount of X and O^JD of Y, and K consumes O^KC(= AM) of X and O^BB (= DN) of Y.

The curve O^JEO^K traces the points of tangency between the two sets of indifference curves. It can be shown that, for any point that is not on the curve O^JEO^K, we can make one individual better off without making the other worse off by moving to some point on the curve. For example if the initial point is H, both individuals will be made better off if we move to

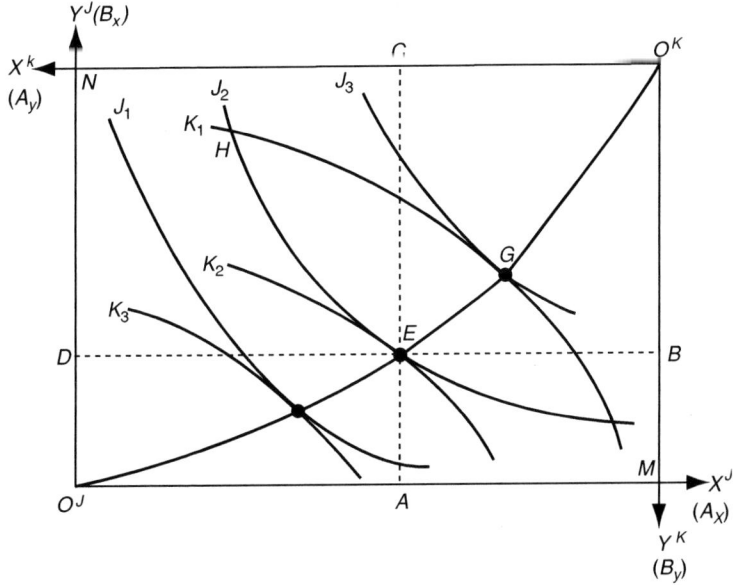

Figure 2.1

any point on the curve between E and G. If we move exactly to E, J stays on the same indifference curve J_2 and K moves from a lower indifference curve, K_1, to a higher one, K_2. On the other hand if we move from H to G, J is made better off and K stays indifferent.

Hence every point between and including E and G is Pareto-superior to H. In fact this is true for all points bounded by the indifference curves J_2 and K_1, that is, the shaded area. But for any point within the shaded area, a further Pareto improvement is still possible until we arrive at a point on the curve.

The curve O^JEO^K is called a contract curve since free contracting will ensure that a point on it will be reached unless our individuals engage in strategic behaviour, each attempting to gain more than the other will concede. If the number of individuals in the free exchange is large and each possesses a small fraction of the total supply of goods, no individual will have any strategic or monopolistic power and a point on the contract curve will be reached by free exchange.[2]

A point on the contract curve is a point of tangency between an indifference curve of J and another of K. The absolute slope of an indifference curve measures the MRS between the two goods for the individual. Hence the MRS is equalised for the two individuals at any point on the contract curve. This links our geometrical illustration to the Pareto condition for exchange.

The second Pareto optimality condition refers to production and states that the MRS between any two factors must be the same for all products and for all production units using these factors. This condition ensures that, with a given factor endowment, the production of each good has been maximised given the amounts of other goods produced. If this condition is not satisfied it is possible to increase the production of some product(s) without reducing that of any other product. The demonstration of this proposition is similar to that of the exchange optimum.

If the MRS between factors A and B is different for products X and Y, the production of one can be increased without reducing that of another. For example, suppose that the marginal rate of substitution of A for B (MRS_{AB}) equals one in the production of X and two in the production of Y. In other words the marginal product of A equals that of B in the production of X but is twice the marginal product of B in the production of Y. Thus if we

---

2. An allocation is blocked if there exists a coalition of traders that can achieve a better outcome for each of its members with their own resources. The core of the economy is the set of all feasible and unblocked allocations. As the number of traders increases, the core shrinks. With a continuum (infinity) of traders the core becomes a single point on the contract curve – the competitive equilibrium. This is called the limit theorem (proved by Shubik, 1959; Debreu and Scarf, 1963; Aumann, 1964; surveyed by Hildenbrand, 1977; first discussed by Edgeworth, 1881).

transfer one A from the production of X to that of Y, and transfer one B from the production of Y to that of X, the production of Y is increased while that of X stays the same. Moreover the output of all other products is unaffected since their inputs are unchanged. With the increased production of Y we can give (divide) this extra amount of Y to some (all) individual(s) in the economy and hence make them better off, while no one is made worse off. Therefore Pareto optimality has not been attained as long as the MRS between any pair of factors is different in the production of different products (and in fact also in the production of the same product in different production units or processes). A geometrical demonstration of this proposition can again be conducted with the help of Figure 2.1 by reinterpreting the indifference curves of J and K as the iso-product curves (or isoquants) of X and Y, and substituting A_X, B_X, A_Y, B_Y (A_X is the amount of factor A used to produce X and so on) respectively for X^J, Y^J, X^K, Y^K. It can then be shown that production efficiency requires the allocation of factors at a point of mutual tangency of the isoquants, which implies equalisation of the MRS between factors.

The third necessary condition for Pareto optimality is called the top-level optimum and relates production to preferences. It requires that, for any pair of goods, the MRS (which is equalised over all individuals, as required by the exchange optimum) be equal to the marginal rate of transformation (MRT). The MRT between any two goods is the marginal rate at which the economy can 'transform' one into the other by allocating more resources to produce one and less to produce the other. If the MRT is not equal to the MRS for any pair of goods, we can produce more of one good and less of the other to make everyone better off. For example if $MRS_{XY} = 1$, and $MRT_{XY} = 2$, then the economy can transform one X into two Y and individuals are indifferent between one X and one Y. Thus by producing two units more of Y and one unit less of X, some or all individuals can be made better off.

To summarise, the three necessary conditions for Pareto optimality are as follows:

- *Exchange optimum*: the marginal rate of substitution (MRS) between any pair of goods must be the same for all individuals consuming the goods. (For those individuals who do not consume a particular good, their MRS of this good for any good they consume must be smaller, or at least not larger, than the MRS between these two goods for those individuals who consume both. Similar inequality requirements hold with respect to the following two conditions.)
- *Production optimum*: the MRS between any pair of factors must be the same for all production units that use the factors.
- *Top-level optimum*: for any pair of reproducible goods the common MRS must be equal to the marginal rate of transformation (MRT). This condition serves to ensure that the set of goods produced is consistent with the preferences of individuals.

The exchange optimum is required to ensure that, for a given collection of goods, the allocation of these goods among individuals fulfils Pareto optimality, that is, the utility of each person is maximised given the utilities of all the others. In other words a point on rather than inside the utility possibility (hyper-) surface (or curve, for the special case of two individuals) is reached. This utility possibility curve (UPC) is depicted in Figure 2.2. It indicates the maximum level of utility one individual can attain, given the level of the other. For example if the level of utility for J stays at OG, the maximum level possible for K is OH, given the fixed collection of goods.

Similarly the production optimum is required to ensure that, with a given endowment of factors, the production of each good is maximised given the amounts produced of all other goods, so that the economy is at a point on the production possibility surface (curve) or on the transformation surface (curve). The production possibility curve, *TPS*, is depicted in Figure 2.3.

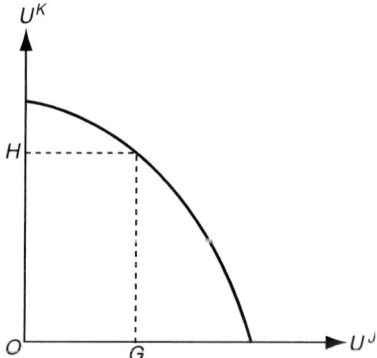

Figure 2.2   Utility possibility curve

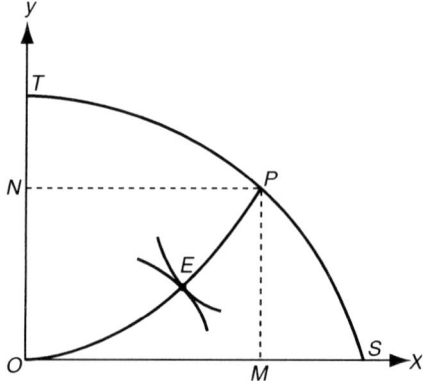

Figure 2.3   Production possibility curve

The absolute shape of this curve measures the MRT between goods X and Y. Each point on the curve (for example P) represents a given collection (OM of X and ON of Y) of the two goods. If we form a rectangular box ($OMPN$ in Figure 2.3) and draw in the two sets of indifference curves, it becomes an Edgeworth box similar to Figure 2.1. By efficient allocation of this collection of goods we arrive at a UPC similar to that in Figure 2.2. It is derived by taking the different combination of utility levels along the contract curve OP in Figure 2.3.

Point P represents only one production possibility among a large number of such possibilities along the *TPS* curve. For each production point or each collection of goods there is a different UPC. If we were to include all such curves in Figure 2.4, the outer envelope of these curves, FF', would be the 'utility possibility *frontier*'. This frontier is sometimes called a '*situation UPC*' (referring to a given situation with a fixed endowment of resources) and a UPC associated with a given collection of goods is called a '*point UPC*'.

As suggested by Bator (1957, p. 26), there is a short cut to the derivation of this frontier. The short cut is based on the top-level optimum, which requires equality between the MRS and MRT. With regard to point P in Figure 2.3, the top-level optimum condition implies that the choice of point P is only consistent with the optimality requirements if the choice of a point along the contract curve, OP, happens to give the indifference curve a slope (= MRS in absolute value) that is equal to the *TPS* slope at P (= MRT in absolute value). As a rule there is only one point (for example E) on OP that satisfies such a requirement (on the uniqueness of this point see Mathur, 1991). Hence for each point on the production possibility *TPS* curve we have only to plot one point in Figure 2.4. By connecting all such points we again have the utility possibility frontier, FF', in Figure 2.4 (some points on the production possibility curve may have a corresponding point *inside* the frontier rather than on it – see Yeh, 1972).

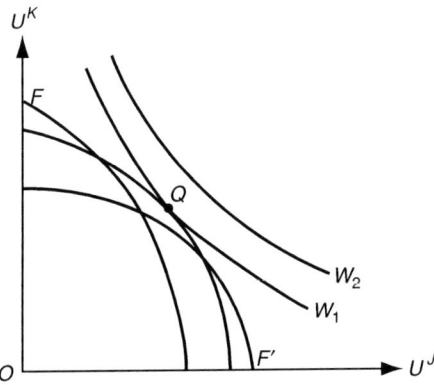

Figure 2.4

All points on the utility possibility frontier (ignoring positively sloped sections) satisfy the Pareto optimality conditions. With the existing production technology and the existing factor endowment, once we are at a point on the frontier it is not possible to make anyone better off without making someone else worse off. Any point on the frontier thus represents *a* Pareto optimum. The choice between these infinite Pareto-optimal points may be made on an ethical level (Friedman, 1980, argues that the Pareto-optimal range is small). This choice is not a problem of Pareto optimality, rather it is usually relegated to a social welfare function (SWF, which specifies the level of social welfare for each combination of factors that affect welfare). If the relevant SWF is represented by the welfare contours, W_1, W_2 and so on, as drawn in Figure 2.4, then a point on *FF'* that touches the highest welfare contour is chosen. Once a point, for example Q on *FF'*, is chosen, we can trace our steps backward to see what pattern of allocation is necessary to achieve it. Each point on the frontier corresponds to a point on the production possibility curve (*TPS*) in Figure 2.3. For example point *P* can be traced from point *Q*. Point *P* again fixes a point *E* on the contract curve, and hence the amounts of both goods going to both individuals are known. Point *P* also specifies that quantities *OM* of *X* and *ON* of *Y* are to be produced. By looking at Figure 2.1 (interpreting the indifference curves as isoquants) we know which two isoquants are to be selected. The tangency of these two isoquants then determines the amounts of both factors to be allocated to the production of the two goods.

It should be noted that the above conditions for Pareto optimality ignore complicating factors such as external effects and transaction or other allocation costs, the presence of which may require modifications to be made to the conditions, such as making the conditions dependent on the starting position.

2.2.2   The second-order conditions

The first-order conditions are necessary but not sufficient for an optimum since they may define a minimum rather than a maximum, so in addition second-order conditions are required to ensure the attainment of Pareto optimality. These second-order conditions are also called the sufficient conditions, and it is only by combining them with the first-order conditions that sufficiency is assured.

To see whether the first-order conditions define a minimum rather than a maximum, let us consider a simple example of one individual and two goods, as depicted in Figure 2.5, where *TS* is the transformation curve and the *J*'s are the indifference curves. In part (a) of the figure, point *P* satisfies the requirement that MRS = MRT and defines a maximum, since J_2 is the highest indifference curve attainable. In part (b), point *P* also satisfies the MRS = MRT requirement but it is a point of minimum utility along the transformation curve. To ensure that our first-order conditions do not lead us to a minimum we require the second-order conditions, as discussed below.

If all the indifference curves and isoquants are convex (to the origin) and all the transformation curves are concave, it is easy to see that the possibility depicted in Figure 2.5b cannot occur. These requirements of convexity and concavity are equivalent to the assumptions of diminishing MRS (for both goods and factors) and diminishing MRT.[3] These conditions, while sufficient (in conjunction with the first-order conditions) for a Pareto optimum, are not necessary. For example consider Figure 2.6a, where the transformation curve, *TPS*, does not satisfy the concavity requirements. Yet tangency point *P* is a maximum rather than a minimum. Hence it can be seen that, in this case, what is necessary is simply that the indifference curve be more convex than the transformation curve.

If the second-order conditions are only satisfied in the vicinity of the point where the first-order conditions are fulfilled, this point may be

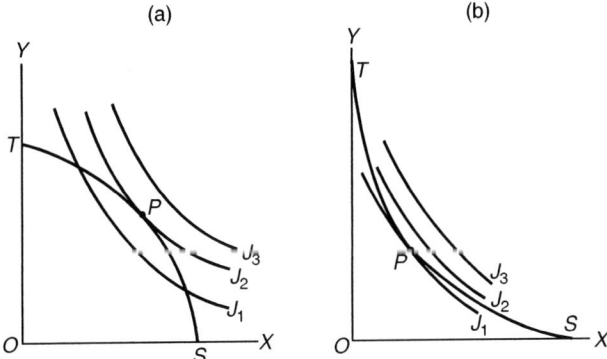

Figure 2.5

---

3. The presence of increasing returns to scale may make the transformation curve convex to the origin (that is, a non-convex production feasibility set) but there may be both increasing returns and a concave transformation curve at the same time. If there are constant returns to scale throughout, the transformation curve will be linear if the factor intensity (or input proportion) is the same for all industries. If the factor intensities are different, the transformation curve will be concave. This diminishing MRT is caused by the fact that, if more than one product is to be produced, increased reliance has to be placed on those factors which are more efficient (in the technical sense) in producing the other product. The degree of increasing returns to scale has to be strong enough to outweigh the effect of different factor intensities before the transformation curve is made convex. However the effects of variable returns to scale on the shape of the transformation curve is complex and has some unexpected properties (see Herberg and Kemp, 1969).

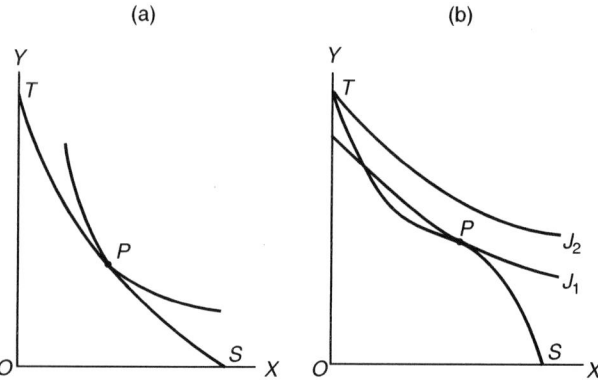

Figure 2.6

maximal only in this vicinity (a local maximum) and the global maximum may lie elsewhere. This is illustrated in Figure 2.6b, where point P represents a local maximum and T the global maximum. If the relevant functions are wholly concave and convex, a local maximum is also the global maximum (Lancaster, 1968, p. 17). In this connection the so-called 'total conditions' (Hicks, 1939, p. 707) should be mentioned. These total conditions require it to be impossible to increase welfare by the complete abandonment/ (introduction) of some existing/(new) commodities or factors of production (in chapter 10 we shall see that this comparison is an essential part of infra-marginal analysis of the division of labour). If the first-order conditions are satisfied not only with respect to the existing but also to the potential commodities and factors, then the total conditions are satisfied, provided that the second-order conditions are also satisfied globally. However this proviso is rather restrictive. In practice such things as economies of scale and so on may cause a violation of the second-order conditions. Hence an all-or-nothing comparison may have to be made. One could also extend Hicks' total conditions to include the introduction of new techniques or production processes. This is related to the argument that the relevant MRT must be that achieved by the most efficient method of production. However, formally, one could argue that any new technique or process of production must be embodied in some factor of production. A technician or manager who knows how to use a better method of production is then regarded as a different and superior factor than one who does not.

2.2.3   Mathematical derivation of the first-order conditions

To assist the mathematically uninitiated, we shall merely derive here the exchange condition in the simple case of two individuals and two goods in given quantities. The mathematically sophisticated can read Appendix 2.1, where all the optimality conditions (first-order) are derived in one maximisation problem, in contrast to the usual procedure of separating them into two problems, one to maximise productive efficiency and the other to maximise consumers' satisfaction.

The utilities of the two individuals are functions of the amounts of the two goods they consume

$$U^1 = U^1\left(x_1^1, x_2^1\right)$$

$$U^2 = U^2\left(x_1^2, x_2^2\right) \tag{2.1}$$

where x_g^i is the amount of good g consumed by individual i. To derive the optimality conditions we maximise the utility level of one individual (U^1), given that of the other individual $\left(U^2 = \overline{U}^2\right)$, subject to the constraint that the aggregate amounts consumed must equal the quantities available, that is:

$$x_1^1 + x_1^2 = X_1$$

$$x_2^1 + x_2^2 = X_2 \tag{2.2}$$

where x_1 and x_2 are the amounts of the goods available.

To maximise a function subject to constraints, we form a Lagrangean function by writing the constraints in the form $f(...) = 0$ and adding them to the objective function after multiplying them with Lagrangean multipliers (λ, α, β):

$$L = U^1\left(x_1^1, x_2^1\right) + \lambda\left(U^2[x_1^2, x_2^2] - \overline{U}^2\right) + \alpha\left(x_1 - x_1^1 - x_1^2\right) + \beta\left(x_2 - x_2^1 - x_2^2\right) \tag{2.3}$$

Setting the partial derivatives of L with respect to $x_1^1, x_2^1, x_1^2, x_2^2$ equal to zero, we have

$$\partial U^1/\partial x_1^1 = \alpha \qquad \partial U^1/\partial x_2^1 = \beta$$

$$\lambda\,\partial U^2/\partial x_1^2 = \alpha \qquad \lambda\,\partial U^2/\partial x_2^2 = \beta \tag{2.4}$$

After simple division, we have

$$\frac{\partial U^1/\partial x_1^1}{\partial U^1/\partial x_2^1} = \frac{\alpha}{\beta} = \frac{\partial U^2/\partial x_1^2}{\partial U^2/\partial x_2^2} \tag{2.5}$$

which specifies the equality of the MRS between the two goods for the two individuals.

The above method works because the constraints are written in a form that equals zero, and the multiplication of anything with zero is still zero. Thus the maximisation of L also maximises the objective function when the constraints are satisfied.

2.3   The attainment of Pareto optimality

Having discussed the conditions for Pareto optimality we shall now consider the possibility of achieving it. It is well established that, under certain classical assumptions such as non-increasing returns, the absence of externalities and so on, a perfectly competitive economy will attain a Pareto optimum. This is the first theorem in welfare economics (on the proof of this theorem see Ng, 1979/83, app. 2B. For a collected volume on general equilibrium see Debreu, 1996). The second theorem states that every Pareto-optimal state can be sustained as a competitive equilibrium by means of an appropriate distribution of resource endowments. This second welfare theorem has to be interpreted carefully to avoid misunderstanding. Suppose that the existing competitive equilibrium, *A*, gives a Pareto-optimal state such that the rich have high utility levels but the poor have low utility levels. One might prefer a different Pareto-optimal state, *B*, where the rich have lower utility levels (relative to *A*) and the poor have higher utility levels. The second welfare theorem states that if the initial distribution of resource endowments (including inherent abilities and the initial ownership of assets) were such that the poor have more (relative to *A*) and the rich less, then the preferred Pareto-optimal state, *B*, could be sustained as the competitive equilibrium with respect to this more equal distribution of resource endowments.

Thus in a sense the second welfare theorem shows that undesirable distribution in terms of utility is not the result of the market mechanism as such, but rather is the result of the equal distribution of resource endowments. However if history and the lottery of birth have already resulted in a distribution of endowments corresponding to state *A*, the second theorem does not mean that state *B* can be achieved from *A* by *redistributing* resource endowments (see Guesnerie, 1995). First, some endowments (such as natural talents) cannot be redistributed. Second, redistribution through tax/transfer may involve administrative, compliance, distortive (including disincentive) and enforcing costs. Hence we may not be able to travel from *A* along the utility possibility frontier to *B*. Rather we can only travel along a utility feasibility frontier that lies inside the utility possibility frontier due to the various costs mentioned above (see Figure 3.2 in Chapter 3 for the relationship between a utility possibility and a utility feasibility curve/frontier).

Neither the two welfare theorems nor the case for the invisible hand shows that as a country/region/individual (or sector) enriches itself through economic growth, its effects on others are beneficial. In fact there are many cases in which the effects are negative. For example a country that lowers the cost of producing some of its imports may make the countries that export these goods worse off. Nevertheless it can be shown that, for the benchmark case of proportionate enrichment (an increased ability to produce all goods proportionately), other sectors as a whole benefit, assuming strong non-inferiority in consumption (weaker than homothetic preferences) (Ng, 1996c). The reason for this is that other sectors have a bigger trading partner with which to trade. The larger volume of exports and imports the enriching sector trades with the other sectors makes the terms of trade move in favour of the rest of the world (this analysis does not take account of benefits of trade through increased division of labour, as discussed in Chapter 10).

The close association between perfect competition and Pareto optimality must not be mistakenly taken to mean that the concept of Pareto optimality is only meaningful in a perfectly competitive economy – the concept can be meaningfully applied to any economy. Moreover an economic system other than perfect competition can also achieve Pareto optimality, on at least in theory. As noted by Wiles (1964, p. 189), efficient resource allocation can in principle be achieved in three ways: via perfect competition, perfect central adjustment and perfect computation (associated respectively with the names of Lerner, Lange and Leontief). It can be added that a system with perfect discriminatory monopolists (which are unlikely to exist in practice) may also achieve Pareto optimality (Pigou, 1932, ch. 17, app. 3). Moreover some rather contrived processes have been suggested that have the required Pareto optimality property. For example the 'greed process', as suggested by Hurwicz (1960), can achieve an optimum even in the presence of indivisibilities and increasing returns, but it calls for more information than the competitive mechanism and is impractical as it conflicts with self-interest. In fact the informational requirement of the competitive market mechanism is minimal in comparison with other processes. This has been stressed by Hayek (1945) and, in connection with other related issues, Stiglitz (1994).

The crucial condition that makes perfect competition under classical conditions capable of achieving a Pareto optimum is that no single buyer or seller of any good or factor is in a position to influence the price appreciably. The profit-maximising and utility-maximising behaviour of firms and consumers, together with the working of supply and demand, will then ensure that the equilibrium position achieved is a Pareto optimum.

To see how the conditions for Pareto optimality are fulfilled in a competitive equilibrium, first consider the equilibrium position of individual consumers. Since they are unable to affect prices their budgetary constraint is linear – a straight line in the case of two goods. Assuming non-satiation of wants, they will maximise their utility by consuming at a point P, where the budget constraint touches the highest indifference curve. Since the (absolute) slope of the budget constraint measures the ratio of prices (p_X/p_Y) and the slope of the indifference curve measures the MRS, we have equality, $MRS_{XY} = p_X/p_Y$. This is true for all consumers, hence:

$$MRS_{XY}^i = P_x/P_Y (i = 1, \ldots, I) \qquad (2.6)$$

where X and Y denote any two goods. (This may not seem to follow from a two-dimensional figure, but we can always use one of the axes for one particular good, and the other axis for all other goods. Since the equality

$MRS_{XY} = p_X/p_Y$ always holds no matter which good we take to be the particular good, the equality must also hold between any two particular goods as well.) Equation 2.6 shows that the exchange optimum is attained, since the same price ratio is faced by all consumers.

Similarly we can show that the production optimum is attained by noting that a producer cannot affect factor prices. His isocost curves are thus linear and he produces at the point where an isoquant touches an isocost curve. We thus have:

$$MRS_{AB}^h = p_A/p_B \; (h = I, \ldots, H) \tag{2.7}$$

where H is the number of producers in all lines of production, and A and B denote any two factors.

It is also not difficult to see that the price ratio between any two goods, p_X/p_Y, must also be equal to the MRT for all producers that produce these goods. Otherwise it would be profitable to increase the production of one and reduce the production of another. Moreover profit maximisation ensures that the chosen methods of production are efficient. The equality of MRT with the price ratio can also be seen in another way. Under perfect competition the price of a product is equal to its marginal cost. Hence the price ratio is equal to the ratio of marginal cost, which is MRT. We have thus seen that all the necessary conditions are satisfied under competitive equilibrium. This depends heavily on there being a large number of price-taking producers and consumers. However even in the absence of large numbers, optimality can still be achieved if entry/exit is free and costless, such that markets become perfectly 'contestable' (examples of highly contestable industries include airlines and road haulage, where the main investments are not sunk and can be resold without substantial losses), even if not perfectly competitive, with potential entrants replacing the part played by numerous competitors to ensure optimality (see Baumol *et al.*, 1982, for a formal analysis and Baumol, 1982, for a survey). The second-order conditions are also satisfied with the assumption of a diminishing MRS (both between goods and between factors) and the absence of increasing returns (hence ruling out convexity in the transformation curve).

We shall now examine some of the assumptions that are made to ensure that a competitive equilibrium is necessarily a Pareto optimum. The first assumption, which seems highly unrealistic, is that consumption and production produce no external effects. In fact the environment is polluted by producers and many consumers do try to keep up with the Joneses. The problem of externalities is so important that a separate chapter (Chapter 7) is devoted to it, and therefore we shall disregard this problem for the moment.

The assumption of a diminishing MRS or convexity of indifference curves is quite weak and is generally used by economists. The assumption of a diminishing MRT or concavity of the transformation curve (or convexity of the production feasibility set), however, generally rules out increasing returns to scale ('generally' does not mean always; see note 3). In the presence of increasing returns to scale there is a natural tendency towards monopoly, and hence the very existence of perfect competition is in doubt. Moreover economies of specialisation and the evolution of divisions of labour have also been largely ignored in orthodox economic analysis. These are discussed in Chapter 10.

The assumption of perfect divisibility seems unrealistic but the inefficiency caused by indivisibility is likely to be small unless the indivisibility involved is very large, and the presence of rental services significantly reduces indivisibility, as a large indivisible unit can be rented for short periods.

The assumption of profit maximisation can be replaced by the more general assumption of utility maximisation by entrepreneurs, since utility maximisation is equivalent to profit maximisation for owner-managed firms (see Koplin, 1963; Ng, 1969a). If there is a separation of ownership from control, then utility maximisation by managers may not result in profit maximisation for the firm (this will happen only if the transaction costs are not negligible; otherwise it will be beneficial for both owners and managers to maximise profit and negotiate a mutually advantageous share of the spoils). Formally, this can be regarded as a type of externality – the external diseconomy produced by managers and borne by owners.

The assumption of utility maximisation is usually employed in economics. If Pareto optimality is defined in terms of the revealed preference of consumers, then the assumption of utility maximisation does not impose any further restriction. On the other hand if Pareto optimality is defined in terms of the actual or *ex post* welfare of individuals, then utility maximisation subsumes perfect foresight, rational choice and so on. Though this is not generally true, it can still be accepted as a working hypothesis unless there is specific reason to believe otherwise, for example in the case of addictive drugs and materialistic bias. These problems have been touched on in Chapter 1 and will be discussed further in Chapters 11 and 12.

There may also be assumptions implicit in the way the analysis is conducted, for example, the analysis deals solely with the allocation of resources and the consumption of goods, and all other activities are disregarded. The extension to these possibly extraeconomic activities need not necessarily show that such choices are non-Pareto optimal, but it might for some choices. For example Ng (2002a) considers parents' choice of the number of children to have. Assuming rational choice[4] and that the

---

4. If we allow for the existence of an irrational urge to procreate, there may be a bias towards excessive family size.

external costs (noise and mischief) and benefits (cuteness and company) to others are negligible, or more likely, largely offsetting, it can be shown that the number of children determined by the free, utility-maximising choice of the family is not Pareto-optimal from the social point of view. Additional people (as a result of more births or immigration – on the latter see Berry and Soligo, 1969) earn their marginal products but also benefit others as a group by enlarging the set of people with whom to trade. It might be thought that this should apply only to additional births and not to migration, which leaves the country of emigration with fewer people to trade domestically. If we ignore distributional issues and take emigration as applicable to anyone, the correct view to take is that of the set of all people before emigration. Then, as a whole group, this set of people are made better off by free, informed and rational emigration, and the people in the country of immigration, as a group, are also made better off.

Since many of the assumptions discussed above are likely to be violated in a real economy that is not perfectly competitive to begin with, attainment of Pareto optimality at the level of abstraction discussed in this chapter is quite impossible. Does this mean that the concept of Pareto optimality is useless? Knowledge about the conditions for Pareto optimality, the relation between Pareto optimality and competitive equilibrium, and so on, not only gives us insights into the economy but may also help us to improve it. However the improvements we make may not necessarily satisfy the Pareto principle. Society may adopt changes that make more people significantly better off at the cost of making some a little worse off. Nonetheless knowledge about the conditions for Pareto optimality and so on may enable us to select changes that are more desirable than others, for example changes that will make a smaller number of people worse off. But if some individuals are made better off and some worse off, by what criterion do we decide that a change is desirable? This leads us to the discussion of welfare criteria in the next chapter.

2.4 Summary

The Pareto principle states that a change is desirable if it makes some individuals better off without making any others worse off. Objections to this principle are usually based on some misunderstanding. The first-order conditions for Pareto optimality in a simple economy involve an exchange optimum, requiring equality of MRS for any pair of goods for all consuming individuals; a production optimum, requiring equality of MRTS for any pair of factors; and a top-level optimum, requiring MRS to equal MRT. The inability of individual consumers and producers to affect prices renders a perfectly competitive economy Pareto-optimal under certain conditions.

Appendix 2.1: The First-Order Conditions for Pareto Optimality*

The optimality conditions for production and those for exchange are usually derived separately in two maximisation problems: one maximising productive efficiency, the other maximising consumers' satisfaction. We shall derive all the first-order conditions in one maximisation problem. We shall also take account of the production of commodities by means of commodities (but we shall ignore the issue of time lags). To simplify the notation we shall disregard the cases of satiation and corner maxima. A corner maximum (or corner solution) is one in which some variables take on the value of the upper or lower bounds (usually zero). For example some goods might not be consumed by some individuals. Corner maxima can be allowed for by changing the equality requirements below into inequality requirements. Divisibility in the variables is assumed throughout and external effects are assumed to be absent (on externalities and public goods, see Chapters 7 and 8). Given the non-economic factors, the utility functions of individuals can be written as:

$$U^i = U^i\left(x_1^i, x_2^i, \ldots, x_G^i\right) (i = 1, \ldots, I) \tag{A2.1}$$

where I is the number of individuals in the economy and x_g^i is the amount of the gth good consumed (or the negative quantity of the particular labour service performed) by the ith individual. The G types of x could either be goods or services *consumed* or productive services (such as labour) *performed*. In the latter case, negative amounts enter the utility function. Hence an increase in the relevant amount means a reduction in the service performed, or an increase in leisure time. The production functions of the various x's can be written as:

$$x_g = x_g(x_{1g}, x_{2g}, \ldots, x_{Gg}; z_{1g}, \ldots, z_{Rg}) (g = 1, \ldots, G) \tag{A2.2}$$

where x_{hg} is the amount of the hth good or service (hereafter we shall refer to this only as 'good'), z_{rg} is the amount of the rth natural resource used in the production of the gth good and R is the number of different types of natural resources. We also have the following accounting identities:

$$x_g = \sum_{i=1}^{I} x_g^i + \sum_{j=1}^{G} x_{gj} (g = 1, \ldots, G) \tag{A2.3}$$

$$z_r = \sum_{g=1}^{G} z_{rg} \quad (r = 1, \ldots, R) \tag{A2.4}$$

The amounts of the R types of resource are given. If x_g is a productive service such as labour, it is not produced and hence $x_g = 0$. Then we have, from

Equation A2.3, $-\sum_{i=1}^{I} x_g^i / \sum_{j=1}^{G} x_{gj}$, or the equality of the aggregate labour performed by individuals and that used in the various industries.

To derive the conditions for Pareto optimality we maximise the utility of one individual given the utility levels of all others. Without loss of generality, we take this individual to be the first person (since any individual can be put in any place). Maximising U^1 subject to $U^i = \overline{U}^i, i = 2, \ldots, I$ and to Equations A2.2 and A2.4, we form the following Lagrangean function:

$$L = U^1 + \sum_{i=2}^{I} \lambda^i \left(U^i - \overline{U}^i \right) + \sum_{g=1}^{G} p_g \left(x_g - \sum_{i=1}^{I} x_g^i - \sum_{j=1}^{G} x_{gi} \right)$$
$$+ \sum_{r=1}^{R} q_r \left(z_r - \sum_{g=1}^{G} z_{rg} \right) \tag{A2.5}$$

where the x's, p's and q's are the multipliers associated with the respective constraints. The p's and the q's may be interpreted as the (shadow) prices of goods and resources respectively, and the X's are the weights attached to other individuals' utility levels relative to U^1. From Equation A2.5 we obtain the following three sets of first-order conditions by setting equal to zero the partial derivative of L with respect to x_g^i, x_{hg}, and z_{rg} respectively:

$$\lambda^i \partial U^i / \partial x_g^i = p_g \ (i = 1, \ldots, I; \ g = 1, \ldots, G) \tag{A2.6}$$

$$p_g \partial x_g / \partial x_{hg} = p_h \ (g, h = 1, \ldots, G) \tag{A2.7}$$

$$p_g \partial x_g / \partial z_{rg} = q_r \ (g = 1, \ldots, G; \ r = 1, \ldots, R) \tag{A2.8}$$

where $\lambda^i \equiv 1$. By division, we can write Equation A2.6 in a proportional form to eliminate λ^i:

$$\frac{\partial U^i / \partial x_g^i}{\partial U^i / \partial x_G^i} = \frac{P_g}{P_G} \ (i = 1, \ldots, I; \ g = 1, \ldots, G - 1, \ldots, G - 1) \tag{A2.9}$$

which is the optimality condition for exchange, requiring equality of the marginal rate of substitution (MRS, ratio of marginal utilities) between any two pairs of goods for all individuals who consume both goods ('goods' here include the negative of services performed). Similarly, Equation (A2.7) can be written as:

$$\frac{\partial x_g / \partial x_{hg}}{\partial x_g / \partial x_{Gg}} = \frac{P_h}{P_G} \ (g = 1, \ldots, G; \ h = 1, \ldots, G - 1) \tag{A2.10}$$

which is a condition for productive efficiency that requires equality of the technical MRS (ratio of marginal productivities) between any pair of goods in all lines of production. Combining Equations A2.9 and A2.10 we have:

$$\frac{\partial U^i/\partial x_g^i}{\partial U^i/\partial x_G^i} = \frac{\partial x_h/\partial x_{gh}}{\partial x_h/\partial x_{Gh}} \quad (i = 1, \ldots, I; \, g, h = 1, \ldots, G - 1) \tag{A2.11}$$

which is a top-level condition that requires equality between the subjective MRS and technical MRS for any pair of goods consumed and used as inputs.
Equation A2.7 can also be written as:

$$\frac{\partial x_G/\partial x_{hG}}{\partial x_g/\partial x_{hg}} = \frac{P_g}{P_G} \quad (g, h = 1, \ldots, G) \tag{A2.12}$$

which can be combined with Equation A2.9 to yield:

$$\frac{\partial U^i/\partial x_g^i}{\partial U^i/\partial x_G^i} = \frac{\partial x_G/\partial x_{hG}}{\partial x_g/\partial x_{hg}} \quad (i = 1, \ldots, I; \, g, h = 1, \ldots, G) \tag{A2.13}$$

which is a top-level condition that requires equality between the subjective MRS and the indirect (that is, through input reallocation) technical marginal rate of transformation (MRT) between any pair of goods. Furthermore, combining Equations A2.7 and A2.9 gives:

$$\frac{\partial U^i/\partial x_h^i}{\partial U^i/\partial x_g^i} = \partial x_g/\partial x_{hg} \, (i = 1, \ldots, I; \, g, h = 1, \ldots, G) \tag{A2.14}$$

which is a top-level condition that requires equality between the subjective MRS and the direct technical MRT between any pair of goods.

We have yet to extend the optimality requirement to the use of resources. Similar to the derivation of Equations A2.9 and A2.10 from Equation A2.7, we derive the following from Equation A2.8:

$$\frac{\partial x_g/\partial z_{rg}}{\partial x_g/\partial z_{Rg}} = \frac{q_r}{q_R} \quad (g = 1, \ldots, G; \, r = 1, \ldots, R - 1) \tag{A2.15}$$

$$\frac{\partial x_G/\partial z_{rg}}{\partial x_g/\partial z_{rg}} = \frac{P_g}{P_G} \quad (g = 1, \ldots, G - 1; \, r = 1, \ldots, R) \tag{A2.16}$$

While Equation A2.16 can be combined with Equation A2.9 to obtain a top-level condition similar to Equation A2.13, we cannot combine Equation A2.15 with Equation A2.9 because we assume that non-reproducible natural resources do not directly enter into utility functions. Should any natural resources directly enter into utility functions, we just define the production function of that 'good' as $x_g = z_r$. We shall then have a top-level condition for it.

In addition to the above, we can also combine Equations A2.7 and A2.8 to extend the requirement for efficiency with respect to the use of goods versus resources. We have thus shown that all the necessary conditions for Pareto optimality can be derived in a single maximisation procedure. Moreover with this approach the MRT is also stated in the explicit form of the technical MRS, the ratio of marginal productivities (indirect MRT) or just a figure of marginal productivity (direct MRT), instead of the usual one stated in the implicit form in terms of the derivatives of the production constraint function.

3
The Direction of Welfare Change: Welfare Criteria

In the previous chapter we noted that the Pareto principle is a sufficient condition for social improvement. However most policy changes make some individuals better off and some worse off, so can we still have a sufficient condition for social improvement? This brings us to the issue of welfare criteria, which has been the subject of considerable debate in the literature on welfare economics.

3.1 The debate on compensation tests

The controversy over welfare criteria is associated with the distinction between the 'old' and 'new' welfare economics. The new welfare economics – marked by (1) the popularisation of the Pareto principle and the associated marginal conditions, (2) Bergson's (1938) paper on the social welfare function and (3) the controversy over compensation tests in about 1940 – is actually not so new. Pareto's original writings (see Tarascio, 1968) were published (in French) before the first edition of Pigou's *Economics of Welfare* (1912, under the title *Wealth and Welfare*), which can be regarded as a pinnacle of the old welfare economics.

The difference between old and new welfare economists lie mainly in the willingness of the former to assume that subjective concepts such as happiness are measurable and interpersonally comparable, and the attempt by the latter to confine themselves to more objective concepts such as choice and to avoid interpersonal comparisons of utility (by this standard I am probably the 'oldest' welfare economist on earth today). For example Pigou regarded it as 'evident' that 'any transference of income from a relatively rich man to a relatively poor man of similar temperament, since it enables more intense wants to be satisfied at the expense of less intense wants, must increase the aggregate sum of satisfaction' (Pigou, 1932, p. 89). Robbins (1932, 1938) argued strongly against interpersonal comparisons of utility in scientific analysis. (I have argued Chapter 1 that interpersonal comparisons of utility are not scientifically meaningless. While I readily admit the practical difficulty of such comparisons I have developed a method for utility measurement that is interpersonally comparable – see Ng, 1996a.) But it is also evident that most policies make some people better off and some worse off, and hence a policy prescription is usually only possible if some interpersonal comparison is made. Kaldor (1939) attempted to get round this difficulty by resorting to the possibility of compensation (on the contribution of Barone, 1908, and Pareto to the compensation principle, see Chipman, 1976; Chipman and Moore, 1978, p. 548n).

In all cases, therefore, where a certain policy leads to an increase in physical productivity, and thus of aggregate real income, the economist's case for the policy is quite unaffected by the question of the comparability of individual satisfactions; since in all such cases it is possible to make everybody better off without making anybody worse off. There is no need for the economist to prove – as indeed he never could prove – that as a result of the adoption of a certain measure nobody in the community is going to suffer. In order to establish his case, it is quite sufficient for him to show that even if all those who suffer as a result are fully compensated for their loss, the rest of the community will still be better off than before (Kaldor, 1939, p. 551).

In effect Kaldor proposed that there is social improvement if the gainers can fully compensate the losers and still be better off (Kaldor referred to improvement from the point of view of production, not necessarily all-round social improvement – see Kaldor, 1947. But the term 'Kaldor criterion' is usually used with reference to a social improvement). Hicks (1939, 1941) supported the criterion (The Kaldor or Kaldor–Hicks criterion) and also proposed a sister criterion, the Hicks criterion, which states that there is social improvement if the losers cannot profitably bribe the gainers to oppose a change (Hicks, 1940).

An important feature of welfare criteria or compensation tests is that only hypothetical compensation is involved, not actual compensation. If the compensation were actually paid there would be no need for these criteria; the Pareto principle alone would be sufficient as everyone would be made better off, or at least no worse off. Hence the compensation tests owe both their strength and their weakness to their hypothetical nature. This weakness was quickly observed by Scitovsky (1941). Using a set of Edgeworth boxes, Scitovsky showed that the Kaldor (and the Hicks) criterion could lead to a contradiction. According to the Kaldor criterion a certain change can be proposed, but the reverse change (that is, changing the situation after the first change back to the original situation) can also be proposed by the same criterion. A logical inconsistency is therefore involved. This inconsistency is illustrated in Figure 3.1. Due to our limitation to two dimensions we either have to assume a two-person community or to assume that the change only

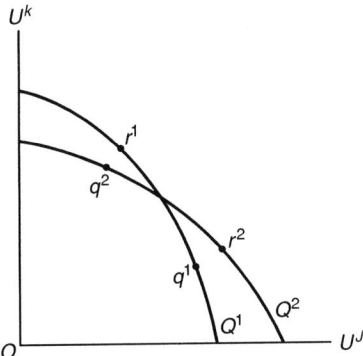

Figure 3.1

affects two persons, J and K, whose utility levels are represented by the two axes. But the essence of the analysis is not affected by this limitation. Moreover the utilities assumed can also be cardinal or ordinal without affecting the analysis. This is so because the relative position of the two curves is not altered by stretching or contracting an axis or one or more parts thereof.

Let the original situation be at q^1 on the utility possibility curve (UPC), Q^1. It does not matter whether a UPC is assumed to represent a given collection of goods (Mishan, 1962a, p. 238, 1969a, pp. 40 ff.), a given endowment of factors of production (Robertson, 1962, p. 227) or a given set of price and output policies (Little, 1957, p. 102). What matters is that movement along the curve is caused only by costless lump-sum transfers. Even if we assume that costless lump-sum transfers are impossible we can still operate with utility feasibility curves instead of possibility curves. Which curve is relevant depends on the context in question (Graaff, 1957, p, 83). Incidentally a utility feasibility curve shows the different combinations of utility levels (of the two individuals) that are attainable, taking into account the cost of transferring income. Hence the shape of a feasibility curve depends not only on the given collection of goods (or factor endowment and so on) but also on the initial distribution of income. Typically the relation of a feasibility curve to its corresponding possibility curve is as shown in Figure 3.2, with A as the initial point. Distribution away from this point will result in a combination of utility levels (such as R) that are lower than that indicated by the UPC (such as S) due to the cost of redistribution.

Returning to Figure 3.1, consider a change that will carry us from q^1 to q^2. This change passes the Kaldor criterion as it is possible, after the change, to redistribute income to reach point r^2 where everyone is better off than at q^1. Starting from q^2, transferring income from K to J (or making K compensate J) will enable us to move along the curve Q^2 to point r^2. Since r^2 is north-east of q^1, both J and K will be better off at r^2 than at q^1. According to the Kaldor

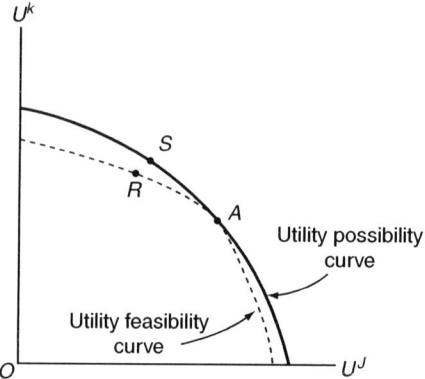

Figure 3.2

criterion, therefore, the change from q^1 to q^2 is a social improvement. However, by exactly the same reasoning the change from q^2 back to q^1 fulfils the
same Kaldor criterion. This is because we can also redistribute income from
q^1 to r^1, which is north-east of q^2. Since the same criterion dictates that q^2
is socially preferable to q^1 and that q^1 is socially preferable to q^2, a logical
inconsistency is involved (for a sufficient condition in which the Kaldor
criterion does not lead to inconsistency see Jerison, 1994).

If one is sceptical about the possibility of contradiction and thinks that
this could just be the result of unrestricted manipulation of UPCs, it should
be remembered that Scitovsky was using an Edgeworth box that consisted
of commodity space with well-behaved indifference maps. The following
simple example by Quirk and Saposnik (1968, p. 121) should be sufficiently
convincing. Imagine a community in which there are just two individuals,
J and K, and two goods, X and Y. In situation q^1 J has two X and K has one Y;
in situation q^2 J has one X and K has two Y. Now suppose that J would
prefer one X and one Y to two X, and would prefer two X to one X; while K
would prefer one X and one Y to two Y, and would prefer two Y to one Y.
These preference patterns are quite reasonable and satisfy the conventional
diminishing marginal rates of substitution. It can easily be seen that the
movement from q^1 to q^2 and the reverse movement from q^2 to q^1 both satisfy
the Kaldor criterion. Thus after moving from q^1 to q^2, if the gainer (K) gives
one unit of Y to the loser (J), J is made better off than at q^1 and K is no worse
off. Similarly, if we move back from q^2 to q^1 and the gainer (now J) gives one
unit of X to K, K is made better off than at q^2 and J is no worse off.

The contradiction in the Hicks criterion can also be seen in Figure 3.3.
Here the change from q^1 to q^2 satisfies the Hicks criterion as it is not possible
to redistribute income from q^1 to reach a point north-east of q^2. By similar
reasoning, the reverse change from q^2 to q^1 also satisfies the Hicks criterion.

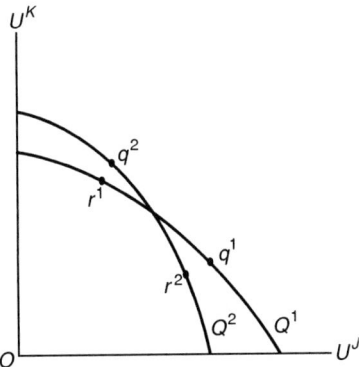

Figure 3.3

The contradiction in the Kaldor and Hicks criteria can also be illustrated by using the Scitovsky community indifference curves (CIC), which show in goods space the minimum bundles of the two goods sufficient to make each individual attain a given utility or indifference level; (see Ng, 1979/83, app. 3A). It can be seen that the contradiction in the compensation test, and indeed in the measurement of consumer surplus discussed in the next chapter, is closely related to the problem of index numbers (Samuelson, 1950).[1]

To avoid contradiction Scitovsky (1941) proposes that a change should be regarded as unambiguously favourable only if it satisfies both the Kaldor criterion and the Hicks criterion (or, equivalently, the Scitovsky reversal test). In terms of UPCs this means that, for the change from q^1 to q^2 to be unambiguously desirable, not only must the UPC through q^2 pass over (north-east of) q^1, but also the UPC through q^1 must pass under (south-west of) q^2. This is satisfied for the movement from q^1 to q^2 in Figure 3.4.

If the change from q^1 to q^2 satisfies the Scitovsky criterion, then the reverse change from q^2 to q^1 cannot satisfy that criterion. The Scitovsky

---

1. For a consistent individual with non-intersecting, strictly convex indifference curves, it can be shown that $\sum_{g=1}^{G} p_g^1 x_g^1$ (abbreviated to $\Sigma p^1 x^1$) $> \Sigma p^1 x^0$ implies that $\Sigma p^\circ x^0 < \Sigma p^\circ x^1$ where the superscripts 0 and 1 denote the old and new price (p) and quantity (x) vectors. From $\Sigma p^1 x^1 > \Sigma p^1 x^\circ$ we infer that x^1 is preferred to x° (assuming there is no change in taste and that more is preferred to less). This is so because, with p^1 ruling, the individual could consume at x° but chooses x^1. If $\Sigma p^\circ x^\circ > \Sigma p^0 x^1$, we similarly infer that x° is preferred to x^1, ending in a contradiction. So $\Sigma p^1 x^1 > \Sigma p^1 x^\circ$ implies that $\Sigma p^\circ x^\circ < \Sigma p^\circ x^1$. However in the case of more than one individual we can have $\Sigma p^1 x^1 > \Sigma p^1 x^0$ and $\Sigma p^\circ x^\circ > \Sigma p^\circ x^1$, leading to difficulties with interpreting national income data and the like.

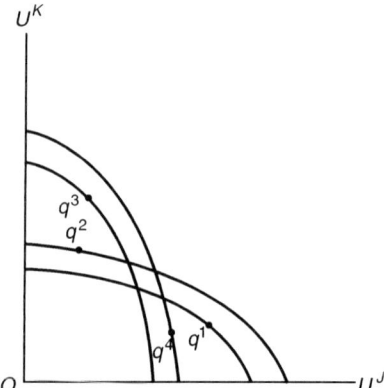

Figure 3.4

criterion is therefore free from contradiction in this sense. However successive applications of the criterion can still lead to cyclicity. Thus the
movements q^1 to q^2, q^2 to q^3, q^3 to q^4 and q^4 to q^1 all satisfy the Scitovsky
criterion but these movements end up at the original position q^1. Also, q^4 is
Pareto-inferior to q^1.

3.2   Taking distribution into account: Little's criterion

3.2.1   Little's criterion and alleged contradiction and/or redundancy

Pointing out that the Kaldor, Hicks and Scitovsky criteria indicate only
potential improvement, Little (1949, 1957, ch. 6) maintains that distributional
effects have to be taken into account for a welfare criterion that purports
to indicate actual improvement.[2] Little's criterion poses three questions:
(1) are the gainers able to compensate the losers fully and still be better off?
(the Kaldor criterion); (2) are the losers unable profitably to bribe the gainers
to oppose the change? (the Scitovsky reversal test); and (3) is any redistribution good? If the answer to (3) is positive (negative) and at least one of
the answers to (1) and (2) is also positive (negative), the change is proposed
(rejected), assuming that direct redistribution is not feasible.

---

2. It may also be noted that the Samuelson (1950) criterion, which requires the new
    UPC to etie *entirely above* the old one, is too restrictive for a potential improvement
    but still insufficient for an actual improvement unless it is assumed that optimal
    redistribution will take place after the change. Readers may wish to confirm this
    assertion by drawing UPCs and welfare contours as an exercise.

The rationale of Little's criterion is based on the following two premises: (a) there is a social improvement if someone is made better off without anyone else being made worse off (the Pareto criterion), and (b) *ceteris paribus*, there is a social improvement if income distribution is made more equal. Consider Figure 3.3. To examine the desirability of a movement from q^1 to q^2, point r^1 is placed on the same UPC as q^1 but is just south-west of (that is, is Pareto inferior to) q^2 and hence 'represents (approximately) the same distribution as' q^2 (Little, 1957, p. 100). Now, if r^1 is regarded as distributionally better than q^1, then the change from q^1 to q^2 must be a social improvement as q^2 is superior to r^1 according to (a) and r^1 is superior to q^1 according to (b).

Little's criterion has been criticised as being conducive to contradiction. In Figure 3.3, if r^2 is also distributionally preferred to q^2, then it can be shown that q^1 is superior to q^2 via r^2 and contradicts the demonstration in the preceding paragraph that q^2 is superior to q^1. How can this arise? If a change from q to q^1 represents a good redistribution, how can a reverse change also represent a good redistribution? When Little says that the change from q^1 to q^2 represents a good redistribution he means that a distributional change that will produce a point (r^1) that is distributionally (approximately) indifferent to q^2 will be a good thing (ibid., p. 101). This means, as Sen (1963, p. 772) explains, that the social welfare contour passing through r^1 is higher than that passing through q^1, which in turn must be higher than that passing through r^2 as long as the social welfare function (SWF) is Paretian, since q^1 is Pareto superior to r^2. As q^2 is again Pareto superior to r^1, r^2 cannot be on a welfare contour that is higher than q^2 unless the welfare contours intersect each other, which is ruled out by consistency. In other words the possibility that r^2 is better than q^2 is ruled out by the very SWF that says that r^1 is preferred to q^1. The alleged contradiction in the application of Little's criterion therefore, cannot arise. However if we have a well-defined, consistent SWF, why do we have to use a welfare criterion? Does not the existence of such a function render welfare criteria redundant? If the society or ethical observers are able to compare the social welfare between q^1 and r^1, why cannot they directly compare the social welfare between q^1 and q^2 (Kennedy, 1953, 1963a, 1963b; Chipman and Moore, 1978)? It is argued here that Little's criterion is neither redundant nor inconsistent.

3.2.2 A defence of Little's criterion*

Little's criterion is based on Pareto improvement and distributional improvement. Does this combined use of two separate value judgments lead to inconsistency, as argued by Kennedy (1963a, b)? If our value system is such that a Pareto improvement is not a sufficient condition for a good change (for example that it must also have better, or at least not worse, distribution), then the Pareto criterion cannot be used independently of other considerations (such as distribution). But Little considers (reasonably) that a Pareto improvement is a good change irrespective of what happens to any other factor (distribution included). Hence there is certainly no problem with respect to the Pareto part of Little's criterion. With respect to the distributional part, Little does not assume (nor is it widely accepted) that a change is good as long as the new situation involves better distribution.

It thus seems that the separate use of the distributional part is the source of the contradiction. But Little confines distributional comparisons to points on the same utility possibility curve. By definition, points on the same UPC differ from each other only with respect to distribution, everything else being held constant. If r^1 is regarded as distributionally better than q^1, and r^1 and q^1 differ only with respect to distribution, then r^1 must be better than q^1 even if everything else is taken into account. Hence the separate use of the distribution part of Little's criterion is also logically valid. If the change from q^1 to r^1 satisfies a sufficient condition for a good change (involves better distribution on the same UPC) and the change from r^1 to q^2 satisfies another sufficient condition (Pareto improvement), then the change from q^1 to q^2 must necessarily be a good change. The combined use of two separate conditions is quite all right as long as each is a sufficient condition. So Little's criterion is not logically inconsistent in itself, but is it redundant, as argued by its critics?

Usually a society does not have a well-defined and logically consistent SWF. This is partly due to the fact that in a democratic system, social decisions are influenced by pressure groups. The whole set of welfare contours in the utility space may be twisted in a certain direction when a pressure group carries out a strategic threat. The choices made after this change may therefore be inconsistent with those made before. This is analogous to consumers' change in taste in the theory of demand. Frequent changes in consumers' tastes do not, however, deter us from assuming a set of nonintersecting indifference curves or the weak axiom of revealed preference. It therefore does not seem unreasonable to assume that there is a well-defined SWF in terms of individual utilities, that is, $W = W(U^1, \ldots, U^I)$. This of course is based on an individualistic premise that what matters are the individuals, not any mythical interest of the state above and apart from the interest of individuals. It is also reasonable to assume that $\partial W / \partial U^i > 0$ for all i's, that is, the Pareto criterion that social welfare is an increasing function of individual utilities.

Does the existence of an SWF in the above form necessarily preclude the usefulness of any welfare criterion? The answer is no. This is so because of a possible lack of knowledge about the correspondence between a social state and a point in the utility space. If we know the exact location of every social state in the utility space, the existence of a specific SWF in the above form means that we can rank all the social states according to this SWF, making any welfare criterion redundant. But such exact and complete information is usually, if not always, unavailable, so a welfare criterion is useful despite the existence of an SWF in terms of individual utilities. Consider a proposal to build a new airport in a certain locality. For simplicity, assume that the choice is between building that airport (q^2) and not building it (q^1). It is known that the people who live in the vicinity of the proposed site, J, will be made worse off and the rest of the community, K, will be made better off. This is the knowledge available to the society, or to ethical observers. Is that knowledge sufficient for these observers to make a rational choice? Not necessarily. Even if it is known that J is relatively richer than K and that the ethical observers favour a more equal distribution of income, it does not necessarily follow that the change from q^1 to q^2 (building the airport) is socially desirable as J may suffer much and K gain only a little by the change, so that even an egalitarian SWF may reject the change. If the ethical observers know the exact position of q^1 and q^2 in cardinal utility space, they also know the extent to which K will be made better off and J worse off. But usually they do not have such precise knowledge. How then can they make a rational decision? It is here that the compensation test (and on a more practical and quantitative level, cost–benefit analysis) enters the scene. The use of a compensation test may reveal that K will not be made sufficiently better off by the change to be prepared to compensate J fully, but J will not made sufficiently worse off to be prepared to pay the required amount to bribe K to oppose the change. Then we know that the two utility possibility curves intersect, although we do not know the precise location of the respective points.

The next step is to ask whether our ethical observers prefer the existing situation (q^1 in Figure 3.3) to the situation after the payment of the bribe (r^1); the two situations differ from each other only by a lump-sum transfer of goods or purchasing power. If r^1 is preferred to q^1, we infer that q^2 is preferred to q^1, since q^2 is Pareto superior to r^1. If q^1 is preferred to r^1, then the ranking of q^1 and q^2 can still be made through r^2. All this, of course, is the application of Little's criterion. The objection is that it could lead to contradiction. If we know the exact location of each social state (or situation) in the utility space, then no contradiction can arise if the SWF is well-defined in terms of utilities. But in this case compensation tests and welfare criteria are redundant. The usefulness of compensation tests arises from our lack of knowledge about the exact position of each social state in the utility space. While compensation tests do not establish the exact location, they do give us the relative position of social states, for example that one is south-west or north-west of the other.

What about the possibility of contradiction? It might be thought that since the ethical observers only have a rough idea of the location of each social state in the utility space, they may prefer r^1 to q^1 and r^2 to q^2 even if they have a well-defined SWF in terms of individual utilities. This inconsistent choice will not occur if our ethical observers have taken account of the information provided by the compensation test. Before the test, since they did not have a precise idea of the location of the respective points, it is quite possible that they ranked r^1 above q^1 and r^2 above q^2 even if they had a well-defined SWF in terms of individual utilities. However the compensation test has shown that r^1 is south-west of q^2 and r^2 is south-west of q^1. Hence no matter whether or not their idea of the position of the four points exactly corresponds to the true picture, as long as they conform to the 'doubt south-west' relationship they will not rank r^1 above q^1 and r^2 above q^2, since they are assumed to have a well-defined Paretian SWF.

What would happen if we relaxed the assumption of a well-defined SWF in terms of individual utilities? The answer is that inconsistency could arise in the application of Little's criterion (without ruling out inconsistent distributional judgments, successive applications of Little's criterion could also lead to everyone being made worse off; see Ng, 1971c, pp. 580–1). This inconsistency would be due not to any logical fault of the criterion but to the inconsistent SWF or the contradictory distributional judgments of the ethical observers. Given the inconsistent SWF, inconsistent decisions could arise even if Little's criterion was not used.

Hence the use of Little's criterion does not create any additional inconsistency, but does it have any positive use? The answer is yes. Without the compensation test the ethical observers may be unable to rank q^1 and q^2, and if they are forced to do so they are even more likely to make an incorrect and/or inconsistent choice. For example, after choosing to move from q^1 to q^2 they may find that they actually prefer q^2 to q^1. Given a third alternative, cyclicity may arise. An inconsistent choice is more likely to occur since, robbed of the compensation test, they have even less knowledge of the position of the respective situations. Hence an inconsistent and/or incorrect choice is more likely as the inconsistent SWF is reinforced by the lack of knowledge.

Our discussion so far can be briefly summarised as follows. If we have a well-defined SWF in terms of individual utilities (but not in terms of social states, as in this case the compensation test is redundant), Little's criterion can assist in the making of a rational social choice without producing an inconsistent result. If the relevant SWF is not consistent, then Little's criterion can still assist social decisions but inconsistent decisions are not completely ruled out. This can be clarified by the following analogy.

Suppose our problem is to compare the sizes of two solid blocks. If we can measure the length of all three dimensions of both blocks, the obvious criterion to use is the product of the three measures. Now suppose that we are allowed only to measure one of the three dimensions and to look at the rectangular area formed by the other two dimensions. The analogy to Little's criterion is the following: block A is larger than block B if A is longer than B in the measured dimension and also looks larger in the rectangle formed by the other two dimensions. Obviously this is a sufficient condition for A to be larger than B unless we are wrong about the relative size of the rectangles, in which case we are even more likely to make mistakes by judging the size of blocks directly without measuring one of the dimensions.

3.3   The inadequacy of purely distributional rankings**

Little's criterion combines compensation tests with distributional judgments in recognition of the fact that purely allocational and purely distributional rankings are inadequate. Purely allocational improvements need not necessarily improve social welfare unless we assume one of the following (or something similar): (1) optimal redistribution of income; and (2) random distributional effects that cancel out in the long run.[3] Similarly, purely distributional improvements need not increase welfare as a small cake will make little difference even if it is optimally distributed. However in his proposed resolution of the unresolved problems with the welfare criterion, Mishan (1973, 1976) downgrades the role of allocational comparison and relies on purely distributional rankings. If this is accepted, the part played by economists will be significantly reduced since economists are predominantly concerned with allocational efficiency. Nevertheless Mishan is intuitively sound in not trying completely to reject dual welfare criteria, that is, criteria based on both allocational and distributional rankings. 'There is always hope that a little more thought may enable us to discover some redeeming features of such criteria' (Mishan, 1973, p. 776). This is in fact what the following argument will demonstrate.

With reference to Figure 3.5 (which is similar to Mishan's figure 2), Mishan argues that if there is another collection of goods, Q^3, whose locus in utility space passes through q^1 and q^2, we can compare q^1 and q^2 directly on distributional grounds, since q^1 and q^2 differ from each other only because there is a different distribution of a single collection of goods. Moreover, by using an ingenious construction involving community indifference curves, Mishan shows that the required collection of goods (Q^3) can in principle always be found, given the divisibility of goods and continuity in preferences (the required collection of goods is simply the case in which the Scitovsky

---

3. According to Polinsky (1972, p. 409), by 'Broadening the notion of compensation to include bundles of changes that have some effective randomness in distribution, it thereby becomes possible to leave particular individuals uncompensated and worse off for single changes, yet assure them that they can (mathematically) expect to be better off as a result of the entire bundle (with the probability of actually being worse off set a value approaching zero).' This proposed criterion enables us to disregard, within certain limits, the unfavourable distributional effect of each single change.

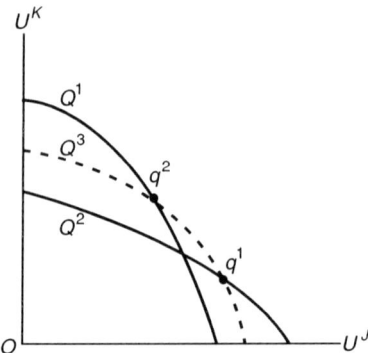

Figure 3.5

community indifference curves corresponding to q^1 and q^2 intersect, since this collection ensures that both the q^1 and the q^2 combination of utility levels can be obtained by appropriate distribution).[4] It is therefore concluded that, 'if society is assumed able to rank distributions of a single collection of goods (which has been the traditional assumption), then "contradictory" collections [those with intersecting UPCs] can be ranked unambiguously albeit only on a distributional scale.... If society is assumed unable to rank the distributions of a single collection of goods, then "contradictory" collections cannot be ranked at all' (ibid., p. 762).

Mishan's conclusion does not, however, invalidate Little's criterion. Mishan concludes that contradictory collections can always be reduced to a distributional ordering. But how do we know that the two collections are contradictory or that the two UPCs intersect each other? This can be revealed by compensation tests. If the answers to questions (1) and (2) in Little's criterion have opposite signs, then the two collections are contradictory. In this case, Little's criterion ranks the two situations according to the answer to question (3), which is precisely the distributional part. Nevertheless there is an important difference between Little and Mishan with respect to distributional ranking. Little uses the intermediate points r^1

---

4. For the case depicted in the solid curves in Figure 3.5, as the UPC of the Q^2 bundle of goods cannot achieve utility combination at point q^1 this means that Scitovsky's CIC through point Q^1 (in a separate figure of goods space) corresponding to distributional point q^1 passes above point Q^2. Similarly, as the UPC of the Q^1 bundle of goods cannot achieve utility combination at point q^2, this means that Scitovsky's CIC through point Q^2 corresponding to q^2 passes above point Q^1. Thus the two CICs intersect each other, and the intersection of the two UPCs implies the intersection of the corresponding CICs and *vice versa*.

and r^2 as a reference point for comparing the distributional desirability of q^1 and q^2, while Mishan uses the direct distributional ranking of q^1 and q^2. Mishan not only makes a direct comparison between q^1 and q^2 as points on Q^3, but also makes a direct comparison between q^1 on Q^1 and q^2 on Q^2. In fact in Mishan's scheme the Q^3 collection need not actually be identified. His 'findings do not...depend on actual identification of the required hypothetical collection of goods [Q^3]. Indeed nothing of significance results from knowing the composition of the hypothetical collection. For the analysis reveals that wherever there are "contradictable" collections there will also be, necessarily, the appropriate hypothetical collection. And the purpose of confirming its existence is only to establish the fact that a comparison of "contradictable" collections can always be reduced to a distributional ranking' (ibid., pp. 762–3).

Given the assumption that the precise location of the relevant social states in the utility space is known, Mishan's argument may appear unassailable. Points q^1 and q^2, as points on Q^3, are exactly the same points in utility space as q^1 on Q^1 and q^2 on Q^2. Since ranking is to be conducted according to the utility levels of individuals, q^1 on Q^1 and q^2 on Q^2 must be ranked exactly as q^1 and q^2 on Q^3, but the latter two points differ from each other only with respect to distribution. Hence if they can be given a direct distributional ranking, so too can q^1 on Q^1 and q^2 on Q^2. However caution is in order, as discussed below.

Consider Figure 3.6, in which the W's are the contours of a consistent and Paretian SWF and the three UPCs depict the actual utility possibilities of the three collections of goods. If these utility possibilities are known, then q^1 will be judged the best distribution of the Q^1 collection since it touches the highest welfare contour. Similarly $q^{2\prime}$ is judged the best distribution of Q^2, and q^2 a not so good distribution. However when q^1 and q^2 are ranked as different distributions of the Q^3 collection, q^2 is ranked a better distribution than q^1. Is this a contradiction? One could say that it is not as different collections of goods are involved, and it is possible that the not so good q^2 distribution of Q^2 may be better than the best q^1 distribution of Q^1, and hence, as a distribution of Q^3, q^2 is a better distribution than q^1. This certainly reminds us that we have to be very careful when making distributional comparisons between points on different UPCs. In particular, making distributional comparisons of points on the same UPC is quite a different matter from making distributional comparisons of points on different UPCs. Point q^2 is ranked higher than q^1, but are we prepared to say that, for a purely distributional ranking, q^2 on Q^2 is better than q^1 on Q^1? It seems that most people are not prepared to say so as q^1 is the best distribution of Q^1, and q^2 is a not so good distribution of Q^2. It is true that, as points on Q^3, q^1 and q^2 differ only with respect to distribution. But as points on Q^1 and Q^2 respectively, q^1 and q^2 do not differ only with respect to distribution. If collection Q^3 is not actually constructed, and the ethical observers, with the welfare contours as depicted, we asked to rank q^1 on Q^1 and q^2 on Q^2 on a purely distributional scale, it is quite likely that they will say that q^1 on Q^1 is superior to q^2 on Q^2 as far as distribution is concerned, though they will rank q^2 above q^1 if they are not restricted to a purely distributional comparison. Hence while Mishan is correct to argue that if society can rank points on the same collection it can also rank points on two contradictory collections, it seems wise not to limit the latter ranking to a purely distributional ranking. Rather society should be allowed to rank q^1 on Q^1 and q^2 on Q^2 directly, taking everything into account (readers are reminded that we have been assuming precise knowledge of individual utilities in this paragraph).

If the Q^3 collection can be found not only in principle but also in practice, and it can be shown which distributions of that collection will result in points q^1 and q^2 in utility space, then q^1 and q^2 can be ranked in a purely distributional ranking as points on the Q^3 UPC. However in the real world of thousands of commodities and millions of individuals, identification of the Q^3 collection is practically impossible, even though it exists in principle. Moreover in practice it is probable that we will not know the precise location of social states in utility space. In this case we have to be even more careful about direct distributional comparisons of points on different UPCs. With imprecise knowledge of individual utilities, distributional ranking is usually made with reference to money income rather than real income. In fact, in the real economy of millions of individuals and commodities, some statistical measure of equality of money income

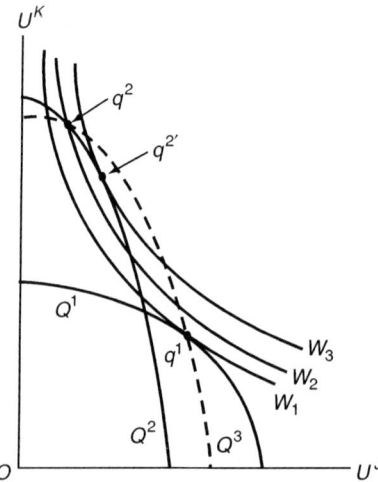

Figure 3.6

is the only practical measure of distributional desirability we can obtain (Mishan, 1963, pp. 345–6).[5] Hence if q^1 on Q^1 and q^2 on Q^2 are ranked with respect only to distribution, it is quite possible that q^1 will be deemed superior to q^2. This is, of course, not a necessary result since there need not be an exact correspondence between the distribution of money and that of real income. But it is quite likely that the (purely distributional) ranking q^1 will be preferred to q^2. If we compare q^1 and q^2 as points on Q^3, it may be that q^2 has a better distribution than q^1. This shows that even if society can rank points (q^1 and q^2) on the same collection (Q^3), it does not necessarily follow that q^1 on Q^1 and q^2 on Q^2 can also be ranked purely on distributional merits.

From the above discussion it can be concluded that, as purely distributional rankings are inadequate, Little's criterion – which combines compensation tests with distributional judgments – is superior. However Little's criterion, like all it predecessors, is cast in static terms. Thus when applying it we have to be careful not to ignore the more dynamic, less immediate effects. For example a change may seem to satisfy Little's criterion, but when account is taken of its disincentive effects it may actually be undesirable. The issue of incentives is considered in more detail in Chapters 6 and 9.

3.4   Retreat to purely efficiency comparisons

In contrast to Mishan's reliance on purely distributional comparisons, and consistent with modern economists' aversion to interpersonal comparisons, Coate proposes that we confine ourselves to the efficiency aspect of policy changes:

> When confronted with a particular policy change, the policy analyst would not investigate whether the social value of the utility gains exceed the social value of the losses or whether the gainers might in principle compensate the losers. Rather, he/she would investigate alternative policy changes that could be made with similar distributional consequences. A policy change would be judged efficient if there did not exist an altern- ative policy change which was better for all…. Efficient policy changes would be deemed sensible ways of achieving the distributional changes that they produce. The policy analyst would take no position on the desirability of these changes (Coate 2000, p. 438).

---

5. If equality in the distribution of money income is representative of equality in the distribution of real income, the application of Little's criterion can never lead to a contradiction (Ng, 1971c).

Coate's point can be illustrated with the help of Figures 3.1 and 3.3 above, with the Q's being interpreted as utility feasibility curves. A change that moves us from q^1 to q^2 in Figure 3.1 is clearly inefficient, as from q^1, we could reach a point r^1 that is Pareto-superior to q^2. This is not the case for the movement from q^1 to q^2 in Figure 3.3. For this movement to be efficient, it must not be possible to have any other policy change that will move us to a point north-east of q^2, possibly a point on a different UFC. If it is possible to have a change that moves us to q^3 on Q^3 (not shown in Figure 3.3), that is, north-east of q^2, it is better to have q^3 than q^2, making q^2 inefficient. If such a change is not possible, then the movement from q^1 to q^2 in Figure 3.3 is an efficient way to achieve that change. Coate calls this 'distributional change', but the movement could involve distributional, allocational, regulatory or other policy changes, or a combination thereof. In terms of the final (distribution of) utility levels, the movement makes J worse off and K better off by the extents depicted in the figures.

However while such changes may be seen by economic policy analysts as efficient, they would take no position on the desirability of these changes. Thus according to Coate's proposal, economists would be confined to the analysis of Pareto efficiency or the lack of it, and would not venture into comparing the social desirability of Pareto-incomparable situations. Thus in terms of welfare criteria no advancement would be achieved beyond the Pareto principle. However for those who were willing to combine Coate's efficiency comparisons with some distributional proviso, the result would become similar to Little's criterion, with the efficiency/allocational part being expanded to consider other changes.

3.5   Quasi-Pareto improvements

Ng (1984a) proposes an extension to the Pareto criterion that amounts to a generalisation of the Pareto and Kaldor criteria. The idea stems from the most important objection to the Kaldor criterion. Even if those who are made better off are willing to pay, say, £10 million while those who are made worse off could be fully compensated with only £7 million, this may not be regarded as a good change if the compensation is not actually paid, especially if the former group is rich with a low marginal utility of income and the latter poor with a high marginal utility of income. The gain may exceed the loss in monetary terms but not in utility or welfare terms. To overcome this objection, Ng suggests that individuals be grouped (perhaps according to their income levels) in such a way that all the individuals within each group are more or less equally poor or rich. Ng then argues that a change should be accepted as a social improvement if the gainers within each and every group can fully compensate the losers in the same group and still be better off. Then the objection to the Kaldor criterion on the ground of divergence between monetary and welfare terms due to the rich–poor contrast does not apply.[6]

It can be seen that the proposed quasi-Pareto criterion will collapse into the Kaldor criterion if the grouping is so broad that the whole economy is lumped into a single group, and it becomes the Pareto criterion when the groups become so small that each individual comprises a distinct group. It is thus clearly a generalisation of both the Pareto and the Kaldor criterion.

The more narrowly the groups are defined, the more difficult it is for the quasi-Pareto criterion to be satisfied. For example analysts may want income groups to be defined not just as rich, average and poor but as extremely rich, very rich, rich, well-off, above average, average, below average, poor, very poor and destitute. With income groups defined narrowly enough to reach agreement that the marginal utilities of income for different people within the same group do not differ significantly (at least as far as income differences are concerned), it might be thought that the quasi-Pareto criterion, though acceptable, is very difficult to satisfy, making the criterion not applicable. However, despite the apparently stringent requirements when groups are narrowly defined, the quasi-Pareto criterion is of important applicability. Ng (ibid.) shows that, no matter how narrowly income groups are defined, the quasi-Pareto criterion can still be used to sanction efficiency-improving changes. This is because some offsetting intergroup arrangement can be combined with the efficiency change to ensure overcompensation within each group. On the other hand, offsetting interpersonal changes to ensure satisfaction of the Pareto criterion is not usually feasible because of the likely existence of differences in preference, even between individuals with the same income. This means that the proposed criterion is of powerful applicability and usefulness.

More importantly, the quasi-Pareto criterion can be used in conjunction with the theory of third best (Section 9.3) and the equality-incentive argument (Appendix 9.1) to obtain the principle that 'a dollar is a dollar'. For each specific issue we can then be exclusively concerned with pure efficiency considerations, treating a dollar as a dollar no matter to whom it goes, leaving equality to be achieved through the general tax/transfer policy. Once this principle of 'a dollar is a dollar' has been obtained with the help of the quasi-Pareto criterion, the latter can be largely be dispensed with and the pure efficiency consideration can be used for each specific issue. Moreover this principle also helps to resolve the paradox of interpersonal

---

6. The slight ambiguity due to the possible inconsistency in the application of the Kaldor criterion discussed with reference to Figure 3.1 is dismissed as practically insignificant if we are confined to cases where the extent of overcompensation is clearly big enough to offset possible ambiguity in data collection; see Ng (1984a).

cardinal utility (that an interpersonal comparison of cardinal utilities is needed for social choice but the required information is usually not available), as discussed in Chapter 5.

3.6 Conclusions

The above discussion on welfare criteria stemmed from the attempt of the new welfare economists to make social welfare comparisons without making interpersonal comparisons of utility. The criteria proposed by Kaldor, Hicks and Scitovsky have all been shown to be inconsistent. Although Little's criterion has been defended, in this chapter, the distributional part of that criterion cannot avoid interpersonal comparisons of utility (not to mention failing to provide answers when the allocational and distributional parts are in conflict). Thus, or at least in the sense of attempting to make social welfare comparisons without making interpersonal comparisons of utility, new welfare economics can be said to be a failure. Nevertheless, for those who are not averse to accepting relevant distributional provisos, Little's criterion is acceptable in some cases. My proposed quasi-Pareto criterion also provides limited advances in some cases. More importantly, its combination with the equality-incentive argument (Appendix 9.1) yields the powerful conclusion that a dollar is a dollar for each specific issue.

3 7 Summary

Different welfare criteria, in terms of compensation tests, have been proposed to deal with cases where some individuals are made better off and some worse off. The criteria proposed by Kaldor, Hicks and Scitovsky are all logically inconsistent. Little's criterion, which specifies distributional improvements in addition to compensation tests, is also regarded as inconsistent and/or redundant, but this chapter has argued that it is not inconsistent since the alleged inconsistency arises from inconsistent distribution judgments, not from the criterion. Moreover it is not redundant even if there is a well-defined SWF in terms of individual utilities, since the SWF may not be well-defined in terms of social states and here the use of Little's criterion can provide useful information. Reliance on purely distributional rankings, as proposed by Mishan, has been shown to be inadequate. Distributional comparisons of points on different utility possibility curves may be more difficult than comparisons of points on the same curve. The proposed quasi-Pareto criterion requires the possibility of full compensation for each income group.

4
The Magnitude of Welfare Change: Consumer Surplus

The discussion of the magnitude of welfare change in this chapter centres on the concept of consumer surplus associated with a price change. But some of the measures of consumer surplus – such as compensating variation, equivalent variation and our proposed measure, marginal-dollar equivalent (see the appendix to this chapter) – can also be used to measure welfare changes that are associated with other changes.

The concept of consumer surplus has given rise to a great deal of debate and confusion. While it has been regarded as superfluous, or at least the theoretical foundation of using consumer surplus as a measure of welfare change is usually regarded as suspect, its use in cost–benefit analyses and policy discussions has been widespread. This chapter reviews the various measures of consumer surplus and discusses some complications, before justifying its use as an approximate measure.

4.1 The origin of the concept: Dupuit and Marshall

The concept of consumer surplus was formulated in about 1850 by the French engineer J. Dupuit, who was concerned with the question as to the amount of worthwhile subsidy towards the cost of constructing a bridge. He was clearly aware of the fact that consumers are usually willing to pay more for a good than they actually pay. Hence the consumer obtains an 'excess satisfaction', or a surplus.

The concept of consumer surplus gained prominence after the publication of Marshall's *Principles of Economics*. Marshall was the first to introduce the concept to the English-speaking world, but it is said that he was less than generous in acknowledging Dupuit's priority (see Pfouts, 1953, p. 316).

Marshall (1920, p. 124) defined consumer surplus as 'the excess of the price which he would be willing to pay rather than go without the thing, over that which he actually does pay'. According to this definition, consumer surplus is the difference between (1) not being allowed to buy any quantity of the good, and (2) buying the chosen quantity of the good at the

65

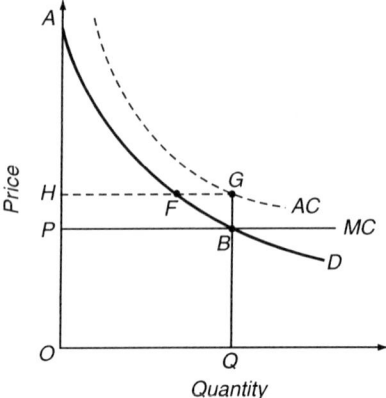

Figure 4.1

prevailing price. As a measure of this, Marshall used the triangular area under the demand curve and above the rectangle that represents the actual money expenditure of the consumer. As shown in Figure 4.1 (for the moment, disregard the dotted lines), this is measured by the curvilinear $\triangle APB$, where OP is the price of the good. As pointed out by Hicks (1940, p. 109), this Marshallian measure is not a definition but a theorem that can be true under certain assumptions. In his mathematical appendix, Marshall mentioned the assumption of a constant marginal utility of money, which could be justified by the fact that expenditure on one particular commodity is usually small relative to total income. Any change in the marginal utility of money is neglected as of the second order of smallness. Marshall spoke in terms of marginal utility since he was interested in consumer surplus as a utility changes. More recently economists have been more concerned with consumer surplus as a more objective measure of willingness to pay.

4.2   Hicks' four measures and the average cost difference

Associated with the attempt to rid economic analysis of the cardinal measures of utility, Hicks (1941) introduced the concept of compensating variation (discussed below). With further clarification by Henderson (1941), four measures of surplus were distinguished (Hicks, 1943). First, in Figure 4.2 we can see how Marshall's definition of consumer surplus is measured in terms of an indifference map. The Y axis represents the amount of money and the X axis the quantity of the commodity in question. If the price of the commodity is represented by the (absolute) slope of the line AP^1 (that is, FP/AF), the consumer will buy ON at a cost of FP since J_1 is the highest indifference curve attainable with AP^1 as the budget line. However the

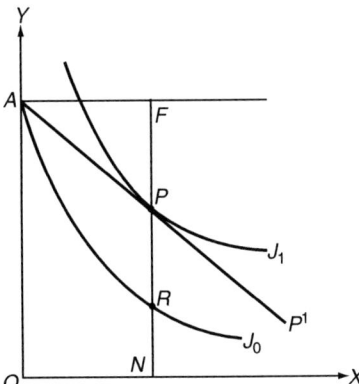

Figure 4.2

consumer is willing to pay as much as *FR* (amount of money) for *ON* (quantity of the commodity) in an all-or-nothing offer. This is because, after paying *FR* and receiving *ON*, he is at the point *R*, which is on the same indifference curve, J_0, as point *A*, his initial position without consuming the commodity. Hence Marshall's definition of consumer surplus – being the difference between the maximum amount the consumer is willing to pay and the amount actually paid – is *FR* − *FP* = *PR*.

The above measure refers to a consumer's surplus when he or she is able to buy a good at a given price, in contrast to the case where the good is not available. Consumer surplus need not be confined to this all-or-nothing situation and may refer to a change in prices. We shall illustrate below the four measures of consumer surplus in the case of a price fall; the case of a price rise can be similarly illustrated.

The four measures of consumer surplus are defined as follows:

- The compensating variation (CV) of a change in prices (or other variables, if we are not confined to price changes) is the amount of compensation (usually in monetary terms) that can be taken from individuals while leaving them just as well off as before the change.
- The compensating surplus (CS) is the amount of compensation that can be taken from individuals while leaving them just as well off as before the change, if they are constrained to buy at the new price the quantity of the commodity they would buy in the absence of compensation.
- The equivalent variation (EV) is the amount of compensation that has to be given to individuals in the absence of a change to make them as well off as they would be with the change.
- The equivalent surplus (ES) is the amount of compensation that has to be given to individuals in the absence of the change to make them as well

off as they would be with the change, if they are constrained to buy at the old price the quantity of the commodity they would buy in the absence of compensation.

If the change in price is a rise instead of a fall, then we cannot take a positive amount of money from the consumers but have to pay them (that is, take a negative amount) to make them as well off as before the price rise. The measures are then negative in sign. (Note that the CV of a price fall, $p^0 \rightarrow p^1$, $= -$EV of the reversed price rise, $p^1 \rightarrow p^0$, and the EV of a price fall $= -$CV of the reversed price movement. The same is true for the CS and ES. As an exercise, readers can verify this after studying Figure 4.3.) It should also be noted that the difference between the variation measures (that is, CV and EV) and the surplus measures (CS and ES) is that, in the case of the former, no constraint is imposed on consumers and they are free to choose any quantity they like. This can be made clearer by the following diagrammatic illustration.

First consider Figure 4.3a. As the price of the good in question falls from p^0 to p^1, consumers move from point A on the indifference curve, J_0, to point B on J_1. It can be seen that, for this price fall, the four measures (all positive) are CV $= Y^0Y^1$, CS $= BC$, EV $= Y^0Y^2$ and ES $= AD$. (For an explanation of why CV and EV are unequal, see the appendix to this chapter.)

In Figure 4.3b, an ordinary demand curve, dd', is derived from the indifference map in Figure 4.3a. When the price falls from p^0 to p^1, the consumers increase their purchase from X^0 (or p^0a) to X^1 (p^1b). If they have to pay the CV of Y^0Y^1 they will end up at E instead of B. Hence the curve *aeg* is the compensated (or Hicksian) demand curve from point a (and refers to the indifference curve J_0). If the good were inferior, *aeg* would lie to the right of dd'. Similarly *bfh* is the compensated demand curve as the consumers we kept on the indifference curve, J_1. It can then be seen that, while in Figure 4.3a consumer surplus is measured as a distance, in Figure 4.3b it is measured as an area, as follows: CV $= p^0p^1ea$; CS $= p^0p^1ea - egb$; EV $= p^0p^1bf$; ES $= p^0p^1bf + afh$.

When the price is p^0 a marginal decrease in price benefits the consumers by p^0a. As the price falls continuously from p^0 to p^1 the total amount of money that can be taken from the individual consumers while leaving them just as well off as without the fall (that is, on indifference curve J_0) is thus the area p^0p^1ea, remembering that, as compensation is extracted from the consumers, they are moving along the compensated demand curve, *aeg*, not the ordinary one, dd'. In order to understand how the area p^0p^1ea measures the CV associated with the price fall p^0 to p^1, note that, for a marginal price fall, the consumers are made better off by the amount of the good consumed, that is by p^0a at p^0. (Intuitively, how much individuals will benefit from a marginal fall in the price of X will depend on how much of X they consume. Formally, from Roy's equality, which is often misnamed 'Roy's identity',

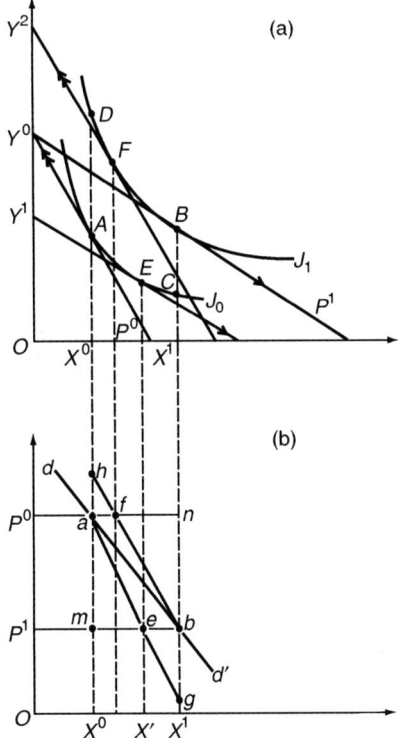

Figure 4.3

$-\partial u/\partial p_i$ divided by the marginal utility of money equals x_i. Roy's identity is discussed in most advanced microeconomics textbooks.) Hence for the whole series of marginal price falls from p^0 to p^1, CV is measured by p^0p^1ea.

For CS, since the consumers are constrained to purchase quantity X^1 when in fact they would prefer to purchase X', they will be made worse off if p^0p^1ea is extracted from them. Hence CS is measured by $p^0p^1ea - egb$; this little triangle being the loss they suffer by having to stick to the constrained quantity. This is because they have to pay the unit price, p^1, while their marginal valuation of the units between X' and X^1 is indicated by the height of the compensated demand curve, *eg*. For ES, they are also made worse off by the constraint. But in this case it relates to the amount they have to be paid, and ES exceeds EV by the little triangle *afh*.

The Marshallian measure is the area p^0p^1ba, which falls somewhere in between the four measures. If the income effect is negligible, consumer demand is not affected by the payment of compensation. Then the compensated demand curve coincides with the ordinary demand curve and all five measures are equal. If readers are not already puzzled by this multiplicity of measures, two further measures can be added (Machlup, 1940, 1957):

- The Laspeyre cost difference of a price change is the amount of compensation that could be taken from the consumers while leaving them just about able (but not necessarily willing) to buy the original bundle of goods they bought before the change.
- The Paasche cost difference is the amount the consumers would have to be paid to have just enough money to buy the new bundle of goods at the original prices.

In the case of the price fall illustrated in Figure 4.3b, the Laspeyre cost difference is measured by the rectangle p^0p^1ma and the Paasche cost difference by p^0p^1bn. A useful exercise for readers at this point would be to indicate the two cost differences (as vertical distances) in Figure 4.3a. While these cost differences do not seem to measure the consumer surplus very accurately, they have the advantage of being easily calculated from actual market data. For most practical purposes, the average of the two cost differences is a good enough approximation. Let us call this the average cost difference (ACD). When the demand curve is linear, ACD equals the Marshallian measure.

4.3   Which measure?

Which of the many measures is appropriate depends partly on the availability of information and partly on the problem in question.[1] For example, since the CS measures involves a quantity constraint but need not directly involve relative prices, it is useful for measuring the welfare cost (loss in surplus) due to quotas, price controls and rationing, or after consumers have made the appropriate purchase and the cost of change is high. On the other hand the CV measure is useful for measuring the cost of distortions in relative prices due to taxes, subsidies, tariffs and so on (Hause, 1975, p. 1148). For example, if we want to compensate for the loss (or extract payment for the gain), CV is the appropriate measure. In the absence of the required information we can use the Laspeyre cost difference if we do not want to overcompensate (overextract) or the Paasche cost difference if we do not

---

1. Information is usually more difficult to obtain for the Hicksian measures than for the Marshallian one. Seade (1978) shows that the Hicksian values of surplus can be computed from not too complicated formulae provided that the Engle curves are linear. This proviso is fairly restrictive. However see Hausman (1981), who argues that the Hicksian values can be derived from the market demand functions (of prices and income) by using Roy's equality to integrate and derive the indirect utility function.

want to undercompensate. If compensation (payment) is not actually intended, CV may not be appropriate. If we want a measure of the gain or loss involved but not actually to pay compensation, then the Marshallian measure has the following advantage over the variation measures, as discussed by Winch (1965).

Consider Figure 4.4, where dd' is the ordinary demand curve and ae is a compensated one. For a fall in price from p^0 to p^1, the Marshall measure of consumer surplus/gain is the area p^0p^1ba, and the CV is the area p^0p^1ea. However let us divide the price fall into two steps: from p^0 to p' and from p' to p^1. For step p^0 to p' the Marshall measure is $p^0p'ga$ and the CV is $p^0p'fa$. For step p' to p^1 the Marshall measure is $p'p^1bg$. The CV depends on whether consumers actually have to pay the amount $p^0p'fa$ for the first step of the price fall. If they have paid, then the relevant compensated demand curve is the section fe and the CV for the second step of the price fall is the area $p'p^1ef$. The CVs for the two price-fall steps will then add up to $p^0p'ea$, the CV of the total price fall. However if they do not have to pay the amount $p^0p'fa$ They will consume at point g if the price is p'; fg being the income effect of the amount $p^0p'fa$. Thus the relevant compensated demand curve for the second step of the price fall is section gh, and the CV of the second step will be $p'p^1hg$. The CVs for the two steps of price fall will add up to p^0p^1hgfa, which is larger than the CV of the total price fall (taken as a single step from p^0 to p^1), denoted by the area $fehg$. If we regard the price fall from p^0 to p^1 as consisting of a large number of small steps, and if the consumers do not actually have to pay the compensation, the CVs will add up to an amount close to the Marshall measure. At the limit, when the number of steps approaches infinity, the two measures approach each other. Thus if we are not interested in the actual amount that we can extract from the consumers (without making them worse off) but in a measure of their gain, Marshall's measure seems to be preferable.

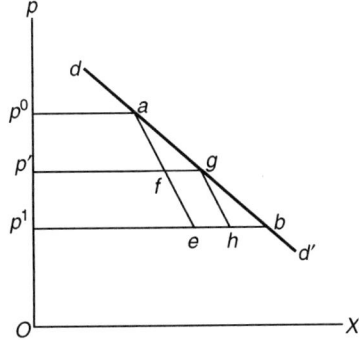

Figure 4.4

Nevertheless Marshall's measure must be taken as no more than an approximate measure of the consumers' gain except in some very restrictive cases (on which see Chipman and Moore, 1976). For each marginal price change, Marshall's measure converges towards the CV (and also the EV) and can be taken as an accurate measure of the consumers' gain. However for a non-infinitesimal price change, although Marshall's measure is just the sum (or integral) of the marginal measures, in general it is just an approximate measure for the following reason. As the price changes the marginal utility of money (MUM) generally changes too. Hence the sum of the marginal measures may no longer be a perfectly accurate measure of consumers' gain (or loss) in utility. The condition of constancy in MUM for the Marshall measure to be accurate must be carefully explained. It is not the constancy of MUM as money income increases but the constancy of MUM as prices change (see Samuelson, 1942; Patinkin, 1963; Currie *et al.*, 1971, p. 751, n. 1). The MUM may stay approximately constant for a particular price change, but to ensure that Marshall's measure is accurate for any price change we need to have constancy in MUM with respect to all prices. This is a rather restrictive condition. Thus in attempting to use the area under the demand curve as a perfect measure, Winch (1965) has been a little overzealous. For one thing, if it were a perfectly accurate measure we would not have the problem of path dependency in respect of the measure for changes in the price of more than one commodity, as discussed below (see Facchini *et al.*, 2001, on the possibly spurious 'deadweight gain' using the Marshallian measure).

4.4   Aggregation over commodities: the issue of path dependency*

The discussion above dealt with changes in the price of a single commodity, but what if the prices of more than one commodity change? How do we measure the change in consumer surplus? To understand this problem with the aggregation of commodities we shall first consider a simple case with two commodities, say tea and coffee (for welfare changes in the presence of new goods, see Bresnahan and Gordon, 1997).

In Figure 4.5 the original demand curve for tea, D_T, is drawn according to a given price for coffee, p_C^0 as well as given prices for all other commodities and the consumer's income. Similarly the price of tea is at p_T^0 for the demand curve for coffee, D_0. Can we say that the consumer's surplus from being able to consume tea and coffee at p_T^0 and p_C^0 respectively, relative to the case where tea and coffee are totally unavailable (which is equivalent to prices being infinite), is measured by $p_T^0\ ab + p_C^0\ cd = (1) + (2)$?

To answer this question, let us conceptually raise the price of tea from p_T^0 to infinity (or make tea unavailable), keeping the price of coffee at p_C^0. Using the Marshallian measure, the loss of consumer surplus is measured by area (1). Let us next raise the price of coffee to infinity. If the demand curve

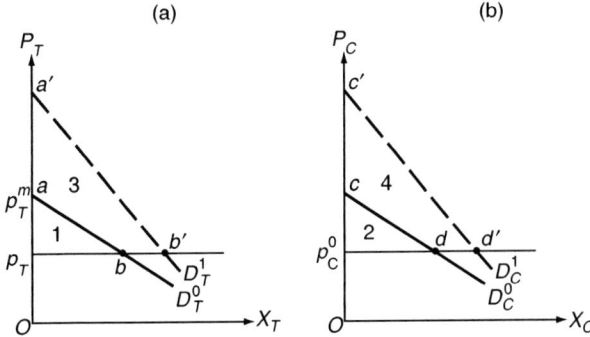

Figure 4.5

for coffee stays at D_C^0 after tea is made unavailable, the loss of consumer surplus is measured by area (2). Thus in comparison with the original situation the total loss in consumer surplus is (1) + (2). However the demand curve for coffee will be unaffected by a change in the price of tea only if the consumption of coffee is independent of that of tea. If coffee is either a complement to or a substitute for tea, then the demand curve for coffee will move as the price of tea changes. In this specific case, it is likely that tea and coffee are substitutes.[2] Hence as tea is not available the demand curve for coffee may move rightward to D_C^1. The loss of consumer surplus when coffee is also made unavailable is thus p_C^0 $c'd'$ = (2) + (4). The total consumer surplus for tea and coffee at p_T^0 and p_C^0 is thus measured by (1) + (2) + (4), which exceeds (1) + (2) by (4). If coffee were a complement of tea, the demand curve D_C^1 would lie to the left of D_C^0 and the measure would be smaller. Thus we cannot measure the consumer surplus of two or more goods by the sum of the areas under the existing demand curves except in the special case of independent goods. Instead we have to take the measure step by step (for an alternative measure using 'total' demand curves see Berry, 1969; Gwilliam and Nash, 1972. See also Kling, 1989; Smith, 1993). This, however, is *not* what is known as path dependency, which is discussed below.

When measuring the total consumer surplus of tea and coffee, we first raised the price of tea to infinity and let the demand curve for coffee move

2. Note, however, that X may be a (gross) substitute for Y and yet Y is not a substitute for X. The same is true for (gross) complementarity. For net substitutes/complements, we cannot have this asymmetry with standard assumptions about the utility function. The difference between the gross and net substitutes/complements is that one includes the income effect and the other does not. It is the possible difference in income effects that gives rise to the asymmetry of the gross substitutes/complements. See Green (1976, pp. 69–70).

in response to this. But we could have taken the logically equivalent method of raising the price of coffee first, in which case we would have arrived at a measure of total consumer surplus of (2) + (1) + (3), where D_T^1 is the demand curve for tea when coffee is unavailable. The two alternative measures of total consumer surplus will be equal if and only if (3) = (4). If (3) ≠ (4) our measure of total consumer surplus will depend on which procedure or path we take. This is what is meant by path dependency (Hotelling, 1938; Silberberg, 1972; Burns, 1977). There are in fact many other possible paths of measurement even in the case of just two goods. For example, we could raise the price of tea by a small amount, then raise the price of coffee, then further raise the price of tea and so on.

Under what conditions will (3) = (4)? It can be seen that if $\partial x_T/\partial p_C = \partial x_C/\partial p_C$ at all sets of prices, then the two areas must be equal. Let us now use the more general notations g and h (instead of C and T) so that we can interpret the results more generally, referring to any two goods. The notation $\partial x_g/\partial p_h$ is the effect of a partial change (that is, other prices and M, the income of the consumer, are being held constant) in the price of good h on the quantity demanded for good g. By means of the Slutsky equation, this can be split into a substitution effect and an income affect

$$\frac{\partial x_g}{\partial p_h} = \frac{\partial x_g}{\partial p_h}\left|U\right| - x_h\frac{\partial x_g}{\partial M} \tag{4.1a}$$

$$\frac{\partial x_h}{\partial p_g} = \frac{\partial x_h}{\partial p_g}\left|U\right| - x_g\frac{\partial x_h}{\partial M} \tag{4.1b}$$

where $|U|$ means that the utility level is being held constant so that the movement is along an indifference contour. If the consumer's utility function satisfies certain mild conditions (such as strict quasiconcavity,[3] and continuous first- and second-order derivatives), it can be shown that $\partial x_g/\partial p_h |U| = \partial x_h/\partial p_g |U|$ (see, for example Malinvaud, 1972, p. 36; Green, 1976, p. 312). Then the condition for $\partial x_g/\partial p_h = \partial x_h/\partial p_g$ boils down to the equality of the income elasticities for the two goods.

$$\frac{\partial x_g}{\partial M}\cdot\frac{M}{x_g} = \frac{\partial x_h}{\partial M}\cdot\frac{M}{x_h} \tag{4.2}$$

---

3. Strict quasiconcavity, together with a number of other conditions, ensures the existence of demand functions; see Malinvaud (1972, pp. 24–9). A (strictly) quasi-concave utility function yields indifference curves or surfaces (strictly) convex to the origin. A real-valued function $f(x)$ defined on a convex set X is quasiconcave if and only if $f(\lambda x + [1 - \lambda]y) \geq \min(f[x], f[y])$ for all $\lambda: 0 < \lambda < 1$ and for any two distinct points x and y in X. If strict inequality holds, we have strict quasiconcavity. The notation 'min' means the minimum of what follows. For quasiconvexity, reverse the inequality sign and change 'min' into 'max'.

If Equation 4.2 holds, the two income effects in Equation 4.1 will be equal. In terms of integrals, area (1) in Figure 4.5 can be written as:

$$\int_{p_T^0}^{p_T^m} x_T \, dp_T$$

where the integration is taken at $p_C = p_C^0$. Thus for a change in the prices of a number of goods, the change in consumer surplus can be measured by:[4]

$$-\int_{p^0}^{p^1} \sum_{g=1}^{G} x_g \, dp_g \tag{4.3}$$

where the initial price vector is $p^0 \equiv (p_1^0, p_2^0, \ldots, p_G^0)$ and p^1 is the new price vector. Some of the prices may be unchanged. The measure in (4.3) depends, in general, on the path of integration. However, with some 'regular' conditions, if Equation 4.2 holds for all g and h whose prices have changed, then (4.3) will give a path-independent measure of the change in consumer surplus. While (4.2) may hold for some goods, it is unlikely to hold for all goods since this implies that all goods have an income elasticity that is equal to unity as the increase in income must be spent. Nevertheless for relatively small changes in prices the income effects, even if unequal, will not be significant. Secondly, even for large changes in the prices of many goods, and even if the income effects are not negligible or equal, they are still likely largely to offset each other in the ways they affect the measures of surplus along different paths such that, while measure (4.3) may be path dependent, the differences involved are likely to be small for most changes and negligible compared with inaccuracies due to statistical and informational problems.[5]

If the shape of the demand curves is not known an approximation can be used. Harberger (1971, p. 788) derives the following approximate measure of welfare change in terms of changes in consumption:[6]

$$\sum_{g=1}^{G} p_g^0 \Delta x_g + \tfrac{1}{2} \sum_{g=1}^{G} \Delta p_g \Delta x_g \tag{4.4}$$

For cases where the income level is unchanged, we have $\Sigma(p_g + \Delta p_g)(x_g + \Delta x_g) = \Sigma p_g x_g$. Hence $\Sigma p_g \Delta x_g = -\Sigma x_g \Delta p_g - \Sigma \Delta p_g \Delta x_g$.

---

4. Hotelling (1938) first generalised the measure of consumer surplus to multiprice changes.
5. Ignoring 'contrived' paths of integration, for example ones that go through a path and back from another many times, thus magnifying the small difference involved.
6. The measure is similar to those in Bennet (1920) and Bowley (1928). Chambers (2001) shows that it is an exact measure if the utility function is of the translation-homothetic generalized quadratic form.

Substituting this into (4.4) yields:

$$-\sum x_g \Delta p_g - {}^1\!/_2 \sum \Delta p_g \Delta x_g \tag{4.5}$$

which is the generalisation of the average cost difference to multiprice changes. In terms of Figure 4.3b, if only the price of X falls we can express the approximate measure either as the area $p^0 p^1\ ba$ (which is Equation 4.5) or as the area $X^0 X^1 ba$ plus the area $(p^0 p^1 ma - X^0 X^1 bm)$, since this is the amount of the change in expenditure on the consumption of other goods.

As the Marshallian measure is path dependent it is not a perfect measure of consumer surplus. This is consistent with our general point that no monetary or any other objective measure of subjective utility gain/loss can be perfect (Section 4.6). However it may still be accepted as good approximate measure, as argued below. In particular, in Appendix 4.2 it is shown that, or at least for the benchmark case of a Cobb–Douglas utility function, starting from any given position, the Marshallian measure of the surplus of a price change is larger than that of another price change if and only if the utility gain of the first is larger than that of the second.

4.5   Aggregation over individuals: the Boadway paradox*

The above discussion concerned only one individual. If more than one person is involved, can we use the area under the market demand curve or the sum of compensating variations (ΣCV) as a measure of the gain or loss of the group as a whole? The problem of distribution arises if the gain or loss is not uniform across all individuals. This is especially so if some individuals gain and some lose. Can we say that, if $\Sigma CV > 0$, the gainers can more than compensate the losers and the change (in prices or other factors) will at least lead to a *potential* Pareto improvement? It is very tempting to give an affirmative answer, but Boadway (1974) discovered the following paradox.

To elucidate the paradox, let us consider a simple case in which the change involves a pure redistribution. For more complicated cases involving changes in the collection of goods, readers are referred to Boadway (1974, pp. 932–4). Consider a simple exchange economy with two goods, X and Y, and two individuals, J and K, as illustrated in the Edgeworth Box (see Chapter 2) in Figure 4.6. Assuming optimal allocation, we are confined to the contract curve $O^J O^K$. A purely distributional change takes us from q^1 to q^2. Since this is a purely distributional change, it is clear that the gainer, J, cannot fully compensate the loser, K, and still be better off. With full compensation we can, at best, move back to the original point, q^1, with no one being any better off. After the movement to q^2 the price ratio of the two goods is indicated by the line cd. Hence in terms of compensating variation, the movement involves a positive CV of ac (using Y as the numeraire) for individual J, and a negative CV of bc for K. Thus $\Sigma CV = ab$ and is positive,

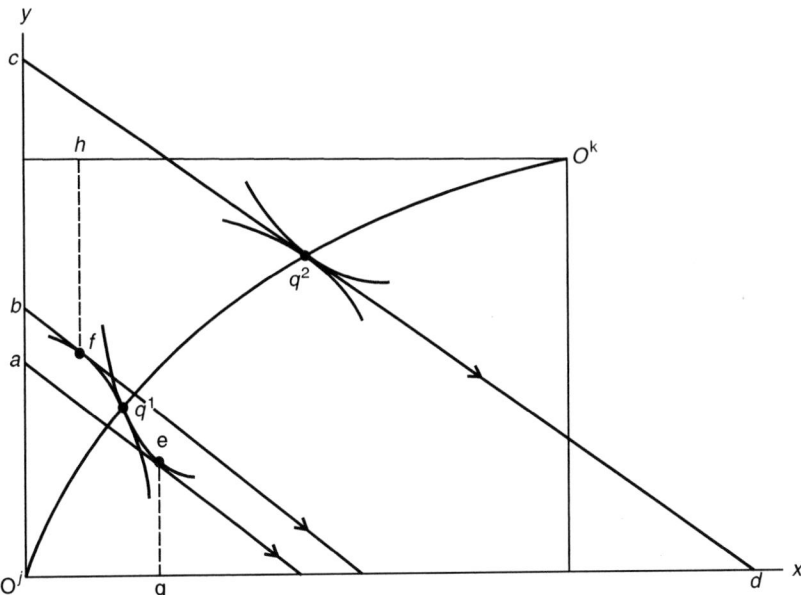

Figure 4.6

despite the fact that *J* cannot fully compensate *K* and still be better off. What has gone wrong with the ΣCV measure? What is the explanation of the paradox?

After paying *ac* amount of compensation, *J* would be no worse off (in comparison with the original point q^1) only if she or he were allowed to consume freely at the unchanged price ratio. She or he would then consume at *e*. Similarly *K* would be not worse off receiving *bc* only if he or she could consume at *f*. However the two points *e* and *f* are inconsistent with each other, since the sum of the amounts of *X* consumed by *J* and $K\left(O^j g + O_h^K\right)$ would add up to more than the total available amount of *X* in the economy. Thus *J* and *K* cannot simultaneously consume at *e* and *f* respectively. The CV measure assumes that the price ratio (the slope of *cd*) can remain unchanged and each individual may choose whatever point of consumption they prefer at this price ratio and given their budget (after compensation). But this may not be feasible (as shown above) if the compensation involved is large enough to change the equilibrium price ratio. If the common slope of the indifference curves at point q^1 is equal to that at q^2, it can be seen that compensation will not change the price ratio. Then ΣCV will be equal to zero, accurately reflecting the fact that full compensation is just about possible if no one is made better off. In general the payment of compensation does tend to change the equilibrium set of prices. Hence the Boadway paradox is logically very real.

Nevertheless in the real economy where a certain change is small relative to GNP, the payment of compensation is unlikely to change prices significantly. Even if prices are changed, the effects of the changes are likely to be mutually offsetting. The remaining net divergence, if any, is likely to be negligible compared with inaccuracies in data collection. Thus if ΣCV is large enough to outweigh data inaccuracies, it is safe to conclude that full compensation is possible. Hence for most cost–benefit analyses the use of ΣCV is quite acceptable. It therefore, seems, that Boadway is too pessimistic in his conclusion that 'If some persons gain and others lose, we cannot interpret a positive surplus as an indication that the gainers could compensate the losers and a negative surplus that they could not. The magnitude and sign of the surplus are not related to the ability to compensate losers' (ibid., p. 938). While the relation is not a perfect one, it is certainly an overstatement to say that the two are unrelated.

4.6   The approximate nature of surplus measurement**

The welfare of an individual is associated with a subjective state of mind, and any non-approximate measurement has to reflect this subjectivity for example the concept of just noticeable difference (see Section 5.4.1). However it is convenient (and in economic calculations, almost essential) to have some objective measures, such as a monetary measure. Nevertheless, since the relation between units of any external yardstick of welfare such as money and the internal unit of welfare (however defined) is in general not a constant, such objective measures, by their very nature, can be no more than an approximate measure of welfare, even abstracting from the problem of inaccuracies in practical data collection. If we recognise that the surplus measurement, and in fact any other objective measurement of welfare, must be regarded as approximate only, then all the problems of path dependency, inconsistency and so on fade into insignificance unless the discrepancies involved are substantial (for a case where this is so, and our proposed measure to overcome the substantial divergence, see Appendix 4.1 on the concept of marginal dollar equivalent).

To illustrate the approximate nature of any surplus measurement, consider the argument by Hause (1975, pp. 1150–1) that the EV and ES measures have the following advantage over the CV and CS measures. Starting from a given initial point, x^0 (say a bundle of goods consumed), the consumer moves to a new point, x^1, due to a certain change (in prices, quotas and so on). Starting from the same initial point x^0, he or she moves to x^2 with another change. An ideal measure of welfare change, ΔW, should possess the following property: $\Delta W(x^0 \rightarrow x^1) > \Delta W(x^0 \rightarrow x^2)$ if and only if x^1 is preferred to x^2. It can be seen that the EV and ES measures possess this property, but in general the CV and CS measures do not. (Readers may attempt this as an exercise before consulting Figure 4.7a, where this point is

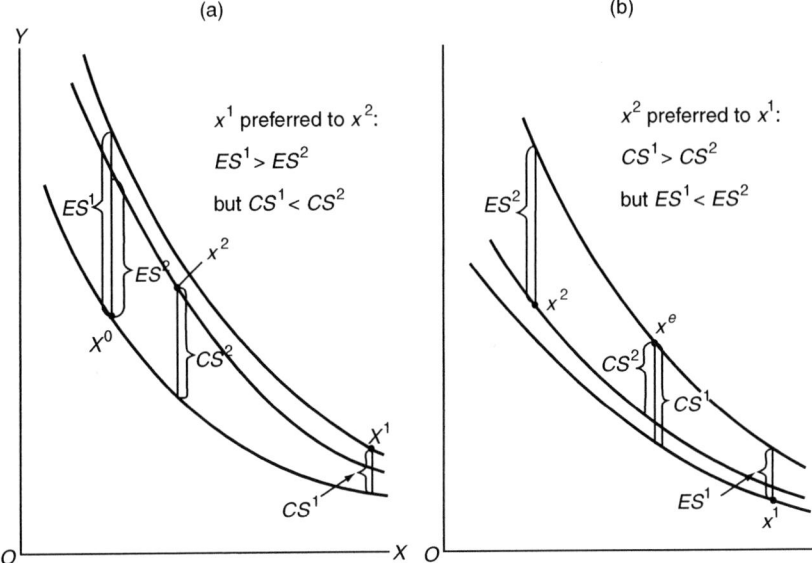

Figure 4.7

shown for the surplus measures. The point can also be shown with respect to the variation measures, using price lines.)

The reason for this is that the equivalent measures use the initial point as the welfare reference point while the compensating measures use the end point as the reference point. In the above comparison, the initial point is fixed but the end points are not. This explains why EV and ES satisfy the required property while CV and CS do not. But this argument by Hause seems to look at only one side of the coin. For any given end point, x^e, the ideal measure of welfare change for different points, x^1, x^2, taken as the original point should possess the following property: $\Delta W(x^1 \to x^e) > \Delta W(x^2 \to x^e)$ if and only if x^2 is preferred to x^1. It can then be seen that CV and CS possess this property but EV and ES do not (see Figure 4.7b). Hence neither pair can be regarded as superior to the other. Both measures may be acceptable as approximate measures for changes whose effects are thinly spread (cf. Appendix 4.1).

It should be noted that we have not discussed the large difference between willingness to pay and willingness to accept due to the unwillingness of many people to pay for something to which they believe they are entitled to the 'endowment' effect or to other similar problems (see for example, Mitchell and Carson, 1989; Tversky and Griffin, 1991; Kahneman *et al.*, 1991; Milgrom, 1993). In such cases there are added practical difficulties in discovering people's real willingness to pay that reflects their intrinsic preference for the items, untainted by the objections to or ill-feelings associated with payment. This difficulty with the intertwining of two different types of preferences or dispreferences is similar to the intrusion of factors such as regret, anxiety, excitement and so on into the process or outcomes of choices involving risk, making the application of the expected utility theory difficult in such cases. However in both cases the principles involved are not invalidated.

4.7   Consumer surplus of diamond goods**

It was argued above that the Marshallian and other measures of consumer surplus are acceptable as approximate measures of welfare change. However even ignoring the possible divergence between preference and welfare (the implications of which are discussed in Chapter 11), there are cases in which the Marshallian measure is completely unusable, for example a case in which it is not just the quantity of the good in question that affects the utility of the consumer but also the price. While Scitovsky (1945) discussed the 'habit of judging quality by price' and Kalman (1968) analyses consumer demand when prices enter the utility function, it appears that the implications for consumer surplus measurement have not yet been discussed. This effect is very complicated for the general case of Kalman, but the specific case of diamond goods is easily analysed. The diamond effect is defined as 'valuing something for its [exchange] value rather than the [intrinsic] consumption effect' (Ng, 1987a, p. 186). Formally, it is the (relative) price multiplied by the quantity of the good that affects utility, rather than quantity itself (quality being held constant). A one-carat diamond is worth thousands of pounds but a zircon that looks exactly like a top-quality diamond is worth only a tiny fraction of it. Someone once mixed a few top-quality diamonds with cubic zircons and presented them to a diamond expert for appraisal. The expert declared all the stones to be imitations. Clearly, people value real diamonds mainly for their exchange value rather than their intrinsic worth. People consume or hold these stone to show off their wealth, to use them as stores of value or to give them away as gifts of value.

The demand curve for a pure diamond good (with no intrinsic consumption effect) is a rectangular hyperbola. This is not difficult to understand. Since it is px (normalising the comparison price index to unity) that enters the utility function, if p doubles the consumer only has to halve x to maintain px unchanged and the ability to consume all other goods remains unchanged. Hence utility also remains unchanged with any change in the price of a pure diamond good. This means that

- The Marshallian measure of consumer surplus is completely unusable.
- Roy's equality ($-\partial u/\partial p_i = x_i \partial u/\partial M$) is inapplicable (which is one reason why it should not be called an 'identity').

- The ordinary demand curve and the compensated demand curves coincide with each other.

Moreover the optimal tax rate on a pure diamond good is arbitrarily high, as consumers suffer no loss and the government gains in terms of tax revenues as the tax rate is raised higher and higher. Taxes on pure diamond goods not only impose no *excess* burden, they impose no burden at all (a tax of £100 million not only involves no additional costs, of say £35 million, but the £100 million of tax revenue is also not a burden on the taxpayers). The pure gain in tax revenue is explained by the saving of resources when producing the diamond goods. However when the price becomes extremely high, the quantity becomes very small for any given value of the pure diamond good, creating inconvenience and making it no longer a pure diamond good. Thus in practice an optimal tax is unlikely to be arbitrarily high, even ignoring such problems as smuggling. Nevertheless very high taxes on diamond goods are efficient, especially if there is international coordination to reduce problems of tax evasion.

With the possible exception of some precious stones and metal, pure diamond goods are uncommon. However mixed diamond goods are quite common. These are goods for which both the value and the intrinsic consumption effects matter. Although some (but not all) of the burden is imposed on consumers, higher (than goods with no diamond effects) tax rates on mixed diamond goods are still efficient. Also, remarkably, the compensated demand curve for a mixed diamond good may be upward-sloping even in the absence of inferiority and a change in the degree of 'diamondness'. This is demonstrated in Ng (1993). Intuitively, a higher price for a mixed diamond good increases px at any given x, and if the diamond effect is strongly complementary to the intrinsic consumption effect the consumer may consume more x. An example may help here. Mr A takes Miss B out for an expensive dinner in the hope that Miss B will be sufficiently impressed to spend the rest of the evening with him. Mr A believes (correctly or not) that the higher the price, the higher the probability that the objective will be met (the diamond effect). He also believes that dinner (with drinks) and evening activities are complementary, for example one has to eat more if one is to stay out later at night; drinking is conducive to an enjoyable evening. An increase in the price of the food/drink increases the probability that the objective will be met. Mr A may thus order more food/drink at higher prices.

The consumer surplus of a mixed diamond good is measured by the Marshallian area multiplied by s, the share of the intrinsic consumption effect (measured by the marginal intrinsic utility of x) in the total effect (the intrinsic consumption effect plus the diamond effect measured by the marginal utility of px) (Ng, 1993). This simple result accords with intuition. However the share s is not available from market transaction data, even given ideal information. Given the prevalence of mixed diamond goods, this is another blow to those economists who insist on using only 'objective' market data. But this should not prevent economists who are willing to use intuition and survey data from attempting to make estimates, although care must be exercised and a lot more studies are needed. Even an imperfect estimate is better than hiding in an ivory tower and pretending that the real world does not differ from a very simple economic model. Estimates based on such models, no matter how accurate the objective market data used, are much worse (differ from the real situation by more) than those based on more realistic models, even if imperfect survey data have to be used.

Another interesting possibility is that consumers may actually gain from a tax on a mixed diamond good, in which case there would not only be no excess burden (or no burden at all), but there would be a positive gain! This possibility exists in cases where the good is consumed for its diamond effect to the point where the intrinsic consumption effect is negative. For example people who drink expensive wines to show off their wealth may drink to the point of harming their health, especially if leaving ordered wine unconsumed is regarded as a bad habit (no free disposal of the intrinsic consumption effect). If wine becomes even more expensive, they do not have to drink as much to show off to the same extent. Likewise if the price of gold rises you do not have to laden yourself with as much gold in order to run away in an emergency with a given amount of liquid wealth.

4.8   Some uses of surplus measurement

In addition to the problems discussed above, there are other complications with the measurement of consumer surplus (see Mohring, 1971; Foster and Neuburger, 1974; Schmalensee, 1976), as well as with the corresponding measure of producer surplus, that is, the area above the supply curve and below the price line. (for surveys see Currie et al., 1971; Berry, 1972). However most of these can be dismissed as being of little practical significance at the policy level since any inaccuracies are likely to be much less than those due to lack of information. Moreover until we derive something better, an imperfect measure is better than no measure at all (for arguments on the use of consumer surplus as a measurement of welfare change see Harberger, 1971; Burns, 1973; Hause, 1975; Willig, 1976; McConnell, 1995. See also Weitzman, 2001, for the argument that the change in present discounted future utility is captured by the difference in current income plus consumer surplus. See also the papers in Creedy 1999).[7] It is true that some prominent

---

7. The claim by Blackorby (1999) that 'if the second-best outcome is not the first-best one, the sum of consumer plus producer surplus cannot lead an economy to its true second-best optimum' is not surprising given the second-best complication (see Chapter 9), which makes many peculiar things possible.

economists once regarded the concept of consumer surplus as superfluous (for example Samuelson, 1947, p. 198) as theoretical analysis could proceed without it. However this was because they were not concerned with practical policy matters where not only the direction of change but also the magnitude of the gains or losses involved were important. In many cases the only feasible means of measuring the gain or loss is to estimate the relevant demand and supply curves. Some simple examples of how surplus measurement can be used to aid policy decisions are outlined below (for a survey of the uses of consumer and producer surpluses see Currie *et al.*, 1971).

Consider an industry with a falling average cost (AC) over the relevant range (a practical example is the provision of electricity to a remote village). As illustrated in Figure 4.1, the marginal cost (MC) curve is horizontal but this is not essential for the problem here. If the demand curve lies wholly below the AC curve, as shown in Figure 4.1, any uniform (non-discriminating) price charged would fail to yield sufficient revenue to cover the total cost. With marginal cost pricing the loss equals *PBGH*. Does this mean that supplying the good in question is undesirable? Not necessarily, even abstracting from questions of externalities (see Chapter 7) and merit goods (see Appendix 12.3). With *OQ* amount of consumption at price *OP*, the amount of consumer surplus is measured by (curvilinear) $\triangle APB$. This is larger than the loss *PBGH* if $\triangle AHF > \triangle FBG$. Thus supplying the good may be desirable despite the loss. A government subsidy or public provision of the good may be called for. However the subsidy or loss has to be financed somehow. Since raising more taxes may involve efficiency and administrative costs, the gain in supplying the good has to be weighed against the costs involved. (There are also other problems such as the need to check to empire-building public investment, rent-seeking, second best and so on, some of which will be discussed in later chapters.)

Now consider the cost (loss in surplus) of a sales tax on a competitive industry. Figure 4.8 shows the pretax demand curve, *dd'*, the supply curve, *ss'* and the corresponding equilibrium point, *e*. The imposition of a per unit tax of *fg* increases the post-tax consumer price to *Oa* and lowers the producer price (net of tax) to *Ob*, and also reduces the quantity from *On* to *Om*. The loss in consumer surplus is measured by the area *cega* and the loss in producer surplus by the area *bfec*. The tax revenue equals *bfga*. Hence the net loss (the total loss in consumer surplus and in producer surplus less the tax revenue, sometimes called the excess burden or distortionary cost of taxation) equals the curvilinear $\triangle feg$. Alternatively we can concentrate on the reduction in the quantity produced and consumed. The reduction by *mn* amount of production saves resources valued at *mnef*. But this same *mn* amount of the good is valued by consumers at *mneg*. The net loss is again $\triangle feg$. This measure is based on the partial equilibrium setting, in which the effects of the tax on the prices of the other goods are taken as negligible.

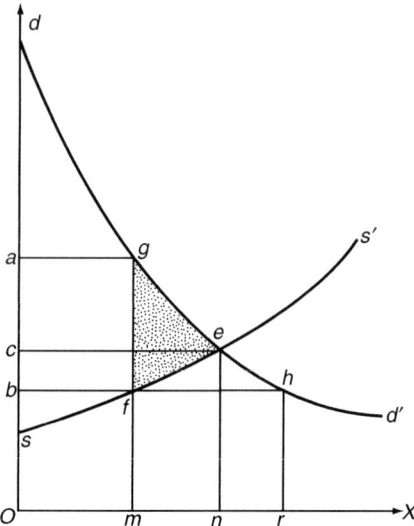

Figure 4.8

However this is not always a permissible assumption, especially if the good in question has close substitutes or complements. Then a correct measure of welfare change has to sum the change in surpluses over a range of goods (see Section 4.4 above). Unless the supply curves for the other goods involved are horizontal and there is no distortion in these goods (taxes/ subsidies are not justified on efficiency grounds, monopolistic power and so on), the measure for welfare loss thus obtained will in general differ from the partial equilibrium measure of Δfeg.

Now consider a legal maximum price of Ob (assumed effective), which reduces the quantity supplied to Om. Will this result in the same welfare cost of Δfeg? The answer is no, even disregarding the general equilibrium problem just mentioned. In the previous case where the price is increased to Oa due to the tax, consumers who continue to consume the good place a marginal valuation on it that is no lower than Oa. Thus the loss in the *mn* amount of consumption is measured by *mneg*. But in the case of a legal maximum price of Ob, consumers who place the marginal valuation as low as rh (= Ob) may also consume the good while those who place a much higher value may have to go without it. Thus the total value of Om amount of consumption will be approximately equal to Om/Or multiplied by the area $Orhd$, assuming that all consumers have an equal chance of obtaining the good. In comparison with the original equilibrium consumption of On, the loss is equal to $Oned - Om/or \cdot Orhd$, which can be shown to be larger than *mneg*, given that the demand curve is downward sloping.[8] Hence the net loss will be much larger than Δ*feg*. In fact it can be shown that the net loss is larger than the area *ced* multiplied by *mr/Or*. If the demand curve has a very high vertical intercept, this could be an amount many times larger than Δ*feg*.

It is true that consumers who value the good highly may arrive earlier in the queue. Hence it is more likely than random that they will obtain the goods. The value of *Om* amount of consumption is then likely to be larger than *Om/Or* multiplied by *Orhd*. On the other hand the additional costs of queuing and so on have to be added. Thus it remains true that the total net loss is likely to be much larger than Δ*feg*.

A similar analysis to the above may also be applied to the case of a quota of *Om*, raising the price to *Oa*. In this case the loss in *mn* amount of consumption is valued at *mneg*. But the saving in resources is no longer measured by *mnef*. With a higher price (*Oa*), less efficient producers may also supply part of the market. While it is true that more efficient producers will enjoy a larger producer surplus or rent and are therefore more likely to obtain the limited quotas, the resources invested in securing the quotas must be included in the calculation of costs (see the end of Appendix 12.1 on rent seeking).

From the above analysis it can be concluded that, for the same amount of quantity adjustment (*mn* in Figure 4.8), the loss is usually much lower if it is achieved *through* the working of the market mechanism (by taxes/ subsidies and so on) than if it is achieved through administrative regulations (such as legal price, quotas and so on).

4.9 Summary

Different measures of consumer surplus (Dupuit–Marshall, CV, EV, CS, ES, Laspeyres, Paasche and average cost differences) are possible. Which measure is appropriate depends on the problem. If compensation is not intended, Marshall's measure has an advantage over CV, as argued by Winch (1965). But Marshall's measure is path dependent. When price changes for more than one good are involved, the measure may give different results depending on which good is measured first, and so on. Since the payment of compensation may affect prices, and since the CV measure is based on a fixed set of prices, a positive ΣCV will not ensure that the gainers will more than compensate the losers (Boadway's paradox). However these complications fade into insignificance if we recognise that any objective measure of subjective welfare must necessarily be approximate in nature, since the differences arising from such complications are small in most practical cases.

---

8. Obviously *Omgd* > (*Om/Or*)*Orhd* given a downward-sloping demand curve. Thus *Oned* − *mng* − (*Om/Or*)*Orhd* > 0, which implies that *Oned* − (*Om/Or*)*Orhd* > *mneg*.

When the differences are large, a different measure (the marginal dollar equivalent – see Appendix 4.1) is proposed. This is the number of times a change is worth a (marginal) dollar in utility terms. The interesting cases of a pure diamond good valued for its exchange value where a change in price does not affect consumer surplus, and that of a mixed diamond good with a possibly upward-sloping compensated demand curve and the possible *increase* in consumer surplus with a higher price, were discussed in Section 4.6. It has also been shown that the loss in consumer surplus due to price control, rationing and so on may be many times larger than the traditional triangular measures (Section 4.7).

Appendix 4.1: CV, EV or Marginal Dollar Equivalent?**

For most practical applications it is likely that the difference between the sum of compensating variations (ΣCV) and the sum of equivalent variation (ΣEV) will be overwhelmed by the inaccuracies in data collection. For changes whose effects are thinly spread, no significant differences are likely to arise. However it cannot be ruled out that, if the effects are concentrated, the two measures may differ by a substantial amount and even differ in sign. As a dramatic example, consider a somewhat eccentric farmer who is content with living simply on his farm (for another example see Mishan, 1971, p. 19). The authorities are considering building a highway and the most suitable route is across his farm. The farmer is not prepared to move for any sum of compensation (that is, $CV = -\pounds\infty$) but is willing to pay £8000 for the benefit of not having to move (EV = $-\pounds8000$) (in terms of Figure A4.1, his marginal utility curve may look like the dotted curve). The only loss he will suffer from moving to another farm is the trouble of moving, which he is willing to pay £8000 to avoid. Since the additional wealth is of little interest to him, he prefers to stay on his farm rather than become a billionaire.

For each individual the CV measure of a change equals the negative of the EV measure of the reverse change, and *vice versa*. Hence the difference between ΣCV and ΣEV means that, whichever measure we decide to use, we may end up with a contradiction. Returning to the example of the eccentric farmer, suppose that ΣCV and ΣEV for the rest of society lie between £8000 and £∞. Thus for society as a whole, ΣCV > 0 and ΣEV < 0. Now consider the reverse change. The decision to build the road has been taken and the proposed change is that the decision be reversed, but again we have ΣCV > 0 and ΣEV < 0. Thus if we use ΣCV as the criterion, we will recommend both the building of the road and that the decision be reversed. Similarly, using ΣEV we will recommend that the road should not be built, but if the undertaking has been made we will recommend that it should not be reversed even if it does not cost anything to reverse the decision.

For an approximate measure, the possibility of a contradiction is not an important objection unless the divergence is large. For cases where CV and EV differ greatly, as in the road-building example, the sum of the marginal-dollar equivalent (ΣMDE) could be used to remove one source of the contradiction, namely the diminishing marginal utility of income.

The difference between CV and EV can be most clearly be appreciated by using a cardinal-utility approach (although this is by no means necessary). In Figure A4.1 the curve *MU* measures the marginal utility of income. Suppose that the individual's income is *OC* and consider a change that will increase his or total utility by the area *IJKL* but leave income and *MU* unchanged over the relevant region (a case in which these are changed is considered in Figure A4.2). By construction, the area *CDEF* = *IJKL* = *CDGH*. Hence the CV for the change is measured by *FC* and the EV is measured by *CH*. Due to the diminishing marginal utility of income, *CH* > *FC*. That EV > CV is usually true but not necessarily so even if we assume diminishing *MU*, unless we also assume that the *MU* curve is not substantially lowered with the change. The size of the (positive) CV is limited by the amount of the individual's income, *OC*, but the size of the (positive) EV can be arbitrarily large. For example the EV of giving blind individuals their sight may be infinite.

If the change that benefits individuals by *IJKL* also costs society an amount *IL*, measured by either CV or EV (if the costs are dispersed, ΣCV = ΣEV), should the change be made? By construction, *CH* > *IL* > *FC*. In terms of aggregate net benefit, the answer could be yes or no, depending on whether ΣEV or ΣCV is used as a criterion. Should we just use an average of the two measures? While this may be the simplest way out in most practical cases of cost–benefit analysis, it is not difficult to think of cases in which it would not do. For one thing half an infinity is still an infinity and scarcely

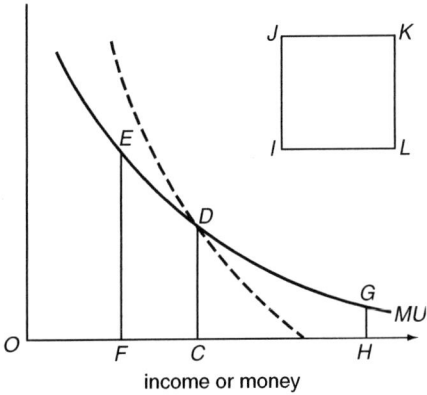

Figure A4.1

anyone would suggest that the world should spend its entire or even half of its GNP to give sight to one blind person, assuming that it can only be done at such a cost.

Before solving the problem of the conflicting ΣCV and ΣEV measures, we shall first examine a more general case in which both the *MU* curve and the income level of an individual may be affected by a change (for example a project). In Figure A4.2 the *MU* curve shifts upward (the case of a downward shift can be analysed similarly) from MU^0 to MU^1 and the income level of the individual increases from Y^0 to Y^1. If the total gain in utility to the individual is equal to *IJKL*, then *C'F'* measures his or her CV and CH his or her EV, where $C'D'E'F' = IJKL = CDGH$ *in area*.

If income is actually to be taken from (or given to) the individual, then the CV (or EV) is the appropriate measure. But if the compensation test is only hypothetical, the CV (EV) usually underestimates (overestimates) the gain to the individual due to the diminishing marginal utility of income. Now we need to derive a monetary measure that is free from such inaccuracy. Since the purpose of the exercise is to determine whether the change is worth making it seems reasonable to use the marginal utility (CD) at the existing income level, Y^0 (OC), as a yardstick (this marginal utility also has significance across different individuals if we accept the incentive argument discussed in Appendix 9.1).

The use of *CD* as a yardstick means that, if the utility gain to the individual is measured by the rectangle *IJKL*, and if by construction $IJ = CD$, then *IL* is the monetary measure we are after. We shall call this measure the 'marginal-dollar equivalent' (MDE) of the gain – the number of times the gain is worth the gain of a marginal dollar. The MDE can be measured in two ways: one via the CV and the other via the EV.

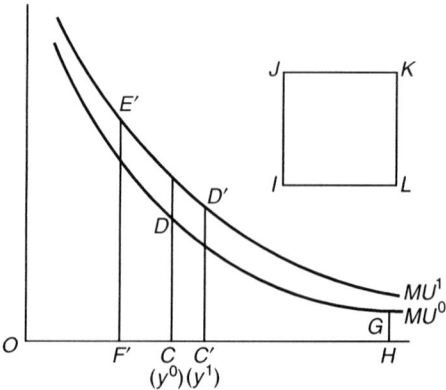

Figure A4.2

$$MDE = \int_{Y^1-CV}^{Y^1} MU^1 \, dY/MU^0 \, (Y^0) \;=\; C'D'E'F'/CD \qquad \text{(A4.1)}$$

$$MDE = \int_{Y^0}^{Y^0+EV} MU^0 \, dY/MU^0(Y^0) = CDGH/CD \qquad \text{(A4.2)}$$

Barring inaccuracies, the two measures should give equal results. If the results diverge the average of the two measurements can be taken to minimise the effect of inaccuracy.

If we know the marginal utilities of individuals over the relevant range both before and after the change we can calculate ΣMDE and make a decision accordingly. But different individuals have different utility functions. In practice we cannot take account of all the differences in individual preferences and have to work in terms of a typical individual and make allowances only for the more obvious and serious cases of abnormality. Both common sense and analytical simplicity suggest that it may be reasonable to assume an iso-elastic form of marginal utility function (that is the marginal utility curve has the same elasticity throughout):

$$MU = Y^{-\rho}; \; U = Y^{1-\rho}/(1 - \rho) \qquad \text{(A4.3)}$$

where Y represents the amount of income and p is a positive constant. In the special case of $\rho = 1$, $U = \log Y$. This has some support from psychological studies that show that, apart from extreme values, sensation $= k \log$ stimulus, where k is a positive constant (the Weber–Fechner law). One of the weaknesses of this function is that utility approaches infinity as income approaches infinity. It is not possible to believe that individuals can have infinite happiness, no matter how great their income. It seems likely that ρ will increase as income becomes very high. But for the relevant range, ρ may be taken to be approximately constant.

The introduction of a policy change (for example a project) may affect MU. However in the absence of specific knowledge of how MU is affected, we shall take (A4.3) to represent the utility functions of individuals both before and after the change. Hence the approximate measures for MDE are:

$$MDE \simeq (Y^0)^\rho \int_{Y^1-CV}^{Y^1} Y^{-\rho} dY \qquad \text{(A4.4)}$$

$$MDE \simeq (Y^0)^\rho \int_{Y^0}^{Y^0+EV} Y^{-\rho} \, dY \qquad \text{(A4.5)}$$

If both measures are available and differ, we take:

$$MDE \approx \tfrac{1}{2} (Y^0)^\rho \int_{Y^1-CV}^{Y^1} Y^{-\rho} \, dY + \tfrac{1}{2} (Y^0)^\rho \int_{Y^0}^{Y^0+EV} Y^{-\rho} \, dY \qquad \text{(A4.6)}$$

A policy measure is then recommended for acceptance or rejection according to whether the sum of MDE over all individuals, that is, ΣMDE^i, is positive or negative.

The ΣMDE measure removes a source of contradiction in the ΣCV or ΣEV measure (due to diminishing marginal utility), but it is still no more than an approximate measure (see Section 4.6 above). In particular, if MU changes due to a shift of the whole curve (that is, $C'D' \neq CD$ in Figure A4.2) a contradiction may still arise (this possible source of contradiction is already present in the ΣCV and ΣEV measure). In principle, if we know all the MU curves before and after the change and can attach social significance to them, we can devise a measure that is free of contradiction. But this would fall a little short of providing a fully defined social welfare function. At any rate it is unlikely that the shift in MU will be an important source of contradiction (the argument in Appendix 9.1 reinforces this assertion).

Appendix 4.2: Acceptability of the Marshallian Measure – The Benchmark Case of a Cobb–Douglas Utility Function**

Despite the fact that the Marshall measure of consumer surplus (using areas bounded by the demand curve and price lines) is not perfect (no monetary or other objective measure is perfect, as argued in Section 4.6), it is an acceptable approximate measure for most cases that involve price changes only. This can be most easily shown using the benchmark case of a Cobb–Douglas utility function. Maximising the following utility function:

$$U = \Sigma_g (\alpha_g \ln x_g) \tag{A4.7}$$

subject to the usual budget constraint $\Sigma_g (p_g x_g) = M$, where M is the budget constraint and p_g and x_g are the price and quantity of good g, respectively, the following demand functions can easily be derived: $x_g = \alpha_g M/\alpha p_g$ for all g, where $\alpha \equiv \Sigma_g \alpha_g$.

Now consider (1) a change in the price of any good j from any given level p_j' to any other p_j'', and (2) a change in the price of any other good k from any p_k' to any p_k''. Is the Marshall measure of consumer surplus associated with (1) larger than that associated with (2) if and only if the utility gain in (1) is larger than that in (2)? This is in fact so, as shown below, where MS stands for the Marshall measure of consumer surplus:

$$MS_j = -\int_{p_j'}^{p_j''} x_j \, dp_j = -\int_{p_j'}^{p_j''} (\alpha_j M/\alpha p_j) \, dp_j = (\alpha_j M/\alpha)(\ln p_j' - \ln p_j'') \tag{A4.8}$$

$$MS_k = (\alpha_k M/\alpha)(\ln p_k' - \ln p_k'') \tag{A4.9}$$

$$\Delta U_j = \alpha_j \ (ln \ x_j'' - ln \ x_j') = \alpha_j (ln \ [\alpha_j M/\alpha p_j''] - ln \ [\alpha_j M/\alpha p_j'])$$
$$= \alpha_j \ (ln \ p_j' - ln \ p_j'') \tag{A4.10}$$

$$\Delta U_k = \alpha_k \ (ln \ p_k' - ln \ p_k'') \tag{A4.11}$$

Hence, $MS_j/MS_k = \Delta U_j/\Delta U_k$ and $MS_j > MS_k$ if and only if $\Delta U_j > \Delta U_k$. QED

Since $MS_j/MS_k = \Delta U_j/U_k$, the Marshall measure gives us not only the correct direction of utility change but also the correct ratio. It is thus an exact cardinal measure of utility change in the present benchmark case. As an exercise, students might like to repeat the above demonstration for the case of a CES (constant elasticity of substitution) utility function, where

$$u \ (x_1, x_2, \ldots, x_G) = \left(x_1^\rho + x_2^\rho + \ldots x_G^\rho\right)^{1/\rho} \quad (0 \neq \rho < 1) \tag{A4.12}$$

5
Social Choice

The concept of Pareto optimality leads to situations in which it is impossible to make someone better off without making others worse off. Moreover it offers no guidance on the choice involved in making some better off and some worse off. In Chapter 3 we discussed welfare criteria that provide sufficient conditions for social improvement. But the results we obtained there are still incomplete in two aspects. First, we have no answer for cases in which the compensation test is met but the distributional one is not, and *vice versa*. Second, the criterion that we find acceptable (Little's Criterion) is based on judgments about distributional desirability. How do we reach such judgments? In Chapter 4 the discussion of the magnitude of welfare changes reduces (but not completely) the inadequacy of Chapter 3 in respect of the first aspect. But the incompleteness of the second aspect has yet to be overcome. The vacuum can be filled by a specific social welfare function (SWF), but how do we obtain such a function? A dictator might say that 'The SWF should just be my preference function. Whatever I prefer or whatever I think is good for society should prevail.' But a dictated solution is not palatable to most people. The problem of social choice is to see whether we can derive a social preference that is based on the preferences of individuals and satisfies certain reasonable conditions. While this seems simple enough and nothing more than the basic requirement of (minimal) democracy, a formidable difficulty is presented by Arrow's impossibility theorem.

5.1 Arrow's impossibility theorem

Arrow (1951b) calls his theorem the general possibility theorem since he first proves another theorem, the possibility theorem, for the special case of two alternatives. However as the answer to the general possibility theorem is negative, it is also called the impossibility theorem or the general impossibility theorem. In simple terms the theorem states that a rule (or a constitution) for deriving – from individual *orderings* of social states – a social ordering that is consistent with reasonable conditions cannot be found in general.

A first glimpse at the content of the theorem can be provided by the well-known 'paradox of voting'. Assume that a three-person group is faced with a choice of three alternatives. A simple and obvious way of arriving at a collective ordering is to say that one alternative is preferred to another if the majority hold such preference. Now suppose that the preferences of the three individuals are as follows:

$$xP^1yP^1z; \ zP^2xP^2y; \ yP^3zP^3x$$

where x, y and z are the three alternatives and P^i stands for 'is preferred to' for the ith individual. It can be seen that a majority prefers x to y and a majority prefers y to z. According to the rule of majority voting we can say that the group prefers x to y and y to z. By transitivity, which is usually accepted as a condition of logical consistency (and a necessary condition for being an ordering), x should be preferred to z. But actually a majority of the group prefers z to x. This shows that the rule of majority voting when making a social or collective choice can result in cyclicity ($xPyPzPx$) and *a fortiori* may fail to satisfy the requirement of transitivity. What Arrow proves in his theorem is that the difficulty illustrated by the paradox of voting is *general*, not just applicable to the majority rule, that is we cannot find *any* method or rule for passing from individual to collective ordering while satisfying reasonable conditions. For example even if we make unanimity our rule, intransitivity may still arise, as follows.

Suppose $xP^1yP^1z; \ zP^2xP^2y$. It can be seen that, according to unanimity rule, xPy and yIz (since we do not have a unanimous preference between y and z, in order to make the social preference complete we have to declare indifference). From transitivity, xPz. But there is actually no unanimous preference of x over z.

We shall now consider Arrow's path-breaking contribution. Arrow defines a social state as:

> a complete description of the amount of each type of commodity in the hands of each individual, the amount of labour to be applied by each individual, the amount of each productive resource invested in each type of productive activity, and the amounts of various types of collective activity such as municipal services, diplomacy and its continuation by other means, and the erection of statues to famous men (Arrow, 1951b/1963, p. 17).

All aspects that may affect the preference of any individual are included. Each individual in the community has a definite ordering of all conceivable social states in terms of their desirability to her or him. 'Desirability' need not be determined only by her or his own commodity bundle. 'The individual may order all social states by whatever standards he sees relevant' (Arrow, 1950, pp. 333–4).

Both individual and social preferences are required to satisfy two rather weak axioms (which are necessary conditions for being an ordering):

- **Axiom A**: completeness – for *all x and y, either xRy or yRx, where R stands for preferred or indifferent to.*
- **Axiom B**: transitivity – *for all x, y and z, xRy and yRz imply xRz. In other words, if x is preferred or indifferent to y and y is preferred or indifferent to z, then x must be preferred or indifferent to z.*

It should be noted that although Arrow discusses his theorem in terms of social states, his argument is generally applicable to the choice of any set of alternatives, be it the set of social states confronting a society, the number of candidates to be elected or the number of alternative actions to be decided by a committee. The two crucial requirements are that more than one individual is involved and that the collective ordering is based on the individual orderings of the alternatives.

Arrow next defines a constitution as 'a process or rule which, for each set of individual orderings $R^l, \ldots, R^I$ for alternative social states (one ordering for each individual), states a corresponding social ordering of alternative social states R' (Arrow, 1951b/1963, p. 23).[1] And Arrow requires the constitution to satisfy the following five 'natural conditions'.

(1) **Free triple**: *there are at least three among all the alternatives under consideration for which all logically possible individual orderings of the three alternatives are admissible.* The purpose of this condition is to ensure that the problem will not be made trivial by being confined to highly restricted sets of individual orderings. For example if the orderings of all individuals over all the alternatives must be exactly the same and no other pattern of ordering is permissible, it would be quite trivial to have a constitutional clause saying that the social ordering can be the same as the common individual ordering. However if we allow our individuals to order the alternatives freely, even if such freedom is allowed for just three alternatives, we are faced with the difficulty of social choice.

---

1. At first Arrow first used the term 'social welfare function'. This was not exactly the same as Bergson's SWF, which is numerical. In the last chapter of the second edition of his celebrated book, Arrow (1963, p. 105) agrees to use the term 'constitution' instead. The concept of social welfare functional (Sen, 1970a, 1977b; D'Aspremont and Gevers, 1977) has also been used. This specifies a social ordering from a set of individual utility or welfare *functions* over all social states. I do not find this concept necessary as 'independence' (see Appendix 5.1) is compelling. On the close connection between the two approaches see Theorem 1 by Roberts (1980b).

(2) **Positive association of social and individual values**: '*the social ordering responds positively to alterations in individual values, or at least not negatively. Hence, if one alternative social state rises or remains unchanged in the ordering of every individual without any other change in these orderings, we expect that it rises, or at least does not fall, in the social ordering*' (Arrow, 1951b/1963, p. 25).

(3) **The independence of irrelevant alternatives (IIA)**: '*the choice made by society from a given environment depends only on the orderings of individuals among the alternatives in that environment. Alternatively stated, if we consider two sets of individual orderings such that, for each individual, his ordering of these particular alternatives in a given environment is the same each time, then we require that the choice made by society from that environment be the same when individual values are given by the first set of orderings as they are when given by the second*' (Arrow, 1951b/1963, pp. 26–7).

This condition has given rise to considerable controversy, partly due to an inadequate understanding of it. Sen (1970a, pp. 89ff.) makes the penetrating observation that there are two different aspects to the IIA. The first is the 'irrelevance' (or 'independence') aspect, which refers to the fact that the social ordering of any two alternatives (or any other subset of alternatives) must depend only on individual preferences for these alternatives, not on individual preferences for other irrelevant alternatives. Many people find this requirement unacceptable. This is probably due to their failure to recognize that each social alternative is a complete specification of *all* the relevant aspects of a social state. Once this is recognised the independence aspect is a very reasonable requirement (see Appendix 5.1). The second is the 'ordering' aspect, which requires the social ordering of any two alternatives to be based only on the individual *orderings* of these alternatives and not on anything else, such as preference intensity or cardinal utilities.[2]

Both aspects of the IIA are reasonable if our knowledge is confined to the *orderings* or ordinal preferences of individuals (Plott, 1972). If the relative intensity of preferences or interpersonally comparable cardinal utilities are known, then the ordering aspect of the IIA need not be accepted. With the introduction of cardinal preferences, however, we have gone outside the scope of the original problem posed by Arrow, since he requires the constitution to derive a social ordering based on individual *orderings*. Nevertheless

---

2. Some writers (for example Quirk and Saposnik, 1968, p. 110) have shown that they are aware of these two distinct aspects of the IIA, but Sen (1970a) has provided a more detailed discussion. The ordering aspect is also involved in Arrow's second condition and in many of the conditions used by other authors. Osborne (1976) divides the ordering aspect into individualism and ordinalism, and somewhat misleadingly calls the irrelevance aspect localism. The IIA may be made even weaker (Quesada, 2002).

the possibility of aggregating cardinal utilities is meaningful and is within the confines of social choice (see Section 5.4).

(4) **Citizens' sovereignty**: *the social ordering must not be imposed. Social ordering is imposed if there is a pair of alternatives, x and y, but society can never express a preference for y over x no matter what the preferences of all the individuals in that society. Even if all individuals prefer y to x, the social ordering is still xRy.*

This condition is very reasonable as it only requires the social ordering of any pair of alternatives to be based on individual orderings or to be not totally independent of these individual orderings.

(5) **Non-dictatorship**: *the constitution must not be dictatorial. The constitution is dictatorial if there is an individual such that if he prefers that individual one of every pair of alternatives the first over the other.*

This definition of dictatorship definitely does not include people like Stalin and Hitler as dictators. The requirement of non-dictatorship is therefore very mild. If we were to allow dictatorship, a constitution could easily be established that required the social ordering to be the same as the ordering of the dictator.

Arrow's original general possibility theorem states that no constitution exists that simultaneously satisfies axioms A and B and conditions 1 to 5 above. To prove this Arrow uses the concept of a decisive set. A set of individuals is decisive for alternative x against y if their unanimous ranking of x as preferred to y is sufficient to establish that x is socially preferred to y, regardless of the orderings of all other individuals. Arrow first proves that, for a free triple, if an individual is decisive for any one alternative against any other, then he or she is also decisive for every pair of alternatives in the free triple (Arrow, 1951b, p. 56). Hence no single individual can be decisive by the requirement of non-dictatorship. On the other hand, since unanimity must determine social ordering by conditions 2 and 4, at least one decisive set can always be found. Select the decisive set that contains the smallest number of individuals, and without loss of generality, let it be decisive for x against y. Divide this decisive set, denoted by V_1, into V', a single individual in V_1, and V_2, the set of all other individuals in V_1. This division is possible since a decisive set cannot contain fewer than two individuals. Suppose the individual orderings are as follows:

V' prefers x to y and y to z;
all individuals in V_2 prefer z to x and x to y;
all individuals in V_3 prefer y to z and z to x,

where V_3 is the set of all individuals not in V_1. This pattern of preference is admissible since x, y and z constitute the free triple.

Since V_1 is decisive for x against y, the social ordering must rank x over y. Individuals in V_2 prefer z to y but all other individuals prefer y to z. If in the social ordering z was preferred to y, V_2 would be decisive for z against y.

But this would contradict the assumption that V_2 is one individual fewer than the smallest decisive set. Thus society must prefer y to z or be indifferent between y and z. By transitivity, x must be socially preferred to z. However all individuals other than the single individual, V, prefer z to x. So she or he is decisive for x against z. But, to satisfy non-dictatorship no single individual can be decisive. This shows that the five conditions cannot be satisfied simultaneously. Before reading on, readers are invited to try to identify any inadequacy in the preceding proof.

The proof is incomplete because it refers only to the free triple. It shows that if other conditions are satisfied, non-dictatorship is violated for the free triple. If we consider the general case of more than three alternatives, then all the five conditions may be satisfied for these alternatives, although not for the free triple. If an individual is decisive over the free triple, this does not mean that he or she is a dictator over all the alternatives. Hence non-dictatorship is not necessarily violated. Arrow's original definition of a decisive set is, strictly speaking, not appropriate, since 'regardless of the preferences of all other individuals' and 'all other individuals have the reverse preference' are not exactly the same thing. A pedantic note can also be added: if the set of individuals is infinite (obviously not relevant), Arrow's theorem does not apply (see Fishburn, 1970a; Kirman and Sondermann, 1972; Hansson, 1976. For a survey of individual and social welfare measurement see Slesnick, 1998).

The inadequacy of Arrow's original proof was first noted by Blau (1957), who shows that the proof can be saved by slightly revising condition 2 and replacing free triple with free orderings.

Free Orderings: *all logically possible orderings are admissible.*

Arrow himself (1963) has replaced the revised condition 2 (2') and condition 4 with a weak version of the Pareto principle.

Weak Pareto Principle: *if every individual prefers one alternative to another, then society also prefers the first to the second.*

This condition is deducible from conditions 2', 3 and 4 and is almost universally accepted. It is weaker than the usual Pareto principle as it requires a strong preference by all individuals. Arrow then proves the revised impossibility theorem: free orderings, IIA, weak Pareto and non-dictatorship are inconsistent. This proof (Arrow, 1963, pp. 97–100) is very similar to the original proof. First it is shown that no single individual can be decisive for any pair of alternatives. This is because if an individual is decisive for any alternative against any other, she or he is also decisive for all pairs of alternatives (with any number of alternatives) by free orderings, IIA and weak Pareto. Then a decisive set with the smallest number of individuals is selected. Using the same argument as in the preceding proof, it is then shown that a contradiction must result.

Another revision of the theorem has been suggested by Murakami (1961), who replaces non-dictatorship with:

Strong non-dictatorship: *among the triples of alternatives that satisfy free triple, there is at least one for which no individual is a dictator.*

Arrow accepts this extension of the notion of a dictator as very reasonable, since its violation implies that there is a dictator for every choice on which there can be real disagreement.

It can be concluded that Arrow's theorem is established under either of the following sets of conditions (with axioms A and B):[3]

- Free orderings, IIA, weak Pareto and non-dictatorship.
- Free triple, IIA, weak Pareto and strong non-dictatorship.

5.2 The impossibility propositions by Kemp–Ng and Parks

Arrow's impossibility theorem has far-reaching implications. For one thing it shows that we cannot have a reasonable rule to derive our SWF or a social ordering from the ordinal preferences of individuals (the existence of an SWF presupposes a social ordering). Since the concept of an SWF is crucial in welfare economics and since many economists are reluctant to use cardinal utilities, a dilemma is posed. Some economists, notably Little (1952) and Samuelson (1967), have attempted to solve this dilemma by rejecting Arrow's theorem as irrelevant to welfare economics. Specifically, it is maintained that what is relevant to welfare economics is an SWF for a given set of individual orderings. It is true that individual preferences may change. But for any new set of individual orderings there is a new SWF. The Arrow impossibility result only applies if the rule used to derive the new SWF (or social ordering) from the new set of individual orderings is the same as the one used to derive the old SWF from the original set of individual orderings. By not restricting ourselves to such interprofile consistency – that is, the same rule for different profiles or sets of individual orderings – we can free ourselves from the Arrow paradox.

The above argument on bypassing Arrow's impossibility result is not really convincing. As individual preferences over social states or alternatives

3. The comment by Bailey (1979) on the Arrow–Murakami proof that no minimum number of alternatives is imposed misses the point that a social-choice rule should give reasonable results for any number of alternatives. His proposed rule (equal endowments with free exchange) is 'imposed', as it fails to base the choice of the distribution of endowments on individual preferences. However his rule shares some common features with my proposal to resolve the paradox of interpersonal cardinal utility (Section 5.5).

change, it is reasonable to assume that society's ordering or SWF over social states will also change. But why should the rule used to derive the social ordering change too? For example, if we use majority rule for a given set of individual orderings, why should we shift to, say, unanimity for another set of individual orderings? It seems unreasonable to change the rule unless it is not acceptable for the original set of preferences.[4]

Nevertheless, even ignoring the requirement of interprofile consistency it can be shown that there does not exist a reasonable rule to derive a social ordering based only on individual orderings. Even if we agree to operate with a fixed set of individual preferences, we still have the impossibility result. This was established almost simultaneously and independently by Kemp and Ng (1976) and Parks (1976), who used different sets of assumptions. Roughly speaking, Parks adopted a stronger assumption with respect to the diversity of alternatives and individual preferences, and Kemp and Ng adopted a stronger assumption with respect to democratic requirement (anonymity in contrast with non-dictatorship). Due to his set of assumptions, Parks' proof is very similar to Arrow's. Hence the elucidation below follows that of Kemp and Ng. (for extensions see Pollak, 1979; Roberts 1980c).

Kemp and Ng (1976) first prove that we cannot construct a real valued SWF based only on individual orderings under a fairly mild set of assumptions. But since the proof of the first proposition is fairly complicated, we shall present their proposition 2, which rules out a reasonable social ordering based only on (a given set of) individual orderings. The assumptions (or conditions) used are as follows:

(1) **Mild diversity of preferences**: there exist three social alternatives x, y *and z, and two individuals, J and K, and (1) these two individuals strongly order (that is, there is no indifference) x, y and z, (2) they differ strongly in their rankings of two pairs chosen from $\{x, y, z\}$ and agree on the ranking of the remaining pair, and (3) other individuals are indifferent between x, y and z.*

By strong difference in preference for a pair of alternatives x and y, we mean xP^Jy and yP^Kx, or *vice versa*. If the allocation of G goods to I individuals is among the variables defining the set of social alternatives, as in welfare economics, it can be shown that mild diversity is a very reasonable condition (Kemp and Ng, 1976, pp. 60–1; see also Kramer, 1973).

4. See, however, McManus (1975, 1978) for the argument that society might give different weights to the preference of an individual depending on whether he or she is a drug addict. But how does society first agree on discounting the preferences of addicts? McManus' proposal does not provide a satisfactory solution to Arrow's impossibility result, not to mention the impossibility propositions by Kemp and Ng (1976) and Parks (1976).

(2) **Strong Pareto principle**: *for any two alternatives x and y, $xR^i y$ for all i implies xRy, and $xR^i y$ for all i and $xP^j y$ for some j implies xPy.*

(3) **Anonymity plus orderings only**: *for any x, y, z and w (which are not necessarily distinct alternatives), if $x\overline{R}^i y$ for all i implies $x\overline{R} y$, then $z\hat{R}^i w$ for all i also implies $z\overline{R} w$, where $\overline{R}^i$ stands for one (not necessarily the same for all i) of P^i, I^i and contra P^i, similarly for $\overline{R}$, and $\hat{R}^1$, $\hat{R}^2, \ldots, \hat{R}^I$ is any permutation of $\overline{R}^1$, $\overline{R}^2, \ldots, \overline{R}^I$.*

The third condition expresses two requirements simultaneously. First, it requires that all individuals be treated anonymously and on an equal footing. This requirement is of course stronger than non-dictatorship (anonymity is not used in Kemp and Ng's proposition 1). However it is still a reasonable democratic requirement. If different weights are to be used, how are they to be decided? Second, the above condition requires that the social ranking of any two alternatives must be based only on the individual rankings of them. Apart from a reasonable independence or irrelevance aspect, this can be split into two requirements: (1) that only *individual* preferences count and not anything else, and (2) that only the ordinal aspect of individual preferences (that is, orderings or rankings) count, and not the intensity of preferences. This last aspect (orderings only) need not be a reasonable condition to impose on the social ordering of anyone who is willing to take preference intensity into consideration. However since our purpose here is to show the impossibility of a reasonable social ordering based on individual *orderings*, this is a natural condition to impose.

> **Impossibility proposition**: *given Mild Diversity of Preferences, there does not exist a social ordering to satisfy the Strong Pareto and Anonymity plus Orderings Only conditions.*
>
> **Proof**: From (1) above, there exist x, y and z such xI^iyI^iz for all individuals $i \neq J$, K and such that either (a) xP^jyP^jz and zP^KxP^Ky or (b) $xP^J yP^Jz$ and yP^Kzp^Kx. Since the proof proceeds in much the same way for each of the two cases, we shall confine our attention to the first. From axiom 2 (Strong Pareto) we infer that xPy. From axiom 3, x and z must be socially indifferent. From transitivity, zPy (an ordering presupposes transitivity). This violates axiom 3 since yP^Jz and zP^Ky while other individuals are indifferent. QED.

This impossibility proposition shows that, even if we confine ourselves to a given set of individual preferences, we cannot construct a reasonable social ordering based on individual ordinal preferences. Thus the Little–Samuelson attempt to escape Arrow's paradox leads us up a blind alley. This is a deadly blow to those who dislike cardinal utilities or believe in the sufficiency of ordinal utilities (see Samuelson, 1947, pp. 227–8, 1967, 1977). But it does not rule out the possibility of constructing an SWF based on cardinal utilities (Section 5.4.1). Of course an aggregating procedure or interpersonal comparison is needed as well. Disallowing interpersonal comparisons, one can establish impossibility results even with cardinal utilities (Sen, 1970a, pp. 123–30; DeMeyer and Plott, 1971; Osborne, 1976; Kalai and Schmeidler, 1977). However, interpersonal comparability without cardinality is not sufficient. For example anonymity is a form of interpersonal comparison. With Orderings Only, we have shown above that it does not provide a reasonable result (see Ng, 1982, for the necessity of interpersonal cardinal utilities, and Roberts, 1980a, for a comprehensive analysis of comparability without cardinality).

Samuelson (1977) argues that axiom 3 (Anonymity Plus Orderings Only) is objectionable. Since no one objects to anonymity, the real issue is ordinalism. For the general social choice problem, ordinalism can be regarded as unreasonable. However, since the point here is about whether ordinalism is a sufficient basis for a single-profile social choice, the axiom is a natural condition to impose. If Samuelson objects to this axiom, he should not continue to insist on the sufficiency of ordinalism.

Some years after the Kemp–Ng–Samuelson debate I discussed the problem with Arrow. He said that if Samuelson insisted on ordinalism he would have to give up independence (that is, irrelevance). I replied that independence is compelling. Later I realised that independence is implied in the Bergson–Samuelson tradition of writing social welfare for any social state x as a function of individual utilities at x only, making the social ranking between any pair x, y independent of any other alternative z (for details see Ng, 2000a, app. F). This tradition is all right if we have interpersonally comparable cardinal utilities. However Samuelson insists that the individual utility indices are only ordinal. This is the crux of the impossibility (for an independent evaluation of the debate see Mueller, 1989, ch. 19; see also Kemp and Ng, 1977).

5.3   Can the paradox of social choice be resolved?*

Arrow's theorem has implications not only for welfare economics but also for political science since it implies that all voting and election methods (including majority rule) based on rankings are imperfect in some sense. Many attempts have been made to overcome or bypass the impossibility result. We have already seen that the attempt by Little and Samuelson led nowhere, but what about the others? Since Arrow's revised theorem is valid, the proposed solutions of the paradox must consist either in relaxing the requirement of (especially social) rationality (that is, axioms A and B) or in relaxing some of Arrow's conditions, especially the IIA and Free Orderings. The latter alternative usually takes the form of imposing restrictions on the admissible sets of individual preferences.

Just before the publication of Arrow's (1950) article, Black (1948) showed that, if the preferences of all individuals are single-peaked, it can be shown that group decisions based on majority rule are transitive. This assumes that the alternatives can be arranged in one dimension (see Grandmont, 1978, for a generalisation to multidimensions) and each individual selects his or her first preference, and the further any alternative departs from this on one side or the other, the less he or she will favour it. The shape of the evaluation curve will then be either an inverted V or monotonically increasing or decreasing, as shown in Figure 5.1. There is no constraint on how to arrange the alternatives. In other words we can arrange the alternatives in any one-dimensional order; as long as there is one arrangement that gives a single-peaked preference curve for *every* individual, the condition of single-peakedness is met.

The assumption of single-peaked preference implies violation of the Free Triple (and *a fortiori*, free orderings). However, single-peaked preference is quite likely for some alternatives, for example the size of a numerical quantity such as the price of a product, the level of a tax and so on. If individuals prefer £10 to £5 (say, for a per unit pollution tax), they are unlikely to prefer £5 to £8. Nevertheless many problems of social choice involve more than one dimension, and individual preferences may be so complicated and diverse that no arrangement of the alternatives will result in a single-peaked preference curve for every individual. Moreover, even for the simple case of choosing a one-dimensional numerical quantity it is still possible that the requirement of single-peaked preference may not be satisfied. Take the case of the number of F-111 planes a country should buy. One individual may feel that the fewer bought the better. Another individual may prefer more planes, say up to 10. The third individual may prefer there to be no planes, but would prefer four planes to three because he or she regards four as the minimum operationally useful number. Rather than waste money on three

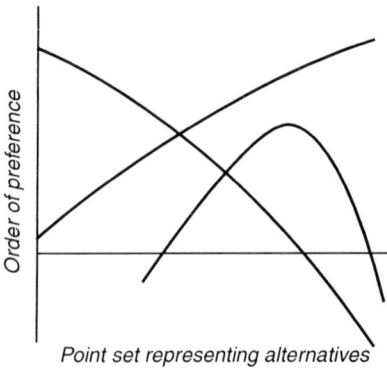

Point set representing alternatives

Figure 5.1

planes, it would be more sensible to spend a little more money and keep a workable fleet of four F-111s. Hence the preference of this individual has two peaks, at zero and at four. If we rearrange the order of the alternatives to give a single peak for this individual, the preference of at least one other individual will be made double-peaked. It can thus be concluded that the assumption of single-peaked preference is likely to be realised in some cases but cannot be taken to prevail generally. As the rule of social choice is to be applied to many alternative sets of preferences, most of which are unknown at present, the requirement of free orderings is very compelling. The attempt to solve the paradox of social choice by imposing restrictions such as single-peakedness on individual preferences does not seem to be very promising (on other restrictions on preferences see Inada, 1970; Pattanaik, 1971; Slutsky, 1977; Grandmont, 1978).

Whilst the requirement for single-peaked preference violates the Free Triple, many of the other solutions presently to be discussed violate the IIA. This condition involves both the 'independence' and the 'ordering' aspects. If the intensity of preferences can be revealed, the 'ordering' aspect need not be accepted. However, many of the attempts to solve the problem by revealing the intensity of preferences (or 'cardinalisation') have violated the independence aspect of the IIA. This is a drawback of such schemes. If the intensity of preferences is known, we would still expect the social ordering or SWF to be a function of the ordinal and *cardinal* preferences of individuals for the alternative in question. The choice between x and y should be a function only of the individual orderings and the intensity of preferences for x and y, and should be independent of an irrelevant alternative, z.[5] The compelling reasonableness of the independence aspect of the IIA has been demonstrated by Hammond (1977), who shows that even if the constant set of individuals has constant and consistent tastes, dynamic social choice will still be inconsistent unless the social choice rule satisfies the independence aspect of the IIA (which Hammond calls a generalisation of the IIA).

To show how both aspects of the IIA are violated in some attempts at cardinalisation, consider the following voting procedure, which is free of intransitivity:

Each elector is asked to vote in the following manner. Faced with a subset of the set x of all conceivable alternatives, he assigns to that alternative which he ranks highest (i.e. from which he expects to get the greatest

---

5. Hansson (1969) shows that if we impose anonymity (or neutrality between persons) and neutrality (between alternatives), no group decision function can satisfy the IIA unless it always declares all alternatives to be equal. While Hansson regards this as an argument against the IIA, it is more reasonably regarded as an alternative impossibility theorem if we stay within the orderings only framework.

utility) the number 'one'. The remaining alternatives are assigned numbers according to the utility expected from them relative to that expected from the most desired alternative.... The numbers assigned to each alternative are summed over all electors and that alternative is chosen which has the greatest total. The alternative with the second highest is ranked second, and so on (Kemp and Asimakopulos, 1952, pp. 196–7; see also Weldon, 1952, p. 452; Hildock, 1953, p. 81).

The procedure clearly violates the ordering aspect of the IIA. It also violates the independence aspect, as shown below. Suppose that my first alternative, x, is ranked very low by all the other voters, who are more or less equally divided between y and z. The utility we expect from y is twice that of z, say 10 units and 5 units respectively. If the utility I expect from x is 100 units, I have to vote 1 for x, 0.1 for y and 0.05 for z. Now suppose that z is preferred by a fractionally larger number of voters than y. In this case, if the utility I expect from x is 20 units we, have to vote 1 for x, 0.5 for y and 0.25 for z. With all other votes unchanged, y may then have a larger total than z. Thus even if all individual preferences (both ordinal and cardinal) with respect to y and z remain exactly unchanged, the social ordering of y and z will be affected by my preference with respect to x, an alternative that will certainly be ranked lower than both y and z. This is certainly an undesirable outcome. Even if all individual preferences are fixed, the social ordering of y and z will still depend on whether x, or some other alternative, is included in the set of alternatives. Again an undesirable outcome. (Observant readers may have noticed that the IIA is stated with reference to a change in individual preferences. But since the example used by Arrow himself to illustrate the spirit of the IIA refers to a change in the set of alternatives, it has frequently been taken to assume this second meaning as well. If we eschew the ordering aspect, both meanings of IIA are just an extremely reasonable property of independence.)

Buchanan and Tullock (1962, pp. 330–2), Coleman (1966) and others propose a log-rolling method of voting, whereby the relative intensity of preferences can be revealed (see also Miller, 1977; Tullock 1998). Basically voters are allowed to enter into vote trading agreements or the actual exchange of votes. For example if J is strongly opposed to alternative z, she may agree with K that she will rank y (her second preference and K's first preference) first, provided K agrees to vote z (K's second preference) last. This increases K's chance of getting his first preference and also increases J's chance of preventing the adoption of her worst alternative (on the prevalence of log-rolling in the US Congress, see Stratmann, 1995).

It has been shown by Park (1967) that in general vote trading cannot produce a stable equilibrium, while Mueller (1967) argues that vote trading agreements cannot be relied upon to reveal the true preferences of individuals and that the resulting set of policy decisions will fall short of being socially optimal. 'If the number of voters is not so large as to preclude the formation of partially stable coalitions, it is too small to remove completely the monopsony power a voter will be able to enjoy over any issue of vital importance to him' (Mueller, 1967, p. 1310). Nevertheless, if vote trading were possible we would tend to move closer to a social optimum, and the social decision would tend to be transitive. Arrow (1963, p. 109) rejects the log-rolling argument on the ground that 'a social state is a whole bundle of issues, and I presupposed that all possible combinations of decisions on the separate issues are considered as alternative social states. That this included log-rolling seemed to me so obvious as not to be worth spelling out.' This argument misses the point that, with log-rolling, the relative intensity of preferences is revealed to some extent and hence we may no longer wish to be bound by the ordering aspect of the IIA (see Hewitt, 1987, on the role of vote trading in improving efficiency both in influencing outcomes in accordance with the intensity of preferences and in providing information to governments). However, social decision with log-rolling violates not only the ordering aspect of the IIA but also its independence aspect. This can be seen most clearly where the alternatives are small in number. A change in individual preferences with respect to some alternatives or the removal of one alternative changes the possibility of vote trading so much that the social ordering of the unaffected alternatives may change (cf. Wilson, 1969, p. 339).

Quite distinct from log-rolling, another proposal along the lines of cardinal utility has been made by Harsanyi (1953, 1955; see also Vickrey, 1945). Each individual indicates 'what social situation he would choose if he did not know what his personal position would be in the new situation chosen (and in any of its alternatives) but rather had an equal *chance* of obtaining any of the social positions existing in this situation,[6] from the highest down to the lowest' (Harsanyi, 1955, p. 316). If the preferences of the individual satisfy a certain reasonable set of rationality axioms, they must define a cardinal SWF that is equal to the sum of the utilities of all individuals in society. But these utilities are those judged by the individual rather than the actual utilities of all the individuals, unless we heroically assume that each individual has perfect information not only with respect to the objective but also the subjective circumstances (psychology, ability to enjoy and so on) of all individuals in different alternatives. Hence the SWFs of different

---

6. 'Or, rather, if he had an equal chance of being "put in the place of" any individual member of society, with regard not only to his objective social (and economic) conditions, but also to his subjective attitudes and tastes. In other words, he ought to judge the utility of another individual's position not in terms of his own attitudes and tastes but rather in terms of the attitudes and tastes of the individual actually holding this position' – (Harsanyi, 1955).

persons thus derived may differ from one another due to the lack of factual information and differences in personal judgments about the utility of other individuals, not to mention the possibility of false preferences. We are still left with the problem of choosing among or aggregating the various individual SWFs, and we have to face the paradox of social choice at this level.

Sen (1969b) shows that if we are interested only in the best social alternative rather than the social ordering of all the alternatives, then the impossibility theorem does not apply. In other words it is possible to have a social *choice* function that denotes the best or chosen alternative while satisfying all Arrow's requirements. However with one additional reasonable condition Sen has been able to revive the impossibility theorem in relation to the social choice function. This additional condition requires that if both x and y are chosen from a set, S_1, then if x is chosen from a larger set, S_2 that includes S_1, y must be chosen (Sen 1969b, p. 384, 1970a, p. 17). The fact that the relaxation of social rationality does not provide a very promising escape route has been confirmed by a number of writers (for example Mas-Colell and Sonnenschein, 1972; Fishburn, 1974; Ferejohn and Grether, 1977b) who have established impossibility results with very mild requirements on social rationality, such as acyclicity (of strict preferences).

Despite Arrow's theorem, the actual functioning of democratic voting systems seems to work well, or at least seems to be acceptable. Why? A number of writers have attempted to provide an explanation, and have questioned, with partial success, the significance of Arrow's theorem. For example Tullock (1967a) has attempted to show that the theorem is not important in practice. While no decision-making process can meet Arrow's conditions perfectly, a very common decision-making process meets them to a very high degree of approximation, and this explains the practical success of democracy. The general impossibility theorem is therefore generally irrelevant in this sense. Arrow admits that Tullock (1967b) has 'argued convincingly that if the distributions of opinions on social issues is fairly uniform and if the dimensionality of the space of social issues is much less than the number of individuals, then majority voting on a sincere basis will be transitive' (Arrow, 1970, p. 19; see also Davis and Hinich, 1966). However MacKenzie (1967, pp. 144–51) and Taylor (1968) argue that Arrow's theorem is still very relevant when dealing with small voting bodies such as committees, which typically consist of a small number of members. In a computer simulation it has been shown that if 'the difference made by adding more dimensions is small ... [the] percentage of cycles declines as the number of committee members increases' (Tullock and Campbell, 1970, p. 101). But 'it has not been demonstrated that cycles in small committees are trivial, nor has it been shown that they are important' (ibid., p. 104; see also Sen, 1970a, pp. 163–6 and the references therein. For more general references on social choice see Rowley, 1993; Arrow *et al.*, 1997).

While majority voting may be acceptable as a workable rule on the level of practical decisions, even a minute probability of cycles is quite disturbing on the level of logic. Though majority voting will be used for a long time to come, theorists will keep searching for a better alternative, if not the ideal. We have examined some representative attempts in this search and have found them wanting in some respect or other. The next section considers two other attempts, both involving ways of revealing the intensity of preferences.

5.4 Revealing the intensity of preferences*

The reason why Arrow's impossibility theorem holds is really rather simple. To make a social choice that involves conflicts of interest (some individuals gain and some lose by choosing different alternatives) we have to know the intensity of each of the relevant gains and losses and compare them interpersonally. Arrow's conditions do not rule out interpersonal comparisons but they (the ordering aspect of the IIA in particular) do rule out the use of intensity of preference and allow only individual orderings. Thus the fact that an individual prefers x to y has to mean exactly the same thing irrespective of whether she or he only marginally prefers x to y or very strongly prefers x to y. It is the exclusion of this important information that causes the impossibility, so the natural way to overcome this impossibility is to reveal the intensity of preferences.

Numerous ways of revealing the intensity of individual preferences (rather than just orderings) have been proposed, some of which are discussed in the preceding section; two further approaches merit special discussion, as follows.

5.4.1 Finite sensibility and welfare aggregate

The first approach is based on the concept of finite sensibility, or recognition of the fact that human beings are not infinitely discriminative. For example suppose an individual prefers two spoons of sugar (x) to one (y) in his or her coffee. If we slowly increase the amount of sugar in one spoon we will eventually reach the point, y' (say 1.8 spoons), at which the individual cannot tell the difference between x and y'. There may exist another point, y'' (say 1.6 spoons), at which the individual is indifferent to y' but prefers x to y''. Hence with finite sensibility a perfectly rational individual may have intransitive indifference.

The concept of finite sensibility was touched on as far back as 1781 by Borda and in 1881 by Edgeworth (when I was giving a seminar at Nuffield College in 1974, upon which my 1975a paper is based, a participant interjected, 'Why can't you wait a few more years until 1981?'). Edgeworth took it as axiomatic, or in his words 'a first principle incapable of proof', that the 'minimum sensible' or just perceivable increments of pleasure for all persons are equitable (Edgeworth, 1881, pp. 7ff., 60 ff.) Armstrong (1951), Goodman and Markowitz (1952) and Rothenberg (1961) have also discussed the problem. It has also been explored in decision theory and the psychological literature, using the term 'just noticeable difference' (see Fishburn, 1970, for a survey).

With intransitivity of indifference, the (explicit) preference of an individual can no longer be represented by a utility function, U^i, such that $xR^iy \leftrightarrow U^i(x) \geq U^i(y)$. However the individual's 'underlying preference' (roughly speaking, her or his preference if she or he were infinitely sensitive) can still be represented by a utility function.[7] In terms of explicit preference, the utility function can be scaled to have the following property: $yP^ix \leftrightarrow U^i(y) - U^i(x) > a$; $xR^iy \leftrightarrow U^i(y) - U^i(x) \leq a$, where a is a constant, that is, any positive number (for example one) that is used to represent a utility difference of a maximal indifference. Using this utility function for each individual and making some assumptions of purely technical nature, Ng (1975a) shows that the only acceptable SWF is the unweighted sum of individual utilities (the utilitarian SWF) if the following value premise is accepted (for other arguments in favour of utilitarianism, see Fleming, 1952; Harsanyi, 1955; Maskin, 1978; Sugden and Weale, 1979; Ng, 2000a, ch. 5):

- **The Weak Majority Preference (WMP) Criterion**: *for any two alternatives x and y, if no individual prefers y to x, and (1) if I, (the number of individuals), is even, at least I/2 individuals prefer x to y, and (2) if I is odd, at least (I − 1)/2 individuals prefer x to y and at least another individual's utility level is not lower in x than in y, then social welfare is higher in x than in y.*

The reason why WMP leads us to the utilitarian SWF is not difficult to see. According to the WMP criterion, utility differences that are sufficient to give rise to preferences in half of the population must be regarded as socially more significant than utility differences that are not sufficient to give rise to preferences (or the reverse) in the other half. Since any group of individuals comprising 50 per cent of the population is an acceptable half, this effectively makes a just-perceivable increment of utility of any individual an interpersonally comparable unit. This is illustrated below.

---

7. Luce (1956) defines a semi-order that effectively requires two levels of preference to outweigh one level of indifference, that is $xPyPzIw \rightarrow xPw$, and so on Fishburn (1973) provides necessary and sufficient conditions for a semi-order to be closed-interval representable. These conditions involve some very technical concepts of countability and density requirements. Ng (1975a) provides sufficiency proof of representation by adopting standard assumptions on explicit preference and showing that the underlying preference must satisfy certain conditions that are known to ensure the existence of utility functions (see also the generalisation by Sichelstiel and Sollner, 1996).

If the number of individuals is even, as long as 50 per cent of the population are made noticeably better off and the other 50 per cent unnoticeably worse off, social welfare increases according to the WMP criterion. Conversely, as long as 50 per cent are made noticeably worse off and the other 50 per cent unnoticeably better off, social welfare decreases. Thus, taking the limit, social welfare remains unchanged as 50 per cent of the population are unnoticeably better off and the other 50 per cent are unnoticeably worse off (reasonably assuming that social welfare is a continuous function of individual utilities).

In Figure 5.2 all the *I* individuals are arranged along the horizontal axis and individual utilities are represented by the vertical axis. Starting from an initial situation, *x*, curve *x* represents the utilities of the various individuals. For example if each individual occupies a distance of one third of a centimeter along the horizontal axis, the utility of the first individual in situation *x* is the shaded area. Curve *x* need not be continuous. This does not affect our argument. Consider another situation, *y*, which in comparison with *x* involves making the first *I*/2 individuals unnoticeably better off and the rest unnoticeably worse off. According to the WMP criterion and the argument of the preceding paragraph, social welfare remains unchanged. Now, starting from situation *y* (see curve *y*), consider another situation, *z*. In comparison with *y*, *z* involves making another 50 per cent (the first individual, and the second half of all individuals except the last one) unnoticeably better off and the other 50 per cent (the last individual and the first half of all individuals except the first) unnoticeably worse off. Hence social welfare again remains unchanged. Since there is no change between *x* and *y*, or between *y* and *z*, social welfare must be the same at *x* as at *z*. Comparing

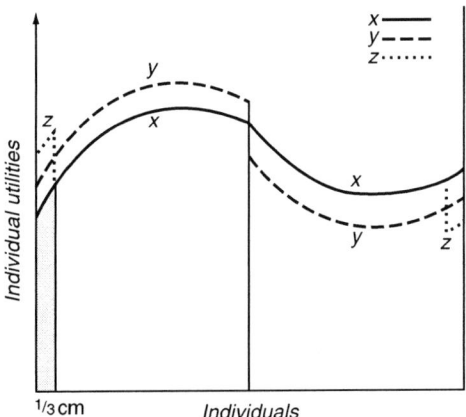

Figure 5.2
Source: Ng and Singer (1981).

x and *z*, we can see that all have exactly the same levels of utility except the first and the last individuals. The first individual's utility has increased by two units and that of the last has decreased by two units. This demonstration does not depend on the choice of these two particular individuals, since WMP applies to any 50 per cent of individuals. Thus we may conclude that, irrespective of the initial situation, if we increase the utility of any one individual by two units and reduce that of any other by two units, holding those of all others unchanged, social welfare must remain unchanged. Effectively this leads us to the utilitarian SWF of the unweighted sum of individual utilities (see Ng, 1975a, for formal proof). But is WMP an acceptable value premise? As Mueller observes:

> WMP is obviously a combination of both the Pareto principle and the majority rule principle that is at once significantly weaker [and hence more acceptable as a sufficient condition for a social improvement] than both. In contrast to the Pareto criterion it requires a majority to be better off, rather than just one [individual], to justify a move. And, in contrast to majority rule, it allows the majority to be decisive only against an indifferent minority. In spite of this apparent weakness, the postulate nevertheless proves strong enough to support a Benthamite [that is, utilitarian] social welfare function (Mueller, 1989, p. 435).

Anyone who accepts either the Pareto principle or majority rule must logically accept WMP. It may be objected that, with finite sensibility, the Pareto principle should refer to underlying preferences and not to explicit preferences. The WMP criterion is not necessarily weaker than this interpretation of the Pareto principle. Nevertheless WMP is a very compelling premise on its own. Ideally, as a variable in the SWF, the preference of individuals should refer to their actual feeling of wellbeing, not to an *ex ante* revelation of preference or actual choice. Although we may have to use revealed preferences except when divergences are significant and obvious, in principle we are referring to actual feeling. Now, when comparing two social states, *x* and *y*, if no individual feels worse off and a majority feel better off at *x*, there seems to be no ground to deny that social welfare is higher at *x* (here we abstract from possible differences in the welfare of other sentients, such as dogs. Personally, I would put them into the SWF). If a majority prefers *x* to *y*, it may be better to choose *y* provided the minority prefers *y* more strongly to *x*. But for the case satisfying WMP, there is no individual in the minority who feels any worse off, not to mention more strongly worse off.

The main objection to WMP and the resulting utilitarian SWF is that it may lead to a very unequal distribution of income. Apart from incentive effects, it is doubtful that differences in sensibility will lead to a great inequality of income if we apply the utilitarian SWF. Psychological studies of pain show that different individuals have very similar pain thresholds (averaging 230 with a standard deviation of ±10), and this also applies to the number of just noticeable differences (Hardy *et al.*, 1952, pp. 88, 157). If there are more differences in the capacity to enjoy income, these are probably due to 'learning by doing' and a long-term SWF will take account of that. If we ask ourselves why we want to give more weight to the poor, we may come up with a number of answers. The most obvious one is that the incomes of the poor have to meet more urgent needs. But this is taken care of by reckoning in terms of utilities instead of incomes. Second, it could be said that the consumption of the rich is self-defeating – because of the snob effect, the desire to keep up with the Joneses and so on – while the consumption of the poor (if spent on, say, education and health) may have very beneficial long-term effects. This again can be taken care of by allowing for all forms of externality and so on. If some inequality still persists after taking all effects into account, this should already be an optimal distribution if it maximises aggregate welfare. Consider the much-cherished principle 'From each according to his ability; to each according to his needs' (which is to be approved of, assuming there is no disincentive effect). Why should this not be 'An equal amount of work from each; an equal amount of income to each'? If a weak person is tired by four hours of work, it is better for a stronger person to work longer to relieve him. Similarly, if a less sensitive person does not enjoy the extra income much, it is better for a more sensitive person to receive more of it. What prevents us from seeing such a simple analogy?

For choices involving risk there is a problem as to whether we should maximise welfare as a function of expected utilities, that is, $WE = W(E^1, \ldots, E^I) \equiv W(\Sigma_s \theta_s U_s^1, \ldots, \Sigma_s \theta_s U_s^I)$, or expected welfare as a function of ex post utilities. $EW = \Sigma_s \theta_s W(U_s^1, \ldots, U_s^I)$, where θ_s is the probability of state s and the summation over s is for all possible states. There seem to be good grounds for adopting either method. If welfare is a sum (unweighted or weighted with constant individual weights, k^i) of utilities, then the two methods are equivalent. Thus $EW = \Sigma_s \theta_s \Sigma_i k^i U_s^i = \Sigma_i k^i \Sigma_s \theta_s U_s^i = WE$. Hence the utilitarian SWF we obtained frees us from the agonising choice of maximising WE or EW, and we may use either one as convenience dictates. Looking at the matter from the opposite sequence, the fact that EW and WE are both appropriate objective functions lends support to WMP and the utilitarian SWF. If welfare is not a sum of individual utilities, then in general the maximisation of EW or WE will not yield the same result.[8] Therefore if either one is a reasonable objective function, the other cannot be so unless social welfare is the sum of individual utilities.

---

8. If WE and EW always yield the same result, we have $WE = W(\Sigma_s \theta_s U_s^1, \ldots, \Sigma_s \theta_s U_s^I) = EW = \Sigma_s \theta_s W(U_s^1, \ldots, U_s^I)$. Differentiation with respect to U_s^i gives $\partial W/\partial E^i = \partial W/\partial U_s^i$ in any given situation. Such an equality cannot hold for every set of θ_s unless W is the sum (unweighted or weighted with constant individual weights) of its arguments.

The acceptance of WMP (and the resulting utilitarian SWF) has far-reaching implications (Ng, 1975a, sec. 8). Here we shall just discuss the implication with respect to social choice. If we adopt the rule of basing our social ordering on the summation of individual utilities, it can be seen that the rule will satisfy all Arrow's axioms and conditions (except the ordering aspect of the IIA) as well as some other reasonable conditions, such as anonymity, neutrality and path independency (on which see Plott, 1973; Ferejohn and Grether, 1977a). Anonymity is satisfied since every individual is treated similarly in the summation of utilities. With the fulfilment of anonymity, non-dictatorship is satisfied *a fortiori*. It is also obvious that the Pareto principle (either the weak or the strong version) is satisfied since xP^iy implies $U^i(x) > U^i(y)$. The utilitarian decision rule can also be shown to be responsive to individual preferences in a stricter sense (Arrow, 1984). However, since the ordering aspect of the IIA is not satisfied, our rule does not constitute a counter example to Arrow's theorem. Nevertheless, having taken account of the intensity of preferences, this ordering aspect becomes irrelevant. Thus our analysis shows that the paradox of social choice can be resolved, on at least in principle, on a rational basis that satisfies reasonable conditions. But the practical problems of doing so remain very real because of the difficulties of utility measurement. In this sense Arrow's theorem is still very significant. However these practical difficulties can be reduced by using the utility unit of just perceivable enjoyment and indirect measurement, as suggested in Ng (1975a) and actually used to derive cardinal and interpersonally comparable utility indices in Ng (1996a). Another way of measuring preferences is the second approach we are going to discuss: the incentive-compatible mechanism for preference revelation, or the demand revealing process.

5.4.2   An incentive-compatible mechanism for preference revelation

The incentive-compatible mechanism for preference revelation was independently proposed by Clarke (1971) and Groves (1970, 1973). (Both presented conference papers in 1970. Vickrey discussed a similar mechanism in 1961 but was not aware of its full significance.) Tideman and Tullock (1976) applied the mechanism to the problem of social choice. Here we shall discuss the simple case of two alternatives – the treatment of the continuous case can be found in Section 8.3 in relation to public goods.

The essence of the preference-revelation mechanism is to ask each individual to state the (maximum) amount of money she would be willing to pay to have her preferred alternative; but instead of actually paying this stated amount she has to pay – if her 'vote' changes society's decision – an amount (that is, the Clarke–Groves tax) that is equal to the cost (of so changing the social choice) to the rest of society. The social choice is simply decided by calculating (summing over all individuals) the total amount of money voted for each alternative and the one with the highest figure is chosen (we shall presently consider a generalisation to avoid the predominant influence of the rich). Consider the simple case of four voters illustrated in Table 5.1. If all voters vote sincerely, alternative x will be chosen since $20 > 19$. Voter 1's stated figure of £8 is effective in shifting social choice from y to x. Voter 1 thus has to pay £7 (= £10 + £9 − £12), the cost of so shifting social choice to the rest of the society. Similarly voter 2 has to pay £11 (= £10 + £9 − £8). Voters 3 and 4 do not have to pay since their votes do not affect the outcome.

Will the above mechanism provide the correct incentive to voters to reveal their true preferences? Take voter 3, who prefers y to x. If £9 reflects his true preference, exaggerating by less than £1 will not change the outcome. To change the social choice into y, he or she has to state a figure of more than £10 (exaggerating by more than £1). But if y is chosen due to exaggeration, voter 3 has to pay £10 (= £8 + £12 − £10) which is more than he or she really wishes to pay to have y. Acting independently, every individual will find it to her advantage to report truthfully (we ignore here the problem of the disposal of the Clarke–Groves taxes, which are discussed in Section 8.3). However if voters 3 and 4 come together they may agree to state the figures of, say, £30 and £40 respectively. If voters 1 and 2 do not engage in such collusion, voters 3 and 4 will have shifted the social choice in their favour at no cost to themselves, as each of them has to pay nothing (since £12 + £8 < £30). It is true that the problem of collusion and strategic misrepresentation is present in other voting schemes as well, but the Clarke–Groves mechanism is especially vulnerable in this respect.[9] In fact if

Table 5.1 Differential values of alternatives

Voter	x	y
1	8	0
2	12	0
3	0	9
4	0	10
Total	20	19

9. In fact all non-dictatorial voting (using only rankings or orderings) on more than two alternatives are manipulatable by misrepresentation (Gibbard, 1973; Satterthwaite, 1975). Most reasonable decision-making processes using only orderings are manipulatable by even a *single* individual. The Clarke–Groves mechanism overcomes this to a large extent. On strategic voting see also Dummett and Farquharson (1961), Farquharson (1969), Barbera (1977), Pattanaik (1978), Sengupta (1978), Barbera *et al.* (1999) and a special symposium issue of the *Review of Economic Studies* (April 1979) on incentive-compatible mechanisms and strategic voting. Blin and Satterthwaite (1978) show the logical similarity of Arrow's theorem and the impossibility of strategy-proof group decisions. For a collection of papers on these and related issues see Laffont (1979).

no other voters engage in collusion, any two voters who prefer the same alternative can always ensure its choice at no cost to them if each states an arbitrarily large figure (the 'optimal mechanism' of Groves and Ledyard, 1977a, is less vulnerable but is not coalition-proof). Thus for the mechanism to work it is essential to ensure non-collusion, a very difficult task in practice (see however Tideman and Tullock, 1981, and Section 8.3 below).

Even forgetting about the difficulty created by collusion, the preference revelation mechanism is still unlikely to be acceptable as a method of social choice as most people would regard it as giving an unduly high degree of influence to the rich. This difficulty is partly solved by generalising the mechanism proposed by Good (1977). Instead of calculating the unweighted sum of (pound) figures by all individuals for each alternative, we calculate the sum using any weight for each individual as desired.[10] For example if we want to discount the figure voted by the rich, their £10 may count only as £5. The reverse weight is used to calculate their tax. If they each had to pay £2 for the unweighted case, they now have to pay £4. This method allows us to use differential weighting without damaging the incentive for preference revelation. Good (1977, p. 66) suggests that a possible weighting system could be inverse proportionality to wealth (financial + human). Since human wealth is very difficult to estimate, it is more practical for income to be used as a proxy. With this inverse proportionality weighting system the rich will have the same degree of influence as the poor. Whether this is desirable depends on the nature of the issue of social choice involved.

For political issues such as the election of a president or a parliament, it is consistent with democratic tradition to let all voters, rich or poor, have the same voting power. For economic issues a distinction between two types of issue is necessary. Problems such as the provision of public (final) goods involve the consumption or enjoyment of the fruit of production. For this class of issue, adoption of the inverse proportionality weighting system would suggest that distribution of the fruit of production should be absolutely egalitarian. However in practice we need some degree of inequality to maintain incentives. Given this, it would be inefficient to adopt a weighting system (a fuller development of this argument can be found in the next section and Appendix 9.1). On the other hand problems such as regulation of the process of production and distribution (patents, tariff, and so on) fall into a different class. The fact that society agrees to let more hard-working people have a larger share of the fruit of production does not mean that they should also have a larger say in future production and distribution. Otherwise those who become rich by luck, illegal means and/or initial hard

---

10. Or, more generally, the original figure for each individual, i, can be transformed into another figure using a continuous, strictly increasing, bounded function, f^i, such that $f^i(0) = 0$.

work may be able to maintain their riches without further effort (see Ng, 2000a, ch. 7 on the rationale for separating politics with a 'one person one vote' rule from economics, where a dollar should be treated as a dollar). As well as the problem of collusion, the Clarke–Groves mechanism is by no means ideal in other ways. For one thing, if the income effects are not negligible, social choice generated by the scheme may be cyclic. This is because the amount of money individuals are prepared to pay to have x instead of z need not be equal to the amount they are willing to pay to have x instead of y plus the amount they are willing to pay to have y instead of z, even given xP^iyP^iz. For example, suppose I am willing to pay £10 000 to prevent the little finger on my left hand from being cut off. If I did lose it I would be willing to pay £11 000 to prevent the loss of the little finger on the right. However I am willing to pay only £19 000 (<£10 000 + £11 000) to prevent the loss of both fingers. This is because the first £10 000 was not actually paid. If I actually had to pay it, I would be only willing to pay £9000 to prevent the loss of the second finger. Thus the cyclicity involved is similar to the contradiction in the Kaldor–Hicks compensation test. In fact the Groves–Clarke mechanism is the application of a compensation test plus an ingenious design to motivate preference revelation (cf. Groves, 1979).

In closing this section it should be reiterated that the practical difficulties of using the cardinal utility approach are very real. However, since this approach seems to provide the most sensible way out of the paradox of social choice and since all practical solutions are not ideal in every respect, further work to reduce the shortcomings of the approach is desirable.

5.5 A dollar is a dollar: a 90 per cent solution to the paradox of interpersonal cardinal utility**

As discussed above, the impossibility theorems by Arrow (1951/1963), Kemp and Ng (1976), Parks (1976) and Sen (1969b, 1970a) prove, and commonsense arguments demonstrate (Ng, 2000a, ch. 2), that interpersonal comparisons of cardinal utility are necessary when making social choices that cannot reasonably be based on individual ordinal preferences alone.

On the other hand there is a long tradition in economics of regarding interpersonal cardinal utilities as impossible or meaningless and scientifically inadmissible (see for example Kolm, 1993). As Wicksteed (1933) and Robbins (1938) put it, each mind is totally inscrutable to any other mind, making interpersonal comparisons of utility mere value judgments without any scientific status. I argue that interpersonal comparisons of utility are not value judgments but subjective judgments of fact, and that economists are capable of making judgments of fact that are closely related to their field of study (Ng, 1972b and Appendix 1.1 above). I also argue (Ng, 1992b) that such views (apparently held by the majority of economists) on the conceptual impossibility of interpersonal comparisons of utility are based on the existence of souls (while the majority of economists, I believe, are philosophical materialists who do not believe in the existence of souls). In my view individual utilities are not only cardinal and interpersonally comparable, but there are also practicable (though imperfect) ways to measure and compare utilities (Ng, 1975a, 1979/1983, 1982, 1996a). However I freely admit that the practical difficulties associated with cardinal utility measurement and comparisons are greater than those for ordinal preferences (which are significant, but ignored by most economists).

If we regard interpersonal cardinal utilities as impossible either in principle or in practice, a paradox is created as they are needed to make social choices. In this section a method is proposed that, to a very large extent, resolves the paradox of interpersonal cardinal utility.

The proposed method of solving the paradox is simply to use individual willingness to pay to obtain information on intensity of preferences, to use the unweighted aggregate willingness to pay when making a social choice, plus the appropriate redistribution of total purchasing power to address the issue of equality. This frees us from having to obtain information on cardinal utilities and to compare them interpersonally, except in the case of decisions on the appropriate redistribution of total purchasing power and the case when willingness to pay cannot be relied upon to reflect individual preferences or welfare due to such factors as ignorance and irrational preference (It is in this sense that our proposal is not a 100 per cent solution to the paradox of interpersonal cardinal utility). Before justifying this solution, a number of clarifications are needed. (Some of these touch on technical concepts, so general readers may choose to skip the rest of this section for the time being. However expert readers will find these clarifications important.)

First, some ambiguities and controversies are associated with the measure of willingness to pay and with the question of whether willingness to pay (CV or compensating variation in income) for something or willingness to accept (EV or equivalent variation), in lieu of something, should be the appropriate measure. This is related to problems with the measurement of consumer surplus, as discussed and resolved in Chapter 4).

Second, when external effects are important, considering only the willingness to pay of individuals who are directly involved may not be sufficient, and externally affected individuals' willingness to pay may also have to be included. Similarly, when factors such as second-best interconnections (Chapter 9) are relevant, they have to be taken into account. These efficiency issues do not change the principle of willingness to pay, they just require the principle to be applied more broadly.

Third, when ignorance on the part of the individuals concerned is involved, the issue becomes more controversial. In my view ignorance that has minor effects should simply be ignored, partly to save administrative costs and partly because violation of free individual choice has indirect costs (for being inimical to freedom). However when ignorance results in large losses, individual willingness to pay may have to be overruled or revised, as in such cases as the prohibition of certain addictive drugs, the fluoridation of water and subsidised milk for school children (see Chapter 11 on excessive consumerism and Appendix 12.3 on the grounds for merit and demerit goods).

Finally, even accepting the use of willingness to pay as a measure of intensity of individual preferences, the acceptability of using *aggregate* (that is, for a number of individuals) willingness to pay is still controversial, *even if* the issue of equality or distribution is ignored. This is because, as shown by Boadway (1974) and Blackorby and Donaldson (1990), a positive aggregate willingness to pay (CV) might not ensure that the gainers will compensate the losers even given the feasibility of lump-sum transfers. This difficulty is discussed in Section 4.5 above. While aggregate willingness to pay does not correspond perfectly with a potential Pareto improvement, it corresponds closely for most cases.

The justification for using unweighted (maximum) willingness to pay as a measure of the preference intensity of any individual (called 'a dollar is a dollar' principle for brevity) is based on the following two arguments. First, abstracting away the difficulties mentioned in the previous section, the amount individuals are willing to pay to obtain a certain item reflects the intensity of their preference. The more intense the preference for a certain performance, the higher the maximum willingness to pay for it. This is less controversial.

Second, the reason why we can use *unweighted* willingness to pay is that It Is more efficient to do so, and whatever redistribution is desired can be achieved through the general tax/transfer system.[11] This point needs more elaboration.

The main reason why people are against the dollar is a dollar principle is that a dollar to the poor or needy is used to meet more urgent needs than a dollar to the rich. Whilst I agree with this and am in favour of helping the poor (provided the costs of doing so are not excessive), unless factors such as ignorance and external effects are involved (making it efficient to subsidise education and health care, for example), it is more efficient to help the poor through the general tax/transfer system instead of overriding the dollar is a dollar principle in specific items, such as using distributional weights in cost–benefit analysis, and adhering to first-come-first-served when allocating car parking spaces. A counterargument to this is that the tax/transfer system involves excess costs in the form of disincentive effects (the problem of administrative, compliance and policing costs is discussed under 'transaction costs' in Section 6.4 below). It is thus believed that it is better to achieve part of the redistribution through the progressive tax/ transfer system, and part through specific equality-oriented measures such as subsidising goods that are consumed predominantly by the poor and using distributional weights in cost–benefit analysis. However this counter-argument (held by most economists, including myself before I analysed the problem carefully) ignores the fact that the use of such specific, purely equality-oriented policies has the same disincentive effects as the tax/transfer system, and also has the additional efficiency cost of distorting choice.

It is tempting for an economist to think that, since the substantial redistributive tax/transfer system has significant (larger than marginal) disincentive effects at the margin, it is better to shift some of the redistributive burden to specific items, for example by taxing (subsidising) items that are consumed predominantly by the rich (poor). Although some *marginal* efficiency costs from distorting choice are incurred, they are believed to be smaller than the reduction in the disincentive effects from relying less on the progressive tax/transfer system. This belief is incorrect because, assuming rational individuals, the disincentive effects are in accordance with the total system of tax/transfer, taxes/subsidies, plus all other redistributive and preferential measures; one does not face a separate and independent schedule with increasing marginal disincentive effects for each of the separate measures. Rational individuals, in their work/leisure choices, do not just ask how much post-tax income they will earn, but also have a rough idea of the utility they can obtain from consuming goods and services purchased with their income. They are trading off the utility of leisure with the utility from work, which consists of the utility from consuming the higher income and the positive or negative utility of work itself. Moreover the utility of consuming the higher income is affected by whatever specific redistributive or preferential measures are in place. Thus discriminatory treatment against the rich in government expenditure and other areas will *add on* to the progressive tax/transfer system to determine the total disincentive effects. Hence even if only a marginal amount of specific equality-oriented measures are used, the disincentive effects involved are not just marginal. For any degree of equality in real income (utility) that is achieved, the same degree of disincentive effects is incurred, irrespective of whether we use only the tax/transfer system or a combination of it and a specific purely equality-oriented system. But the latter alternative has the additional efficiency cost of distorting choice, and is therefore inferior.

The following proposition has been proved by Ng (1979, 1984a) and is discussed further in Appendix 9.1.

- A dollar is a dollar: for any alternative (designated *A*) using a system (designated *a*) of purely equality-oriented preferential treatment for the

poor there exists another alternative, *B*, which does not involve preferential treatment, makes no one worse off, achieves the same degree of
equality (of real income, or utility) and raises more government revenue,
which can be used to make everyone better off.

Under alternative *B* a more (than alternative *A*) progressive tax/transfer
system (designated *b*) may have to be used. By definition, progressivity in
the tax/transfer system is not classified as 'preferential treatment'. As argued
in Appendix 9.1, complications such as administrative costs, political constraints, ignorance of benefits distribution and so on either strengthen the
proposition or do not significantly affect its main thrust.

In fact the above proposition can be generalised to any efficiency-
inconsistent alternative (A), and is not just applicable to equality-oriented
preferential treatment. The proof of the proposition is unaltered even if the
preferential treatment is inequality-oriented rather than equality-oriented.
That is, instead of counting a dollar to the poor as worth *less* than a dollar
to the rich in cost–benefit analysis, it is better to tax the rich less and tax
the poor more (or subsidise them less). Similarly an alternative based on
random treatment, tradition and so on can be shown to be inferior to
some alternative *B* that is designed to compensate for the gains and losses
from dismantling efficiency-inconsistent methods. Then, ignoring practical
difficulties, individual ignorance, irrationality and procedural preferences
(on the last item see Ng, 1988), alternative *B* must be Pareto superior.
(On the inconsistency between welfare maximization or the Pareto principle
and fairness, see Kaplow and Shavell, 2002.)

5.6 The possibility of a Paretian liberal

Since readers who are encountering the topic of social choice for the first
time may have found this chapter a little hard going, I shall try to placate
them by closing it with a light discussion of the 'impossibility of a Paretian
liberal', as proposed by Sen (1970c).

The (weak) Pareto principle states that if everyone prefers *x* to *y*, society
should prefer *x* to *y*. However liberalism insists that there are certain matters
on which individuals should have a decisive say, irrespective of the preferences of others. 'Whether you should sleep on your back or on your belly
is a matter in which the society should permit you absolute freedom, even
if a majority of the community is nosey enough to feel that you must sleep
on your back' (ibid., p. 152). Both principles seem extremely reasonable, but
according to Sen is impossible to adhere to them simultaneously. He illustrates this with the following interesting example.

There is one copy of a certain book, say *Lady Chatterley's Lover* (or indeed
Portnoy's Complaint), which is viewed differently by two individuals, *J* and *K*.
The three alternatives under consideration are: (1) *J* reads it (*j*), (2) *K* reads

it (*k*) or (3) no one reads it (*n*). Madam *J*, who is a prude, would prefer no one to read it, but if either she or *K* must read it she would prefer to read it herself than to expose the gullible Mr *K* to such a bad influence (prudes, as Sen was told, tend to prefer to be censors rather than being censored). Meanwhile *K* feels that one of them should read the wonderful book rather than neither. As he takes delight in the thought of prudish *J* having to read the book, his first preference is that *J* should read it. The set of individual orderings is therefore

$$nP_j^J P_k^J; jP^K kp^K n$$

For the choice between *j* and *n* (that is, between *J* reading the book or no one reading it), liberalism dictates that *J*'s preference should be decisive as no one should be forced to read a book they do not like. Therefore society should prefer *n* to *j*. Similarly, for the choice between *k* and *n*, *K*'s preference should be decisive, so society should prefer *k* to *n*. According to the Pareto principle, society should prefer *j* to *k* since all individuals prefer *j* to *k*. So social preference becomes cyclic, as *jPkPnPj*. Hence liberalism seems to be inconsistent with (even the weak) Pareto principle.

I still profess to be a Paretian liberal, as most readers probably would, despite Sen's impossibility result (in fact I have generalised it to be the impossibility of a Paretian *X*, where *X* is any principle of social choice not based on interpersonal comparisons of cardinal utilities; see Ng, 1982), Cf. Kaplow and Shavell, 2002 on the inconsistency between welfare and fairness. Partly because of space limitation and partly as an exercise, I shall leave it to readers to think of a way out of Sen's paradox. The interested reader is referred to the discussions by Ng (1971b), Gibbard (1974), Farrell (1976), Sen (1976, 1992), Aldrich (1977), Rowley (1978), Riley (1988), Seidl (1990), Gaertner *et al.* (1992), Craven (1996), Deb *et al.* (1997), Campbell and Kelly (1997). Readers who are interested in the topic of social choice are referred to the surveys by Mueller (1976, 1989), Sen (1977a), Kelly (1977) and Roberts (1980a, 1980b, 1980c). For questions of interpersonal comparison, cardinality and inter- versus intraprofile approaches, see Blackorby *et al.* (1984) and Ng (2000a).

5.7 Summary

Arrow's impossibility theorem shows that any rule used to derive a social ordering from individual orderings is undesirable in some respect. Majority rule does not provide a consistent social ordering since it may be cyclic. Little and Samuelson's attempt to dismiss Arrow's theorem as irrelevant to welfare economics is countered by Kemp and Ng (1976) and Parks (1976), who have established impossibility results even operating with a given set of individual orderings. Other attempts to bypass Arrow's paradox by restricting individual preferences, relaxing social rationality and so on have been shown to be restrictive and/or undesirable in some respects. A more promising pursuit is to attempt to reveal the intensity of individual preferences, and hence to operate beyond just individual orderings. Using the concept of finite sensibility, a measure of marginal indifference can be used as an interpersonally comparable unit of utility. The weak majority preference criterion states that x should be preferred to y if no one prefers y to x and at least half the population prefer x to y. With this criterion it has been shown that the rule of social choice must be the utilitarian SWF of the unweighted sum of individual utilities. The relevance of the 'incentive-compatible mechanism' for social choice has also been discussed. Even without using cardinal utility and its interpersonal comparison, most problems of social choice can be solved by using the dollar is a dollar principle for specific issues, leaving only the balance between efficiency and equality in the general tax/transfer system to be decided by an interpersonal comparison of cardinal utility.

Appendix 5.1: The Incompatibility of Individualism and Ordinalism**

In the proof of their impossibility proposition that there does not exist a reasonable SWF or a social ordering based only on individual ordinal preferences, Kemp and Ng (1976) use a condition (Orderings Only – the second requirement of condition 3 in Section 5.2) that can be seen as objectionable (Samuelson, 1977). However it does reflect the requirement that social ordering should only be based on individual *orderings*. The fact that, in combination with other reasonable conditions, Orderings Only gives an impossibility result means that if there is to be a reasonable social ordering it cannot be based only on individual orderings. Either cardinal preference information or something other than individual preference will be needed. In other words, either Ordinalism or Individualism has to give way. Let us first discuss this informally before proving a formal proposition and commenting on a related paper by Mayston (1980). First we shall formally state the condition of Orderings Only:

- **Orderings Only**: *the social ordering of any two social alternatives depends only on the I individual orderings of the alternatives. Formally, for any (not necessarily distinct) x, y, z, w, if ($x\bar{R}^{i}y \leftrightarrow z\bar{R}^{i}w$ for all i) then ($x\bar{R}y \leftrightarrow z\bar{R}w$), where $\bar{R}^{i}$ stands for one (not necessarily the same for all i) of P^{i}, I^{i} and contra P^{i}, and R stands for one of P, I and contra P* (see Kemp and Ng, 1976, where there are minor notational differences; note also the unconventional notation $\bar{R}$, which may stand for *contra* preference).

To understand the implication of this condition, consider Samuelson's (1977) example of a society with 100 units of chocolates to be distributed to two self-centred individuals who prefer more chocolates to less. The Orderings Only condition implies that if it is socially preferable to take, say, one or 50 chocolates from *J*, who has all the chocolates, in order to give them to *K*, who has none, then it must be socially desirable to give all the chocolates to *K*. This is clearly a very unreasonable implication. I place myself with Samuelson to be ranked among the last group of persons on earth to accept it – indeed I shall never accept it. The only acceptable alternative is to reject either Individualism or Ordinalism.

Most people would find it reasonable to take some chocolates from *J* (who has all 100 units) and give them to *K* because otherwise *K* will starve. The chocolates given to *K* will meet a more urgent need than if they are consumed by *J*. But this is speaking in terms of cardinal utility. In purely ordinal utility terms, we cannot distinguish whether individuals prefer 50 units to no units more strongly than they prefer 100 units to 50 units. However for those (myself included) who find it sensible to speak in terms of intensity of preference, it is quite sensible to use the cardinal utility approach. It is the pure ordinalists who cannot accept this.

Is there an alternative way out of the Kemp–Ng impossibility? Yes, by rejecting Individualism. Social preference then need not be based only on individual preferences (cardinal or ordinal). In particular social preference may depend on the objective specification of social states, such as the amount of commodities consumed by individuals. For example the social state (50, 50) – that is 50 units of chocolates for each individual – can be selected as the best alternative based on the objective amount of chocolates consumed and not on the cardinal utility approach of urgent versus not urgent need mentioned in the previous paragraph. But it is clearly unreasonable to base social choice on the objective specification of social states irrespective of individual preferences. What if the 100 units of chocolates are very essential to *J*, who needs them to cure a curious disease, while *K* only slightly prefers more chocolates to fewer and throws them into the river for fun instead of using the slightly inferior substitute of stones, which are in abundant supply? Should not (100, 0) be socially preferable to (50, 50)? What if *K* is not self-centred and both individuals prefer (100, 0) to (50, 50)?

Clearly, social preference based on the objective specification of social states could violate the Pareto principle. To avoid this violation, the so-called social preference over the objective specification of social states has to be carefully designed to be consistent with individual preferences, especially in a multicommodity society with diverse individual preferences. To be consistent with the Pareto principle, social choice has to be confined to the Pareto optimal frontier determined by individual preferences. If the social ranking of a pair of alternatives on this frontier is based only on individual orderings, we have the orderings only condition (more on this below). If it is based on intensity of preferences as well, we have to reject Ordinalism. It cannot be said to be based on the objective specification of social states since what social states are in this Pareto-optimal frontier depends on individual preferences. If we want to stick to Individualism, the only relevant differences between different social states are individual ordinal and cardinal preferences. Hence objective specification cannot be used or can only be used as an indirect indicator of cardinal preferences if we want to stick to Individualism.

Let us now establish the incompatibility of Individualism and Ordinalism more formally. Let the set of individuals be denoted by $N = \{1,\ldots,i,\ldots,I\}$ and the set of social alternatives be denoted by S. Let μ be the set of all numerically bounded functions that may be defined on $S \times N$. Any *set* of individual preferences (cardinal or ordinal) is then represented by some u in μ. In other words, $u(x, i)$ is the utility of individual i in state x. The problem of social choice is to rank each pair of alternatives such that the overall ranking of R over S is logically consistent.

- **Weak Individualism:** *social choice is a function of and only of individual preferences, $R = f(u)$. Non-preference variables do not affect the form of f.*
- **Independence:** *given non-preference variables, the social ranking between any pair of alternatives (x, y) is a function of and only of individual utilities at these two alternatives. $R(x, y) = g\{u(x), u(y)\}$, where $u(x)$ is the vector $u(x, i)$, $i = 1,\ldots,I$. The form of g may be affected by non-preference variables.*

Independence captures the irrelevance aspect of Arrow's independence of irrelevant alternatives, but does not demand its ordering aspect (Sen, 1970a, p. 89ff.). It is therefore extremely reasonable (Plott, 1972). Since social alternatives are mutually *exclusive* and each alternative is a complete specification of all the relevant aspects of a social state, one naturally does not want the choice between x and y to be affected by preferences with respect to z.

Combining weak individualism and weak independence, we have:

- **Individualism:** $\forall x, y \in S, R(x, y) = g\{u(x), u(y)\}$ *with the form of g fixed.*

The relative social desirability of any pair of alternatives depends only on the desirability (utility) of these alternatives to the individuals. This is extremely reasonable if one recalls the mutually exclusive nature of social alternatives.

- **Ordinalism:** *if $u^1, u^2 \in \mu$ are such that $u^2(x, i) = \phi^i\{u^1(x, i)\}$ for all x and all i, where ϕ^i is a positive monotonic transformation for each i, then u^1 and u^2 are two equivalent pieces of information (written $u^1 \approx u^2$) and are to be treated similarly.*

- **Proposition:** *Individualism and Ordinalism imply* the Ordering Only condition.

- **Proof**: If the precondition of Orderings Only is satisfied, $x\overline{R}^i y \leftrightarrow z\overline{R}^i w$ for all i. If the social ranking is $x\overline{R}y$, we have to show that $z\overline{R}w$. Take a $u^1 \in \mu$ that represents the given set of individual preferences (remembering that each μ is defined over $S \times N$). Then from individualism, $g\{u^1(x), u^1(y)\}$ dictates $x\overline{R}y$. Since $x\overline{R}^i y \leftrightarrow z\overline{R}^i w$ for all I, we may select a $u^2 \in \mu$ such that $u^2 \approx u^1$ and $u^2(z) = u^1(x)$, $u^2(w) = u^1(y)$. From Ordinalism, u^1 and u^2 are to be treated in the same way. Then from individualism $g\{u^2(z), u^2(w)\}$ will dictate $z\overline{R}w$. QED.

The above proposition shows that Individualism and Ordinalism imply orderings only, which presumably no one accepts. If we want to reject the latter, which we should, we must either reject Individualism (which would be unreasonable) or reject Ordinalism (the only reasonable way out).

Some professed individualistic ordinalists may attempt to get away with the above proposition by saying that there is an element of independence in the above definition of Individualism. By accepting just Weak Individualism and Ordinalism without accepting independence, Orderings Only need not be implied. However those who understand the true meaning of independence will certainly accept it provided they also understand that social states are mutually exclusive and each state is a complete specification of all relevant factors. Most people reject independence because of a misunderstanding. For example it is often said that whether one (and society) preferred Gore or Bush to be elected president depended on whether a potential third candidate (L) was alive or dead. For example one might have believed that Gore would be a better president if L was around to do some mischief, and Bush would be better if L was not around (although one might have changed one's mind after Bush's refusal to sign the Kyoto Protocol and to reject the idea of an international criminal court, but that is another story). Then one's choice between two alternatives might have depended on a third. This, however, would have been based on an incomplete specification of social states. If L being around was a relevant consideration, then a complete specification would not just have involved Gore versus Bush, but also Gore with L around, Gore without L, Bush with L and so on. This might have posed some practical difficulties in the actual election of candidates, but it does not pose a problem at the level of generality on which we are operating.

Since social states are mutually exclusive it is perfectly reasonable that, if social preference is to depend only on individual preferences, the social ranking of any two alternatives must be a function only of the individual rankings and/or intensity of preferences between these two alternatives. In other words Individualism as we define it might be said to incorporate an element of independence, but it is true individualism and is quite reasonable.

Due to the lack of perfect information on the intensity of individual preferences, we might wish to use the number of intermediate alternatives (or rather steps of preference) to give us a rough guide to the intensity of preference (Goodman and Markowitz, 1952; Mayston, 1975), but the use of intermediate alternatives is reasonable only if it gives us some indication of intensity of preference. Then independence is not really violated. Rather the availability of the intermediate alternatives just gives us more information on the intensity of individual preferences for the relevant alternatives. The social ranking of any two alternatives is still a function of the individual preferences of these two alternatives. In fact, with finite sensibility and enough information on the intermediate alternatives, we could go all the way and construct fully cardinal utility functions, and base our social choice on these cardinal utilities (Section 5.4.1). On the other hand, if the intermediate alternatives do not provide or are not regarded as providing an indication of the intensity of preferences, then it is unreasonable to use the number of intermediate alternatives or any other aspect of other alternatives to determine the social ranking of any given two alternatives. For example, suppose that xP^JyP^Jz and yP^KzP^Kx. Is it reasonable to say that y should be socially preferred to x since J prefers x to y in one step but K prefers y to x in two steps? If we introduce more alternatives we may find that the one step becomes 10 steps and the two steps remain at two steps, even if the individual ordinal and cardinal preferences with respect to all the alternatives remain unchanged. Thus unless intermediate alternatives can give us some indication of preference intensity, they should not alter social ranking. This can be seen even more clearly in the following case.

Consider the divisible case with an uncountable infinity of alternatives and infinite sensibility. Let us also confine our attention to the intermediate range (in which no individual is in bliss or in hell), which is usually the only relevant range in practice. (If one believes in the general possibility of individualistic ordinalism, then presumably one has to tackle this case.) Then for any individual, and for any relevant social alternative, x, there is an uncountable number of alternatives preferred to, indifferent to and inferior to x. And for any two relevant alternatives, x, y, such that not $x\,I^iy$, there is an uncountable number of alternatives between x and y. Thus if we eschew information on the objective amount of commodities and so on, and consider only individual orderings, we can see that, for any two pairs of alternatives x and y, z and w, if xP^Jy, zP^Jw, yP^Kx, wP^Kz (no other individual or all others are indifferent) the standing of x against y with respect to individual orderings is exactly the same as that of z against w, even if account is taken of the number of alternatives or steps of preference between, above and/or below. Then if we choose xRy, how can we not choose zRw if social choice is to be based only on individual orderings? Hence, unreasonable as it is, the Ordering Only condition has to be accepted if social choice is to be based only on individual orderings.

Consider Figure A5.1a, where the arrows indicate the direction of individual preferences. Suppose that social choice is xIy. Mayston (1980) argues

(a)   (b)

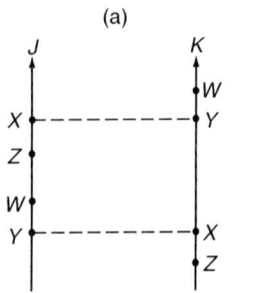
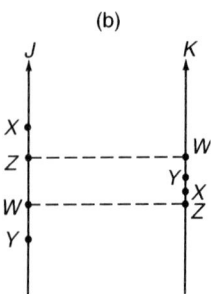

Figure A5.1

that, contrary to the Orderings Only condition, which requires zIw, we should have wPz due to 'secondary Pareto dominance'. This is very reasonable (given xIy), since the difference between z and w is less than the difference between x and y for J but the reverse is true for K. If society regards the preference of x over y by J as just outweighed by the lack of preference for K and declares xIy, then it is reasonable to require wPz, as argued convincingly by Mayston. However Mayston fails to see that, unless we rely on information on intensity of preference (violating ordinalism) and/or non-preference information (violating individualism), we simply cannot declare xIy without also committing ourselves to zIw, and thus violating secondary Pareto dominance. To understand this, consider Figure A5.1b, which is derived from Figure A5.1a by compressing the scale of K. Since absolute scale is arbitrary for ordinal preferences, both figures give us exactly the same ordinal information. Then instead of declaring xIy, why not declare wIz, which implies xPy from secondary Pareto dominance? As far as individual orderings are concerned, the standing of x against y is exactly the same as the standing of z against w. Unless we use something other than individual orderings (intensity of preference for non-individualist procedures such as tossing a coin or relying on objective specification), there is no way of discriminating between the two pairs (in Mayston's terms, the required social weighting function or social marginal rates of equivalence cannot be constructed at all).

From the above discussion it can be concluded that if we do not want to accept the Orderings Only condition and its unreasonable implications, we must reject either Individualism or Ordinalism. A reasonable individualistic ordinalist exists only under illusion. (At the risk of being redundant, it can be added that the above argument against Ordinalism in no way affects the adequacy of Ordinalism for the analysis of a consumer's choice instead of a social choice.)

6
The Optimal Distribution of Income

6.1 Conceptual determination of optimal distribution

What is the optimal distribution of income? As with any constrained optimisation problem, this depends on the form of the objective function and of the constraint. Since we are interested in optimality from the social point of view, the relevant objective function is the SWF. Since a reasonable SWF does not exist without an interpersonal comparison of cardinal utility (Chapter 5), the interpersonal cardinal utility approach is used in this chapter. The relevant constraint can be expressed as a utility possibility frontier if we agree that social welfare is a function of individual utilities (or individual welfares – abstracting away the differences between preference and welfare, the two are equivalent; see Section 1.3). Factors other than individual utilities are either regarded as not relevant to social welfare or are held constant. In Section 2.2.1 we derived a utility possibility frontier by taking the outer envelope of the numerous utility possibility curves, each corresponding to a specific collection of goods. This could be regarded as rather restrictive or purely economic, since by varying only the collection of goods other factors (social and so on) must be held constant. By changing these other factors, a different utility possibility frontier may emerge. Conceptually this generalisation can easily be taken into account by taking the outer envelope of the various utility possibility frontiers and calling it the grand utility possibility frontier. Second, we could also take account of the possible costs of and constraints on redistribution, which would reduce the grand utility possibility frontier to the grand utility feasibility frontier (GUFF) (on the relationship between utility possibility and utility feasibility curves or frontiers, see Figure 3.2).

Given a GUFF, the point of optimal distribution will depend on the form of the SWF. This is illustrated in Figure 6.1 for the simple case of two (or two groups of) individuals. The given GUFF is the curve UU'. It does not extend beyond points U and U' as, for example, a constraint on GUFF is that no individual must be pushed lower than his or her 'misery point'. The frontier has an upward-sloping section at each end (UD and $U'A$), reflecting the

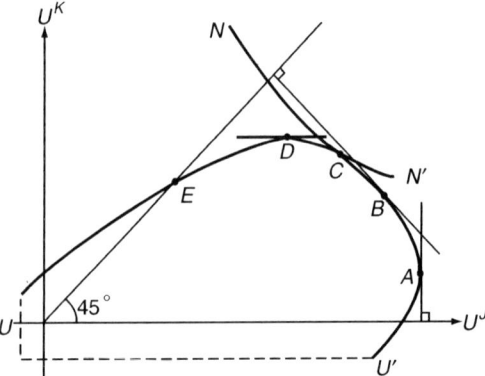

Figure 6.1

fact that as one individual is made much worse off the other suffers as well, perhaps due to sympathy or fear of a revolution. If we accept the Pareto principle, the upward-sloping sections are ruled out and the choice is confined to section *AD*. Point *A* will be chosen by the élitist (maximax) SWF, maximising the utility of the best-off individual (*J*). In contrast point *D* will be chosen by the 'Rawlsian' (maximin) SWF, maximising the utility of the worst-off individual (*K*). Clearly both these points are extreme choices since they imply zero trade-off, or vertical and horizontal welfare contours respectively. For example a policy maker who is acting in accordance with the maximin SWF will be prepared to sacrifice enormous quantities of the utilities of other people (including the second worst off) even if that will only marginally increase the utility of the worst off. The maximax SWF goes to the other extreme. The utilitarian SWF selects a point somewhere between these two extremes, specifically point *B*, where the GUFF touches the highest, negatively sloped 45° line (a utilitarian welfare contour).

While maximin point *D* is an extreme choice within the confine of Paretian SWFs, overly egalitarian people might may go beyond it and choose point *E*. This would involve the blind pursuit of equality *per se* without regard to its contribution to individual well-being, since it would mean opting for equality even at the expense of making all individuals worse off.

A more appealing choice is point *C*, the outcome of maximising the product of individual utilities, with welfare contours (e.g. *NN'*) as rectangular hyperbolas. An operational disadvantage of this Nash solution,[1] in

---

1. Nash (1950). To be fair it must be noted that Nash was dealing with the more positive problem of the outcome of bargaining, using the initial position as the origin. But the principle of maximising the product of utilities has been used by others in a normative context (for example Fair, 1971).

comparison with the utilitarian solution, is that it is based on individual utility functions with known origins, whilst the utilitarian solution is invariant with respect to shifts in these origins. Conceptually the Nash SWF is open to a stronger objection, especially in the general case of I individuals. If one individual has zero utility, it does not matter whether the other 999 999 individuals have extremely high or extremely low utilities, since the product of utilities in both cases is the same. When an individual utility becomes negative the Nash SWF becomes ridiculous. Even if we are confined to non-negative utilities, its acceptability is still doubtful since, according to the Nash SWF, $W(U^1 = 1000, U^2 = 1, U^3 = 1,\ldots,U^{1\,000\,000} = 1)$ $> W(U^1 = 1000, U^2 = 0, U^3 = 1000, U^4 = 1000,\ldots,U^{1\,000\,000} = 1000)$. But it is clearly ethically desirable to provide a decent life for 999 998 fairly miserable individuals even if this involves making an equally miserable Mr 2 a little bit worse off still. Similarly, according to the Nash SWF, $W(U^1 = 2000, U^2 = 1,\ U^3 = 1,\ldots,U^{1\,000\,000} = 1) > W(U^1 = 0,\ U^2 = 1000,\ U^3 = 1000,\ldots,$ $U^{1\,000\,000} = 1000)$. But we will be prepared to sacrifice 2000 utilities of well-off Mr 1 (no matter who he is) if the rest of the million miserable individuals can be made fairly happy. Even if we exclude zero utility, the above results still follow since any sufficiently small utility will do.[2]

The forms of SWF discussed above are of course only a few out of a large number of possible SWFs. The main point of this section is to show that, given a GUFF, the optimal point depends on the specific form of the SWF. Once a point in the utility space is chosen, not only is the optimal distribution of income determined, but the optimal set of non-economic policies are also determined, if they are included as variables affecting the feasible combination of utilities. It is possible, though not very likely, that the same point in the utility space can be achieved by two or more different combinations of income distribution and non-economic policies. If such is the case, society will be indifferent between these combinations

6.2 Utility illusion

Since there are numerous forms of SWF, which one should we select? In Section 5.4.1 it was noted that acceptance of a very reasonable value premise, the weak majority preference criterion, implies that we must subscribe to the utilitarian SWF. When the utilitarian philosophy was first propounded it was regarded as a radical principle to justify such measures as progressive income taxation. Nowadays egalitarianism has won so much support that many people want to go beyond utilitarianism and adopt a strictly quasiconcave SWF with welfare contours strictly convex to the origin of utility space, such as the Nash welfare contour NN' in Figure 6.1.

---

2. Kaneko and Nakamura's (1979) support of Nash's SWF is based on the objectionable Condition II; see Ng (1981a).

However it is possible that this is due more to some kind of illusion than to genuinely rational ethical radicalism. It is true that problems such as choosing the 'right' form of SWF have to be solved by resorting to value judgments that cannot be true or false. Nevertheless certain value judgments can be shown to imply, or to imply the rejection of, certain other value judgments. Moreover one might also be able to convince some people that their adherence to certain value judgments may be based on illusion. The possibility that strictly convex welfare contours may be based on 'utility illusion' (Ng, 1975a) is discussed below.

If we have to draw our welfare contours not in a utility space but in an income space with axes representing the income levels of different individuals (holding other relevant variables constant), most people will agree that the contours should be convex to the origin (similar to a normal indifference curve of an individual between two goods). This is due to the belief that, for any given individual, a marginal pound meets more important needs when income is low than when income is high. Hence the marginal income of an individual is given a diminishing weight as her or his income increases and we have strict convexity in the welfare contours (in an income space). If we use utility not only as an ordinal indicator of choice but also as reflecting the degree of subjective satisfaction, we have, for each individual, a diminishing marginal utility of income. Given interpersonal comparability of utility and equal capacity for enjoyment, the unequal distribution of a given amount of total income (abstracting from incentive effects and so on – more on this in the next section) diminishes total utility by denying more urgent needs and satisfying less urgent ones. This egalitarian ethic may, however, be carelessly carried over to the distribution of utilities. Since an unequal distribution of income usually implies an unequal distribution of utilities, the two are sometimes regarded as equivalent. Thus an unequal distribution of utilities is condemned along with an unequal distribution of income.

Consider a simple example. Given a fixed total income of £100, we may prefer (£50; £50) (that is, £50 to each of the two individuals) to (£70; £30), assuming a similar capacity to enjoy income. Then, when asked to choose in terms of utilities, we may say we prefer (50 utils; 50 utils) to (70 utils; 30 utils), believing that the former is just a more equal distribution of the same total income as the latter. However, given a diminishing marginal utility of income and a similar capacity for enjoyment, the former must involve a smaller total income. If our preference for equality in the distribution of a given total income is based on the diminishing marginal utility of income, it does not follow that a more unequal distribution of a *larger* total income is inferior.

If the objection to the unequal distribution of a given total income is based only on the diminishing marginal utility of income (plus, perhaps, such arguments as externality or utility interdependency, which can be taken account of by reckoning in terms of utilities), then the preference for a more equally distributed but smaller aggregate utility over a larger aggregate utility must involve double counting (or double discounting). A larger but less equally distributed total income is already discounted by reckoning in terms of utilities rather than incomes, with diminishing marginal utility, interpersonal comparability, utility interdependency and so on. If the unequal distribution of utilities is again to be discounted, this second level of discounting cannot be based on the diminishing marginal utility of income or utility interdependency.

6.3 Theories of optimal income distribution and taxation: Lerner and Mirrlees

Classical economists, including Pigou, seem to be quite free of utility illusion; they justify equal distribution of income mainly on the ground of diminishing marginal utility, assuming equal capacity to enjoy income. Abstracting away such questions as incentive effects, that equal distribution maximises total utility and hence the utilitarian SWF is an obvious implication of such assumptions. The assumption of diminishing marginal utility of income, which is implied by the Weber–Fechner law (see Section 6.5), is regarded by most people as reasonable. The assumption of equal capacity to enjoy income is more open to criticism. However Lerner (1944) successfully relaxes this assumption. Even if different individuals have quite different capacities to enjoy income, it can be shown that the equal distribution of a given total amount of income will maximise expected total utility, provided that we have no knowledge about the capacity levels of different individuals. This argument is illustrated in Figure 6.2 for the case of two individuals.[3]

The given total amount of income is O^JO^K. The amount given to J is measured rightward from O^J and that given to K is measured leftward from O^K. It can clearly be seen that, with diminishing marginal utility and equal capacity – that is, when both individuals have the same MU curve, such as $MU^{J'}$ and MU^K – equal distribution at point E maximises total utility. However if J has a lower MU curve, say MU^J, total utility is maximised at point A. Starting from the equality point, point E, if we transfer AE amount of income from J to K, this increases K's utility by $ACDE$ but reduces J's utility only by $ACFE$, with a net gain of CDF. However if we do not know (even on a probabilistic level) who is more capable of enjoyment, we could

---

3. For a critical discussion of Lerner's argument see Friedman (1947). For formal statements of Lerner's argument see Sen (1969a) and McManus *et al.* (1972). For the generalisation of Lerner's argument to any SWF that is quasiconcave in individual utilities, see Sen (1973b). For variable production see Bennett (1981).

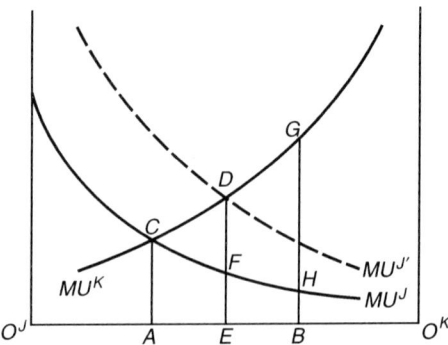

Figure 6.2

equally give *EB* (= *AE*) amount of income from *K* to *J*. This would increase
J's utility by *EFHB* but reduce *K*'s utility by *EDGB*, with a net loss of *FDGH*.
Since *FDGH* > *CDF*, the expected gain of an unequal distribution of income
with no knowledge of the actual distribution of capacity is negative.

The above argument is based on the assumption that the total amount of
income is independent of its distribution. This ignores the costs of achieving
the desired distribution, including the disincentive effect. Since factors
affecting the ability to earn income (inheritance, intelligence, motivation,
luck and so on) are not equally distributed, the pretax distribution of income
is usually far from equal. Consider a principle method of redistribution –
income taxation. The more progressive the income taxation the more equal
the post-tax distribution, although the disincentive effect is likely to be
higher. If people have to pay a larger proportion of their extra income in
taxes, they will tend to work less and undertake less risky but profitable
ventures. While empirical studies are vague about to the extent of the
disincentive effect of taxation, they refer to what could be called the gross
disincentive effect, which includes the income effect. When the post-tax
wage rate is reduced, individuals may tend to work less due to the substitution effect; conversely they may tend to work more due to the income
effect, as leisure is probably viewed as a non-inferior good. The gross effect
depends on the balance between these two opposing tendencies. The
excess burden of taxation, however, depends on the net disincentive effect,
that is, the pure substitution effect. This net disincentive effect is almost
necessarily negative. Given their post-tax income, individuals will probably
choose to work more if their is income/leisure trade-off has not been
distorted by taxation. Taking account of this excess burden, what is the
optimal schedule of income taxation? This problem has been tackled by
Mirrlees (1971; see also 1997), a mathematician who became an economist.
The problem may appear to be an ordinary simple maximisation problem,

but it is really much more complicated as a government's choice of a tax *schedule* (equivalent to an infinite number of variables, instead of just one or a few) to maximise an SWF is subject to the *freedom* of taxpayers with respect to their work/leisure choices. Each individual knows his or her earning ability but the government only knows the ability distribution function and not who is more able (the so-called informational asymmetry). Recognising fully the nature of these complications, one does not question why the problem was not tackled before Mirrlees and why his analysis was worthy of a Nobel Prize.

To make the problem tractable, Mirrlees adopts a number of simplifying assumptions, including a common utility function for all individuals who depend only on the amount of post-tax income and the amount of work. 'Differences in tastes, in family size and composition, and in voluntary transfers, are ignored. These raise rather different kinds of problems, and it is natural to assume them away' (Mirrlees, 1971, p. 175). The SWF is utilitarian, that is, the integral of individual utilities (since individuals are distributed along a continuous scale of different earning skills). Maximising the SWF by choosing an appropriate tax schedule is subject to the requirement that a given amount of tax revenue is raised. Thus the amount of government expenditure is regarded as a separate problem. Without assuming a specific form of utility function (which determines the work/leisure choice, given the level of skill and the tax schedule) and a specific form of distribution of skills, it would be too much to expect stronger results than the following obtained by Mirrlees: (1) the marginal tax rate lies between 0 per cent and 100 per cent; (2) in a large class of cases, consumption and labour supply vary continuously with the skill of the individual; and (3) there will usually be a group of people at the lower end of the scale of earning abilities (the disabled?) who ought to work only if they enjoy it. 'The optimum tax schedule depends upon the distribution of skills within the population, and the labour-consumption preferences of the population, in such a complicated way that it is not possible to say in general whether marginal tax rates should be higher for high-income, low-income, or intermediate-income groups' (ibid., p. 186). However the two equations that Mirrlees uses to characterise the optimum tax schedule are of a reasonably manageable form, so the schedule can be calculated without great difficulty once the forms of the utility and skill distribution functions are specified.

Taking a specific example (with a positive revenue requirement) where the utility function is the sum of the (natural) logarithm of consumption and the logarithm of leisure, and the skill distribution is lognormal, Mirrlees (ibid., p. 202, table II) calculates the optimum tax schedule, which is progressive in terms of average rates (increasing from negative to 14.5 per cent for the top 1 per cent) and regressive in terms of marginal rates (decreasing from 23 per cent to 17 per cent). Mirrlees expected that the rigorous analysis of income taxation in the utilitarian manner would provide an argument for the use of high tax rates to achieve equality, and he expresses surprise that it has not done so (ibid., p. 207). It is true that the specific results depend on the specific functional forms chosen and a different choice will yield different rates (see for example Atkinson, 1973, table 2; Atkinson 1995, ch. 2). Moreover the choice of a different SWF will also affect the outcome (see Helpman, 1974). But the regressivity of marginal rates is still present (see Tuomala, 1990, for a review). The presence of uncertainty and imperfection in observing true incomes reduces the optimal tax rates, which is intuitively agreeable (Mirrlees, 1990).

The regressivity of marginal tax rates is not too surprising if we realise that, in Mirrlees' model, the optimal marginal tax rate for people with the highest earnings is zero (for experimental support of the positive work effort of a zero top marginal rate, see Sillamaa, 1999; see also Gruber and Saez 2002). The reason for this apparently astonishing result is not difficult to see. For any tax schedule that does not involve a zero marginal tax rate for the top earners, let us amend the schedule to make the marginal rate zero after the income level of the top earners. This will induce them to engage in a little extra work since they now have to pay no tax for the extra earning. (This assumes smooth indifference curves, but at least they will not work less. For a geometrical illustration see Sadka, 1976, fig. 4.) This makes them better off and no one else worse off (due to the use of a utility function that rules out utility interdependency). The total amount of tax revenue collected is not smaller than before since the tax schedule has been amended only in the range in which no one was operating before. Although no tax is imposed on the marginal income of the top earners, that income was not earned before and hence no tax was collected on that income level despite a positive tax rate. Some readers may wonder, if this argument is valid, why we do not make the marginal tax rate zero for all persons instead of just for the top earners. The explanation is that the tax schedule has to apply to all individuals simultaneously: there is not a separate schedule for each individual. If we make the marginal rate zero at a lower income level than the income of the top earners, this will reduce the amount of tax collected from the latter (and the taxpayers in between). Such amendments to the tax schedule may then not be feasible. (If the number of individuals is finite, it is possible to design a complicated discontinuous tax system whereby every taxpayer is faced with a zero marginal rate at the relevant income level. Ignoring administrative and informational costs, this is indeed a necessary condition for optimality.)

With every step down the income scale, the above point applies with stronger and stronger force, especially over the range of middle-income levels, where most taxpayers are. This explains the regressivity of the marginal rates. The objective of equality is then achieved through progressity in the average rates (cf. Mirrlees, 1997, p. 1319, on the intuitive reason for regressivity). However Mirrlees' 'expectation that the minimum consumption level would be rather high [implying a higher degree of progressivity in the average tax rates] has not been confirmed' (Mirrlees, 1971, p. 207). This is largely due to his allowance for a high marginal utility of income even at fairly high income levels, contrary to later results on the negligible values at the social level (this is discussed in Chapter 11). Mirrlees' intuition may be more trustworthy than his numerical result here.

Should we then advocate marginal tax rates that are regressive to zero at the top end? The answer is no, or at least not necessarily, for the following reasons. First, in practice the incomes of the very rich are largely unearned and it is doubtful whether making the marginal tax rates regressive to zero would induce the very rich to work appreciably harder. Second, the above analysis ignores utility interdependency and external effects. Increased earnings by the rich could make the non-rich worse off as individual utility is not only a function of absolute income but also of relative income. The failure to account for this is a major weakness in Mirrlees' analysis. (Boskin and Sheshinski, 1978, analyse optimal linear income taxation with utility dependent on relative income. See also Chander and Wilde, 1998; Hammond and Myles, 2000; Widmalm, 2001; Boone and Bovenberg, 2002; Corneo, 2002; Saez, 2002; and the related references in these works) In private correspondence in 1975, Mirrlees agreed that the problem of utility interdependency was an interesting one but remarked that utility interdependency need not necessarily remove regressivity since envy might make people work harder. Having a high income group may make other people feel worse off but it could also make them do more work to keep up with the rich. Since the whole income tax system has a strong disincentive effect, inducing people to work harder produces a positive result. However if my (subjective) judgment is right, the negative effect of high incomes is likely to predominate. Nevertheless if poverty is a public bad, negative marginal tax rates on low incomes or income subsidies (such as the recently introduced Working Tax Credit in Britain) may be desirable (Wane, 2001).

Kolm (1996a) suggests a just system of income taxation with fewer disincentive effects. A standard duration (say 35 hours per week) is fixed. Incomes earned within this duration are subject to a tax/subsidy that completely equalises over all individuals, but incomes earned after this duration are totally untaxed. Viewed in terms of full income (income plus leisure), this is just. As the marginal tax rate (after the fixed duration) is zero, it is also efficient. In practice there will be those who exaggerate the hours of work done to earn a given income or who fail to disclose their actual income (the latter problem applies also in the present system). Nevertheless the proposal has some merit and justifies further exploration.

6.4 Discussion

Mirrlees' analysis concentrates on the choice of a tax schedule to strike an optimal balance between the need to provide incentives to work and the reduction of inequality due to differential earning skills. This is one of the most important issues, but it is not the only relevant one: differences in skills are not the only cause of inequality, income tax is not the only means of achieving equality, equality of income distribution is not the only problem in economic justice and so on. Due to space limitation these issues cannot be discussed in detail, but interested readers are referred to the following works and the references therein: Pen (1971), Phelps (1973), Sen (1973a), Hochman and Peterson (1974), Atkinson (1975, 1976, 1995), Okun (1975), Rivlin (1975), Taubman (1975), Tinbergen (1975), Meade (1976), Atkinson and Harrison (1978), Griliches *et al.* (1978), Juster (1978), Krelle and Shorrocks (1978), Kolm (1996b), Apps and Rees (1999), Silber (1999), Atoda and Tachibanaki (2001), Bénabou and Ok (2001), Fernández and Rogerson (2001), Ho (2001), Acemoglu and Ventura (2002), Castello and Domenech (2002), Corneo and Grüner (2002), Fleurbaeya *et al.* (2002), Lundberg and Squire, 2003. What is presented below is no more than a brief resumé.

Since work is not the only source of income, it is obvious that skill differentials are not the only source of inequality. In fact the reverse misconception – the belief that property incomes account for more than they really do – is more likely to prevail (Pen, 1971, p. 10). Recent empirical studies show that property incomes in advanced economies account for a small and declining share of total income, and that inequality in the personal distribution of income has been narrowing over the last one or two centuries, although this has reversed in recent decades. While not doubting the basic validity of these studies, it must be noted that they do not reflect hidden illegal income. Inequality due to such income is regarded by most people as even more contrary to economic justice. But such income has existed for a long time, and it is likely that inequality has narrowed even if it is taken into account. However it remains true that if inequality due to dubious forms of income can be reduced, it will be even more conducive to the attainment of economic justice. But this is easier said than done (Pen, 1971, section vii4).

One reason for the reversal of the trend towards greater equality in the last few decades is probably the movement towards the right in the economic policies of many countries that emphasise efficiency and the free market. Another reason could be the increasing importance of mass production, mass communication, globalisation and the knowledge economy, which gives winners a bigger share of the total pie. To a significant extent these developments have increased the contribution of the winners by enabling what they offer to reach more consumers. However they may be taking much more than their marginal contribution warrants. Many people like to watch the performance of top superstars such as Olympic gold medalists, Wimbledon winners, or Miss Universe. Although the difference between the talent, entertainment value and so on of the winner and runner-up may be minimal, with victory largely being decided by random and irrelevant factors, most people are still willing to pay a significant premium for getting the top person rather than the runner-up. While real talent counts, as far as the preference for the top superstar is concerned, who gets to be the top person is not really important and the earnings of that person tend to be much more than his or her actual contribution. This divergence is magnified by the ability of modern technology to make performances accessible to an audience of millions by such devices as television, cassettes, CDs and the like (Borghans and Groot, 1998; see also Frank and Cook, 1995). The use of well-known superstars to advertise products of course further increases the income of these winners. The superstars draw viewers' attention to the products being advertised and possibly give credence to the quality of the products. Thus the advertising incomes of these superstars are justified by their high value to the advertisers. However they are unlikely to be justified by their value to the society as a whole because of the following considerations:

- The attention of viewers is largely relative: if they pay more attention to an advertisement featuring a gold medalist they tend to pay less attention to other advertisements, imposing an external cost on other advertisers.
- The credence given to products is largely unjustified, and therefore misleading.
- Most advertisements are largely competitive in nature rather than purely informative, imposing an external cost on the producers of close substitutes.
- Commercial advertising fosters materialism (as discussed in Chapter 11), causing a divergence between preference and welfare.

On the other hand there are areas in which superstars do not earn more than their marginal contribution, or even earn far less. For example people who have contributed significantly to the advancement of knowledge and civilisation, such as Aristotle, Beethoven, Copernicus, Darwin and Einstein, earned only a tiny fraction of the value of their long-term contribution. There are at least two reasons for the contrast between them and superstars in the mass entertainment world. First, unlike in competitive areas such as sport and pop music, contributions in knowledge or even in the business areas have a lower fraction of the pure 'being top in name only' effects (as discussed above), but have substantial contribution. It is true that, even in knowledge production, there is still a competitive element, especially with respect to who gets there first: the first inventor takes all. If she or he is ahead of others by a significant length of time (someone else would have eventually come up with the same invention, but not for a long time), her or his contribution is very large. If she or he is only slightly ahead of the rest, the contribution is much smaller. However the reward depends more on the usefulness and appropriability of the invention. Thus the reward is unlikely to correspond to the marginal contribution in all cases. If we take the expected average reward and average contribution of a researcher of a given calibre in a given field, it is likely that the contribution will far exceed the rewards (this is the second reason for the contrast between the worlds of knowledge and entertainment). Due to the difficulty with appropriability and the global public-good nature of knowledge, investment in knowledge production, especially in fundamental research, is well below the optimum level from a world point of view. But for inherent human curiosity, the rate of knowledge production would be miserably low.

Because of the large divergence between contribution and reward in different areas, should income redistribution measures such as taxation be structured to reflect negative or positive divergences?[4] There is a problem here in that the effectiveness of taxation is limited by the existence of evasion.

With regard to tax evasion, a simple system of linear income tax (a so-called 'flat tax', with constant marginal rates but increasing average rates) would not only reduce administrative costs but would also reduce tax evasion substantially. Mirrlees' analysis shows that the optimal tax schedule is regressive (in marginal rates). If we were to take account of utility inter-dependence, this regressivity could be eliminated or even reversed. But when we consider administrative costs and tax evasion, it may be the case that a linear income tax is not far from the optimum, which only leaves us to choose the fixed marginal rate and the level of exemption or minimum post-tax income (Atkinson, 1973; Davies and Hoy, 2002). When tax evasion is taken into account the progressive income tax systems of many countries are not actually very progressive as, with progressivity in marginal rates, there are more incentives and opportunities for evasion by higher earners. A constant marginal rate would reduce the scope for tax evasion by income-splitting. Any residual loss of equality could be outweighed by the gains in incentives and reduced administrative costs (including the time costs of tax evasion). This would be especially so if measures were introduced to reduce inequality in pretax incomes and create equality of opportunity.

Some people believe that equality of opportunity is more important than equality of income as (1) equality of opportunity can lead to equality of income, and/or (2) inequality of income is not unjust if there is equality of opportunity. The latter is especially true if income inequality is the result of differences in motivation and in choices about work/leisure, risk/security, pecuniary/non-pecuniary matters and so on (Friedman, 1953; Taubman,

---

4. The divergence between marginal productivity and monetary reward due to the status reward of being relatively high in the pay scale of an organisation (analysed by Frank, 1984) does not have the same policy implication as total reward in utility terms is in fact consistent with marginal productivity.

1975). However even if we use a broader concept of income (full income?) that takes account of non-monetary factors, it is still unlikely that equality of opportunity will lead to complete equality of (full) income since people are not born equal in terms of physical fitness and mental ability. Should this type of inequality be tolerated or removed? Different persons may have different answers to this ethical question. If we accept the utilitarian ethic, it is likely that such inequality should be reduced but not removed. The difficulty lies in the choice of degree and the methods used. To avoid undesirable side effects, the appropriate method is likely to lift the lower and rather than to suppress the higher end.

Where there are indivisibilities or increasing returns (resulting in the violation of convexity of the feasible sets), efficiency and equity may be inconsistent with freedom and fairness (Ng, 1985). For example, due to the costs of training and increasing returns it is usually desirable to have specialised armed forces to defend a country. In times of war, when the need for soldiers is large, paying soldiers at the point where the demand and supply curves intersect might mean that soldiers will have very high incomes. This may make the marginal utility of income of soldiers much lower than non-soldiers. This situation need not be equitable. Many countries then choose to sacrifice freedom by introducing conscription.

Even if we opt to achieve equality of opportunity alone, this will by no means be simple. For one thing the concept of equality of opportunity is not very precise. For example, with regard to education, does equality of opportunity mean that each student should pay the same fee or that each student should receive the same amount of education? And what do we mean by 'the same amount of education'? Do we measure education by the amount of input or by the amount of output? With differences in intelligence and motivation, equality in educational input implies inequality in output, and equality in output (if at all possible) implies inequality in input. The application of the utilitarian principle seems to suggest that there should be output regressivity (with the able ending up better off) with input progressivity or regressivity depending on the utility function (Arrow, 1971b). In respect of optimising education and income redistribution policies simultaneously, Ulph (1977) shows that optimal education policies are more regressive than is suggested by Arrow. It may also be noted that, while many supporters of the principle of equality of opportunity believe that equality in educational input will produce a substantially equal output, or at least that substantial equality in output can be achieved by input progressivity, empirical and theoretical studies suggest the reverse. Education may do little to change innate differences in ability, and may serve mainly as a screening process to sort out the intelligent from the less intelligent (Jencks *et al.*, 1972; Arrow, 1973; Spence, 1973; Stiglitz, 1975; Taubman, 1976; Battalio *et al.*, 1977; Riley, 1979; Liu and Wong, 1982; Cohn and Johnes, 1994).

Ambiguity may also arise when applying the principle of horizontal equity, which requires the equal treatment of people in the same circumstances. The difficulty lies in the interpretation of 'the same circumstances'. For example if Mrs J, who has one child, receives £x in child endowment, should Mrs K receive the same amount as she also has one child? Or should the family income be taken into account when defining people's circumstances, such that the well off will receive no child endowment? If we admit all factors into the definition the concept of horizontal equity becomes vacuous since no two persons are exactly alike. Alternatively, if we do not include all factors the different criteria of horizontal equity may be inconsistent with each other. Moreover each may be inconsistent with the Pareto principle (Stiglitz, 1982). What about vertical equity, which requires different but appropriate treatment of people in different circumstances? This depends very much on the criterion used to judge the appropriateness of treatment. Should we go for 'from each according to their choice, to each according to their contribution', or for 'from each according to their ability, to each according to their needs'? A fundamental liberal might insist on 'choice' instead of 'ability' since no people should be forced to work against their will. (Fundamental liberals believe in liberalism as an ultimate moral principle; instrumental liberals believe in liberalism because it is generally consistent with some ultimate end, such as utilitarianism.) A utilitarian can only be an instrumental liberal and must at least allow for a hypothetical exception to the freedom of choice. But taking account of the harmful effects of forced labour (especially in the long term), utilitarians may be practically identical to fundamental liberals with respect to freedom to work. With regard to remuneration, the utilitarian principle will probably settle at something between 'contribution' and 'needs', taking account of incentive effects and so on. In other words the utilitarian SWF trades efficiency for equality to some extent. But what are appropriate ways to achieve a favourable trade-off? We have discussed Mirrlees' approach to the use of income taxation and have briefly touched on the provision of equality of opportunity. We shall now briefly discuss some other forms of taxation.

If the government were omniscient and knew the potential of all individuals, it could design a system of lump-sum taxes for different persons to achieve the objective of equality without any loss of efficiency. This is an unobtainable ideal, but it has been suggested that it could be approached by taxing individuals according to their measured capabilities (such as IQ) instead of their incomes (see for example Tinbergen, 1972). Unfortunately the practical difficulties – especially the problem of evasion, with people hiding their real capabilities – would be overwhelming. Mirrlees (1971, p. 208) believes that 'high values of skill-indexes may be sought after so much for prestige that they would not often be misrepresented'. But it might be suspected that, if these indices were used for taxation purposes, most people would take pride in being able to register a low value (however consider the proposal of women being tolled on their beauty, men on their valour, with self-assessment as the rule!)

Other taxes to achieve equality (especially of opportunity) include death and gift duties. To achieve the objective of equality without damaging efficiency, it has been proposed that progresse duties should be based not on the size of the estate but on the size of the individual bequest, the wealth of the beneficiary and/or the total amount of the bequest or gift received by the beneficiary. This would produce very few disincentive effects since one could reduce the tax rate by leaving a moderate amount to each of a number of persons who were poor and/or had not received much in the way of inheritance or gifts. In particular it would encourage people to distribute their estate among relatives and friends instead of concentrating on a favourite. While there would be some practical difficulties with implementing this proposal, they would not be insurmountable (Meade, 1964, pp. 55–8).

Taxation is not, of course, the only means to achieve equality. Other measures can be divided into two groups: the first consists of measures to remove man-made, institutional barriers in order to create equality of opportunity; the second consists of measures that impose restrictions on activities that lead to inequality even when there is equality of opportunity. The second type of measure not only results in a substantial loss of efficiency but also usually leads to infringements of freedom (Bauer, 1976). While the pursuit of equality may have significant side effects. Recent cross-national studies (for example Scully, 2002) show that economic freedom is positively associated with both economic efficiency/growth and equality.

6.5 Concluding remarks

In the first section of this chapter it was noted that optimal distribution can be put in terms of an SWF and a GUFF. Different people may disagree widely on the form of both the SWF and the GUFF. Section 5.4.1 argued in favour of a specific SWF – the unweighted sum of individual utilities. But the shape of a GUFF is much more difficult to ascertain. The following factors are relevant here: (1) the degree of diminishing marginal utility of income, (2) the extent of incentive effects, (3) the nature and extent of utility interdependency, (4) the social rate of discount, and (5) the administrative and other costs of pursuing equality (for example time spent on evading taxes, infringements of freedom and so on).

There is evidence in psychological studies that, apart from extreme values, the noticeable increment to any stimulus value is a constant proportion of that value. Written as the Weber–Fechner law, sensation = k log stimulus.[5]

---

5. Luce and Edwards' (1958) criticism of Fechner does not apply to this particular function.

If we take this general law as applicable to the utility of individuals as a function of their income, then we can write $U = k$ log income. The marginal utility of income then diminishes by the same proportion as income increases. Economists have also conducted studies on the marginal utility of income, usually based on simplifying assumptions (Fisher, 1927; Frisch, 1932; van Praag, 1968; Clark, 1973; van Herwaarden *et al.*, 1977. See also van Praag and Frijters, 1999, for a survey of the 'individual welfare functions' approach). Recent studies on happiness (Veenhoven, 1993; Diener and Suh, 1997; Cummins, 1998; Kenny, 1999, Kahneman *et al.*, 1999; Blanchflower and Oswald, 2000; see also Chapter 11 below) suggest that, after a certain level (around US$5000 per person per year), the long-term marginal welfare of income may be close to zero (the significance of this is discussed in Chapter 11). While studies have also been conducted on the extent of disincentive effects, no definite conclusion has been drawn. Recent studies have emphasised factors that make efficiency/growth and equality go together rather than being either/or trade-offs, due, for example, to such considerations as the physiological effect of income on work effort (Strauss and Thomas, 1995), principal-agent problems and imperfection in the credit market due to informational asymmetry, which may be lessened by (1) the use of collateral that the very poor lack (Binswanger *et al.*, 1995; Hoff and Lyon, 1995; Hoff, 1996), (2) the effects of tax progressitivity in moderating the wage demands of unions (Hersoug, 1984; Creedy and McDonald, 1990; Lockwood and Manning, 1993), (3) the discouragement of investment of high inequality which increases the difference between median and average incomes and hence the median voter demand for a higher tax rate (Persson and Tabellini 1994; but see Perotti, 1996, on the negative empirical evidence for the mechanism, although the negative relationship between inequality and growth appears to be valid – see Birdsall *et al.*, 1995. However Li and Zou, 1998, Forbes, 2000, and Scully, 2002, show positive relationships), (4) the crime-reduction effect of equality (Eaton and White, 1991; Grossman, 1994; Keefer and Knack, 2002), and (5) limited behavioural responses (Blank, 2002). (For a summary of empirical evidence on the relationship between inequality and growth see Benabou, 1996. On other related issues, see Haveman, 1988; Murphy *et al.*, 1989; Schmid, 1993; Bowles and Gintis, 1996; Baland and Platteau, 1997; Breen, 1997; Le Grand, 1997; Devins and Douglas, 1998; Nagel, 1998; Putterman, *et al.*, 1998; Aghion and Williamson, 1999; Lee and Roemer, 1999.)

The nature and extent of utility interdependency is even more elusive, especially if long-term effects are taken into account. When there are intertemporal considerations, the social rate of discount becomes relevant. Some people argue that while it is reasonable to discount future consumption if future generations will be richer, it is unreasonable to discount future utility from the social point of view. This argument ignores the fact that we are not completely sure of the continued existence of human society.

Thus a small uncertainty discount can be justified, although it would be difficult to agree on a precise value. We are on similarly imprecise territory when we move to the matter of freedom and other non-economic factors. We have a long way to go before the practical choice of distributional policies is based mainly on more objective factors.

6.6 Summary

Given a utility possibility or feasibility frontier, the choice of an optimal point (related to income distribution) depends on the form of the SWF. The common 'egalitarian' inclination to adopt welfare contours that we convex to the origin may be due to a 'utility illusion', the double discounting of the incomes of the rich. With a given total income, diminishing marginal utility and no knowledge of individual utility functions, equal distribution maximises the expected sum of utilities. Some degree of inequality is usually needed to maintain the incentive to work. The choice of an income tax schedule to strike an optimal balance between incentive and equality, as analysed by Mirrlees (1971), shows that, for a particular choice of the relevant functional forms, the average tax rate is progressive but the marginal rate is regressive. Since Mirrlees' analysis ignores utility interdependency and administrative costs, perhaps a linear tax schedule over a significant income range would not be too far from optimal. The recent reversal to the long-term trend towards greater equality may be partly due to the winner-take-all effect, which is related to the very high incomes of, for example, media superstars, who earn far more than their true marginal productivity, in contrast to contributors to knowledge.

7
Externality

It was noted in Chapter 2 that an equilibrium situation of a perfectly competitive market economy is Pareto optimal under certain conditions. One of these conditions is the absence of (unaccounted for) external effects. However external effects are pervasive. External effects in the form of environmental disruption have attracted both academic and public attention for decades (see for example Papandreou, 1994; Stavins, 2000). This chapter considers how external effects can cause non-optimality, and how this can be alleviated. But first we shall discuss the concept and classification of external effects.

7.1 The concept and classification of externalities

Obviously, for an external effect to be present there must first be an effect. Some party, K (the affecting party) must produce an effect on some other party, J (the affected party). The effect must not just be present but must also have a positive or negative welfare significance. For example if water from my neighbour's garden hose flows into my garden, a physical effect is there. But if I do not care about it one way or the other, it cannot be said that an externality exists. Second, the affecting party is usually a person, a group of persons or something that is under the control of persons (animals, institutions and so on). It is possible to speak of the external effects of, say, wild animals and use this to justify certain measures against them. But the usual methods of tax/subsidy, bargaining and so on will not be applicable. The affected party is also usually a person/group of persons or something owned by persons. However if the welfare of non-human beings, such as animals, enters into our objective function, then it is quite logical to include them as possibly affected parties.

The mere presence of a welfare-relevant effect by one party on another does not necessarily constitute an externality; additional conditions are needed for the effect to be considered external. For example when you buy oranges from a shop there is presumably a positive effect on your welfare.

However this is an exchange relationship rather than an external effect as you are paying for the oranges. Externality refers only to benefits or damages that are not paid for; market relationships are not external effects. Another possible condition is to require externality to refer only to incidental effects and not to primary or intended effects (Mishan, 1971, p. 2). Thus the factory does not emit smoke for its own sake, rather the smoke is incidental to the production process. On the other hand one's welfare can obviously be affected by murder, robbery, friendship, companionship and so on. But these are primary, intended effects and are not usually described as externalities. Rather, they are either outright illegal activities or social activities. However the distinction between primary and incidental effects is blurred one. If a group of hooligans enjoy themselves by throwing stones, some of which happen to break a window, is the breakage a primary or an incidental effect? If air pollution becomes so severe that we ban all forms of smoke, will not emitting smoke be as much of an illegal activity as the breaking of a window? Moreover could not the effect upon the victim of an illegal activity such as rape be regarded as the incidental effect of a drastic attempt by the rapist to achieve (perhaps psychopathic) sexual fulfilment? Factory managers are interested in production, not in polluting the atmosphere. Similarly the rapist may be interested only in his sexual satisfaction, not in inflicting harm on the victim. It therefore seems quite logical to speak of the external effects of offenders on victims or society in general. In fact according to this general interpretation of externality, most illegal activities have been made illegal because of their harmful external effects.

More formally, we shall say that an externality exists when the utility function of individuals (or the cost or production function of a firm) depends not only on the variables under their control but also on variables under the control of others else when the dependence is not effected through a market transaction. Thus:

$$U^J = U^J(x_1^J, x_2^J, \ldots, x_G^J, x_1^K) \tag{7.1}$$

where U^J is the utility of individual J, x_g^J is the level of the gth activity by J. In this case the first activity of K has an external effect on J.

Assuming differentiability, the externality at $x_1^k = x_1^{-k}$ (where x_1^{-k} is a particular given level of the activity) is said to be marginal if $\partial U^J/\partial x_1^K{}_{/x_1^K = \bar{x}_1^K/} \neq 0$, and an inframarginal if $\partial U^J/\partial x_1^K{}_{/x_1^K - \bar{x}_1^K/} \neq 0$ but $\neq 0$, for some $x_1^K < x_1^{-K}$. Thus if $\partial U^J/\partial x_1^K$ is as depicted in Figure 7.1a, it is a marginal external economy (benefit) over the range OC, an inframarginal one over the range CD, and a marginal external diseconomy (cost) after D. It is of course possible for some externality to be a marginal diseconomy or economy throughout its entire range.

The usual definition of inframarginal externality as $\partial U^J/\partial x_1^K{}_{/x_1^K = \bar{x}_1^K/} = 0$, $\int_0^{x_1^{-k}} \partial U^J/\partial x_1^K \, dx_1^K \neq 0$ leaves the cases illustrated in Figures 7.1b and 7.1c

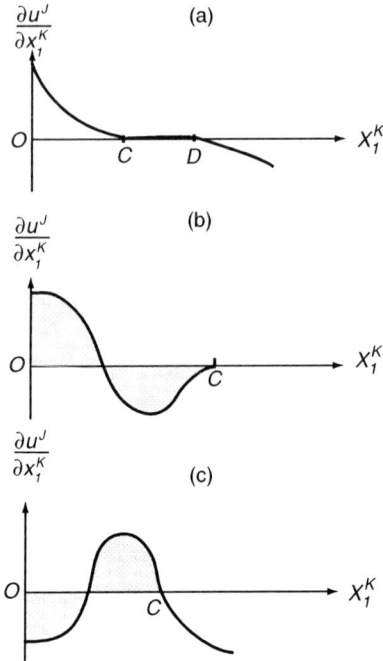

Figure 7.1

without a name. Here the two shaded areas are equal in size, and therefore $\int \partial U^J/\partial x_1^K \, dx_1^K$ is equal to zero after/at point C in Figures 7.1b and 7.1c. While such cases are unlikely to occur often in practice, they are logically quite possible and may be termed inframarginal mixed externalities. An example of mixed externality is high-pitched laughter. The first few bursts are usually regarded as amusing, but further bursts are often regarded as irritating until people get used to them.

If activity x_1^K affects not only the total utility of J but also the marginal utility of some relevant activity of J, it is said to be a non-separable externality. We now have $\partial^2 U^J/\partial x_g^J \, \partial x_1^K \neq 0$ for some x_g^J. On the other hand if $\partial U^J/\partial x_1^K \neq 0$ for some value of x_1^K but $\partial^2 U^J/\partial x_g^J \, \partial x_1^K = 0$ for all relevant x_g^J, it is a separable externality. An example of a non-separable externality is an emission of smoke that reduces people's preference for wearing white shirts.

If K's activity affects J but J's activity does not affect K, there is a unidirectional externality. If they are mutually affected, there is a reciprocal externality. A classic example is the case of an apple grower and a beekeeper – both benefit from the activity of the other as the bees pollinate the apple flowers and the flowers provide the bees with nectar to make honey.

The concept of externality here is confined to real external effects and does not include a 'pecuniary' external effect, which works through changes in prices. For example if some people substantially increase their demand for a certain good, this may push up the price of that good, making other consumers worse off. However, at least in the case of a perfectly competitive economy with no distortion, this decrease in consumer surplus is fully offset by the corresponding gain in producer surplus, and hence no inefficiency is caused by such pecuniary external effects (for complications arising from the presence of increasing returns, see Section 10.3.2).

7.2 Divergence from optimality and the tax/subsidy solution

The analysis of externalities can most easily be undertaken with a partial equilibrium approach, assuming an existing unidirectional externality (Ng, 1980a, justifies corrective taxes/subsidies for normal cases in a general equilibrium setting). This is done in Figure 7.2, which differs from Figure 7.1 in two respects. First, in order to speak in monetary terms the (net) marginal utility curves have been converted into (net) marginal valuation (MV) curves. This is done by dividing $\partial U^j/\partial x_1^K$ by the marginal utility of money. Second, while the MV of K is measured on the vertical axis in the normal direction, that of J is measured in the opposite direction (southward from the origin). In the case depicted in Figure 7.2 there is an external diseconomy and hence J's valuation of K's activity is negative. Due to the way in which J's valuation is measured, her MV curve (MV_J) lies in the upper section of the figure.[1]

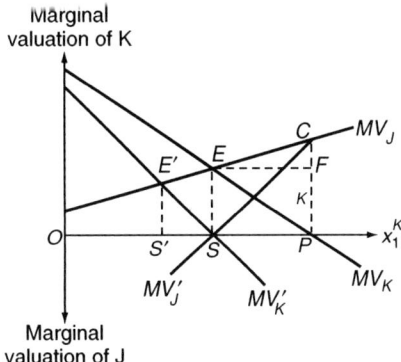

Figure 7.2

---

1. If MV_J depends on some activity under J's control, the curve MV_J should trace out the MV_J for the utility-maximising (or profit-maximising) choice of J for each given x_1^K.

Since K undertakes the activity x_1^K himself, his MV is positive over some range of the activity. However, since his MV curve is measured net of the costs of undertaking the activity, it must meet the horizontal axis somewhere or K will extend his activity indefinitely. As drawn in Figure 7.2, MV_K cuts the horizontal axis at P. Assuming that K maximises his utility (and ignoring the conscience effect discussed in Section 7.4), he carries his activity up to P. At this point his net MV of the activity is zero. But he is imposing a marginal damage of PC on J. This is therefore not a socially optimal solution. The latter occurs at S, where the two MV curves intersect.[2] The traditional Pigovian solution to this divergence between private and social optima is to impose a tax on the activity (on a subsidy in the case of an external economy). The marginal tax rate is equal to the negative marginal valuation of J. After the imposition of this tax, K's new net MV curve will be MV_K'. K will then be induced to reduce his activity level to the socially optimal point S, ignoring income effects. In the presence of income effects, the marginal valuation curve of K may move slightly due to his payment of taxes. Hence the socially optimal point, S, may also move slightly. However the solution remains Pareto optimal.

A major difficulty with the Pigovian solution is estimating the extent of the external costs involved, in particular the value of ES in Figure 7.2. While this difficulty is very real, it has probably been exaggerated. For an important external cost such as environmental damage, a Pigovian tax based on a rough estimate is likely to be better than doing nothing. Moreover, as shown by Ng (2001a), for most cases where some abatement of pollution is desirable, the problem of estimating an efficiency-improving tax can be easily solved. It is desirable to tax pollution at the marginal cost of abatement, which is easier to estimate than the marginal cost of damage. Moreover such a tax will normally yield a total revenue that is in excess of the amount of abatement spending. However, due to the global aspect of this, international cooperation is necessary (Ng and Liu, 2002, have called for the United Nations to take ownership of unowned resources such as the Earth's atmosphere and to enforce Pigovian taxes on environmental damage).

---

2. A lump-sum transfer may be assumed to side-step the distributional issue. However, according to the argument in Appendix 9.1, this assumption is not really necessary. We have also been assuming the satisfaction of second-order and total conditions (on which see Section 2.2.2). For the argument that the presence of external diseconomies tends to push the production possibility curve inward except for points of specialisation, hence making the violation of the second-order condition more likely see Baumol and Bradford (1972; cf. Starrett, 1972; Otani and Sicilian, 1977). For an analysis of total conditions see Gould (1977). On the impossibility of decentralised, finite-dimensional mechanisms to guarantee Pareto optimality in the presence of externalities and the possibilities for Pigou taxes see Hurwicz (1999).

However it has been argued that full optimality cannot be attained by the imposition of a unilateral tax (Buchanan and Stubblebine, 1962, p. 383). At point S, J's (absolute) marginal valuation of the activity is not equal to K's marginal valuation (net of tax). Hence there is an incentive for them to bargain to achieve a new level of the activity, S', although this is not the socially optimal point. By moving from S to S', J gains the area $S'SEE'$ and K loses $S'SE'$. So there is a net gain of SEE' to be shared between J and K. But this is not a social improvement since there is a loss in tax revenue, $S'SEE'$. To prevent this non-optimal outcome, Buchanan and Stubblebine propose that J should also be taxed to ensure that she will take into account the costs imposed on K. This second tax on J should be positively correlated with K's reduction of his activity level from point P, or negatively correlated with x_1^K, thus shifting MV_J to MV_J', intersecting MV_K' at the socially optimal point, S. If this tax on J is positively correlated with K's increase in his activity level, it will shift MV_J upward (recall that J's marginal valuation is measured southward from the origin), making its intersection with MV_K' further away from the socially optimal point, S.

The proposed bilateral taxation may be superfluous. If bargaining between the parties is possible, a Pareto optimum can be achieved without any taxation. If bargaining is impossible (owing, for example, to the high cost of coming to an agreement and enforcing it), a single tax on K may be sufficient to achieve the optimum (Ng, 1971a; Shibata, 1971). Nevertheless bilateral taxation may be relevant when bargaining is possible but is deemed unjust or too costly. But of course the costs of administering the bilateral taxation must also be taken into account.

Bilateral taxation can also serve two other purposes. In the example illustrated in Figure 7.2, if J can avoid the external diseconomy (for example by moving to another place) at a cost that is less than K's cost of reducing the nuisance (that is, ESP in Figure 7.2), then it would be desirable for J to do so rather than for K to reduce his activity level. But with the enforcement (or expected imminent introduction) of the unilateral tax, J is not motivated to do this unless she is required to pay an amount equal to the cost (or the reduction in utility) incurred by K to reduce the externality. Second, the amount of diseconomy borne by J is difficult to determine in practice. Under a unilateral tax system she is motivated to exaggerate her damage so as to raise the rate of tax on K and hence further reduce the activity of K. But if J is required to pay a tax that is equal to the cost borne by K to reduce the externality, J will not benefit from the reduction of K's activity beyond S. J will therefore be motivated to report her damage function truthfully (Ng, 1971a, pp. 1973–4).

Similarly, since K also has to pay for the damage sustained by J, he too will be motivated to report his MV function truthfully. In fact one can show that, even given an exaggerated report by one party, the other party will still find that honesty is the best policy under the bilateral tax arrangement.

Dishonesty not only harms the other party but also the dishonest party itself. Unfortunately this happy result does not generalise to the case where J and/or K consists of a number of individuals/firms with different MV functions. For example suppose that K is a polluting firm and J consists of a large number of affected individuals. First take the case in which these individuals have identical MV curves. As illustrated in Figure 7.3, each individual MV curve is MV_J^i. Hence the vertical summation of these n individuals' MV_J^i gives $\sum_{i=1}^{n} MV_J^i = nMV_J^i$, whose intersection with MV_K gives the socially optimal point, S. If each individual is required to pay $1/n$ of the cost imposed on K by having to reduce the externality (curve PD in Figure 7.3), they will all be motivated to reveal their MV curve truthfully, provided they believe that the others will on average report truthfully. Thus for any single individual j, if she believes that all other individuals' reported MV curves sum to $\sum_{i \neq j} MV_J^i = \sum_{i=1}^{n-1} MV_J^i$, she will figure that, if she also reports truthfully, the aggregate reported MV_J will intersect MV_K at S. If she exaggerates or underreports her MV, the actual level of x_1^K will diverge from point S. Since she is required to pay for $1/n$ of the cost imposed on K and since her own MV is equal to $1/n$, the aggregate MV, it will be to her advantage to have x_1^K reduced to point S, where $\sum_{i=1}^{n} MV_J^i$ intersects MV_K and MV_J^i intersects $1/nMV_K$.

The above analysis is based on the assumption that the true MV_K curve is known – if we relaxed this assumption would the result change? The answer is no. For any given reported MV_K', whether it is the true one or not, each individual will be motivated to make the level of x_1^K occur at the intersection

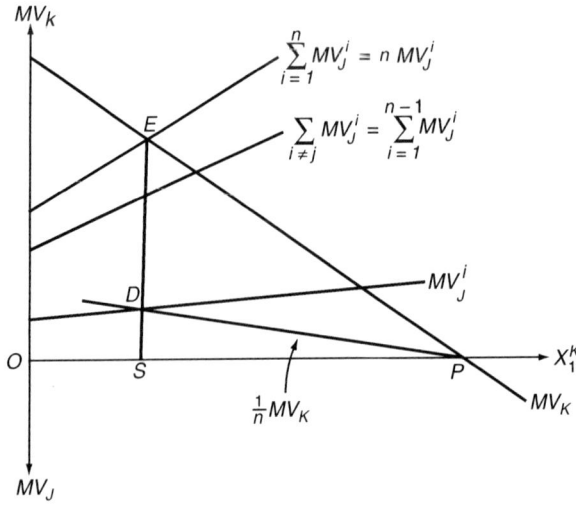

Figure 7.3

of $\sum_{i=1}^{n} MV_j^i$ with the reported MV_K. Hence the above conclusion will not be affected by a false revelation by K. Moreover since K has to pay a tax equal to $-\sum MV_j^i$, he will be motivated to reveal MV_K truthfully.

Unfortunately, if we introduce differences in individual MV curves we run into trouble. Individuals with a high (absolute value) MV will be motivated to exaggerate and those with a low MV to underreport their true MV. We cannot count on these two opposite tendencies precisely offsetting each other to produce a true aggregate MV. If we try to avoid this difficulty by making each individual pay according to her reported MV, we run into trouble in another direction. Each individual may then try to underreport her MV in order to reduce her own payment. This is the well-known free-rider problem in the literature of public goods. This difficulty can be overcome by using a more complicated mechanism, as shown below (for a more detailed discussion of and relevant references for this mechanism, see Section 8.3. Beginners may skip the following paragraph).

Basically the scheme consists of (1) asking each individual to report her marginal valuation function, (2) summing the reported marginal valuation functions for all individuals in J and taxing individual (or firm) K according to the negative of this sum, that is, $-\sum_{i=1}^{n} MV_j^i$, and (3) taxing each individual j in J according to $MV_K - \sum_{i \neq j} MV_j^i$, positively correlated with the reduction in x_1^K from the point where $MV_K = \sum_{i \neq j} MV_j^i$. These three points are illustrated in Figure 7.4. Given the reported MV of all other individuals, an individual j in J has to pay taxes according to T_j as x_1^K is reduced beyond the point Q. If she reports her true MV_j^i, the sum of the reported MV_j^i will intersect MV_K at R, where MV_j^i is equal to T_j. Thus at this margin she has no incentive to exaggerate or underestimate her damage. If she exaggerates (underestimates) her damage and reports her MV curve as being higher (lower) than her true MV_j^i curve, then $\sum_{i=1}^{n} MV_j^i$ will intersect MV_K at a point

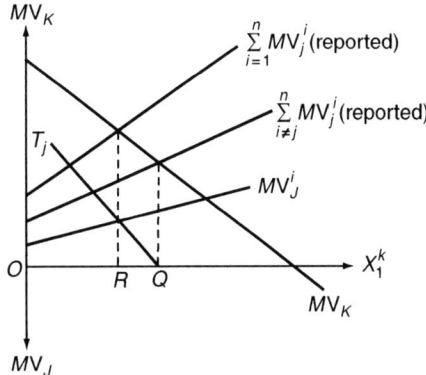

Figure 7.4

to the left (right) of R. She will gain from the resulting reduction in x_1^K (taxes), but the gain will be more than offset by the increase in taxes (x_1^K). This is true whether other individuals report truthfully or not. Moreover since this is true for each individual (j can be any one in J), each will in fact be reporting truthfully. Similarly, since K has to be taxed according to MV_j^i, he is also motivated to report truthfully. Therefore the resulting bilateral taxes may lead to an optimal level of x_1^K (for some complications, see Section 8.3).

7.3   Other solutions

In passing we have mentioned bargaining, which is one of the possible ways of solving the problem created by externality. In the example illustrated in Figure 7.2 above, J and K could come to a mutual agreement. K could agree to reduce his activity to point S. By doing so he would lose the area ESP and J would gain the area $ESPC$. So the net gain would be EPC. If J also agreed to pay K an amount of money equal to, say, the area $ESPF$, then both parties would be made better off than at the initial position, P. Hence, provided that the costs of coming to an agreement and enforcing it (loosely referred to as transaction costs) were not too high, both parties would have an incentive to do so. One possible objection to this solution is that many people might think it unjust that J, the sufferer of K's activity, should have to pay K to reduce the activity. This equity question can be taken care of by the appropriate assignment of property rights. If J had the 'amenity right', then K would have to pay J in order to undertake the activity. As will be shown in Section 7.5, a Pareto optimal outcome might still emerge if the transaction costs are not too high (see Klibanoff and Morduch, 1995, on the difficulties of reaching an agreement).

Apart from transaction costs there is another significant difficulty in reaching voluntary bargaining agreements. Referring again to Figure 7.2, suppose that J is interested in reducing the amount of payment to K towards the minimum amount, ESP, and that K is interested in increasing it towards the maximum amount, $ESPC$. In between these maximum and minimum amounts there are a large number of possible payment amounts that will still make both parties better off. The actual outcome will depend on their relative skill and toughness in bargaining. It is possible that they may not be able to come to an agreement at all. While it is true that some agreement is better than no agreement, both of them may act on the assumption that the other party will give in first. This sort of strategic behaviour may prevent the reaching of an agreement. Such a prospect would reduce the incentive for both parties to enter into negotiations.

If we take account of game-strategic behaviour, K might carry his activity beyond his private optimal point, P (Shibata, 1971). This would mean that he would sustain a net loss at the margin. He might do it in the belief that

J would be damaged even more and would therefore be willing to settle on terms that are more favourable to himself (*K*). While such unethical behaviour is not likely to be engaged in by many people, the possibility that some persons may act very unscrupulously cannot be ruled out. This poses a further problem to the bargaining solution. Another shortcoming of the bargaining approach is its effect on future decision making, including the possibility of encouraging blackmail. This will be discussed in Section 7.5 below.

If the parties concerned are both business firms, then bargaining may go beyond an agreement to reduce/increase the level of activity involved. The two firms may agree to merge into one firm, effectively internalising the pre-existing external effect. With a single management, the pre-existing external effect can be taken into account and will no longer be an external effect. But the informational and organisational costs may increase (Alchian and Demsetz, 1972; Chu and Wang, 1998). A Pigovian tax that encourages such mergers, while apparently solving the externality problem, may not really be efficient when organisational costs are taken into account. However the external costs of one producer on another producer could be solved by negotiation plus proper operation of the law. Moreover the more important forms of external cost in the real world are probably environmental damage and relative competition between consumers (keeping up with the Joneses), neither of which is an external cost of one producer on another producer. Hence the relevance of the Pigovian tax, especially in the form of bilateral taxation, remains relevant.

Another way of tackling the problem of externality is for the government to impose some form of direct control. This could be outright prohibition, making the activity completely illegal, or milder regulations, such as the zoning of residential areas so that no factory can be built, the division of smoking and non-smoking areas in public places, compulsory installation of pollution-reduction devices and so on. In particular a certain quota on the maximum permissible amount of externality could be specified. Economists are generally in favour of making quotas freely transferable. Thus if the government did not want a certain pollutant to exceed *X* units it could issue *X* units of quotas, which could either be distributed proportionally or, better still, sold to the polluters, who could later exchange them for money if their circumstances changed. Producers who could only reduce their pollution at a high cost would be motivated to pay for quotas, while those who could do so at a low cost would be motivated to reduce their pollution levels. Thus an overall reduction in the pollution level could be achieved at a lower cost to society as a whole (see for example Parish, 1972; Baumol and Oates, 1975; on solving the problem of siting unwanted facilities see Quah and Tan, 2002).

When choosing between alternative methods of tackling the externality problem, it is necessary to consider not only their ability to achieve the desired result but also the costs (informational, administrative and so on) of their implementation. It is likely that different external effects will best be solved by different methods, including doing nothing.

The various methods of tackling externalities discussed above are applicable only to normal external effects. There is a special type of externality that is inherently not amenable to the usual solutions, even assuming there are no informational, administrative or transaction costs. This externality usually involves non-economic activities such as social interactions that change their character when taxes/subsidies and so on are introduced. For example if I received a subsidy for being friendly to my neighbours, they might regard my friendliness as bogus and I might reduce my contact with them to avoid being accused of being friendly only because of the subsidy. For a discussion of these non-amenable externalities and the associated indirect externalities see Ng (1975d).

7.4 The conscience effect**

The above analysis of externalities was based on the assumption that there is no divergence between welfare and preference. We shall now relax the assumption that individual K is self-centred with respect to activity x_1^K. (Self-concerned individuals' utility or preference is affected only by their own welfare, although their welfare may be affected by others' welfare; self-minded individuals' welfare is not affected by others' welfare; self-centred individuals are both self-minded and self-concerned – see also Section 1.3 above.)

Consider Figure 7.5. The curve MV_K^a is the (net) marginal valuation of K if activity x_1^K does not have any external effects. Now introduce the external

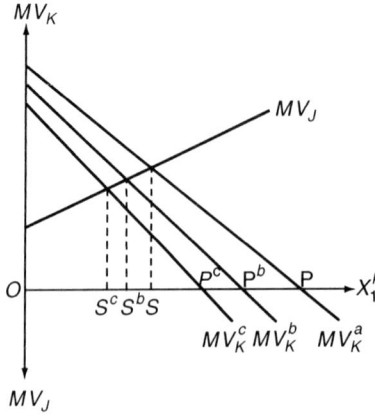

Figure 7.5

effect represented by MV_J. If K is self-centred his MV curve remains unchanged and the above analysis applies. However if K is not self-minded, the fact that J is adversely affected by x_1^K may reduce MV_K even if K is self-concerned. Suppose this reduces his MV curve (in terms of his own welfare) to MV_K^b. Moreover if K is not self-concerned his MV (in terms of his preference) may be further reduced to MV_K^c. He will then carry the activity up to point P^c, which may be to the right or the left of S. But is S still the point of social optimum? Since in terms of welfare the MV curve of K is MV_K^b, it seems that the socially optimum point is now S^b. It is likely that S^b still lies to the left of P^b because K, even if he is not completely self-concerned, is unlikely to have equal concern for J's welfare as for his own. If K *is* self-concerned, then MV_K^c and MV_K^b coincide. It may then seem that the analysis of previous sections applies, provided that MV_K^b and not MV_K^a is taken as the relevant marginal valuation curve for K. However, as will be shown below, some interesting new results emerge even for self-concerned individuals provided they are not also self-minded.

Consider Figure 7.6, where K's marginal valuation curve is reduced from MV_K^a to MV_K^b due to the presence of an external diseconomy, as indicated by MV_J. The socially optimal point is apparently at S^b, where MV_K^b intersects MV_J. If we were to impose a Pigovian tax on K, would this move MV_K^b down to $MV_K^{b'}$ to intersect the horizontal axis at S^b, as in the analysis in the preceding sections? Not necessarily, even ignoring income effects. In fact it could move up to $MV_K^{a'}$. K's MV curve would be reduced from MV_K^a to MV_K^b due to the external diseconomy imposed on J. Now that he had to pay a tax (or some other form of compensation) to account for the externality, his MV curve could well revert to MV_K^a, which, after subtracting the tax, would give

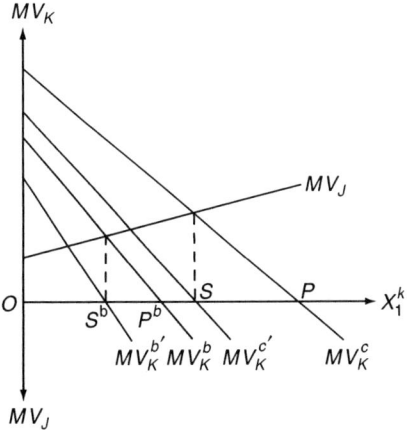

Figure 7.6

$MV_K^{a\prime}$. K would then carry the activity up to point S, which would be socially optimal since his MV curve had reverted to MV_K^a.

Two interesting observations can be made here. First, the diseconomy-producing activity could increase (from P^b to S in Figure 7.6) after the imposition of the optimal Pigovian tax. This should not be confused with the argument by Buchanan and Kafoglis (1963) and Baumol (1965) that 'the presence of external benefits may very conceivably call for reduced output and activity levels on the part of those who produce these economies' (Baumol, 1965, p. 32). This is due to the reciprocal nature of some externalities – such as communicable diseases. Thus a public health programme could reduce medical expenditure, in contrast with uncoordinated private health programmes, where many individuals – fearing that they are unprotected – may be apt to take very strong self-protective measures. 'However, the reduction of aggregate resources is not caused by the reduced output and activity levels on the part of those who produce the external economies, but rather by a reduction in resources committed by those who are benefited by the external economies' (Ng, 1971a, p. 180). In contrast, for the case illustrated in Figure 7.6, it is the party who produces the externality (K) who makes the 'counternormal' adjustment. Second, the affecting party may be made either better off or worse off by the tax, and the same applies to the affected party. In the analyses in the previous sections, the affected party was always made better off (ignoring the unlikely Giffen effect) and the affecting party was always made worse off. (If the tax proceed is used for compensation, then of course both parties could be made better off.) Referring back to Figure 7.6, the possibility that the affected party (J) might be made worse off is due to the fact that the activity level may increase after the imposition of the tax. The possibility that the affecting party (K) might be made better off is due to the fact that he may gain more than the amount of the tax as he can no longer engage in an activity that is detrimental to someone else without paying for it. This can be called the conscience effect.

As drawn in Figure 7.6, P^b lies to the left of S. This could be regarded as impossible, but consider the following real-life example. After learning that a vacant plot of land in our street was a common dumping ground, I started to dump grass clippings from my front lawn onto the plot. Being aware that this was someone else's property. I refrained from dumping grass from my back lawn. However if my next-door neighbour was right in saying that the dumped grass would quickly decompose and would not do any harm, the optimal Pigovian tax on dumping would have been much less than a dollar. If something like a dumping meter had been installed so that people dump legally by putting a coin in the meter, I might have been prepared to pay to dump grass from my back garden as well.

Factors other than a feeling of guilt can serve to reduce the value placed on an activity that produces an external diseconomy. The value to the owners of a polluting factory may be reduced not only by the guilt felt by the owners themselves, but also by that of their employees since the latter will, presumably, require some wage premium to compensate them for the unpleasant feeling. If the labour market is not sufficiently perfect for such a premium to exist, then the value to the owners might not be reduced but the producers' surplus of the employees will be. Moreover the employees will be more likely to engage in industrial disputes, either to obtain wage increases or in protest at the pollution. The decision by the unions to ban the building of the Newport power station in Victoria, Australia, on the ground of its environmental impact involved many factors but can be at least partly analysed using our framework. Had the principle of Pigovian taxes been enforced the State Electricity Commission (SEC) might have taken the environmental effects more into account. An independent body could have estimated the external costs involved, which the SEC would have been required to pay. If it had still regarded Newport as the best site, then the decision might have been accepted as socially optimal and the costly dispute between the unions and the government might not have happened. (It may be true that the real motive of the unions was power politics rather than concern for the environment, but without a reasonable pretext they would not have been able to initiate the dispute.) A smaller power station that took adequate account of environmental consequences could have been built despite the Pigovian tax. In fact the tax was not imposed and a stalemate ensued between the unions and the Victoria government, which was probably much more costly.

The case depicted in Figure 7.6 can also be doubted on the following ground. If K's valuation of the activity is reduced by more than the external cost due to the conscience effect, why does he not pay for it voluntarily? This can be explained by imperfect knowledge and transaction costs. (Lack of amenability may also come into the picture. Who would dare to approach their neighbours and offer to pay for their permission to allow noisy after-midnight parties?) But if the transaction cost is prohibitive for a voluntary payment, is it not likely that it will be prohibitive for the taxation scheme? This may be so for many cases, such as the grass-dumping example above, but for many other cases the reverse may be true, especially if the number of individuals affected by an external effect is large. The transaction cost of paying for the damages is then likely to be very high. Yet it may not be too costly to impose a tax based on a reasonable estimate of the total damages.

We have argued that a Pigovian tax may actually increase the level of a diseconomy-producing activity due to the conscience effect. But such examples can be seen as extreme. Cases that are more likely to occur in practice are shown in Figure 7.7, where P^b lies to the right of S and the imposition of the tax reduces the activity. While this has a less startling effect on the activity level, it is noteworthy in another regard: both parties to the externality may be made better off without any compensation from the tax revenue. Party J gains from the reduction of the activity from P^b to S.

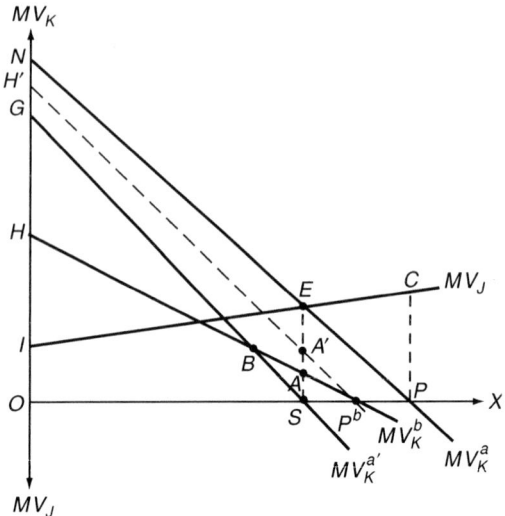

Figure 7.7

K also gains if $\Delta OGS > \Delta OHP^b$, or equivalently if $NHAE > NGSE + ASP^b$. ($\Delta OGS > \Delta OHP^b$ implies that $\Delta GHB > \Delta BSP^b$, which in turn implies that $NHAE > NGSE + ASP^b$.) The right-hand side is the amount of tax K pays plus his loss from reducing his activity from P^b to S, and the left-hand side is his gain due to the conscience effect. This can still be regarded as an extreme case since the total conscience effect is larger than the external effect. A more likely case is for the conscience effect to move K's marginal valuation from MV_K^a to the dashed curve. Then $NH'A'E < NGSE = IOSE$. K will then be made worse off by the tax, but his loss will be less than the amount indicated by the traditional analysis due to the conscience effect. The area $NH'A'E$ is ignored in the traditional analysis. For cases where the conscience (and the associated disturbance) effects are significant, corrective taxes do not just lead (after accounting for the tax revenue but ignoring transaction costs) to gains in triangular areas such as ΔEPC, but also to gains in trapezoid areas, such as $NH'A'E$. If the conscience (including the associated disturbance) effects are not insignificant, the importance of the externality problem is greatly enhanced. Even if the conscience effect is relatively small, it should not be ignored as it is of first-order magnitude in comparison with the traditional second-order cost of a marginal misallocation.

7.5 The Coase theorem and liability rules*

One of the most controversial topics in connection with the problem of externality involves the so-called Coase theorem (Coase, 1960). In essence, it is argued that the problem of externality is a two-way one. Avoiding harm to *J* will inflict harm on *K*. In the absence of transaction costs the two parties will agree to an optimal outcome irrespective of who has to pay compensation. Hence the assignment of property rights does not affect the outcome (the presence of even very small transaction costs may cause problems – see Dixit and Olson, 2000).

Referring back to Figure 7.2, suppose that a certain activity by *K* affects *J*, say through the emission of smoke. If *K* has the right to emit smoke he will carry his activity up to *P*. But in the absence of transaction costs *J* will agree to pay *K* to reduce his activity to level *S*. On the other hand if *K* does not have the right to emit smoke he will pay *J* to let him do so. The optimal level of the activity will still be arrived at. At this optimal point, *S*, where the two *MV* curves intersect, no further gain is possible.

There are several qualifications to the above argument. First, if the income effects are not negligible the *MV* curve of each party will be different, depending on whether she or he has to pay or to receive compensation. Thus the point of intersection of the two curves may differ according to the assignment of property rights. However, while the presence of income effects will affect the activity level it will not affect the Pareto optimality of the outcome. It just means that a different Pareto optimum will be reached due to a change in distribution effected through different assignments of property rights (Ng, 1971a, pp. 176–7).

Second, the proviso 'in the absence of transaction costs' is important. If the transaction costs are not negligible a Pareto optimal outcome may not necessarily be achieved by mutual agreement. Moreover even in the absence of transaction costs, as observed in Section 7.3, the presence of game-strategic behaviour alone might prevent an optimal solution from being reached. It is possible to extend the definition of transaction costs to include the cost arising from game strategic behaviour or any other factor that impedes the attainment of Pareto optimality. Then Coase's theorem will be formally valid but will become just a tautology (Calabresi, 1968; Swan, 1975; Bernholz, 1997). In the real world where transaction costs, strategic behaviour, blackmail and so on are all present or possible, the optimum assignment of property rights is a tremendously complicated matter even if only the efficiency and not the equity aspect of the problem is being considered (Walsh, 1975; Ng, 1975b). As an example, consider the first-party priority rule.

Barring strategic behaviour, if the transaction costs of reaching an agreement between the parties to an existing externality are negligible, a Pareto-optimal outcome will emerge no matter how the property right is assigned. However the assignment of property rights will affect future decisions. For example if parties affected by factory smoke are entitled to receive compensation, this will tend to encourage people to build houses close to the factory without regard for the smoke effect, since they will be compensated.

This may result in socially inefficient decisions. Moreover blackmailers who actually have no intention of building houses nearby may threaten to do so in order to extort payment from the factory. In the absence of transaction costs (in the all-inclusive definition), all relevant parties will come to a Pareto-optimal agreement. But while the assumption of negligible transaction costs between two parties may be reasonable for some cases, the transaction costs between one party and all potentially affected parties (including blackmailers) must be enormous. Hence inefficiency is likely to result.

To overcome the above weakness of the bargaining solution it has been proposed that, in order to avoid inefficiency and blackmail, in general it should be the second party rather than the affecting party who should have to pay compensation (Ng, 1971a, p. 171). The following discussion shows that the first-party priority rule is not without limitation. While the affected-party priority rule encourages people to pretend to be affected, the first-party priority rule may encourage people to pretend to be first parties. For example, in anticipation of an expansion of a city's residential area, shrewd but unscrupulous people may set up smoke-emitting factories on the outskirts of the city and wait to profit from the compensation paid by future residents. However, since it is usually more difficult to distinguish true second parties from blackmailers than it is to identify true first parties, the first-party priority rule may still be of some merit, although many other factors must be taken into account. One of the main difficulties of the bargaining solution is that, no matter how property rights are assigned or what liability rule is adopted, it tends to be *one-sided* and fails adequately to tackle the two-sided nature of the externality problem. The payment of compensation only makes the payer take into account the cost he or she imposes on others, and fails to make the receiver and prospective receivers of compensation take account of the cost they impose on the payer. In this regard it seems that the bilateral tax/subsidy scheme is superior, provided it is not too costly to administer.

Third, the Coase theorem ignores the conscience effect. Consider Figure 7.8, where K's MV curve is MV_K^a if the activity does not involve any unpaid-for external cost. The presence of this cost, represented by MV_J, reduces K's MV curve to MV_K^b. If J compensates K to reduce his activity from P^b to S^b, the net gain of the activity (not the change in the activity level) after this mutual agreement is $\Delta HIL = HOS^bL$ (K's benefit) $- IOS^b L$ (J's loss). On the other hand if K compensates J for damages sustained he will have a better conscience and therefore his MV curve will be MV_K^a. The activity level will occur at S. More importantly the net gain will now be ΔNIE, which is larger than ΔHIL by $NHLE$. This extra gain is due to the conscience effect. In fact the gain from the conscience effect may be larger than $NHLE$ because the valuation K places on the payment by J may be less than its face value. It is likely that one would rather receive money from some neutral source

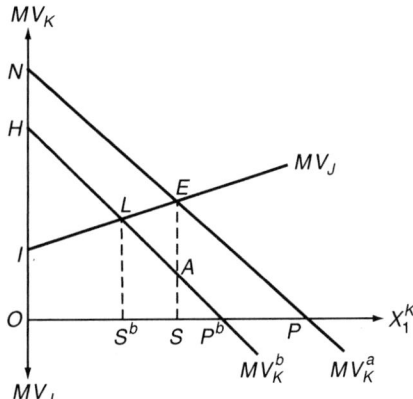

Figure 7.8

than from someone who is externally affected by one's activity. On the other hand the conscience effect is unlikely to operate if the affected party (say, a householder) receives compensation from the affecting party (say, a smoke-emitting factory). Thus even in the absence of transaction costs and strategic behaviour it may be better that the affecting party rather than the affected party pays compensation, even if we ignore the question of equity. However this may contradict the first-party priority rule, which again suggests the possible superiority of the bilateral taxation scheme. At the risk of repetition, it must be noted that the actual choice of a method to tackle an externality has to take many factors into account, including the costs of administration.

Coase's analysis has been interpreted to mean that the Pigovian solution is incorrect by being only one-sided (see for example He, 2000). Thus my proposal for imposing pollution and congestion taxes on cars and petrol was criticised for ignoring Coase's analysis. He (2000, p. 4) writes, 'Obviously... [Ng] is wrong. His mistake is exactly the Pigovian tradition criticized by Coase. He considers only the damage on one side, that of external costs of the usage of private cars.... But he forgets to calculate another account: the restriction of the usage of private cars results in how much losses on individual utilities, the car and other related industries in China?' This pervasive influence of Coase prompted me to reconsider his criticism of the Pigovian tradition. This reconsideration (Ng, 2001b) was as follows. While Coase is correct to emphasise the reciprocal nature of an externality problem (avoiding harm to J will inflict harm on K), he ignores an important asymmetry. At the initial private equilibrium, before accounting for the external effect (either by agreement, taxation or some other method), the incremental harm to J (the sufferer of the external cost, say, pollution) is supramarginal (that is, significantly larger than infinitesimally small – CP

in Figure 7.2), while the harm to K (the polluter) of marginally reducing the damage-causing activity is infinitesimal. This is because K has optimised with respect to the level of the activity under his control but J has no control over it. This ignored asymmetry renders a Pigovian tax welfare-improving, as shown in a mathematical model that even gives J recourse to reduce the damages of the external effects, at some cost to herself. Coase's failure to notice the asymmetry is probably due to his style of argument, using only verbal reasoning and examples with all-or-nothing comparisons. In terms of Figure 7.2, Coase compares point P with point O, and with the case where J moves elsewhere or installs some preventive device that completely avoids all external costs. He does not compare point P with an intermediate position, such as S. Not using mathematical models frees Coase from being captured, like many other theorists, by pure techniques (for an example see Section 10.3 below). This partly explains his success in concentrating on the important conceptual issues. Nevertheless, foregoing both mathematical and graphical methods does take a toll in that it makes the analysis too rudimentary and fails to uncover the simple asymmetry. To be a good economic analyst one has to learn the proper use of techniques but not be blinded by them and fail to see the real issues.

Despite the reciprocal nature of the externality emphasised by Coase, a case for amenity rights (or the principle of polluter pays) can be made on the following grounds (Ng, 2001b): (1) the Coase theorem is invalid in the presence of conscience effects; (2) The likely effects on future decisions; and (3) the underprovision of environmental quality due to its global public-good and long-term nature and the relative unimportance, at least in rich countries, of additional material production in comparison with environmental quality (the last point will be discussed in Chapter 11).

7.6   Summary

An externality is present when a utility/production function depends on a variable that is not under the control of the relevant consumer/producer and this dependence is not effected through the market relationship. If a person's activity puts an external diseconomy (economy) on others, the level of the activity tends to be higher (lower) than socially optimal. Different methods can be used to tackle this problem: a Pigovian tax (subsidy) on the external diseconomy (economy) according to the marginal external cost (benefit) involved; mutual agreement with compensation between the parties involved; government regulations and so on. The Coase theorem states that, in the absence of transaction costs, a Pareto-optimal outcome will be arrived at by mutual agreement irrespective of whether the affecting or the affected party is liable to pay compensation. However some tax on pollution is efficient as the marginal damages caused by pollution exceed its marginal benefits, an asymmetry ignored in Coase's all-or-nothing comparison. Liability rules may also be important if we take account of issues such as blackmail, equity and the 'conscience effect', whereby the affecting party's welfare may be reduced by the fact that she or he is adversely affecting the welfare of others without paying compensation. This conscience effect may make the problem of externality much more important than is suggested by traditional analyses.

8
Public Goods

In the previous chapters, especially Chapter 2, we were mainly concerned with an economy of private goods. But public goods are an increasingly important part of the overall economy, and in a certain sense are a special kind of externality in consumption. We discussed problems of externality in the previous chapter but our discussion mainly concentrated on one party affecting another. Significant external effects such as pollution (public bads) affect large numbers of individuals and can be regarded as involving an external diseconomy aspect and a public aspect. Hence this chapter is relevant not only to the more traditional subject of the provision of public goods but also to solving the problem of public bads, as well as other social issues that involve a large number of individuals simultaneously (issues such as the environment, health, knowledge and peace are public goods at the global level – see Kaul *et al.*, 1999).

8.1 Basic characteristics of public goods

What is the basic characteristic that distinguishes public goods from private goods? Of the several that have been suggested, two have been widely discussed. First, the same unit of a public good can be consumed by many individuals: its availability to one does not diminish its availability to others. This is called 'non-rivalry in consumption'. Examples of goods that possess this characteristic are national defence and radio and television broadcasting. My tuning in to a certain broadcast in no way reduces its availability to other listeners. Conversely once I have eaten an apple it can no longer be consumed by others. Two persons may share an apple but they will each eat only half. Hence such goods as apples, bread, and so on are private goods. However there are goods that fall between the polar cases of purely public and purely private. For example books in libraries can be borrowed by different readers over different periods but not at the same time. In fact even the books on my own shelves have some degree of publicness since my students and colleagues quite often drop in to borrow them. However in this case, since there is a prime beneficiary/owner, they are best regarded as goods with external effects – that is, a common consumption externality – instead of public goods (the borrowing imposes negligible costs on me except when, occasionally, some borrowers forget to return the books and I forget who borrowed them).

The second proposed characteristic of public goods is 'non-excludability'. That is, once a good is provided to some individuals it is impossible, or at least very costly, to exclude others from benefiting from it. Defence is again a good example. It is also difficult to exclude people from receiving television signals. But licensing can be used as a (usually not very effective) method and cable television as an effective but costly method of exclusion. Moreover the exclusion cost is almost never zero, even for purely private goods, since the production and distribution of all goods require the maintenance of law and order.

A characteristic that is both similar to and the opposite of non-excludability is 'non-rejectability'. Defence can again be cited as an example. If your country has been defended from foreign invasion you too are defended, even if you would prefer the chaos created by invasion. But non-rejectability is more important in respect of public bads (pollution and so on).

If a good is perfectly non-rivalrous, once provided it can be made available to all the individuals concerned at no additional cost. If a good is both perfectly non-excludable and non-rejectable it must be consumed by the same amount by all individuals concerned. The qualification 'concerned' here refers to the distinction between local, national and global public goods. For example certain forms of broadcasting can be received only within a given geographical area while others can be picked up almost all over the world.

A characteristic that is of relevance here is that of decreasing average costs, as discussed by Baumol (1977). Quite often a good is not perfectly non-rivalrous, for example broadcasting (given the programme, the place and the strength of transmission), but once some units of it have been produced additional units can be supplied at very low cost. For example the marginal cost (MC) of supplying your copy of this book was probably only a small fraction of the price since the bulk of the cost of publication consists of the fixed costs of writing, typing, editing, administration, typesetting and so on. However, many economists regard the question of decreasing costs as a separate issue from that of public goods since the production of both public and private goods may be subject to decreasing, increasing or constant costs. Basically this is due to two different dimensions of the good involved. For example the publication of a book involves both the length (and/or quality) and the number of copies printed (or more generally the number of consumers served). For a pure public good the MC with respect to the second dimension is zero, but it may be decreasing, increasing or constant with respect to the first dimension. In the following paragraph the first dimension is held constant.

Average costs (ACs) may be decreasing due to a substantial fixed cost component or to decreasing MCs. The latter case, however, is very rare and unimportant (in this case 'decreasing costs' as such need not have anything to do with publicness). Let us therefore concentrate on the case of substantial fixed costs. For concreteness, consider the publication of a book such as this. Once it is decided to publish the book the fixed costs are committed and the book can serve any number of readers without diminishing its availability to others. It clearly possesses the characteristic of non-rivalry. It is true that the MC of printing and distributing additional copies is not zero but it can be treated as a separate part. Moreover this is true for most public goods. Take television, the broadcasting part of which is a pure public good. But you need a TV receiver (plus electricity) to benefit from the broadcast. Clearly a TV set is not costless and is a private good. It corresponds to a copy of this book while the broadcasting corresponds to the writing and publication of the book. The main difference is that TV broadcasting and TV sets are usually produced by quite separate groups but the same is not true for the publication of books. Nevertheless, in some cases of cable broadcasting, both the broadcasting and the TV sets are provided by the same organisation. On the other hand it is also conceivable that the public good aspect of books is recognised, so that books approved by independent selection committees may have their fixed costs paid for, be supplied to competitive distributors at marginal cost and may be freely copied. In fact some universities and research institutions are fulfilling a small part of this function by subsidising the publication of books, although because of their limited funds they usually price their books so as to minimise their losses rather than at marginal cost (which may involve more losses).

It could be objected that, if we regard the fixed cost component of a good as a public good, virtually all goods are public goods or possess a public good aspect. It is true that the production of most goods involves fixed costs (for example capital equipment) in the short run. But if the capital equipment is utilised close to capacity, output cannot increase without significantly increasing the MC. If the total market demand is large relative to the output of a firm, perfect competition ensures a long-run equilibrium of price = MC = AC. This is, then, a clear case of a private good. Even if the efficient size of production is large and there is a monopolist operating at the range of decreasing AC, the industry may still be more efficiently run privately, though the fixed-cost component can be regarded as possessing a public good aspect. This is partly a problem of the relative importance of the fixed cost component and partly a problem of the relative efficiency of private versus public production.

Some economists (notably Musgrave, 1959, 1969a) emphasise the non-excludability aspect of public goods, arguing that, with excludability, non-rivalrous goods can be effectively provided by private production.

But if we do not regard public production as a necessary and sufficient condition for a public good, it seems analytically more fruitful to regard non-rivalry as the basic defining characteristic and accept other characteristics, such as non-excludability and non-rejectability as factors that make the good more difficult to be provided by private production. According to this view we can then have excludable public goods, non-excludable public goods and so on.

8.2 Optimality conditions and the financing of public goods

8.2.1 The traditional simple condition

Due to the nature of a public good the (top-level) optimality condition for its provision is quite different from that for private goods in the form $MRS^i = MRT$, as discussed in Chapter 2. In the case of a pure private good, the sum of the amounts consumed by various individuals equals the net amount produced. In the case of a pure public good the total amount produced is (or at least can be) simultaneously consumed by all individuals. Because of this difference it can be shown (see Appendix 8.1) that the Pareto-optimality condition for the supply of a public good is characterised by $\sum MRS^i = MRT$, that is, the sum over all individuals of the marginal rate of substitution (of the public good for a numeraire private good) is equal to the marginal rate of transformation (Samuelson, 1954, 1955). The reason for this optimality condition is not difficult to see. Once a public good is provided it can be enjoyed by all individuals. Pareto optimality requires that it be made available to all, and it is the sum of the marginal benefits for all individuals that should be compared with the MC of providing it when determining the optimal amount of the public good. The MRS and MRT are just respectively measures of the marginal benefits (or marginal valuations) and marginal costs in terms of the numeraire good.

The condition for the optimal supply of a public good is illustrated in Figure 8.1. For simplicity, assume that there are only two individuals whose marginal valuations of the public good X (measured along the horizontal axis) are represented by MV^J and MV^K respectively. Abstracting from income effects, these MV curves also correspond to individual demand curves.[1]

---

1. Income effects may shift the *MV* curves. Strictly speaking, therefore, the optimal supply of a public good is not independent of the way it is financed – see Strotz (1958), Samuelson (1969), McGuire and Aaron (1969), Bergstrom and Cornes (1981). However for most cases, within the relevant range of cost shares, the degree of indeterminacy is trivial.

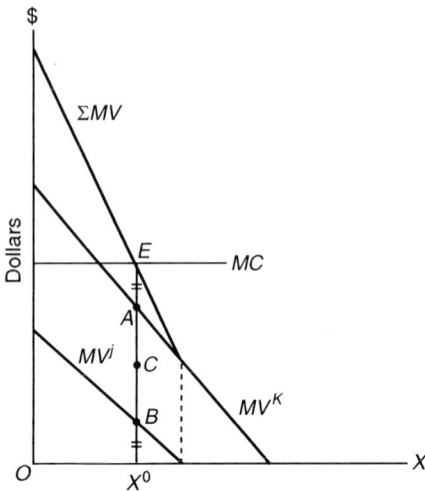

Figure 8.1

The vertical sum of the individual MV curves (denoted ΣMV) intersect the MC curve at the point E. This determines the optimal amount, X^0, of the public good. At this amount of the good, $\Sigma MV (= BX^0 + AX^0 = EX^0) = MC.$[2]

8.2.2 Accounting for excess costs in financing public goods: Pigou versus Kaplow

Once a pure public good is produced it does not cost anything to make it available to more individuals. Thus it seems desirable to make it available to all. But should those who have access to the good pay for the cost of producing it? Suppose we charge each individual a price equal to $1/I$ of the cost of producing the good, where I is the number of individuals. Then those individuals who benefit only slightly from the good may choose not to consume it. This may be undesirable, since the cost of making the good available to them is zero. We could charge these individuals a low price and charge those who benefit more a higher price (ideally, each individual would face a marginal price that was equal to her marginal valuation, which

---

2. The MC curve is drawn as horizontal in Figure 8.1, which is not essential for the analysis. A horizontal MC = AC curve may be due to constant costs of production. Alternatively we can define the units of X so as to make the cost curve horizontal. If there is a significant fixed cost element there will be an initial section of X that is subject to an all-or-nothing choice. If the MC of producing the 'natural unit' of the public good is decreasing, this may outbalance the diminishing MV to result in increasing MV curves in X, defined to make the cost curve horizontal.

would achieve a Lindahl equilibrium),[3] but then consumers might try to conceal their true MV in order to qualify for a low price, resulting in an undersupply of the public good. This is the problem of preference revelation, often referred to as the 'free-rider' problem, which will be discussed further below.

What about making the public good free and financing it from general taxes? The problem here is that the collection of taxes may involve costs, the so-called 'excess burden' of taxation (however, as argued below, economists may overestimate the costs of public spending). Taking account of the budget constraint of the public sector, it might be better to charge a positive price even for pure (but excludable) public goods. A positive price would reduce the amount that has to be financed from taxes and hence reduce the excess burden of taxation, though at the cost of discouraging some consumers from consuming the full amount of the public good in question. It is a matter of striking an optimal balance between the two inefficiencies. Moreover, without charging a price how can we ascertain the extent to which the public benefits from the public good? In the case of a private good, consumers have to pay for it and hence their preferences are revealed through their willingness to pay. If they do not have to pay directly for the consumption of public goods, how can we know that it is worth the cost of supplying them? (Again the problem of preference revelation.) Therefore making consumers pay for public goods may be superior to the alternative of supplying them free, despite involving some inefficiencies in comparison with the ideal. The problem of the optimal provision of public goods is more complicated than the simple condition $\sum MRS = MRT$ discussed above.

Even if the provision of public goods is financed by general tax revenues we still have to consider the possible excess costs of taxation. For a dollar of public spending, non-economists typically cost it at one dollar. However economists typically cost it at well in excess of one dollar. A prominent economist (Feldstein, 1997) puts it at \$2.65. Such a high estimate of the cost of public spending suggests that public goods should be expected to yield very high benefits if their provision is to be worthwhile. This conception probably partly accounts for the world-wide trend towards cuts in public spending.

The costs of public revenue include not only its direct cost (the amount of taxes imposed) but also the costs of administration, compliance, policing

---

3. For an exposition of Lindahl's analysis see Johansen (1963). For a generalisation see Vega (1987). For the achievement of this Wicksell–Lindahl solution through cooperation between individuals and competition between governments see Khanna (1993) and Breton (1996) respectively. For a mechanism to implement the Lindahl allocation see Tian (2000).

and distortion. While the first three types of cost are substantial they do not vary significantly from the amount of tax revenue raised. Hence, concentrating on the marginal costs of public spending, economists emphasise distortionary costs or the excess burden of taxation due to the fact that taxes distort the free choice of individuals, especially in terms of discouraging work effort, that is, the disincentive effect. At least since the time of Pigou (1928), economists have insisted that the benefits of public goods must exceed their direct costs by a sufficient amount to outweigh the excess burden of taxation. An authoritative textbook (Stiglitz, 1988, p. 140) puts the Pigovian principle this way: 'Since it becomes more costly to obtain public goods when taxation imposes distortions, normally this will imply that the efficient level of public goods is smaller than it would have been with nondistortionary taxation.' It is known that this general rule is subject to qualifications due to the presence of considerations such as complementarity/substitutarity between public and private goods (see, for example Atkinson and Stiglitz, 1980; King, 1986; Batina, 1990; Wilson, 1991; Chang, 2000). Specific cases or conditions under which the efficient level of public goods is not affected have also been identified (Christiansen, 1981; Boadway and Keen, 1993; Konishi, 1995).

In contrast to minor qualifications and special cases, a wholesale onslaught on the Pigou principle has been made by Kaplow (1996), who argues that public goods can be financed without additional distortion by using an adjustment to the income tax that offsets the benefits of the public good.

> [The] preexisting income tax schedule is adjusted so that, at each income level, the tax change just offsets the benefits from the public good. By construction, an individual's net reward from any level of work effort will be unaltered; any reduction in disposable income due to the tax adjustment is balanced by the benefits from the public good. Because an individuals' after-tax utility as a function of his work effort will thus be unchanged, his choice of work effort – and utility level – will also be unaffected (ibid., p. 514).[4]

For example if the benefit of a public good is proportional to the income level of the taxpayers it could be financed by a proportional income tax or an increase in income tax. While the proportional income tax may involve

---

4. The adjustment in income tax is similar to the use of a more progressive tax/transfer schedule to replace preferential treatment of the poor in our argument for treating a dollar as a dollar in each specific issue (Appendix 9.1). Thus the Kaplow principle of using the simple benefit/cost rule of unity can be viewed as an application of the principle of a dollar is a dollar. However I was unaware of this application for years after proving the more general principle.

a disincentive effect, when the tax and the public good are taken together there is no disincentive effect. For example suppose that the benefit from police protection of property is proportional to the income level of taxpayers. With a higher degree of police protection financed by a higher proportional income tax, individuals benefit more (in comparison with a lower degree of protection and lower tax) and pay more by the same amount if they earn more, leaving the incentive structure unaffected.

While Kaplow's argument has to be qualified in the presence of tax evasion, heterogeneity among individuals at the same income level, benefits from public goods being a function of people's ability rather than their income and so on, its main thrust is valid, as argued in Ng (2000b). How do we reconcile this with the orthodox position regarding the high costs of public spending? First, Feldstein (1997) obtains his high estimate of $2.65 by including policy-intended effects as unwanted distortions. He emphasises that higher tax rates may not only reduce the supply of labour and capital, but could also change the forms in which individuals take their compensation, including more spending on things that are tax deductible. While correctly including tax-induced expenditure on luxurious working conditions, he also includes other tax-deductible items such as charitable gifts and health care as involving distortions. However these items are what society/ the government wants to encourage either on external benefit grounds (for example the prevention of communicable diseases), or on the grounds of poverty reduction and perhaps merit wants (though the last ground is more controversial – see Appendix 12.1). Provided the extent of tax deductibility is not excessive, either no net distortion is created or the extent of the distortion is offset by the benefits, as demonstrated more formally in Ng (2000b).

Second, Feldstein's high estimate ignores the argument by Kaplow (1996) that while the cost of a dollar of public spending on the revenue side may be much higher than $1, the excess can be largely offset by the positive incentive (or negative disincentive) effects of the spending side. If the benefits of public spending are not positively correlated with income such that there are no positive incentive effects on the spending side and only disincentive effects on the revenue side, there is a distributional benefit since the rich pay more and the poor pay less.

Since high tax rates also encourage tax avoidance and evasion, and since some of the higher benefits of public goods are related more to unobservable earning ability than to observable income levels, the positive incentive effects on the spending side generally do not completely offset the distortive effects on the revenue side, making a dollar of public spending cost in excess of a dollar, taking both sides into account. However, as argued below, other considerations suggest either that the cost of a dollar of public spending should be significantly reduced (possibly to below one dollar or even towards zero) or that the benefits of public spending should be significantly increased from those normally estimated by economists.

8.2.4   Accounting for environmental effects, relative-income effects and burden-free taxes

Even before taking account of Kaplow's (1996) argument, as discussed above, the costs of public spending are overestimated due to the failure to take adequate account of environmental effects, relative-income effects and burden-free taxes.

The production and consumption of most goods and services have a significant effect on the environment either directly or indirectly through input usage, including various forms of pollution, congestion, deforestation and so on. Ideally taxes should be imposed in accordance with the estimated costs to society of the environmental damage caused. However, largely speaking this does not happen. General taxes on income and consumption, though designed mainly to raise revenue, could in fact serve to counteract the environmental effects involved. Thus far from being distortive, taxation could be corrective; instead of imposing excess burdens or distortionary costs, taxation could serve to improve efficiency. Given that tax rates are around 30 per cent in most countries and given the severity of the environmental effects, this might well be the case, especially if a long-term global view is taken. At the very least the distortive costs of taxation are much lower than those estimates that fail to take account of environmental damage. Most such estimates (for example the one by Feldstein, 1997, mentioned above) do not consider environmental effects.

The importance of relative incomes (an individual's income relative to those of others) is beyond doubt and was discussed as long ago as the 1800s by economists such as Rae (1834). However their relevance to the costs of public spending has been ignored. Leaving aside concern for the poor, most people (with the exception of those at starvation level) would not like everybody else's income to double while their income increased only by 5 per cent. For an individual, an increase in income increases both their absolute and their relative incomes and is therefore very important. If the friends/ schoolmates of your child receive expensive birthday gifts, you may also feel obliged to give your child an expensive one. If all your friends have luxurious cars, you may feel less satisfied with your standard one. In the case of public goods, however, as these are simultaneously consumed by all individuals there are no such relative pressures. This causes a bias in favour of private spending or against public spending. The benefits of public spending are often underestimated and are effectively equivalent to an overestimation of the costs. In most estimates the marginal benefit of private expenditure is likely to include the absolute-income and intrinsic-consumption effects *plus* the internal or direct relative-income effect (as these two taken together constitute the worth of private consumption as it appears to each individual), but not to include the negative-external or indirect relative-income effects. This creates an overemphasis on private expenditure, leading to a suboptimal level of public spending, as demonstrated by Ng (1987b; see also Chapter 11).

Economists regard a tax of $1 million as generally imposing on the economy a burden in excess of $1 million – say, $1.35 million (the $2.65 million estimated by Feldstein is remarkably high; $1.35 million is about the average estimate). One million dollars of the burden is exactly offset by the tax revenue, while the $0.35 million represents an excess burden or a deadweight loss created by the distortion of choice. While most economists realise that corrective taxes on, say, pollution involve a negative excess burden or a positive efficiency gain burden-free taxes are regarded as existing only in fairyland. However there are goods taxes that create not only no *excess* burden (the $0.35 million) but also no burden at all ($1 million). These are pure diamond goods, or goods valued for their actual value rather than their intrinsic consumption effects. As discussed in Section 4.7, taxes on pure and mixed diamond goods impose either no, less or even a negative burden, not to mention an excess burden.

In addition to the above factors, recent evidence shows that higher incomes do not significantly increase happiness or other quality-of-life indicators. If increased private consumption does not increase happiness, the provision of public goods that reduce private consumption through taxation may be costly in monetary terms but may have a negligible, if any, cost in happiness terms. As happiness is our ultimate objective but money is not, drastic reconsideration of the costs of public spending may be needed.

According to the various factors discussed above, the costs of public spending have been grossly overestimated. While it is desirable to do away with inefficient public spending, increased public spending, especially on research and environmental protection, could substantially increase our welfare. Therefore the recent trend to check the growth in public spending could be extremely counterproductive. In fact Ng and Ng (2001) show that economic growth increases the optimal share of public spending, and that, if environmental damage is not dealt with head-on, economic growth may reduce welfare even if the shares of public spending and environmental protection are optimised.

In addition to the above considerations, public spending on research on environmental protection is likely to continue to be grossly suboptimal, due to its long-term, global, public-good nature. A cleaner environment would benefit the whole world for generations to come, but decisions taken by national governments have a relatively short time horizon, resulting in suboptimal spending in this area. This suggests the need for an international cooperative drive to increase funding for research on environmental protection. However the relative-income effects at the individual level discussed above also apply to the national level, resulting in international competition for income growth, a bias against public spending and disregard for environmental degradation. This further strengthens the argument for international cooperation, the success of which would partly depend on widespread appreciation of the points presented here.

8.3   An incentive-compatible mechanism for preference revelation*

As discussed above, preference revelation is a very important issue in the provision of public goods. But the free-rider problem was long regarded as unremediable in a world of imperfect knowledge and individual self-interest. Hence the discovery of an *incentive-compatible* mechanism whereby self-interested individuals would be induced to reveal their true preference for public goods could rightly be hailed as a landmark in the theory of public goods, and in economics in general. Nonetheless Tideman and Tullock (1976), while regarding the proposed mechanism as of vital importance, warned their readers that it would not cure cancer or stop tides!

The mechanism was discovered independently by Clarke (1971, 1972) and Groves (1970, 1973, 1976; see Groves and Loeb, 1975; Groves and Ledyard, 1977a; Groves *et al.*, 1987; Page, 1988). Hence we shall call it the Clarke–Groves mechanism.[5] While the mechanism takes account of such complicated matters as general equilibrium (see Groves and Ledyard, 1977a; Pethig, 1979) and dynamic procedures (Green and Laffont, 1978a), we shall just consider the more essential parts of the mechanism, mainly following the exposition by Tideman and Tullock (1976). Consider Figure 8.2a, where X (measured along the horizontal axis) may be taken either as the number of units of a public good at a cost of $1 each, or the total dollar expenditure on the public good. The horizontal line through the $1 mark represents the MC curve. The Clarke–Groves mechanism can be broken down into the following steps.

In step 1 each consumer is allocated a percentage share of the total cost of providing the public good, with $\Sigma s^i = 1$, where s^i is the cost share of individual *i*. Thus the cost of producing the good (irrespective of the amount produced) is adequately covered by the levies. For the moment we shall take the method of determining the shares as given, either by convention, by equal shares or determined arbitrarily.

In step 2 consumers are asked to report their MV curves (they need not be linear), which are then summed vertically to give $\sum_{i=1}^{I} MV^i$, whose intersection with the MC curve determines the amount of the public good to be supplied as X^0.

---

5. Green and Laffont (1977a) show that this is the only class of mechanism with the desired properties. Earlier Vickrey (1961) described a similar mechanism in connection with an optimal counterspeculation policy and price auction procedure, but was not fully aware of its significance. On various alternative versions of the mechanism see Loeb (1977). For a fairly comprehensive bibliography of the literature on demand-revealing mechanisms, see the introduction to the special issue on the topic of *Public Choice* (Spring, 1977). A monograph specifically tackling the problems of incentive-compatible mechanisms is Green and Laffont (1978b).

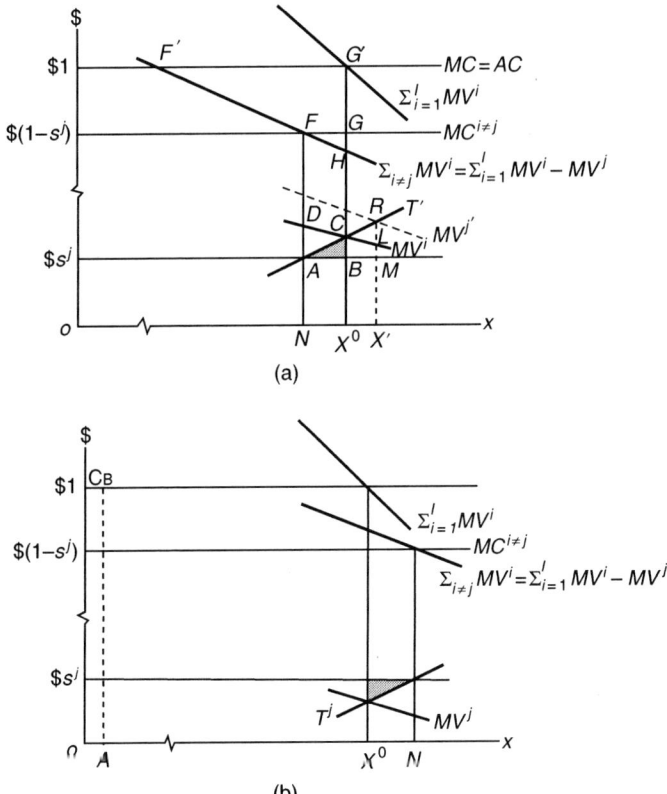

Figure 8.2

In step 3 each consumer, j, in addition to her or his share of the total cost of production discussed in step 1, has to pay a Clarke–Groves tax, which is determined in the following manner. A horizontal line is drawn through point $\$(1 - s^j)$. This line is labelled $MC^{i \neq j}$ since it is the marginal cost to all consumers other than j. The curve $\sum_{i \neq j} MV^i = \sum_{i=1}^{I} MV^i - MV^j$ is then drawn in. This is the aggregate MV of all consumers other than j. It intersects the $MC^{i \neq j}$ curve at a point (F) to the left of X^0 since the MV^j curve lies higher than the line through $\$s^j$ at point X^0 the reverse case is illustrated in Figure 8.2b. The Clarke–Groves tax on consumer j is then the difference between $MC^{i \neq j}$ and $\sum_{i \neq j} MV^i$ from point N to X^0 or (the curvilinear) ΔFHG. Drawing T^j as the mirror image of $\sum_{i \neq j} MV^i$, the tax also equals the shaded area ΔABC, where $BC = HG$. For the case in which MV^j lies below s^j at point X^0, illustrated in Figure 8.2b, $\sum_{i \neq j} MV^i$ intersects $MC^{i \neq j}$ at a point to the right of X^0. The Clarke–Groves tax is then the difference between $\sum_{i \neq j} MV^i$ and $MC^{i \neq j}$ from point N to X^0, or the shaded triangle.

The three steps described above are the basic outlines of the Clarke–Groves mechanism. We should now examine its rationale and the reason why it works. Point N is the amount of the public good that would be supplied if individual j were to report her MV as identical with her cost share, that is, the horizontal line through $\$s^j$. This is the level of supply preferred by all consumers other than j as a group, given s^j, since it is at this point (N) that $\sum_{i \neq j} MV^i$ intersects $MC^{i \neq j}$. By reporting a MV^j curve either above or below $\$s^j$, consumer j causes the amount of the public good provided to differ from N. Thus all other consumers suffer a loss measured by the shaded triangle. By making consumer j pay precisely this shaded triangle, she is motivated not to attempt to increase or reduce the supply of the public good from point N, unless by doing so she gains more than the loss to the other consumers. She will then find it in her interest to report her MV truthfully. To see this more clearly, suppose that j overstates her MV as $MV^{j\prime}$ (Figure 8.2a). This will cause the public good to be supplied at X'. Her MV on the extra amount, X^0X', is area $CX^0X'L$. But she has to pay an extra $X^0X'MB$ in cost share plus an extra $CBMR$ in the Clarke–Groves tax. Thus the net loss of misreporting is ΔCLR. Similarly, if she underreports her forgone benefit exceeds her saving in cost share and tax. Thus the best strategy for her is to report her MV curve truthfully. This argument for individual j is true for any $j = 1, \ldots, I$. Hence all individuals will be motivated to reveal their true preferences.

It should be noted that the purpose of assigning cost shares is to ensure adequate finance to cover the cost of providing the public good. If this cost could be met in a way that would not affect individual motivation, then the cost share would not have to be preassigned. The Clarke–Groves tax would still induce the revelation of true preferences, as shown towards the end of Section 7.2 with respect to externality (where no cost of production need be met). The Clarke–Groves tax for a typical consumer would then be a larger amount, being $\Delta F'HG'$ (Figure 8.2a) for consumer j.

Since the cost of providing the public good is already adequately met by the cost-sharing arrangement, the Clarke–Groves tax constitutes a surplus. In cases where the number of individuals is large, this surplus can be used to benefit the group as a whole without any significant effect on incentives to reveal true preferences. However, sophisticated individuals might take into account the effect of their reported MV curves on the amount of Clarke–Groves taxes others have to pay. If they have a share of the benefits of the surplus they may be motivated to misrepresent their preference. This is consistent with the impossibility finding by Hurwicz (1972) that in general no resource allocation mechanism can yield individually rational Pareto optima that are also incentive-compatible for each individual. But this finding was derived by ignoring the costs (time, trouble and conscience) of behaving in a strictly rational fashion. Therefore, or at least in the case of large numbers, the surplus produced by the Clarke–Groves tax can safely be used for the group as a whole without any adverse effect on preference revelation. Otherwise there would not be a correct preference revelation for private goods either. However in the case of a small number of individuals this adverse effect may be significant, for two reasons: each individual will have a larger share of the benefits from the surplus; and the surplus itself will be much larger as the Clarke–Groves tax on each individual decreases rapidly with the number of individuals (Green *et al.*, 1976). How can this difficulty be overcome?

Tideman and Tullock (1976) have made an interesting suggestion for the disposal of the Clarke–Groves surplus. They suggest that the surplus should be wasted and be regarded as a cost of the process of preference revelation. They justify this partly on the ground that, in the case of a large number of individuals, the surplus is only a small amount relative to the cost of providing the public good. Nevertheless, as argued in the preceding paragraph, it is when there are small numbers that the problem of surplus disposal is a real problem as small numbers usually mean a relatively larger surplus. This difficulty can largely be solved by slightly revising the assignment of cost shares discussed in Step 1. Right at the beginning a lower estimate is made for the total amount of Clarke-Groves tax to be collected. Out of the total cost of production, an amount equal to this estimate (say, *OABC* in Figure 8.2b) is set aside. In other words, costs in excess of this estimated amount are shared by the various consumers. In this revised scheme the amount of the surplus is still likely to be positive since the estimate is lower (to avoid losses of confidence), but it will only be a small amount. This can either be wasted or, better still, donated to an outside body.

Tideman and Tullock also have an interesting proposal for the assignment of cost shares, whereby a Lindahl equilibrium can be approximated.[6] An official is appointed to assign the cost shares,

> with the stipulation that from his pay we are going to subtract some multiple of the sum of the triangles [that is, the Clarke–Groves tax] for all the voters [that is, consumers]. The person assigning the fixed [cost] share would be motivated to try to minimise the triangles. In the limit, if he were able to perfectly achieve his goal, there would be no triangles and no loss (or surplus); we would have a perfect Lindahl equilibrium, with each voter paying for public goods according to his marginal evaluation' (ibid., p. 1156).

---

6. Compare the use of unanimous auction election to achieve a Lindahl equilibrium, as discussed by Smith (1977). This method has the advantage of making no one worse off (each individual has veto power) but also the possible disadvantage of a stalemate, as happened in one of the five experiments conducted by Smith (ibid., p. 1132). Smith and others have also conducted experiments with the incentive-compatible mechanism – see Smith (1979, 1980). See Ledyard (1995) and Chen (forthcoming) for surveys on recent literature in experimental tests of these mechanisms. For an alternative practical method of revealing preferences for public goods see Bohm (1984).

With an advanced econometric method, Tideman and Tullock believe that the official would be able to do quite well (though not perfectly, otherwise there would be no need for preference revelation) despite the fact that there is one piece of information he is not allowed to use when assigning the cost share of any individual: that individual's reported MV curves in previous choices. Otherwise the individual may be motivated to understate his or her MV curve in order to obtain a lower cost share in the future.

Having discussed the theory of the Clarke–Groves mechanism, what about its practicability in actual decision making? One difficulty that is regarded as serious by Tideman and Tullock is the fact that, in the case of a large number of consumers, each has very little incentive to go to the trouble of putting in a report since each report has very little effect on the amount of the public good supplied. This difficulty is relatively easy to resolve as long as a section (especially if it is a representative one) of the population does report, which is likely to happen. For those who fail to report, their MV curves are just taken to be their assigned cost shares (that is, the horizontal line through $\$s^j$). In terms of purely economic incentives it is those whose cost shares differ more from their MV at the margin (in either direction) who have a greater incentive to report, since the gain to each from reporting (such as $\triangle ACD$ in Figure 8.2a) will be larger. Thus it could be expected that the reporting section will be non-representative of the population in this sense. However it could be representative in the following sense. As long as the divergence is equal in each direction (that is, the proportion of reporting people with low MV relative to cost shares is as high as the proportion of reporting people with high MV relative to cost shares), the resulting supply of the public good will still be optimal from the view of the whole population. Even if the reporting section is not representative of the population in this latter sense, the resulting supply of the public good will still be optimal from the view of the reporters since non-reporters still have to pay their cost shares. A possible source of non-representativeness among the reporting section is the epistemological problem discussed below. It could be that the more educated section of the population will have a higher percentage of reporters. If they also have a higher than average MV, this could exaggerate the aggregate MV. However this bias will not be present if these better educated people have already been allocated higher cost shares in accordance with, say, econometric estimates of their MV. This is because, when estimating the aggregate MV, we add all the reported MV curves and the cost shares of non-reporters. This estimated aggregate MV will be less steep than the true one but will still intersect the MC curve at approximately the same place. If desired, econometric methods could also be used to correct (approximately) the divergence in the steepness. If the better educated people are not allocated higher cost shares, the estimated aggregate MV might not be representative of the whole population. Whether we should then use statistical methods to adjust for this bias will depend on whether we want to achieve optimality for the reporting section or for the whole population, or whether the failure to report should be taken as giving up one's potential gain of ΔACD.

Apart from the basic difficulty of coalition (see Section 5.4.2), the more important practical difficulties with the preference revelation scheme are epistemological, political and administrative.[7] Participants not only have to know how to reveal their preference by drawing their MV curves correctly, they also have to understand the full rationale of the scheme and therefore know that it will be advantageous for them to report truthfully. Anyone who has marked undergraduate examination papers will doubt that the average citizen will be able to achieve such an understanding. Perhaps what can best be hoped for is that they will trust the assurance of experts and draw their MV curves to the best of their ability. Second, the assignment of cost shares may not be politically acceptable. Whether the assignment is equal, arbitrary or decided by the Tideman–Tullock official, it is likely that many individuals will claim that their shares are excessive. Perhaps a politically more acceptable method of cost assignment would be to tie the cost shares to some extent with income levels since income is one of the major determinants of MV and this would be more consistent with the present method of financing public goods. Third, the costs of administering the scheme for large-number cases would be prohibitive. Nevertheless these costs could be significantly reduced by requiring only a sample of the population to report their MV curves (Green and Laffont, 1977b). While all individuals would have to pay the assigned cost shares, only those in the sample would have to report and pay the Clarke–Groves tax.

The sampling method has another advantage in that it could be used to mitigate the coalition difficulty by making the sample secret. If only 2000 out of 200 million individuals had to report it would be rather costly for any individual in the 2000 to find a partner, especially if attempts at coalition forming were declared illegal. In addition, if the time of sampling and the time of reporting were made as close as possible, coalitions might well be nigh impossible. Another method of preventing coalitions would be to disallow vertical MV curves. In our present continuous case, the counterpart

7. Groves and Ledyard (1977b, p. 107) also 'present five warnings intended to dampen any premature urge to adopt a constitutional amendment to institute one of these demand-revealing mechanisms'. Except with respect to the difficulty created by coalitions, I agree with the argument by Tideman and Tullock (1977) that these limitations are not very significant. While all known group decision mechanisms are subject to manipulation by coalitions, the demand-revealing mechanisms seem particularly vulnerable – see the second half of Section 5.4.2 above. For some practical issues see Bohm (1979). For a comparison of the survey and hedonic approaches to the empirical measurement of the value of public goods see Brookshire *et al.* (1982).

of reporting an arbitrarily high value (see the discrete case discussed in Section 5.4.2) would be for the coalition members to report the same vertical *MV* curve. For most public goods it can be reasonably assumed that it would be impossible for vertical MV curves to prevail. If individuals were constrained to report reasonably downward sloping MV curves, there would be a cost (in terms of the Clarke–Groves tax) to each coalition member who stuck to the agreed false MV curve. Hence if the reports were also classified confidential, each coalition member would have an incentive to betray the coalition and report truthfully (for other difficulties with coalition forming see Tullock, 1977).

As well as the difficulties mentioned above, there is the additional problem that many publicly provided goods, such as education, are not pure public goods. The reason these goods are publicly provided may be based more on the grounds of external benefits, merit wants, distributional considerations and so on than on the ground of non-rivalry in consumption. Hence we cannot simply rely on the Clarke–Groves mechanism discussed above to determine the optimal provision of public goods. For one thing, even if one were prepared to accept that individuals are the best judges of their own interest with respect to the consumption of private goods, one might reasonably be sceptical about the average citizen knowing the extent to which he or she would benefit from additional expenditure on preventive public health care to, among other things, reduce the outbreak of communicable diseases. Moreover the beneficiaries of the expenditure on health care would include the as yet unborn, who of course could not report their MV curves.

While the possibility of actually using the Clarke–Groves mechanism for most public goods is remote, its potential for application in specific cases cannot be denied. Moreover even if the Clarke–Groves mechanism has rather limited practical applicability, it must still be regarded as an important theoretical contribution since it shows that the problem of preference revelation is essentially one of practical difficulty rather than intrinsic intractability.

8.4   Income distribution as a peculiar public good: the paradox of redistribution*

While the concept of public goods is an important one, few practical examples of a pure public good can be found. However it has been suggested that, since some people may have a preference for the distribution of income (excluding the effects on their own income level), income distribution can be regarded as a pure public good (for empirical applications of the concept of income distribution as a public good, see Orr, 1976; Morawetz, 1977). Indeed income distribution can be seen as the purest of all public goods as it meets all the tests of a pure public good: 'Exclusion is impossible, consumption is nonrival; each individual must consume the same quantity' (Thurow, 1971, pp. 328–9). It can, however, be shown that income distribution as a public good has a peculiar nature that renders traditional analysis inappropriate in some sense. This peculiar nature can be called the paradox of redistribution (Ng, 1973a), which refers to the fact that, on counting the compensating or equivalent variations, it may seem as though a Pareto redistribution of income (that is, one that makes someone better and no one worse off due to utility interdependency – see Hochman and Rodgers, 1969, and the ensuing discussion) is possible, but in fact it is impossible. The Pareto optimality condition for a public good must correspondingly be revised as it is no longer in the simple form of the aggregate MRS. A verbal and geometrical discussion is provided below; the mathematics is in Appendix 8.1.

A Pareto improvement requires that no one be made worse off. If some individuals are made worse off by the production of a public good, for example a superhighway, the Pareto criterion may be met if they are sufficiently compensated and the rest of the community is still better off after paying the compensation. In other words if the maximum amount of money the gainers are willing to pay for a public good exceeds the cost of production plus the amount necessary to compensate the losers, a Pareto improvement is still possible. While this is true for other goods, it is not so for income distribution. In order to arrive at an income distribution without making anyone worse off, those who will be made worse off must be compensated. But once this compensation is paid, income distribution itself is changed.

A highly simplified example may be helpful. In a community of one rich man and two poor men, suppose that the poor men are strong egalitarians and each of them values each dollar transferred from the rich man to be shared equally by the two poor men at one dollar, that is, 50 cents in excess of what each of them receives. Suppose also that the rich man is self-centred and cares only for his own income. The aggregate benefit of the transfer of one dollar is therefore $2, which is larger than the cost of $1 to the rich man. The poor men are willing to pay a higher sum ($2) to buy a unit of the public good 'distributional equality' than that which is necessary to compensate the loser (the rich man). Assuming negligible administrative and efficiency costs, a Pareto improvement should be possible in the production of this public good if it is a normal public good. But as income distribution is a peculiar public good, Pareto redistribution may be impossible. Therefore as the rich man is self-centred he has to receive exactly one dollar in compensation for each dollar transferred to the poor. Society may decide to supply the public good 'equality' since the amount people are willing to pay exceeds the cost of production (which is negligible in this case) plus the necessary amount of compensation. However if the redistribution is to remain Pareto optimal the rich man has to be paid back exactly the same amount as that transferred. This leads back to exactly the initial situation, thus illustrating the fact that, with the peculiar public good 'income distribution', a Pareto improvement may not be possible even though the counting of compensating or equivalent variations suggests the reverse. (For a more elaborate graphical illustration see Ng, 1973a or 1979/1983. This paradox of redistribution is not the same as the Broadway paradox, which is due to a change in price, as discussed in Section 4.5.)

The above argument is not based on the fact that the rich man is self-centred. Even if he were to derive some satisfaction from a more equal distribution, a Pareto redistribution would still be impossible unless he (or they, in the case of many rich men) placed a higher valuation on more equal distribution than the amount of money he had to give up. If this were so, the Pareto redistribution would be automatically achieved in the case of one rich man just by his voluntary transfer. However in the case of many rich men, some coordinated action would be necessary and a Pareto optimal redistribution might not be realised in the free market because of problems with strategic behaviour, negotiating costs, information and so on.

8.5   Economic theories of clubs*

As not many goods are *pure* public goods, generalising to account for different types and degrees of 'impurity' is desirable. One such generalisation is the recognition that, for any given amount (and/or quality) of a public good, each consumer's satisfaction may be a function of the number of individuals consuming it. While some individuals may prefer to swim alone, most seem to prefer the presence of others. However if the capacity of the pool is overtaxed, most swimmers will suffer a loss of enjoyment. Thus after a certain point an additional consumer imposes a cost, in the form of reduced utility, on existing consumers. The number of consumers then becomes a variable to be optimised in the 'economic theory of clubs', as analysed by Buchanan (1965) and Ng (1973b, 1974a). The relevant Pareto optimality condition requires that any individual in the club (that is, consuming the public good) must derive a total benefit that is in excess of (or at least equal to) the aggregate marginal cost imposed on all other consumers in the club, and that the reverse holds for any individual who is not in the club. Instead of directly focusing on the number of consumers, Oakland (1972) takes as the crucial variable the degree of congestion, which in turn depends on the capacity of the public good and its degree of utilisation. (For a discussion of impure goods see De Serpa, 1978. For a geometric review of the economics of congestion see Porter, 1978.)

An alternative framework for the theory of clubs is to assume that an infinite number of individuals will form themselves into many clubs of the same or different sizes depending on assumptions about homogeneity or heterogeneity in tastes (Tiebout, 1956; Pauly, 1970; McGuire, 1974).

Under certain conditions the assumption of an infinite number of individuals allows each individual (club) to maximise her (its) benefit (average benefit) without violating the requirement of Pareto optimality since each individual can join the club that best suits her preference (Caplan, 2001a, questions the feasibility of this with respect to choice of the place of residence due to the high costs of movement). The assumption of an infinite number of individuals is crucial for this result. To understand this, consider a simple contrasting example of a finite number of individuals, zero congestion and the positive benefit of joining additional clubs. Thus ideally any club should be made available to any willing consumer. It then becomes clear that decentralised, non-discriminating financing cannot simultaneously meet the cost of production and the requirement of optimality. The proposition by Auster (1977, pp. 425–6) that competitive production results in the optimal provision of public goods in long-run equilibrium under the condition of imperfect information is therefore, at best, of limited applicability since there are usually not enough consumers to ensure the optimality of a competitive solution even if one exists.

The framework of an infinite number of individuals is suitable for problems where the number of clubs for the same good is large and the population is mobile across clubs, as in the case of group segregation in housing. The previous Buchanan–Ng framework, which concentrates on each particular club, is preferable when these conditions are not satisfied, for example when the location of consumers is given and transportation is not costless, and/or when there is just one or only a few clubs (on the application and generalisation of the Buchanan–Ng framework see Dodsworth, 1975; De Serpa, 1977; Sandler, 1977, 1997; Cornes and Sandler, 1996). Berglas's (1976) criticism of Ng (1973b) is based on the failure to distinguish between the two frameworks. Ng's analysis, which aims at Pareto optimality or maximising the total benefits of the entire population, has also been mistaken as maximising the total benefits of one club, which can be shown to be, in general, non-Pareto optimal (Helpman and Hillman, 1977; Brennan and Flowers, 1980). The last section in Ng (1973b) attempts, apparently not very successfully, to clarify this and similar confusions.

8.6 Summary

Non-rivalry in the consumption of a public good means that the optimality condition is couched in terms of the sum of the marginal rates of substitution. The question of whether the cost of providing public goods should be inflated to reflect the excess burden of taxation has been discussed in this chapter. The negative excess burden of public spending and the prevalence of relative income effects, environmental damage and burden-free taxes suggest that the costs of public spending have been grossly overestimated. The incentive-compatible mechanism whereby individuals might be motivated to reveal their true preferences has been examined in some detail and its practicability discussed. Viewing income distribution as a public good raises the paradox of redistribution, in which, on counting the compensating variations, it may seem that a Pareto redistribution is possible but in fact it is impossible. Two contrasting frameworks for the economic theory of clubs have also been outlined.

Appendix 8.1: The Paradox of Redistribution and the Paradox of Universal Externality**

The paradox of universal externality refers to the impossibility of expressing the Pareto optimality conditions in the simple terms of MRS.

The Pareto optimality condition for a pure public good is derived in the following model of one public good, X, and G private goods (the number of public goods can easily be increased). First, the utility functions of I individuals can be written as

$$U^i = U^i(x_1^i, \ldots, x_G^i, x)(i = 1, \ldots, I) \tag{A8.1}$$

where x_g^i is the amount of the gth private good consumed by individual i. The production constraint is written as

$$F(x_1, \ldots, x_G, X) = 0 \tag{A8.2}$$

where $x_g \equiv \sum_{i=1}^{G} x_g^i$. Note the difference between public and private goods: the total amount of the public good, X, enters the utility functions of all individuals simultaneously. Note also that, for simplicity, the production constraint is written in the implicit form, in contrast to Appendix 2.1.

To derive the Pareto optimality conditions we maximise U^1 subject to $U^i = \overline{U}^i$, $i = 2, \ldots, I$ and to the production constraint (Equation A8.2). Defining $\lambda^1 = 1$ and $\overline{U}^i \equiv 0$, the relevant Lagrangean function is

$$L = \sum_{i=1}^{I} \lambda^i(U^i - \overline{U}^i) - \theta F(x_1, \ldots, x_G, X) \tag{A8.3}$$

The first-order conditions are

$$\lambda^i U_g^i = \theta F_g \quad (i = 1, \ldots, I; g = 1, \ldots, G) \tag{A8.4}$$

$$\sum_{i=1}^{I} \lambda^i U_X^i = \theta F_X \tag{A8.5}$$

where $U_g^i \equiv \partial U^i/\partial x_g^i$, $U_X^i \equiv \partial U^i/\partial X$, $F_g \equiv \partial F/\partial x_g$, $F_X \equiv \partial F/\partial X$

As in Appendix 2.1, Equation A8.4 can be written in the proportional form:

$$U_g^i/U_G^i = F_g/F_G \quad (i = 1, \ldots, I; g = 1, \ldots, G - 1) \tag{A8.6}$$

which is the equality of the MRS across all individuals and with the MRT. To see that $F_X/F_Y = MRT_{XY}$, we totally differentiate $F(X, Y) = 0$ to obtain $F_X dX + F_Y dY = 0$, which yields $F_X/F_Y = -(dY/dX) = MRT_{XY}$.

Since $\lambda^i U_G^i$ is equal to θF_G for all i, Equation A8.5 can also be written in the proportional form by dividing it by $\lambda^i U_G^i$ and θF_G.

$$\sum_{i=1}^{I} (U_X^i/U_G^i) = F_X/F_G \tag{A8.7}$$

which is the equality of aggregate MRS with the MRT, the standard optimality condition for a public good, as illustrated in Figure 8.1.

Instead of a normal public good, now consider X as some measure of income distribution. The utility functions A8.1 are unchanged. But we have

$$X = X(M^1, \ldots, M^I) \tag{A8.8}$$

where $M^i = \sum_{g=1}^{G} p_g x_g^i$ is the income of individual i and p_g is the price of the gth good.

Ignoring the costs of redistribution for simplicity, the production constraint can be written as

$$F(x_1, \ldots, x_G) = 0 \tag{A8.9}$$

The relevant Lagrangean function in our maximisation problem is now

$$L = \sum_{i=1}^{I} \lambda^i (U^i - \overline{U}) - \theta F(x_1, \ldots, x_G) \tag{A8.10}$$

The corresponding first-order conditions are

$$\lambda^i U_g^i + \sum_{k=1}^{I} \lambda^k U_x^k X_i p_g = \theta F_g \quad (i = 1, \ldots, I; g = 1, \ldots, G) \tag{A8.11}$$

where $X_i \equiv \partial X/\partial M^i$, $U_X^k \equiv \partial U^k/\partial X$.

In proportional form, Equation A8.11 can be written as

$$\frac{U_g^i + p_g \sum \lambda^k U_x^k X_i/\lambda^i}{U_G^i + p_G \sum \lambda^k U_x^k X_i/\lambda^i} = \frac{F_g}{F_G} \quad (i = 1, \ldots, I; g = 1, \ldots, G - 1) \tag{A8.12}$$

which can be written as

$$\frac{U_g^i \left(1 + p_g \sum \lambda^k U_X^k X_i/\lambda^i U_g^i\right)}{U_G^i \left(1 + p_G \sum \lambda^k U_X^k X_i/\lambda^i U_G^i\right)} = \frac{F_g}{F_G} \quad (i = 1, \ldots, I; g = 1, \ldots, G - 1)$$

given the utility-maximising choice of consumers, $U_g^i/U_G^i = p_g/p_G$. Thus we may substitute $p_g = p_G U_g^i/U_G^i$ into the above equation, which then simplifies into

$$U_g^i/U_G^i = F_g/F_G \quad (i = 1, \ldots, I; g = 1, \ldots, G - 1) \tag{A8.13}$$

or the equality of MRS over all individuals and with MRT.

However Equation A8.13 gives us only the first-order conditions for private goods and says nothing about income distribution. Since we have ignored the costs of redistribution we should be able to derive the condition $\Sigma\text{MRS} = \text{MRT} = 0$, or $\Sigma U_X^k/U_G^k = 0$ if X were a common public good. From A8.11 we have

$$\sum\lambda^{.k}U_x^k = (\theta F_g - \lambda^{.i}U_g^i)/X_i\,p_g \qquad (A8.14)$$

But we cannot even express the LHS in the form of ΣMRS. We cannot divide it by $\lambda^{.k}U_g^k$ since, from Equation A8.11, $\lambda^{.i}U_g^i$ may vary over i due to the term X_i, which in general differs over i. This impossibility of expressing the Pareto optimality conditions in the simple form of MRS or ΣMRS has been called 'the paradox of universal externality' (Ng, 1975c). For the present case, the difficulty involves only one good, X. The conditions for all other goods can still be expressed in the simple form of MRS, as shown in Equation A8.13. But in the presence of complete universal externality, where the consumption of each good by each individual enters into the utility function of at least one other individual, no Pareto optimality condition can be expressed in the simple form of MRS. The Lagrangean multipliers $\lambda^{.i}$ (which convert one individual's utility into equivalent units of another's) can be eliminated from the Pareto conditions only by a complicated process that makes them extremely complex. If we wish to avoid this complexity, we are left with the paradox that we have to retain the λ's, which signify interpersonal comparison of utility, just to express the conditions for Pareto optimality, which is free of interpersonal comparisons. This paradox of universal externality is analysed in some detail in Ng (1975c).

9
First, Second or Third Best?

In Chapter 2 we discussed the necessary conditions for Pareto optimality and how these conditions could be fulfilled. A factor that makes fulfilment of the necessary conditions difficult in a market economy is monopolistic power, which is quite impossible to eliminate in the presence of the increasing returns to scale and product differentiation that are characteristic of many sectors of the economy. The presence of external effects (Chapter 7) makes things even more complicated. In principle there may exist a tax/subsidy system that enables all the necessary conditions to be fulfilled and a first-best Pareto optimum achieved. But this may not be politically or institutionally feasible. (In the presence of 'non-amenable' externalities, the first best is inherently impossible to achieve, even abstracting from the problems of political feasibility, costs and information. Non-amenable externalities include those external effects, such as social interaction, which change their character once tax/subsidy, regulation, bargaining and so on are introduced to internalise the effects. See Ng, 1975d.) If the necessary conditions cannot be satisfied for some sectors of the economy for one reason or another, what is the best we can do for the rest of the economy? This is the problem of second best.

For example, first-best Pareto optimality requires equality of the marginal rate of substitution (MRS) and the marginal rate of transformation (MRT) for every pair of goods produced and consumed. Under certain conditions this will be fulfilled if perfect competition prevails in every sector of the economy (Section 2.3). Suppose however that industry X is competitive and industry Y is monopolised. The price of $X(p_X)$ is then equal to its marginal cost (MC_X) but p_Y exceeds MC_y. The MRS_{XY}, being equal to p_X/p_Y due to the utility-maximising behaviour of atomistic consumers, is therefore not equal to MRT_{XY} ($= MC_X/MC_y$). Assuming that we have no way of affecting the decisions in these two industries, $MRS_{XY} \neq MRT_{XY}$ is then a constraint that prevents the achievement of a first-best Pareto optimum. We are then left to do the next best thing, that is, to achieve a second-best Pareto optimum, which is subject not only to the usual technological constraints on production possibilities but also to the additional constraint created by the presence of a monopoly. (The necessary conditions for a second-best optimum are still optimal in the Pareto sense given the additional constraint. The usual contrast between Pareto conditions and second-best conditions can give the misleading idea that a second-best optimum is not optimal in the Pareto sense.) To achieve a second-best optimum, should we make the MRS equal to the MRT for every other pair of goods? Given that some first-best conditions cannot be fulfilled, is it better to fulfil as many of the rest as possible? In particular, if the government cannot control the distortive private sector, should it put its own house in order by pricing public utilities at MC? According to the theory of second best the answer is a firm no. This has devastating implications for the practicability of welfare economics. In particular there seems to be very little scope for the valid application of piecemeal welfare policies. We shall first discuss the theory of second best and the various attempts to salvage welfare economics from its full implications before presenting a theory of third best.

9.1   The theory of second best

In the 1940s Samuelson (1947, pp. 252–3) was already aware of the principle contained in the theory of second best, but it was not widely discussed until the 1950s, when a number of writers working in different branches of economics (for example Viner, 1950, Meade, 1955a, 1955b, and Ozga, 1955, on custom unions and tariffs; Little, 1951, and Corlett and Hague, 1953, on taxation) encountered the problem of second best. Lipsey and Lancaster (1956) generalised the principle into the celebrated 'general theory of second best'.

The theory of second best usually refers to the achievement of Pareto optimality, although it is applicable to other optimisation problems. For simplicity, a simple constrained maximisation problem is used for enunciation. In maximising a differentiable objective function of n variables

$$F(x_1, x_2, \ldots, x_n) \tag{9.1}$$

subject to a differentiable constraint on the n variables

$$G(x_1, x_2, \ldots, x_n) = 0 \tag{9.2}$$

the necessary conditions can readily be obtained as

$$F_i/F_n = G_i/G_n (i = 1, \ldots, n - 1) \tag{9.3}$$

where a subscript after a functional notation denotes partial differentiation, that is, $F_i \equiv \partial F/\partial x_i$ and so on, and corner solutions are ignored. Equation 9.1

can be interpreted as a social welfare function since the n variables can represent the allocation of G goods to I individuals, that is $n = I \times G$. Here $W = W(U^1, \ldots, U^I) = F(x_1^1, x_2^1, \ldots, x_1^1; x_1^2, \ldots, x_G^I)$. Equation 9.2 can be interpreted as a production constraint and take the form $G(\sum x_1^i, \ldots, \sum x_G^i) = 0$. Equation 9.3 specifies the equality of the MRS and MRT.

A second-best problem arises if there is an additional constraint(s) in the form, such as

$$F_i/F_n = kG_i/G_n, \quad k \neq 1 \tag{9.4}$$

Maximising Equation 9.1 subject to Equations 9.2 and 9.4, we can form the following Lagrangean function:

$$L = F(x_1, \ldots, x_n) - \lambda G(x_1, \ldots, x_n) - \mu (F_1/F_n - kG_1/Gn)$$

where λ and μ are the Lagrangean multipliers.[1] The following necessary conditions are obtained by equating to zero the partial derivatives of L with respect to the x's and by writing the resulting equations in the proportional form:

$$\frac{F_i}{F_n} = \frac{G_i}{G_n} \cdot \left[\frac{1 + \frac{\mu}{\lambda G_i}(Q_i - kR_i)}{1 + \frac{\mu}{\lambda G_n}(Q_n - kR_n)} \right] \quad (i = 2, \ldots, n-1) \tag{9.5}$$

where $Q_i \equiv (F_n F_{1i} - F_1 F_{ni})/F_n^2$, $R_i \equiv (G_n G_{1i} - G_1 G_{ni})/G_n^2$ and a double subscript denotes second-order differentiation, for example $F_{1i} \equiv \partial^2 F/\partial x_1 \partial x_2$.

In general the expression in square brackets in Equation 9.5 is not equal to unity. This means that the conditions for second-best optimality differ from the conditions for first-best optimality even for variables that are not subject to the additional constraint(s). In terms of marginal analysis, if we are unable to equate the MRS and MRT for some pair of goods, it is then better to deviate from this equality for all pairs of goods except when the bracketed expressions happen to equal unity.

To show the principle of second best vividly, the following diagrammatic illustration is useful. Consider a simple economy that produce, three goods X, Y and Z, under conditions of constant cost. By means of a suitable choice

---

1. Allingham and Archibald (1975) argue that, with an additional constraint, strictly speaking it is not valid to assume in advance that the economy should still operate at the boundary of the production constraint, Equation 9.2. However they show that productive efficiency is still optimal in the second-best solution. Hence we shall ignore this technical methodological point.

of units for the three goods, one unit of each can be transformed into one unit of any other. The aggregate amount of the three goods produced is then constant. Any combination of the three goods produced can be represented by a point in the equilateral triangle XYZ in Figure 9.1, with the amount of X produced being measured by the (perpendicular) distance of the point to the side facing the vertex X, and so on. For an equilateral triangle, the sum of the distances of any point in the triangle to the three sides is a constant. (Students with logical minds may wish to prove this as an exercise to revise their secondary school geometry. As I found out a few years ago, there is an elegant simple proof. However before then I was not clever enough to discover it and conducted a very complicated proof that took half an hour. After that I thought that I could easily prove it again within a few minutes and threw the proof away. A decade later, when I tried to redo my complicated proof, it took me nearly an hour. I was scared by the deterioration of my intellectual capacity and carefully wrote out the proof in detail and put it in a safe place. Another decade passed and I decided to look at the written proof to make sure that I could still understand it. However by that time my intellectual capacity had deteriorated so much that I could not remember where I had put the proof. Moreover I dared not attempt to prove it again. However I can still remember the simple elegant proof. Long live simplicity! (A hint for this elegant proof: use areas.) Assume that the SWF can be represented by a community indifference map on ΔXYZ. This involves some restrictions but is used purely for simplification (to reduce the number of variables in order to facilitate geometrical treatment) and does not affect the essence of the argument.

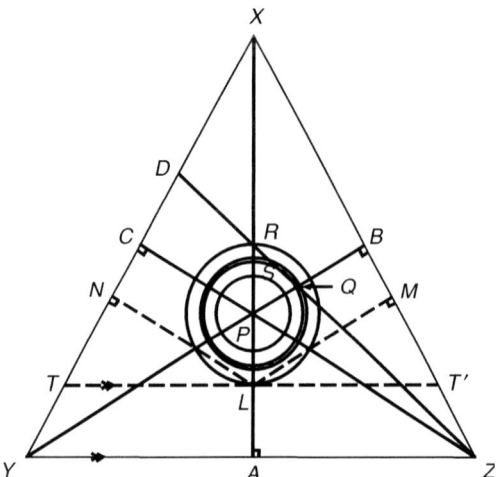

Figure 9.1
Source: Adapted from McManus (1959) and Winch (1971).

Typically point P of the highest level of community indifference occurs in the interior of $\triangle XYZ$. Given continuity of preference, lower levels of indifference are represented by 'rings' (not necessarily circular) enclosing point P, as shown in Figure 9.1.[2] For a given amount of X, represented by the distance between TT' and side YZ, TT' is the locus of the various combinations of Y and Z that can be produced. Recall that the amounts of Y and Z are measured as distances to the sides XZ and XY. For example if the economy is operating at point L, the amount of Y equals LM and that of Z equals LN. Along TT', point L touches the highest community indifference curve (CIC). It is therefore the point at which, for the given amount of X, the community's MRS_{YZ} equals MRT_{YZ} (which equals unity in this simple case). If we translate the different combinations of Y and Z along TT' into an ordinary two-dimensional figure (not shown), with Y and Z being measured along the two axes, the production possibility or transformation curve for Y and Z (with the given X) is a 45°, negatively inclined straight line. If we draw in the CICs in the figure, L will correspond to the point where the transformation line is tangent to the highest CIC. The curve XA (not necessarily perpendicular to YZ) is the locus of all points, such as L, where for a given amount of X the corresponding transformation curve (such as TT') touches the highest CIC. Hence along XA we have $MRS_{YZ} = MRT_{YZ}$. Similarly along YB we have $MRS_{XZ} = MRT_{XZ}$, and along ZC we have $MRS_{XY} = MRT_{XY}$. The three curves intersect at a common point, P. This is because the MRS must equal the MRT for the remaining pair of goods if they are equal for any two pairs. Point P is the first-best optimum where the MRS equals the MRT for all pairs of goods.

Now let us introduce a second-best complication. Suppose that, for one reason or another, MRS_{XY} cannot be made equal to MRT_{XY}. Instead of operating at a point along ZC, we are constrained to operate at a point along, say, ZD, where $MRS_{XY} \neq MRT_{XY}$. Given this constraint, what is the best we can do? Should we try to make the MRS equals to the MRT for as many other pairs of goods as possible? Obviously we cannot achieve such equality for both the remaining two pairs of goods (that is, X, Z and Y, Z) since the fact that the MRS equals the MRT for any two pairs implies the same for the remaining pair, but $MRS_{XY} \neq MRT_{XY}$ is given as a constraint. In other words MRS $\neq$ MRT for any one pair of goods implies inequality for at least one other pair. But it is possible for the MRS to equal the MRT for one pair of goods, either X, Z (that is, at point Q) or Y, Z (at point R). But either Q or R is on a lower CIC than point S, where the constraint ZD touches the highest CIC.

---

2. This is true despite the fact that a special method of measuring the various amounts of goods (distances to sides) is used since a small movement in the plane of Figure 9.1 corresponds to a small movement in the ordinary three-dimensional commodity space.

Point *S* is the second-best optimum which generally involves *MRS* ≠ *MRT* for all pairs of goods unless the constraint *ZD* happens to touch the highest CIC at point *Q* or *R*, which is unlikely. We have thus illustrated diagrammatically the second-best principle that, once some necessary conditions cannot be fulfilled, in general it is no longer desirable to fulfil the rest, even if it is feasible.

Given a second-best constraint, the resulting necessary conditions are different from the first-best necessary conditions even for the free sector. If the second-best conditions were simple and easy to fulfil the problem of second best would not create much difficulty. Unfortunately the second-best conditions (Equation 9.5 above) are generally very complicated, involving not only first-order derivatives but also second-order, cross-partial derivatives. In economic terms this means that the second-best conditions depend not only on the values of (ratios of) marginal costs and marginal rates of substitution, but also on the degrees of complementarity or substitutability between goods in the constrained sector and those in the free sector, and the effects of increased production of a good on the marginal costs of another. This involves much more complicated information than that related to the first-best conditions. Moreover this is so even if the second-best constraint applies only to one pair of goods. In the real economy, where there are second-best constraints (due to monopolistic power, externalities, taxes/ subsidies and so on) in many sectors of the economy, the resulting second-best conditions are well-nigh impossible to define, let alone to fulfil.

The principle of second best is not difficult to comprehend intuitively. If some goods produce important external diseconomies their price to (social) MC ratios will be lower than others, *ceteris paribus*. These sectors are there-fore overexpanded from a social point of view. If the government cannot do anything directly to affect the private sector, it may no longer be desirable to price its own products (for example public utilities) at MC. For example, for those public products which are highly complementary to the products of the overexpanded sectors, it may be better to price above MC in order indirectly to discourage their overexpansion.

The difficulty that arises from insufficient knowledge of the relevant inter-relationships (complementarities and so on) is only part of the problem of second best. For example, even if we had the required information it might still be practically impossible to fulfil all the complicated conditions as the administrative costs might be prohibitive (see Allingham and Archibald, 1975, on the difficulty of attaining a second-best optimum through decen-tralisation). Although we can achieve neither first best nor second best, this might not be too bad if we can at least make some improvements to the existing state. Unfortunately, according to the theory of second best, by trying to satisfy as many conditions as possible we could make matters worse. This is true not only with respect to the first-best conditions but also to the second-best conditions. Given some second-best constraints, the conditions for optimality in the free sector become the complicated second-best conditions. Unless we can satisfy all these second-best conditions, in general it is not desirable to satisfy as many as possible. This can be shown to be true by forming a second-stage second-best (or 2.5th best) problem whereby the non-satisfaction of some second-best conditions is taken as an additional constraint. One can then apply the theory of second best all over again to arrive at the above negative conclusion with stronger force, since the second-stage second-best conditions are even more complicated.

Most if not all economic analyses are based on the assumption that the first-best optimality conditions are satisfied in the rest of the economy or for other aspects of the economy. For example, when analysing the appropriate policy for a particular sector it is analytically useful to assume that optimality prevails in other sectors. Even for general equilibrium-type analyses where all sectors are taken into account, usually only one or two problems are considered and other problems are assumed to have been solved. For example, when analysing externality it is assumed that problems of monopolistic power and so on will not arise, and *vice versa*. According to the theory of second best it seems that all these analyses are useless. By adjusting the economy to take account of externalities alone, we may be making matters worse if there are other distortions in the system. Similarly, by studying a (proper) subset of the economy, even considering all problems including externality, monopoly and so on, the resulting policy recommendation may be worse than doing nothing unless the complicated interrelationships of this subset and the rest of the economy are taken into consideration. It seems that, to make any improvement at all, we must analyse the whole economy and take every problem into account. We must leap right to the summit to be sure of an improvement, but it is clear that this would be epistemologically, administratively and politically impossible.

Before readers conclude from the negative results above that welfare economics is useless and therefore decide to throw away this book, they are advised to read the rest of this chapter on the ways out of the second-best difficulty.

9.2   Softening the blow of second best

First, not all constraints give rise to complicated second-best conditions such as Equation 9.5 (Mishan, 1962b). For example some constraints take the form that a certain variable (for example the output of an industry) must not exceed or fall short of a certain value, such as

$$x_1 \leq \bar{x}_1 \tag{9.6}$$

Maximising Equation 9.1 subject to Equation 9.2 and 9.6, we still obtain the first-best conditions (9.3) except for $i = 1$, for which we have

$$\frac{F_1}{F_n} = \frac{G_1}{G_n} + \frac{\theta}{\lambda G_n} \tag{9.7}$$

where θ, the multiplier associated with Equation 9.6, is equal to zero if Equation 9.6 is ineffective and λ need not have the same value as in the previous second-best problem. Hence only the constrained sector needs to be adjusted; piecemeal welfare policy is sufficient here. This is true even if there are several constraints of the Equation 9.6 type. Constraints that place maximum or minimum values on certain variables, such as the amount of consumption, production, imports, exports, input usage and so on, will in general reduce the maximum value of the objective function, but will not lead to complicated second-best conditions.

The point that constraints of the Equation 9.6 type do not lead to complicated second-best conditions is illustrated in Figure 9.1. suppose that the constraint is that the value of X must not be greater than the distance between TT' and YZ. It can then be seen that the highest indifference curve is reached at point L, where $MRS_{YZ} = MRT_{YZ}$. In fact the constraint, if effective, confines the economy to the line TT' and simple first-best condition for the pair YZ confines it to the line XA. Hence these two equations (together with the production constraint) already define the maximum point, L, and therefore the corresponding values of X, Y and Z. In this simple case of three variables we cannot add another effective constraint (such as a constraint on the value of Y) without causing the economy to have no degree of freedom. But in a many variable case a number of constraints of the Equation 9.6 type can be added without affecting the necessary conditions of the unconstrained variables. However, complicated necessary conditions will result if the added constraint is specified in the form of an inequality in an original first-best condition such as Equation 9.4. Since the real economy does not lack constraints of this type, we still have to face the difficulty of second best.[3]

---

3. Since this involves a pair of goods, McManus (1959) regards it as really 'two constraints for the price of one'. This is a problematic interpretation. It is true that if the additional constraint takes the form of, say, $p_1 = kMC_1$, $k \neq 1$, we can still achieve a first-best optimum by making $p_i = kMC_i$ for all i if the economy is vertically integrated, that is, there are no interfirm transactions for intermediate goods (see Kahn, 1935. With intermediate goods, some complication is present – see McKenzie, 1951). In a constrained maximisation problem where the constraint is effective, there are only $n - 1$ degrees of freedom. The $n - 1$ necessary conditions in Equation 9.3, together with the constraint equation, determine the n variables. A constraint of the form $p_1 = kMC_1$, need not violate any of the conditions for $MRS = MRT$, provided other sectors price appropriately. But if the additional constraint is due to the monopolistic power of the first industry, it will make $p_1 > kMC_1$ after we have made $p_i = kMC_i$ (Lipsey and Lancaster, 1959). This problem of the number of constraints seems to be better handled in Allingham and Archibald (1975).

There is a special case where the first-best conditions still apply in the second-best solution for all variables other than those which are subject to additional constraints of the Equation 9.4 form. This is the case where the objective and constraint functions (that is, Equations 9.1 and 9.2) are separable functions. A function $f(x_1, x_2, \ldots, x_n)$ is separable if it can be expressed as $f^1(x_1) + f^2(x_2), \ldots, + f^n(x_n)$. For example the function $z = 2x^2 + 3y^4$ is separable but the function $z = 2x^2y^3 + 4$ is not. The function $z = \log x^2y^3$ is separable as it can be expressed as $z = \log x^2 + \log y^3 = 2 \log x + 3 \log y$. It is clear that every second-order cross-partial derivative of a separable function is zero. Thus if (9.1) and (9.2) are both separable functions, we have $F_{ij} = G_{ij} = 0$ for all $i \neq j$. Then Q_i and R_i in Equation 9.5 are all zero for $i = 2, \ldots, n - 1$. The square-bracketed expression in Equation 9.5 becomes unity for $i = 2, \ldots, n - 1$, and therefore first-best conditions are retained.

The above happy result follows from the assumption of separability; the issue is the interpretation of this assumption. Davis and Whinston (1965, pp. 3, 12) emphasise that 'separability is not an unduly restrictive assumption. If there are no technological externalities, there must be separability in terms of the decision units (consumers and producers) in the general equilibrium model....In such situations "piecemeal policy" is all that is required.' If this conclusion is true, then the second-best theory loses a great deal of its significance. As a welfare economist, one very much hopes that this is so. Unfortunately the assumption of separability is actually much more restrictive than the mere absence of externality (Ng, 1972a), as shown below.

If (9.2) is interpreted as a production constraint, then the mere absence of externalities will not, in most cases, make it a separable function. Take a very simple example of three goods, X, Y, Z, with the production functions

$$X = A_X, \ Y = B_Y, \ Z = A_Z B_Z; \ A_X + A_Z = \overline{A}, \ B_Y + B_Z = \overline{B} \tag{9.8}$$

where $\overline{A}$ and $\overline{B}$ are the fixed quantities of the two inputs. No externality is involved as the output of each commodity is only a function of its own inputs. From Equation 9.8 we have $X = \overline{A} - A_Z = \overline{A} - Z/B_Z = \overline{A} - Z/(\overline{B} - B_Y)$. The production constraint is then

$$X - \overline{A} + Z/(\overline{B} - Y) = 0 \tag{9.9}$$

which is not a separable function in terms of X, Y and Z. It is possible to separate any one variable but not all three. The presence of non-separability in this example of simple production functions indicates that the assumption of separability is very restrictive in the real economy of thousands of products and inputs.

Turning to the objective function (9.1), if it is an individual utility function the assumption of separability is equivalent to (Edgeworth) independence for *all* goods. This of course is a very restrictive assumption since complementarity and substitutability are very common phenomena in consumption. If (9.1) is an SWF or a community preference function, in general F_{ij} will still be non-zero, even in the absence of externality, as the complementarity and substitutability at the individual preference level will be reflected at the social preference level. It can be concluded that the absence of externality alone is far from sufficient to ensure separability in both the objective and the constraint functions. Separability is too restrictive an assumption to make the special case by Davis and Whinston (1965) interesting. Similarly the analysis by McFadden, 1969, is misleading. His definition of 'externality-free' is much more restrictive than the absence of technological externalities. His 'externalities' include normal forms of economic interdependency whereby the production or consumption possibility of an economic agent depends, through the market, on the production and consumption of others.

Green (1961), assuming a single primary resource and constant returns to scale, shows that if all goods are substitutes, the second-best optimum involves price to MC ratios between the largest and smallest constrained ratios. A similar result is obtained by Kawamata (1977) using more general assumptions (for an open economy see Lloyd, 1974). Hatta (1977), integrating the contributions by Green (1961), Foster and Sonnenschein (1970), Bruno (1972) and Kemp (1968), shows that, in an economy of linear production constraint (constant costs), a policy that uniformly reduces all price distortions will improve welfare if the economy is stable in the Marshallian sense. Moreover a policy that brings the highest distortion to the level of the next highest will improve welfare if the good with the highest distortion is substitutable for all other goods and the economy is Marshall-stable. The requirement of substitutability is not difficult to see. If the good with the highest distortion has a perfect complement, the two together may be regarded as a single good, which need not then have the highest level of distortion. It should also be noted that the linear constraint assumption nullifies the effect of G_{ij} in Equation 9.5 and therefore concentrates the effect of F_{ij}, that of complementarity or substitutability. These assumptions involve fairly strong restrictions. Moreover some of the measures, such as uniform reduction of all distortions, may not be politically feasible. Hence although the above results provide some useful insights, they are not sufficient to overcome the difficulty of second best. In the next section we shall examine a quite different approach to the solution of the second-best problem (the following two sections are based on Ng, 1977a).

9.3   A theory of third best

When maximising the objective function (9.1) subject to the constraint (9.2), the first-order necessary conditions, ignoring corner solutions (which can be allowed for), are the $(n - 1)$ conditions in Equation 9.3.[4] If the second-order conditions are also satisfied throughout, Equation 9.3 defines a global maximum. Thus if we satisfy Equation 9.3 for all $i \neq j$, the value of the objective function will attain the maximum value as Equation 9.3 is also satisfied for j, as illustrated by the curve F^1 in Figure 9.2. Hence we have the following trivial proposition.

Proposition 1: first-best rules for first-best worlds

In Figure 9.2 the curve F^1 relates the value of the objective function to the direction and degree of divergence from the first-best rule for the variable under consideration and may be called the relation curve for short. In most cases it is reasonable to expect that the relation curve is concave. As we diverge more and more from the first-best rule, the marginal damage increases. Take a specific example of the first-best rule of price equals MC. The relation curve will be concave (in a first-best world) if the demand curve is downward-sloping and the MC curve is either upward, constant or downward-sloping but everywhere less steep than the demand curve. To put it more concisely, we have concavity if the algebraic slope of the demand curve is everywhere smaller than that of the MC curve. Of course, it is, possible to

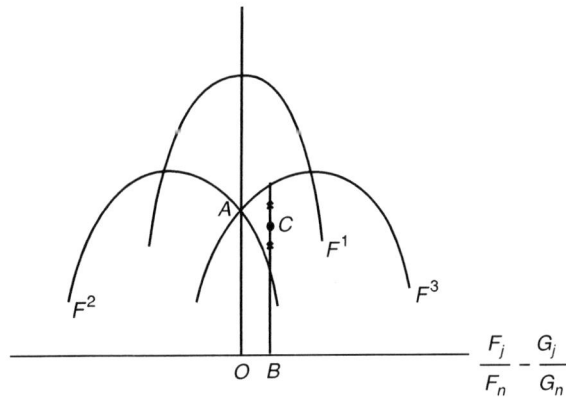

Figure 9.2

4. Although we have only $n - 1$ first-order conditions in a system of n variables, the system is not indeterminate since there is the constraint in Equation 9.2. While the variables in the whole system are simultaneously determined, if one likes one may regard each of the first $n - 1$ variables as directly determined by the corresponding first-order condition and the last variable (that is, the numeraire or money supply) as directly determined by the resource constraint equation, that is, the need (for feasibility + optimality) to operate at full employment.

construct cases where the concavity condition is not satisfied. But the condition may be violated on either side of the curve. In the absence of more precise knowledge it is reasonable to say that the *expected 'average' curve* is concave.

Now suppose that a distortion is preventing fulfilment of the first-best rule for a set of variables. The theory of second best states that in general the value of the objective function is no longer maximised by observing the first-best rule for variables when this is feasible. If the distortion is truly of second-best nature, the second-best rules (first-order conditions) are typically extremely complicated (see Equation 9.5). However if all the relevant information can be obtained costlessly and we apply the second-best rules without significant additional costs, then we have the (again trivial) following proposition.

Proposition 2: second-best rules for second-best worlds

Here a 'second-best world' is defined as the situation in which some second-best distortion is present but the costs of information and so on are negligible. But first-best and second-best worlds are not of much practical interest. Though the second-best solution has been termed 'optimal feasible', it is neither optimal nor feasible if we take account of administrative costs and inadequate information. What is really optimal feasible can be called the third best since the real world is better characterised as a third-best world in which both distortions and information costs exist. When the costs of acquiring information are significant an integral part of tackling the optimisation problem is choosing the amount of information to acquire. In general this problem with the economics of information is not independent of the other aspects of the optimisation problem. However, to deal with one issue at a time, let us for the time being assume that the information problem has been solved. In other words we have already decided the amount of information we will acquire. This will be termed the available amount of information.

The available amount of information can range continuously from perfect information to perfect ignorance, but it is convenient to adopt the following discrete classifications:

- *Informational poverty* exists when the available information is insufficient to provide a reasonably probabilistic judgment about (a) the direction and extent of the divergence of the second-best optimum from that resulting from the application of the first-best rule in the presence of the second-best distortion, and (b) the shape and skewness of the relation curve, apart from its general concavity.
- *Informational scarcity* exists when the available information is sufficient for such a judgment but is not perfect.

- *Informational abundance* equals perfect information. Informational abundance was dealt with in proposition 2, so we shall now consider informational poverty and informational scarcity.

With informational poverty, what is the appropriate policy to adopt in the presence of second-best distortion? It was noted earlier that the relation curve in a first-best world is likely to be concave, attaining its maximum at $F_j/F_n - G_j/G_n = 0$. With the introduction of second-best distortion, the relation curve may of course change its position as well as its shape. However under informational poverty we do not know in which direction it is likely to move. Moreover we do not know whether it is skew, or the sign of its skewness. Under these conditions, it is not difficult to establish proposition 3.

Proposition 3: first-best rules for third-best worlds with informational poverty

To understand the reason behind this proposition, consider Figure 9.2 where F^1 is the relation curve under first-best conditions. With a second-best distortion the relation curve will, in general, diverge from F^1. But with informational poverty we do not know in which direction it is likely to move. As a representation, F^2 and F^3 are drawn as two equally likely curves. Moreover both curves are symmetrical as we do not know the sign of skewness, if in fact they are skew. It is then easy to see that, if we stick to the first-best rule, the expected value of the objective function is OA. If we diverge from the first-best rule in any direction and any degree, for example to point B, the expected value of the objective function is BC, which is smaller than OA.

Of course, it is not necessary that, in the face of risk, we should maximise the expected value of the objective function. However it is reasonable to assume that what we are maximising is a concave function of the possible values of function F. In other words we are either risk-neutral or risk-averse. With this additional reasonable assumption, proposition 3 follows.

We shall now examine the case of informational scarcity. Suppose, for some reason, that the relation curve is skew, as shown in Figure 9.3. A right-hand or positive divergence from the first-best rule causes a sharper reduction in the value of the objective function than a left-hand or negative divergence. Then the expected value of the objective function with first-best rule, OA, is smaller than BC, the expected value resulting from a negative divergence from the first-best rule. Furthermore if we have reason to believe that the relation curve is more likely to move leftward than rightward, there is another reason to prefer a negative departure from the first-best rule. Of course this second consideration might counterbalance the first consideration (that of skewness). An optimal policy is taken by considering the effects of these factors as well as the degree of risk-aversion we possess. We shall call such policies third-best policies. This brings us to proposition 4.

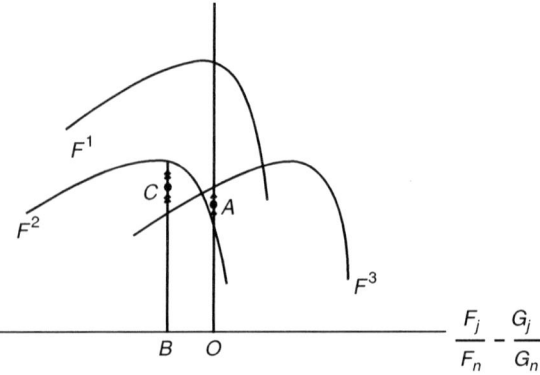

Figure 9.3

Proposition 4: third-best rules for third-best worlds with informational poverty

Third-best policies depend on the available amount of information as well as the administrative costs involved. With informational poverty, third-best policies converge with first-best ones. With perfect information and negligible costs of administration, third-best policies converge with second-best ones. Hence both first-best and second-best policies are special, polar cases of the general third-best policies. Thus if we relax the assumption that the available amount of information is already given, the latter becomes an important variable in the system. As a simplified illustrative model, we can write our objective function as dependent on the amount of information ι and the policy to be pursued, π, that is, $Q = Q(\iota, \pi)$, where the functional form reflects the cost of obtaining information, the administrative costs of carrying out the policies and the given economic environment. In the presence of uncertainty we do not know what will definitely happen for any particular choice of ι, π. But Q can be regarded as the expected utility or whatever is being maximised. Thus the subjective probability estimates and the attitude towards risk will also influence the form of the Q function, and therefore the Q function may differ from the F function in Equation 9.1. Assuming differentiability and a non-corner solution, Q is maximised at $Q_\iota (= \partial Q/\partial \iota) = 0$, $Q_\pi = 0$, as illustrated in Figure 9.4a, where M is a typical third-best solution.

The shapes of the contours are determined by the costs of obtaining information, administrative costs, and other factors mentioned above. The two ridge lines trace out the loci of the optimal value of one variable (ι or π) given the other. Both lines can be expected to be positively sloped. If the cost of information is sufficiently high, we could have a corner solution of 0 in Figure 9.4b.

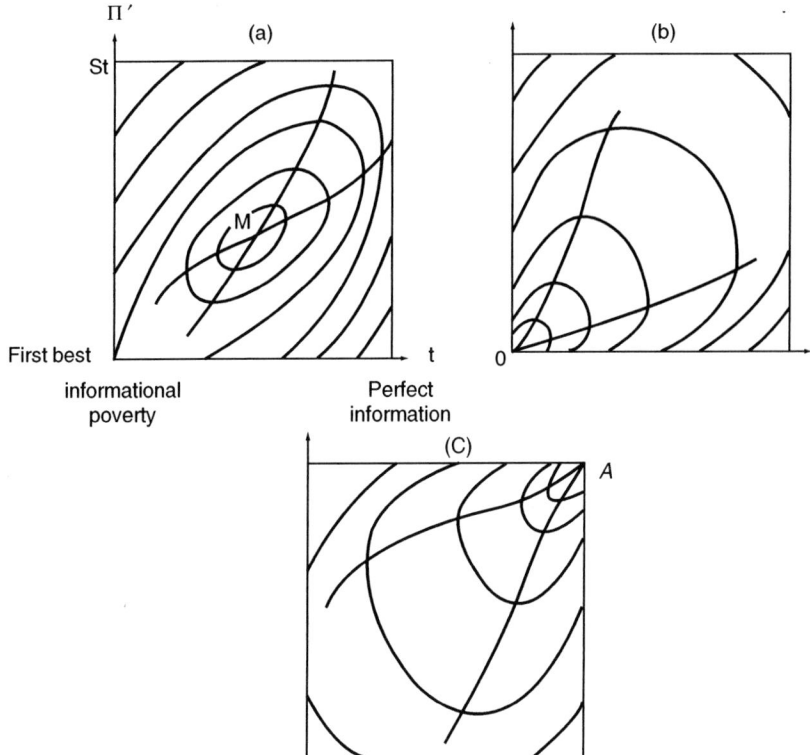

Figure 9.4

However it is not possible to have a corner solution at any other point on the vertical axis. Given informational poverty, the best policy is to stick to first best. If the costs of obtaining information are very low (unlikely to prevail), there may be a corner solution diagonally opposite to the origin at *A* in Figure 9.4c. It is, however, logically possible to have a solution along the vertical line below *A*: because of administrative costs, perfect information does not necessarily mean that a second-best policy is optimal.

In practice neither ι nor π are likely to be unidimensional and the functional relationships are known only very imperfectly. But since the theory of third-best deals precisely with situations in which precision is lacking, the above simple model can at least be accepted as a first approximation. To illustrate further the difference between informational poverty and informational scarcity, let us consider a specific example.

Suppose that a good, *X*, has an important external diseconomy that justifies, assuming a first-best world, a Pigovian tax of $*M* per unit. We know that the actual economy is not first-best, so the $M tax may actually worsen the situation if, for example, X is highly complementary to Y and Y produces important external economies that for some reason cannot be dealt with directly. A situation in which we have knowledge about the characteristics of goods closely related to X corresponds to our case of informational scarcity, and the first-best rule will have to be appropriately revised in view of this knowledge. On the other hand, if X does not have any clearly identifiable close substitute or complement, or if the goods that are closely related to X do not exhibit any marked characteristics (such as strong non-amenable external effects or a high degree of monopoly), then the appropriate policy is to adopt the first-best rule of $M tax on X, unless there is some other reason to justify a specific divergence. It is possible that, if we know all the detailed interrelationships and characteristics of the whole economy, the second-best tax on X will be $(M + N). But it is also possible that it will be $(M - N). We cannot know which way to diverge from $M unless we have such detailed knowledge. A marginal increase in our knowledge of the rest of the economy is likely to be of no help at all. For example the additional knowledge that good Z is closely related to V is of no use at all unless we also know of other interrelationships that lead us back to X.

It can be argued that, in the presence of informational poverty, we do not know whether the adoption of first-best rules will improve matters even in a probabilistic sense. Since we have no information we know nothing, and we may as well stay with the *status quo* rather than impose the $M Pigovian tax. (This is the line taken by Brennan and McGuire, 1975. I am grateful to Brennan for clarifying his position during private discussions and in correspondence.) This argument ignores the fact that while we do not have enough information on the rest of the economy to form reasonable judgment, we do have specific information that good X imposes an external *diseconomy* (instead of just an externality with no knowledge of its sign, that is whether it is a benefit or a cost) of about $M per unit. To refuse to impose the tax on the ground of second-best would be to fail to make use of this specific piece of information and the policy would not be optimal according to our theory of third-best. This theory shows that piecemeal policies can be justified and that analyses based on first-best assumptions about the rest of the economy can be useful. Thus despite the theory of second best, welfare economics can still be a worthwhile field of study.

We shall now discuss, in a very loose way, some of the factors that can affect the nature of third-best policies, taking account of the efficiency aspect of the problem. The distributional aspect is considered in Appendix 9.1, which attempts to justify the separate consideration of efficiency and equity on third-best grounds, hence tremendously simplifying economic policy making.

9.4 Towards a third-best policy

What a third-best policy is depends, of course, on the specific case under consideration. What can be given here is no more than a general discussion of a few factors that are likely to be important for most cases. We shall first consider the shape of the relation curve under first-best conditions and then examine the effects of second-best distortions.

Consider the demand (or marginal valuation) curve for a commodity and its MC (marginal cost) curve. If both are linear, the relation curve is concave as well as symmetrical over the neighbourhood of the first-best rule. If we reasonably rule out negative quantities and prices, then the extreme values of the relation curve will not be equal unless the MC cuts the demand curve at mid-point. For example, with MC^1 in Figure 9.5a, if there is a positive divergence from the first-best rule (that is, price > MC) the loss cannot be larger than the triangle ABC. But the maximum loss from a negative divergence is much larger. On the other hand if we have MC^3, then the reverse is true. If we have MC^2, which cuts the demand curve at its mid-point, or if we do not know the likely position of the MC with respect to the demand curve, the relation curve may be taken to be symmetrical.

However, the demand curve is, more likely to be iso-elastic than linear over the relevant range, as shown in Figure 9.5b. If the MC is either MC^1 or MC^3 and intersects the demand curve in the middle of the range, say, AB, which is regarded as relevant, then the relation curve is again symmetrical. If we instead have MC^2, then the relation curve will be somewhat skewed, but not to a significant degree.

The main sources of second-best distortion seem to be the existence of differential degrees of monopolistic power, uncorrected externalities, taxation, and government intervention.

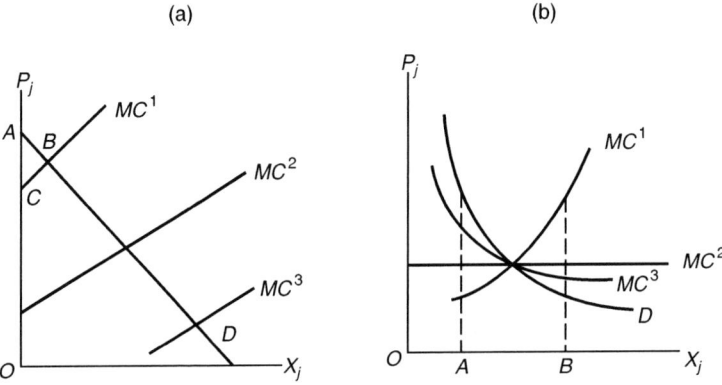

Figure 9.5

In a first-best world, optimality requires equality of prices and MCs. In the presence of uncorrected monopolistic distortion, formulation of the second-best pricing rule requires detailed knowledge of cost and demand relationships (including cross relationships). However on third-best grounds it can be argued that, unless a particular commodity is known to be highly complementary to or competitive with some commodities produced under highly monopolised conditions, it is not far from optimal to make its price to MC ratio equal to the estimated average in the economy (cf. Green, 1961; Mishan, 1962b; Ng, 1975d). Since this ratio is likely to be larger than one, this third-best rule requires the price to be above the MC. This offers a way out of the optimal pricing dilemma for public utilities with decreasing average costs (another way out is to adopt a multipart tariff – see Mayston, 1974; Ng and Weisser, 1974; Marchand *et al.*, 1984; Bousquet and Ivaldi, 1997; DeBorger, 2001). When the MC is smaller than the average cost (AC), pricing at MC involves losses, the financing of which – by non-lump sum taxes – again involves inefficiency (for some of the difficulties involved in MC pricing, see Ruggles, 1949–50; Farrell, 1958). However if optimality requires not MC pricing but above MC pricing, then one would not be too far out by setting the price at the AC, unless the MC is very much smaller than the AC.

Some qualifications to the above argument for average cost pricing are necessary. First, monopolistic distortions need not be left uncorrected. If idealised subsidies plus a lump-sum tax can be costlessly administered, the presence of monopolies need not cause any distortion. While in practice such a perfect 'cure' for monopoly is quite impossible, some rough treatment may be feasible. Let us divide the economy into three sectors: the very competitive, the very monopolised, and the intermediate. If the competitive sector is taxed according to its output, the monopolised sector according to its profit, and the intermediate sector by a combination of the two, then the restrictive effect of monopoly can be partially remedied. Second, there may exist areas in which prices are below MC – for example the public provision of goods on political rather than efficiency grounds, and expenditure that is subject to tax deductions. The deductions might initially be provided on grounds of efficiency or equity but then become outdated or subject to abuse, but are difficult to withdraw for political reasons. If sectors with prices below MC are so important as to roughly outweigh the MC pricing practice of monopolistic firms, it may be optimal for public utilities to adopt the first-best rule of MC pricing. However other considerations, such as the need to prevent empire building by public enterprises, may also have to be taken into account.

As well as monopolistic distortion there is taxation distortion (however this distortion may be far less significant than is commonly believed – see the argument below). For example commodity taxation, increases the divergence of (consumer) prices from MC. Hence even for public utilities whose

MCs are well below their ACs, average cost pricing may still not be far from optimality – exemption from taxation may be all that is needed.

Now consider externality. An external effect can be either an external economy or an external diseconomy. If both these beneficial and detrimental externalities are equally prevalent in the economy, it can be argued on third-best grounds that unless a good is known to have a significant externality or is highly complementary to or competitive with other goods with important externalities, then the first-best rules are applicable (Ng, 1975d). However it seems reasonable to say that, on the whole, detrimental external effects are likely to outweigh the beneficial ones – think of pollution, congestion, keeping up with the Joneses and so on. If public goods are included as externalities, beneficial externalities may be just as important, but this is not of much relevance to our purpose here. For example, when determining the amount of expenditure on defence, presumably account is taken of the beneficial effect on all citizens. Also, education may have important favourable external effects, but it is provided free or heavily subsidised. For the problem of second versus third best, it is unaccounted-for externalities that matter. If we confine our consideration to unaccounted-for externalities in the production and consumption of goods and services, it is quite certain that detrimental externalities predominate. Most production processes directly or indirectly (through input usage) have detrimental external effects on the environment. Moreover the consumption of many goods has detrimental external effects due to people's desire to keep up with or surpass their neighbours and fellow citizens. Thus the appearance of new fashions and new models renders their predecessors 'older', and the building of bigger houses makes the existing ones 'smaller'.

If we agree that detrimental externalities predominate, this gives rise to an interesting consideration. The necessity to raise government revenue through non-lump-sum taxes has always been regarded as a form of distortion we have to live with.[5] But with the predominance of detrimental externalities, most goods and services have to be taxed to achieve the first-best optimum to start with. This first-best system of taxes involves, of course, complicated rate structures to account for the different degrees of externality. However, taking account of the informational and administrative costs of devising such a complicated system, it might not be far from optimal to impose a general tax (in the form of an income tax, a value-added tax or some other tax)

---

5. The problem of minimising the cost of this distortion has given rise to a considerable amount of very sophisticated literature – see for example Baumol and Bradford (1970); Dixit (1970); Lerner (1970); Boiteux (1971); Diamond and Mirrlees (1971); Stiglitz and Dasgupta (1971); Atkinson and Stiglitz (1972); Bradford and Rosen (1976); Mirrlees (1976); Sandmo (1976); Wilson (1992); Cremer and Gahvari (1995); Quigley and Smolensky (1996/2000); Cremer *et al.* (1998); Kleven *et al.* (2000).

on all goods and services, with special adjustments only to account for particularly severe forms of externality. If this average rate of taxes is not much different from that required to finance government expenditure, there need not be any real distortion as a result of government taxation. Considering the degree of such externalities as environmental pollution and keeping up with the Joneses, and the fact that the government sector accounts for around 30 per cent of GNP, it seems likely that such might well be the case. Due to the progressive structure of income taxation, the marginal tax rates are well above the average rates and the tax rates on the rich are well above those on the poor. This may involve some distortion, but at least part of the differentiation in tax rates can be regarded as an unintended corrective of differential externalities. The detrimental externalities of consumption due to utility interdependence (keeping up with the Joneses and so on) are likely to be more pronounced for the rich than for the poor. Hence even on efficiency grounds alone, the rich may have to be taxed more anyway.[6]

The validity of the above subjective judgments of fact (on which see Ng, 1972b, and Appendix 1.1) is of course an empirical question, and until such information is available all we have is a rough estimate. However we must act on the best information we have. Decisions based on rough estimates are better than random choice or indecision (if that is an option). It is true that many difficulties are associated with the collection of relevant information, but further study seems to be justified in view of the importance of the issue.

For our purpose here, government intervention can be divided into two types: corrective and distortive. Corrective intervention is undertaken to offset distortions due to externalities and so on. Distortive intervention leads to inefficiency and is undertaken for purposes of income distribution, political handouts and so on. Corrective intervention need not concern us here. For distortive intervention, it seems that some forms (such as farm-price maintenance, quotas and so on) result in a positive distortion, with price being higher than MC, and others (such as a free national health service) result in a negative distortion. In the absence of empirical studies it is difficult to judge the relative importance of the two opposite effects.

With regard to government intervention and the problem of second best, there is an interesting argument that should be considered:

Suppose that, in accordance with a second-best solution, we subsidise those sectors which we ought to, and encourage those which must

6. Thompson (1974, 1979) argues that, due to the defence burden of capital accumulation and the effect of wartime price controls, the US tax/subsidy structure is roughly efficient. In the text I have not taken account of this defence burden argument for taxation/subsidization.

become more monopolistic in their behaviour to do so. As time goes by, other constraints will appear and some of those which were effective in the past may cease to be so. All this will involve us in a process of extending subsidies and monopolisation on the one hand and trying to dismantle them on the other. While, however, it is easy thing to start subsidising or encouraging restrictive practices, it is not so easy to take the reverse of these steps. In general, one can justifiably expect that some of the imperfections which we might have encouraged in the past according to a second-best solution may harden out after some time and become constraints in their own right, at least according to the logic of the theory [of second best]. In this way we run the danger of a proliferation of constraints and the efficiency of the system will become very poor (Athanasiou, 1966, p. 86).

In reply to the above argument, a theorist might say that what we need to do is to pose a long-run maximisation problem that takes account of possible changes in the constraints over time. Despite the possible effects on the set of constraints, it can be seen that a second-best policy is in general different from a first-best one. In fact, due to interactions between policy and constraints, the second-best solution will be even more complicated. For example it may be optimal (on second-best grounds) to give tariff-compensating subsidies to agricultural products at lower rates than a static second-best solution would suggest. (Given that the tariffs on industrial imports cannot be eliminated due to political reasons, a subsidy on agricultural production has been advanced as a second-best solution to compensate for the adverse effect of tariffs on agriculture. For an argument against this proposal see Warr, 1979.) It may even be optimal to vary the rates of subsidy over time (perhaps increasing slowly) according to a complicated formula.

The above 'second-best' reply to the argument by Athanasiou is formally correct if we ignore the problem of informational and administrative costs. Taking account of these, it is obvious that a dynamic second-best solution is even more utopian than its static counterpart. Thus if we combine our argument for a third-best policy that recognises informational and administrative costs with Athanasiou's argument on the danger of the proliferation of constraints, a powerful case can be made for ignoring second-best considerations and adopting simple first-best rules for most cases. It is true that Athanasiou's argument involves an asymmetry between taxes and subsidies, that is, it is easy to withdraw taxes but difficult to withdraw subsidies. However, because of the necessity of raising government revenue, most sectors are subject to various forms of tax. Therefore it may not be far from optimality to impose taxes according to first-best rules in order to correct for significant distortions (such as the $M tax on an external diseconomy discussed above), refrain from introducing subsidies that can be justified only on temporary grounds, waive taxes instead of giving subsidies that can be justified on more permanent grounds, and give subsidies only if amply justified (cf. Bos and Seidl, 1986).

9.5 Summary

The theory of second best shows that the presence of irremovable distortions renders the second-best conditions exceedingly complicated – by satisfying some optimality conditions, an improvement is not ensured. However the complicated second-best rules are neither optimal nor feasible if informational and administrative costs are taken into account. The simple first-best rules are the optimal feasible in an important class of situations (informational poverty), implying that analyses based on first-best assumptions are still relevant for practical policy making. This is so because, with a reasonable concavity assumption, staying with the first-best rules maximises expected benefit. With more (but not perfect) information, third-best policies are appropriate. Some informal illustrative applications of this third-best theory have been provided in this chapter. In particular, average cost pricing for public utilities may not be far from the third-best optimum and the necessity to raise government revenue through non-lump-sum taxes need not impose any real distortion.

Appendix 9.1: A Dollar is a Dollar – Efficiency, Equality and Third-Best Policy

The conjecture that 'a dollar is a dollar' was originated by Ross Parish. Despite my assurance that the conjecture is worth 50 per cent of this appendix, Parish has modestly declined my invitation to share joint authorship (he has outlined his argument elsewhere – see Parish, 1976. It does not include the third-best equity-efficiency argument of this appendix). I was converted to Parish's conjecture during my attempt to convince him that it was wrong. This shows that this appendix is free from ideological motivation. In fact this is an example of the very widespread phenomenon that many economists are very sympathetic – at the intuitive and/or ideological level – to many ideas of the left that unfortunately turn out to be unacceptable upon closer analysis.

In economic policy in general and cost–benefit analysis in particular, there are two different approaches. One takes distributional issues explicitly into account by using, for example, distributional weights, such that a dollar to the rich is worth less than a dollar to the poor (on the efficiency costs of the application of distributional weights see Harberger, 1978). The other approach concentrates only on the efficiency aspect of the problem, with an explicit or implicit understanding that the result is subject to distributional qualifications (Harberger, 1971, seems to believe that no such qualification is required but does not provide a convincing justifying argument). I argue that, in general, no distributional weights need to be used – that is, analysis based on efficiency alone is worth its face value and there is no need for a distributional proviso. In short, a dollar is a dollar. This argument, if accepted, provides a powerful simplification for the formulation of economic policy in general and cost–benefit analysis in particular.

The pursuit of equality by progressive income taxation is usually limited by the consideration of incentives (thus the progressivity of the Australian income tax system was reduced in 1978 and in 2000, partly on the ground of incentives). But for the disincentive effect it is likely that most people would prefer a more equal distribution of post-tax income. Hence it is believed that a dollar to the rich should count as less than a dollar to the poor; rationing is regarded as more equitable than the price mechanism and so on. What most people fail to see is that distributional weighting, preferential treatment, rationing and so on will also produce disincentive effects. Therefore these measures are inferior to income taxation as they have efficiency costs in addition to the disincentive effect. This may not be true if the measures are used as a second-best policy to counteract the disincentive effect of taxation. However they are used not for this second-best efficiency purpose but for equality purposes. Moreover the scope for pursuing the complicated second-best policy, if at all possible, is severely limited by informational and administrative costs. Hence the optimal feasible or third-best policy is to treat a dollar as a dollar, leaving the objective of equality to be achieved by income taxation (this does not of course rule out measures that reduce inequality without creating my disincentive effect, such as the removal of man-made barriers to equality of opportunity). Instead of using income weighting, rationing and so on to achieve the objective of equality, it is better to get rid of such efficiency-reducing measures and substitute a more progressive income tax system. The removal of income weighting, rationing and so on will make the rich better off. Hence the compensating increase in taxes will not reduce their incentives. In fact everyone could be made better off by the introduction of such a system.

A9.1.1 The third-best equality-incentive argument

In an ideal first-best world where costless and neutral lump-sum transfers (fixed according to potential rather than actual incomes) are feasible, a dollar is a dollar. A dollar must be treated as a dollar to achieve efficiency, and any desired level of equality can be achieved by lump-sum transfers. If we introduce some second-best constraints that rule out lump-sum taxes and taxes on leisure, the resulting second-best system of taxation/pricing rules is very complicated, even if only the efficiency consideration is taken into account. (If taxes on all goods including leisure are possible, no inefficiency need be involved in taxation since a system of proportional taxes can be devised that is effectively equivalent to lump-sum taxes.)

To illustrate the point that in a second-best world a dollar need not be a dollar, consider a simplified economy with three sectors: goods X and Y, and leisure L. Suppose that the degree of substitutability between X and Y is not strong and X is highly complementary to L. It may then be better to impose a higher tax on the consumption of X by the rich instead of just relying on income tax, which is equivalent to taxing X and Y at the same rate. In the real economy of thousands of goods, the second-best optimal rates of taxation require information far in excess of what is available. Taking account of informational and administrative costs, it was argued in Section 9.3 that second-best policies are not optimal. In fact first-best rules (such as price equals marginal cost) may be optimal if the available information is very inadequate and third-best rules (less complicated than second-best rules but not as simple as first best rules) may be desirable with more information. For our purpose here, we cannot of course rule out the possibility that the amount of information may be sufficient to justify some third-best rules instead of the first-best rule of a dollar is a dollar. However such departures from the first-best rule are justified, as will be argued below, not on equality grounds but on efficiency grounds, depending on the degree of complementarity with leisure and other interrelationships. (For simplicity I shall refer only to the degree of complementary with leisure in the following discussion – this will not affect the essence of the argument. On the importance of complementarity with leisure see Corlett and Hague, 1953; Atkinson and Stiglitz, 1972.)

As lump sum transfers are impracticable, the actual redistributive mechanisms take such forms as progressive income taxation, rationing, preferential treatment in government expenditure and so on. The fact that redistribution is not pursued to achieve complete equality can be explained by the disincentive effects involved. Ideally, then, the pursuit of equality should stop at a level that involves an optimal balance between equality and efficiency (or incentive). I wish to argue that:

- Assuming that we have already achieved such an optimal balance, a dollar should be a dollar.
- If not, it is better to achieve such a balance by manipulating the income tax schedule (that is, by making it more or less progressive) instead of using rationing, preferential treatment of the rich or the poor and so on – a dollar should still be a dollar.[7]

---

7. As real tax liabilities depend on non-income characteristics such as age, marital status, home ownership and so on, the evaluation of effective income tax progressivity may not be simple. However see Hayes *et al.* (1995) for an algorithm to evaluate effective income tax progression.

- For any balance (optimal or not) between equality and incentives using preferential treatment, there exists a superior alternative system: one that provides the same balance between equality and incentive without using preferential treatment.

The last proposition is the more interesting one and in fact subsumes the first two. Our argument differs from the well-known negative income tax proposal in that the latter is based on the first-best partial equilibrium framework, which ignores the second-best complication. The analysis here takes this complication into account but justifies the principle of a dollar is a dollar on third-best grounds. Nevertheless our argument does lend support to the negative income-tax proposal and also to the attempt by Musgrave (1969b) and others to separate the equality and efficiency issues.

Consider rational individuals with no money illusion. In their choice between work and leisure they will take into account not only the amount of income they can earn by working extra hours (or extra hard) but also what they can obtain with this extra income. If having a higher income will not enable them to buy more parking space but instead means that they will have to pay more for the same thing, and/or that projects in their favour are less likely to be undertaken, then the extra income will be worth less than it would otherwise be. It is as though the tax rate has increased. The same degree of disincentive will apply unless income is valued not so much for its purchasing power but mainly as a status symbol. However among those individuals for whom status considerations are important, it is more likely that the pretax rather than the post-tax income will be used as an indication. Hence the same degree of incentive still applies. But the use of rationing, preferential treatment, income weighting in cost–benefit analysis and so on will, in general, result in additional inefficiency unless they are designed as second-best measures that require detailed information. For example by using the unequal income weighting system we may, by chance, choose a project with the greatest unweighted aggregate net benefit. But in general we will choose one with a lower aggregate net benefit.

To illustrate this point, suppose that a society is so adamantly against the inequality involved in the market mechanism (with unequal earning abilities) that it replaces the market with a system of complete, equal and permanent rationing. Then, even if labour is not rationed so that people still have the freedom to work, the remaining incentive (if any) to work can no longer be explained by differential earnings, since extra income will not enable people to buy anything extra at all. Even if the resulting incentive is sufficient to keep the system going, it is better to introduce a system of taxation that completely equalises post-tax incomes or a system of completely equal wage payments and let the market perform its allocative function. The objective of equality is achieved all the same but the undesirable effects of rationing need not be incurred.

In the real world, complete equality in post-tax incomes will result in an intolerably low incentive level. Hence some degree of inequality has to be accepted. But whatever the combination of equality and incentive aimed at, it is better to achieve it by means of income taxation than by using preferential treatment and/or dispensing with the market mechanism. With appropriate income taxation, a dollar is a dollar. More precisely, consider the following proposition:

- *For any alternative (designated A) using a system (a) of pure equality-type preferential treatment between rich and poor, there exists another alternative, B, that does not use preferential treatment, makes no one worse off, achieves the same degree of equality (of real income, or utility) and raises more government revenue, which can be used to make everyone better off.*

This proposition is true even in cases where the pure equality-type preferential treatment just happens to be consistent with second-best efficiency considerations. This is because alternative *B*, which does not incorporate pure equality-type preferential treatment but instead uses system *b*, which is designed for efficiency purposes only, will already, within system *b*, incorporate the second-best efficiency considerations with which system *a* just happens to be consistent.

However the existence of alternative *B* does not necessarily mean that it can be identified and implemented. If system *a* is designed to take account of second-best considerations, then system *b* can also be so designed. But system *a* may only be consistent with second-best considerations by chance rather than by design. In addition the informational costs of designing a system consistent with the second-best considerations may be prohibitive.[8] Then we might not be able to identify system *b*. Thus while alternative *B* may exist, implementing it may not be feasible. Therefore if we wish to strengthen the above proposition and make it about the existence of a feasibly superior alternative *B*, it will apply only in a probabilistic sense. That it (the strengthened proposition) will still apply in a probabilistic sense is due to the theory of third best. Just as it may be consistent with second-best considerations, system *a* may also be opposite to the requirement of second best. The argument in Section 9.3 can then be used to show that the expected gain is negative. Hence as far as the second-best

---

8. Second-best taxation pricing rules are typically very complicated, even if only the efficiency consideration is taken into account. For optimal taxation, see Mirrlees (1976, 1986), Sandmo (1976, 1999), Quigley and Smolensky (1994/2000). Conditions that make second-best considerations ineffective are rather stringent, for example separability in the utility function (see Atkinson and Stiglitz 1980; compare Bergstrom and Cornes, 1983).

consideration is concerned, the use of system *a* involves negative expected gains. For simplicity we may therefore assume that system *a* is neutral with respect to second-best considerations (this in fact gives it an advantage). To establish our proposition we shall adopt the following simplifying assumptions:

- There is no political constraint on redistribution through taxation.
- The administrative cost of the pure taxation system is no higher than that of its alternative for any degree of equity attained.
- All individuals know the relevant taxation scale, details of government expenditure and so on.
- There is no money illusion or similar 'irrational' preference.

In Section A9.1.2 we shall see that relaxation of these assumptions does not affect our argument significantly.

Consider Figure A9.1, where curve *Q* represents a given income-tax schedule relating post-tax to pretax income levels. For example individuals who earn *OC* (= *CE*) will be taxed *DE* and left with *CD* as their post-tax income. With the operation of preferential treatment and so on the rich will be made worse off and the poor may be made better off. Let this be equivalent to a more egalitarian tax system, β, but without the preferential treatment.[9] Now, instead of adopting alternative *A* – tax schedule α with

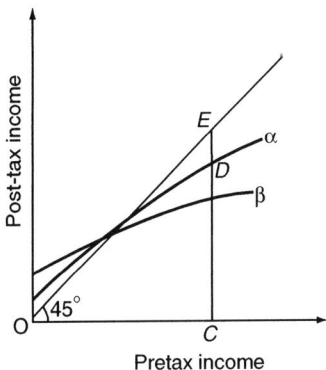

Figure A9.1

---

9. In Section A9.1.3 it is shown that a common tax schedule (with no preferential treatment) can be devised that all individuals will regard as equivalent to alternative *A*, assuming a common utility function, as in Mirrlees (1971). If this assumption is relaxed we have to work with representative individuals, but the main thrust of our argument will not to be affected.

the given system of preferential treatment a – let us adopt alternative B: tax schedule β without preferential treatment. Assuming there is no money illusion, alternative β offers the same incentives as well as the same degree of equality in real income (with 'real income' including the effects of preferential treatment) or utilities.

To understand this, consider *any* individual or group of individuals. Under alternative A, suppose they choose to work to the extent that their pretax income is OC. Their post-tax income is CD. They could have chosen any other point along the α curve within the range of their earning capacity. Hence D is their utility-maximising point subject to their earning ability. Next consider alternative B. The individuals are now faced with curve β. For any level of pretax income, post-tax income is, in general, different from that under A. However in terms of utility they are the same by construction. Hence the individuals will still find it most advantageous to work to earn the pretax income of OC. This applies to any individual. Hence alternatives A and B offer the same incentive as well as the same level of equality of real income.

The argument in the preceding paragraph is based on the assumption of perfect preferential treatment. In other words the degree of preferential treatment is taken to be a monotonically decreasing function of incomes across all individuals. In practice preferential treatment in government expenditure cannot be perfect. For one thing some expenditure benefits all people in the same geographical area. The government may choose to spend more on poor areas but rich people living in a predominantly poor area will benefit as well. People are not likely to change their place of residence each time their incomes are increased. Hence in the case of government expenditure that is geographically specific, those living in the area in question will not be appreciably adversely affected if they earn more. The increase in their income will not increase the average income of the whole area appreciably, but for the purpose of income taxation it is their individual incomes that count and not the average income of the whole area. It follows that the disincentive effect of pure income taxation (alternative B) is greater than that of income taxation with lower progressivity but imperfect preferential treatment (alternative A'). Does it follow that alternative B is inferior to alternative A'? No, as the following paragraph shows.

The reason why we have to make do with imperfect preferential treatment is the infeasibility or very high costs of effecting perfect preferential treatment; it is not that we prefer imperfect preferential treatment (alternative A') to perfect preferential treatment (alternative A) as such. Abstracting from the problems of feasibility and implementation costs, alternative A is preferable to A'. But it was argued above that alternative B is preferable to alternative A, so it follows that alternative B must be preferable to A'. This is so despite the fact that the disincentive effect is higher under *B*. The imperfection of alternative *A'* involves a welfare loss in terms of inequity that must be larger than the cost of the higher disincentive effects of *B* or *A* (which have the same incentives), otherwise *A'* would be preferable to *A*. Since the problem of imperfection in preferential treatment does not affect our conclusion, let us henceforth concentrate mainly on perfect preferential treatment.

It remains to be seen whether tax schedule β will collect no less an amount of net government revenue than schedule α. If the preferential treatment under alternative *A* is designed as a second-best measure by taking account of the different degrees of complementarity with leisure and so on, then ignoring the problems of information and administrative costs, alternative *B*, without using such an efficiency-improving method of transfer, will yield a smaller net revenue. However this second-best measure of preferential treatment is justified on grounds of efficiency. This is similar to the argument that a commodity that produces an important negative externality should be taxed more. The usual case for preferential treatment, rationing and so on is based on equality grounds. First-home buyers are given a special subsidy not because of consideration of the degree of complementarity of housing with leisure but because their incomes are usually low. If it can be shown that adequate housing has significant external economies or is a merit good, then perhaps the tax concession can be justified on this ground. But purely on equality grounds, if some people are still too poor to buy a house after the operation of the optimal income tax subsidy, then it is optimal for them not to own a house. If we think we have not done enough to achieve equality, it is better to make the income tax system more progressive instead of meddling with all manner of interventions, unless these are justified on grounds of externality, second best, merit-want and so on. If measures of preferential treatment, rationing and so on are not selected on efficiency grounds, they may still be justified by chance on efficiency grounds after all. But it is more likely that they will not be so justified. Moreover according to the principle of increasing marginal damages (Section 9.3) the expected gains from such policies are negative. Hence, at least in a probabilistic sense, tax schedule α without preferential treatment will collect more net revenue than tax schedule *Q* with preferential treatment. The increased revenue collected is a measure of the superiority of alternative *B* over *A* (for a more precise demonstration of this result, see Section A9.1.3 below).

Before concluding this section we shall illustrate our argument with a utility possibility map. In Figure A9.2, U^J and U^K represent the levels of utility of two groups of individuals in a society. Staring from the initial position *D* on the utility possibility curve *I*, consider a project (or any change) that involves a negative aggregate net benefit (the possibility curve moves

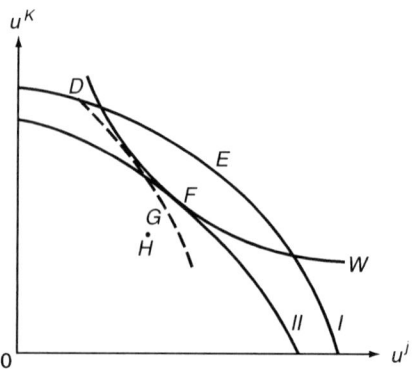

Figure A9.2

inward to *II*),[10] and a more equal distribution at point *F*. If the welfare contour *W* to *F* passes above *D* the change seems to be desirable. Income weighting in cost–benefit analysis that sanctions such changes seems to be justified. However to achieve the degree of equality represented by point *F* it would be better to do so by changing income taxation, effecting a movement along curve *I* from *D* to *E*. But income taxation has disincentive effects and thus point *E* is not sustainable.

The disincentive effect will lead to an inward contraction (not drawn in the figure) of the utility possibility curve, *I*, to pass through, say, point *G*. In other words we cannot in fact move along the utility possibility curve but have to move along the utility feasibility curve, *I'*, in redistribution through income taxation. As drawn, *G* is inferior to *F*. But what is not commonly recognised is that point *F* is also not sustainable. If redistribution through income taxation from *D* to *E* will lead to contraction of the utility possibility curve, so will redistribution through cost–benefit weighting from *D* to *F*. Abstracting from second-best considerations, *II* will contract by roughly the same amount as *I*. Hence instead of point *F* we will end up with *H*, which is

10. We are confined to unambiguous cases in which the net benefit measure shows a negative (or positive) result irrespective of whether compensating variation or equivalent variation is used (the utility possibility curves do not cross in the relevant region). Cases in which they do cross give rise to well-known theoretical problems when using compensation tests. However it is clear that the differences between compensating and equivalent variations are likely to be overwhelmed by inaccuracies in the process of information collection and aggregation. Thus for cases in which we can be sure that the aggregate net benefit is positive, it is likely to be positive irrespective of which measure we use. This is especially true if the redistribution effects are not very large. For cases in which this is not true, see Appendix 4.1.

inferior to *G*. In the presence of second-best factors we are uncertain about which point we will end up with, but the expected average is somewhere below point *H*.

A9.1.2   Some complications

We shall now discuss factors that may render inapplicable our general argument that 'a dollar is a dollar'. While these considerations will qualify our conclusion, the main thrust of the central argument will be little affected.[11]

Political constraints on redistribution through taxation

It was argued above that, if we have already achieved an optimal balance between equality and incentive in our taxation system, a dollar should be treated as a dollar. If not, it is better to change the taxation schedule instead of using preferential treatment, quotas, income weighting and so on. What if the taxation schedule cannot be changed to the desired structure because of political constraints? If it is true that we cannot change the taxation schedule but we can effect redistribution by other means, our conclusion may have to be qualified accordingly, though there is still the ethical question of the desirability of doing good by stealth. However why should the political constraint act only to prevent redistribution through taxation and not by other means? This could be because voters are rather irrational, but in this respect they tend to be quite rational and practical. The upper and middle classes will vote a government out of office not only for carrying out drastic changes in taxation but also for carrying out other drastic redistributive measures. Especially in the long term, the forces that operate to prevent redistribution through taxation will also operate to prevent redistribution by other means. If we are thinking about a distributional equilibrium, the distribution should be in terms not so much of money income but of real income. Naturally if the rich are penalised in other ways they will be less tolerant about the progressivity of taxation.

Implementation costs

Our analysis is based on the assumption that implementation costs are negligible, or at least that the additional implementation costs associated

---

11. It might be thought that the possible efficiency effects of different distributions of endowment in the presence of increasing returns (Brown and Heal, 1979) may also serve to qualify our argument. However such efficiency effects relate to first-best efficiency, which is not really feasible in the presence of increasing returns. Our argument refers to the optimal feasible method of achieving whatever degree of equality is being aimed at, and is not affected by the above effects. See also the discussion of the practical absence of the Smith dilemma in Section 10.2. See Vohra (1992) on the compatibility of a weaker (than the no-envy criterion) equity notion with Pareto optimality in general non-convex economies. Cf. Moulin (1996).

with redistribution through more progressive income taxation are not higher than the implementation costs of its alternatives. Apart from the disincentive effect (which has been taken into account and is not subsumed under implementation costs), the costs associated with income taxation are mainly (1) the costs of administration on the part of taxpayers and collectors, (2) the costs involved in tax evasion and enforcement, and (3) the costs of tax lobby activities and the like. All these costs are very substantial. But the relevant amounts are not the total but the marginal costs. For good or bad, income taxation will be with us for the foreseeable future. The incremental costs of administering a more progressive tax schedule seem trivial. The costs of a change from one schedule to another may not be trivial but are unlikely to be substantial. However in the long term the relevant comparison is between the costs of administering two alternative schedules, the difference between which is probably quite negligible. A more progressive tax schedule, however, may incur higher costs by encouraging evasion and lobbying activities. But the increased progressivity is in lieu of some system of preferential treatment, which itself is subject to evasion and lobbying. While this is a matter for which precise conclusions can hardly be expected, it does not seem likely that the costs involved in the latter (preferential treatment) will be much lower. On the other hand the cost of administering a pure taxation system is almost certainly significantly lower than that of administering a system of taxation combined with preferential treatment in government expenditure. Hence for implementation costs as a whole our central conclusion is strengthened, not weakened.

Ignorance of benefit distribution

Our argument is based on the assumption that individuals have knowledge of the distribution of costs and benefits in government expenditure across income groups and the details of preferential treatment, so the incentives are the same as for an equivalent pure income taxation system. In practice such knowledge is unlikely. On the other hand most individuals do know the scale of income taxation (however de Bartolome, 1995, shows that at least half of taxpayers underestimate their real marginal rates by confusing them with their average rates). Does this asymmetrical knowledge mean that the disincentive effect of income taxation is stronger than that for an equivalent preferential expenditure system, as in effect argued by Feldstein (1974, p. 152)?

In the absence of perfect knowledge, individuals have to base their choice on their estimates. From the fraction of knowledge they possess they are as likely to overestimate as to underestimate the degree of progressivity implied in a given preferential expenditure system, depending on the psychology of the individuals in question. Hence on the whole the degree of incentive is likely to be similar for the preferential expenditure system and the pure income taxation system.

Illusion and dogmatism

We have already mentioned money illusion (which may qualify our result in the short term but is unlikely to be significant in the long term) but there could be other forms of illusion and/or dogmatism. For example some individuals may insist on rationing the limited parking space (or any other scarce good) by quota and are quite ignorant of or unable to see the inefficiency involved and its futility in respect of achieving greater equality. If these individuals would genuinely feel hurt or frustrated if we abolished the quota system, even with a compensatory increase in the progressivity of income taxation, then it might not be true that such a move would increase social welfare.

This complication is not peculiar to our specific problem here but also applies to many economic and social policies. The long-term solution to this (at the risk of being too optimistic, or even idealistic) could be to educate the public to free them from their naive and dogmatic beliefs. In the meantime policy makers will have to take such complications into account, but it is very difficult for theorists to incorporate them formally into the analysis.

The redistributive effects of the project

Our argument shows that a dollar is a dollar irrespective of whether it accrues to the poor or the rich. But this argument does not show that a billion dollars is a billion dollars. Consider two alternative projects: project M, which will increase the incomes (after allowing for cost share) of all million individuals by $1000 each; and project N, which will increase the income of a single random individual by $1 billion. Ruling out costless lump-sum transfers (which would make us indifferent between the two projects), it is clear that project M will be preferred to project N by all egalitarian SWFs. This preference will not be based on making a marginal dollar to the rich of lower value than a marginal dollar to the poor. Rather it will be based on treating the first dollar as more valuable than the 1 billionth dollar, to whomever it goes. Hence the equality-incentive argument used above does not apply here. However this argument can be used to dispel the belief that, since a project that creates inequality is inferior to one with the same aggregate net benefits, a project that creates equality must be preferable to one that has the same aggregate net benefit but is distributionally neutral. Consider another project, O, which will yield the same aggregate net benefit of $1 billion but distributed across the economy in such a way that the poor will have much higher benefits and the rich will have negative benefits. While this may seem to be a good thing, the incentive argument will show that project O is in fact inferior to project M.

From the above it can be said that, for projects whose redistributive effects are marginal, we can simply choose in terms of the aggregate net benefits; for projects whose redistributive effects are significant, we should prefer the one with fewer redistributive effects, given the same aggregate net benefits. This seems to lend support to Corden's (1974, p. 107) concept of a conservative SWF.

Preference for working and so on

If individuals prefer to earn their income rather than receive it as a transfer welfare payment, then a cost–benefit analysis that does not take this preference into account may be misleading (this has been emphasised by Skolnik, 1970; for an analysis of the social norm of living on one's work, see Linbeck *et al.*, 1999). The main thrust of this complication can be taken care of by appropriate shadow pricing. For example, in the particular case considered here the main difference is the preference some individuals may have for earning their income instead of receiving some kind of unemployment benefit. This can largely be taken care of by putting an appropriate shadow price on employment. For single people without dependants, income from a low-paid job is likely to be sufficient to preclude them from receiving a subsidy (negative income tax). All that is needed is a low or zero income tax so that they will not have to suffer the stigma of being on the dole. For people with dependants, the negative income tax could be effected in the form of, say, substantial child-endowment payments, differentiated according to income level. A fixed child benefit/endowment is paid in Britain and Australia, and where no one feels shame in receiving it and the introduction of differentiation would be unlikely to change this substantially.

Preferential treatment based on an index of earning abilities

It might be thought that our argument against preferential treatment for the poor does not extend to preferential treatment according to characteristics that account for people being poor. For example preferential treatment based on an index of earning ability, such as IQ (by, say, spending on education until the marginal returns on the less/more capable are less/more than that justified by pure efficiency considerations) or skin colour (by subsidising Afro haircuts, as suggested to me in a seminar), could be regarded as desirable as it is very difficult or impossible for people to acquire (or not to acquire) such characteristics as a high IQ. However this only means that, instead of basing our equity tax/subsidy on income levels that are liable to be affected by disincentive effects, it might be better to base it on some index of earning ability, such as IQ (see, for example Viard, 2001). Instead of subsidising Afro haircuts it would be better directly to subsidise the individuals concerned. Instead of stopping the education of the capable when the discounted net marginal returns are still positive, it would be better to continue to educate them but impose higher taxes on them (according to IQ). However if the practical difficulties of taxing intelligence (on which see Section 6.4) would be too prohibitive and preferential treatment in educational spending would be more feasible, an exception to our general principle on this practical ground might be justified. (This is in fact a question of asymmetrical implementation costs, not a failure of our principle as such. The exception would be justified on the efficiency grounds of lower implementation or implementation costs. The desirability of subsidising goods preferred by the poor if it is difficult to identify who are the poor but fairly efficient to subsidise these goods due to self-selection and low substitutability is based on a similar consideration – see for example Besley and Coate, 1991.)

Unexpected emergencies
In times of unexpected emergencies such as earthquakes, wars and so on, certain necessities may be in very short supply. In principle we could impose higher taxes on the rich and those who happen to own the goods in short supply and pay subsidies to the poor and the victims of the disaster. Then the policy of 'a dollar is a dollar' could still be best even in such emergencies. However due to time lags, imperfect information and so on it might be practically infeasible to effect the changes in taxes/subsidies in time. Rationing basic necessities such as medical supplies (which would also involve external economies) might then be the best practical solution. However the possible desirability of deviating from the 'a dollar is a dollar' principle in emergencies does not mean that the same is true for normal times.

From the above discussion it can be concluded that none of the complications significantly changes the central argument of this appendix. In fact proposition *A* can be generalised to any efficiency-inconsistent alternative, not just equality-oriented preferential treatment. The proof of the proposition is also unaltered if the preferential treatment is not equality-oriented but inequality-oriented. Instead of counting a dollar to the poor as worth *less* than a dollar to the rich in cost–benefit analysis, it is better to tax the rich less and tax the poor more (or subsidise them less). Similarly an alternative based on random treatment or tradition and so on can be shown to be inferior to an alternative (*B*) that is designed to compensate for the gains or losses from dismantling the efficiency-inconsistent methods used. Then, ignoring practical difficulties, individual ignorance, irrationality and procedural preferences (on the last item see Ng, 1988), alternative *B* must be Pareto superior.

A9.1.3 Is β the tax schedule we want?
With reference to the argument in Section A9.1.2, we wish to show that a common tax schedule, β, can be constructed that, with the elimination of the preferential system, *a*, makes no individual worse off and also increases government revenue. We have to assume a common utility function (with respect to leisure, consumption and the preferential system) and shall comment on the relaxation of this assumption later. Suppose that each individual has a given income-earning ability. Subject to this earning ability,

each may choose a different level of pretax income by varying the hours and intensity of work. Their choice will depend, of course, on their subjective preference, the tax schedule and the system of preferential treatment. Even with the assumption of the same preference or utility function, individuals with different earning abilities may have different indifference maps, as defined in Figure A9.3 (this is similar to Mirrlees' model of optimal income taxation – see Seade, 1977, for a diagrammatical illustration). Given some mild assumptions, income varies positively and continuously with earning ability (Mirrlees, 1971). Geometrically, a person with higher earning ability has a flatter indifference curve at a given point. The equilibrium points (E^1, E^2, E^3) of three individuals under alternative A (tax schedule α and preferential system a) are depicted in Figure A9.3.

Now let us dismantle the system of preferential treatment, a. This will make the rich better off and may make the poor worse off. If system a is so inefficient that its dismantling will make everyone better off, we have a stronger case for its removal. Therefore let us take the case where the poor will be made worse off by its removal. A system of perfect preferential treatment involves a degree of preferential treatment that is monotonically decreasing in terms of income (non-perfection in preferential treatment does not affect our conclusion, see the third last paragraph in Section A9.1.1 above). Thus if the rich are made better off and the poor worse off by the removal of system a (assumed perfect), there exists an intermediate income level (say C^2) at which an individual will remain indifferent by the removal of system a. This individual must exist in a model of a continuous distribution of individuals, but may not exist in the discrete case. But the actual

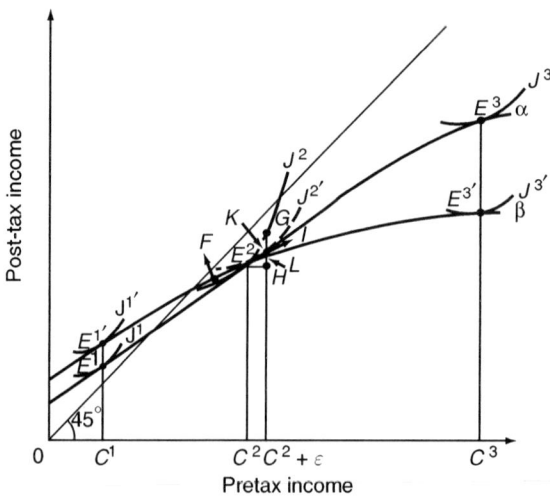

Figure A9.3

existence of this individual is of no consequence to our argument. After the removal of system *a*, the new indifference curve of this individual, which corresponds to the same level of utility as J^2, must still pass through point E^2. On the other hand individual 3, who is made better off by the removal of system *a*, must have a new indifference curve $(J^{3'})$ that corresponds to the same level of utility, J^3, passing through a lower point, $E^{3'}$. With no preferential treatment against this individual, he or she only needs a lower level of post-tax income to attain the original utility level at the same level (*DC*) of pretax income.[12] Conversely the new indifference curve $(J^{1'})$ for individual 1 passes through a higher point, $E^{1'}$. Tracing through all points, such as $E^{1'}$, E^2 and $E^{3'}$, we arrive at the new tax schedule, β. With the usual continuity assumptions, this schedule will also be continuous and smooth, (continuity and smoothness are not really necessary for our central proposition, but they make the illustration easier and enable it to be put in terms of the familiar tangency condition for maximisation). Let us call the tax schedule β with no preferential treatment alternative *B*. If the government can collect at least as much revenue as before to maintain public expenditure, it is clear that everyone will remain at least as well off as under alternative *A*. This is because each individual can choose to earn the same amount of pretax income and attain the same level of utility as before. However if alternative *B* has greater disincentive effects, many individuals may choose to earn less and government revenue may be lower than before. Let us examine this possibility.

The preferential system may in fact be a system of second-best measures to counteract the disincentive effects of the income tax schedule, α. Since the rich are confronted with higher tax rates, these second-best measures could include, say, higher taxes on goods consumed by the rich that are highly complementary to leisure. They may therefore appear to be preferential, but in fact they can be justified on efficiency grounds and need not be preferential treatment designed to achieve equality. If this is the case, then system *a* is not really preferential and can therefore be incorporated into alternative *B*, making alternatives *A* and *B* equivalent. Our purpose is not to argue against preferential treatment that is justified on second-best grounds (or some other efficiency grounds such as externality, merit goods and so on). Rather we are arguing against preferential treatment to achieve

12. This is obviously true with the assumption of given earning abilities. With the relaxation of this assumption, it could be thought that $J^{3'}$ will pass above E^3 (and $J^{1'}$ below E^1) if the wage rate of individual 3 (individual 1) is sufficiently increased (reduced) by the operation of preferential system *a*. If this is so, it means that preferential system *a* in fact favours the rich rather than the poor when its full effects (including the indirect effect on earning ability) are taken into account. This possibility can therefore be disregarded. It is also clear that the indirect effect is unlikely to outweigh the direct effect.

equality as such. A system of truly equality-type preferential treatment might happen to go in the same general direction as required by second-best considerations. But it could also go in the reverse direction. Hence we shall assume that it is neutral in this respect. (In Section 9.3 it is argued that the expected gain of a movement towards or away from the second-best direction is probably negative. Therefore by assuming that preferential treatment is neutral in this respect, we in fact give it an advantage.)

If the new indifference curve of individual 2 not only passes through E^2 but also stays unchanged at J^2 (or at least in the neighbourhood of E^2), the new tax schedule, β, being flatter than α, must cut this indifference curve, J^2. Individual 2 will then choose to earn a lower level of pretax income, say at point F. However the actual new indifference curve ($J^{2'}$) must be flatter than the old one, J^2, at point E^2. With no preferential treatment, individual 2 will need less/more post-tax income if she or he earns a higher/lower level of pretax income (otherwise β would not be flatter than α to begin with). Moreover it can be shown that β must be tangential to J^2 at E^2. Tax schedule α touches the (highest) indifference curve, J^2. Both J^2 and α are reduced in slope to become $J^{2'}$ and β respectively. Moreover the reduction in slope must be the same at point E^2. Hence alternative B touches $J^{2'}$ at E^2. To make this clearer, consider a slightly higher level of pretax income of $C^2 + \varepsilon$. The slope of J^2 at E^2 (denoted by S^2) can be approximated by GH/E^2H. This approximation will become exact equality as ε approaches zero, given smoothness in the curve. Similarly the slope of $J^{2'}$ at E^2 (denoted $S^{2'}$) $\approx IH/E^2H$, and the slope of α at E^2, $S^\alpha \approx KH/E^2H$. Similarly $S^\beta \approx LH/E^2H$.

Since the denominators of all these slopes are the same we shall concentrate on the numerators. S^2 is larger than $S^{2'}$ by (approximately) GI, ignoring the denominator. GI measures the extent to which individual 2 will be made better off by the removal of preferential system a if she or he chooses to earn $C^2 + \varepsilon$ instead. (This is so because of the argument in the preceding paragraph, abstracting away the possible second-best effect of a preferential system. Otherwise GI may partly reflect this second-best effect, which could, however, go either way.) S^α is larger than S^β by KL, which measures the extent to which the individual who actually earns $C^2 + \varepsilon$ under alternative A will be made better off by the removal of preferential system a if he or she keeps earning $C^2 + \varepsilon$. It must be recognised that GI need not equal KL. Although the pretax ($C^2 + \varepsilon$) incomes of both individuals are the same if the above hypothetical conditions prevail, they have different earning abilities. The same pretax income must then imply different hours or intensities of work. The difference in hours of work may make them willing to forgo a different amount of post-tax income to remove the same system (and the same degree) of preferential treatment. However as ε approaches zero, not only do the above approximate slope measures become exact, the difference between the earning abilities of the two individuals also approaches zero. Given continuity, the amount by which S^2 is larger than $S^{2'}$ will then be equal to the amount by which S^α is larger than S^β at point E^2 as the measures of these slopes are made exact. Since $S^2 = S^\alpha$ at E^2, so $S^{2'} = S^\beta$ at E^2. It is then not difficult to see that, under alternative B, not only can individual 2 attain the same level of utility as before by earning the same income as before, but she or he has no incentive to earn a different income. Given some convexity assumption she or he will be positively worse off to operate at a different point.

Let us now consider the position of individual 3. Now $S^{3'}$ (the slope of $J^{3'}$ at $E^{3'}$) may differ from S^3 for two reasons. One is the same as that which makes $S^{2'}$ differ from S^2, that is, the removal of preferential treatment tends to make the slope flatter. But since E^2 and $E^{3'}$ are now on two different points, there is an additional reason why $S^{3'}$ may differ from S^3. The difference in post-tax income may cause the individual have a different trade-off between consumption (or post-tax income) and leisure (related to pretax income). However S^β (at $E^{3'}$) also differs from S^α (at E^3) for these two reasons. It is therefore not difficult to see that S^β must equal S^3 at $E^{3'}$. Individual 3 will choose to earn the same amount of pretax income as before. Similar reasoning shows that under alternative B all individuals will choose to earn the same amounts of pretax income as under alternative A. Alternative B thus provides the same degree of incentive and the same degree of equality in the distribution of real income (utility) as alternative A.

Even if all individuals earn the same amount of pretax income, can we be sure that government revenue will be no less under alternative B? In Figure A9.3, suppose that C^1 (it could be zero) is the lowest pretax income earned and C^3 is the highest. The change in government revenue by changing from alternative A to alternative B equals the area $E^2E^3E^{3'}$, weighted by the population density function along the horizontal axis, minus the area $E^1E^1E^2$, which is similarly weighted. It is clear that the weighted area $E^2E^3E^{3'}$ must be larger than the weighted area $E^1E^1E^2$. The former measures the aggregate amount by which all individuals who earn more than C^2 are made worse off by preferential system a. The latter area measures the aggregate amount all individuals who earn less than C^2 are made better off by system a. If the former area were smaller than the latter, system a would be justified on pure efficiency grounds to start with. Thus if system a is truly preferential the former area must be larger than the latter. For example the use of unequal income weighting in cost–benefit analysis may sanction projects with positive unweighted aggregate net benefits. But such projects would be sanctioned without the use of unequal income weighting and would be undertaken under alternative B too. Hence the difference in tax schedules α and β is caused by the effects of preferential measures, such as unequal income weighting, when they are effective in sanctioning projects with negative unweighted aggregate net benefits.

From the above discussion it can be seen that alternative B not only provides the same degree of incentive and the same degree of equality, it also generates more government revenue than alternative *A*. This extra amount of revenue is a measure of the superiority of *B* (no preferential treatment but more progressive income taxation) and can be used to make everyone better off by increasing public expenditure and/or lowering taxes all round.

Our argument is based on the assumption that all individuals have the same preference. If individual preferences differ with respect to leisure, consumption and preferential treatment, the removal of system *a* may make individuals who earned the same income better off or worse off by different amounts. Their new indifference curves will then pass through different points and we cannot construct a new tax schedule (such as β) that will keep every individual as well off as before and earning the same income as before. Hence we have to work with average individuals and construct a tax schedule that will make these average individuals (one at each income level) indifferent. Some non-average individuals will be made better off and some worse off. However at each income level those who are made better off could in principle pay compensation to those who are made worse off so as to make everyone better off. If such compensation were actually paid the change would be Pareto superior. However in practice such compensation would be difficult if not impossible to effect. Nevertheless, even without actual compensation the change satisfies the quasi-Pareto criterion proposed by Ng (1984a; see also Section 3.5 above). Thus even if we accept the divergence of preference at the same income level, we can still use the quasi-Pareto criterion to show that alternative *B* is superior to alternative *A*. (A mathematical demonstration that each individual will choose the same amount of work under alternatives *A* and *B* is available from the author.)

A9.1.4 Economists should be in favour of reversed weighting!

At the risk of repetition, it should be emphasised that our argument for using the *unweighted* sum of willingness to pay or for treating 'a dollar as a dollar' is not based on valuing a dollar to the poor the same as a dollar to the rich. In fact I put a much higher value on the former than on the latter. If manna were to fall from heaven (and were regarded as a one-off, or at least as unrelated to income), I certainly hope that it would fall at the feet of the poor. However if we adopt a policy of treating a dollar to the poor as worth more than a dollar to the rich, this will create disincentive effects and will therefore be inferior to using the tax/transfer system to reduce inequality. I am not against an attempt to reduce inequality, just against the use of an inefficient method to do so.

While governments may not actively and optimally pursue distributive justice through income taxes and transfers, in the long run some degree of distributive balance is maintained. Even if this does not lead to an optimal trade-off between equality and efficiency, it would be wrong to ignore the fact that some degree of balance is being maintained. It seems that all those in favour of using distributional weights or inequality-averse criteria effectively ignore such a balance, or at least they have not shown their awareness of its implication in respect of the appropriate distributional weights. This balance implies that the distributional weights should be less unequal (for example a dollar to the poor should be counted as only $1.20 instead of $2) than in the absence of a balance. In the presence of an optimal balance, no weights (or only equal weights) should be used. In the presence of an excessive balance (that is equality pursued at excessively high incentive costs) the distributional weights should be reversed (that is more weights to the rich than to the poor). Nevertheless, it appears that no advocate of distributional weights or inequality-adverse criteria has explicitly shown awareness in this respect. Many people probably believe that the distributional weights should be proportional to the social marginal utility of a dollar. However this can only be justified if the use of distributional weights has no disincentive effects (efficiency costs over and above their direct distortive costs). It can be strongly suspected that many of those in favour of distributional weights simply ignore these disincentive effects.

It is possible that, despite some degree of balance between equality and efficiency, some economists regard the balance as far too inadequate. They may think that much more equality should be achieved despite the inefficiency costs involved. While this is certainly possible, the reverse case that an economist may believe that too many efficiency costs are being incurred to achieve equality is even more likely, or at least as likely. As a group, economists are unlikely to be more equality-inclined than politicians, bureaucrats or voters whose inclinations influence government policies (in fact there is evidence to suggest that economists are much more right wing that the general public – see for example Ng, 1988). Moreover economists are more aware of the efficiency costs of pursuing equality, including the administrative, compliance, policing and disincentive costs. Thus one should expect more economists to think that the actual trade-off between equality and efficiency is excessively in favour of equality, rather than the other way round, and therefore be in favour of using reversed distributional weights rather than normal distributional weights. However it seems that not a single economist has come out in favour of reversed weighting. The most radical person in this respect is probably Posner (1981), a judge who is in favour of wealth maximisation (my argument of treating 'a dollar as a dollar' differs from Posner's as I allow for the achievement of equality through taxes/transfers beyond wealth maximisation). These considerations support my suspicion that many economists who are in favour of distributional weights simply ignore the disincentive effects involved, and not just because they are more egalitarian.

What about the minority of economists who are genuinely more egalitarian than the prevailing policy? As economists, they should not be in favour of using distributional weights and purely equality-oriented policies, however as citizens they should campaign to move government policies towards increased equality (preferably by using more efficient methods), while the majority of their fellow economists, as citizens, should campaign for less equality if, as argued above, they view the equality–efficiency trade-off as having been pursued to excess.

A9.1.5 Concluding remarks

The argument in this appendix has far-reaching implications as it justifies the separation of equality and efficiency considerations in public policy. In all specific areas, public policy needs only to be concerned with efficiency, leaving equality to be achieved through the general tax/transfer system. This will considerably simplify the formulation of all public policies, and cost–benefit analysis in particular.

However the argument presented here does not deny the possibility that some measures could improve efficiency and equality simultaneously and some measures could harm them simultaneously, due, for example, to such considerations as the physiological effect of income on work effort (Strauss and Thomas, 1995), the principal-agent problem and imperfection in the credit market due to informational asymmetry, which could be lessened by (1) the use of collateral that the very poor lack (Binswanger *et al.*, 1995; Hoff and Lyon, 1995; Hoff, 1996), (2) the effect of tax progressivity in moderating the wage demands of unions (Hersoug, 1984; Creedy and McDonald, 1990; Lockwood and Manning, 1993), (3) discouraging investment that increases the difference between median and average incomes and hence the median voter demand for a higher tax rate (Persson and Tabellini, 1994; but see Perotti, 1996, on the negative empirical evidence for the mechanism, though the negative relationship between inequality and growth appears valid – see Birdsall *et al.*, 1995), and (4) the crime-reducing effect of equality (Eaton and White, 1991; Grossman, 1994). (For a summary of empirical evidence on the relationship between inequality and growth see Benabou, 1996. On other related issues see Haveman, 1988; Murphy *et al.*, 1989; Schmid, 1993; Bowles and Gintis, 1996; Baland and Platteau, 1997; Breen, 1997; Le Grand, 1997; Devins and Douglas, 1998; Nagel, 1998; Putterman *et al.*, 1998; Aghion and Williamson, 1999; Lee and Roemer, 1999;) Our argument is also consistent with the idea of regulating or taxing more heavily the incomes of superstars in sports and entertainment. This is because they earn more than their marginal contribution in that their role can be assumed by their runners-up without significant losses (Borghans and Groot, 1998). Borghans and Groot attribute discrepancy/inefficiency to some form of monopolistic power. However in my view the insignificant losses involved in the replacement of superstars by their runners-up can be regarded as more important, making the discrepancy/inefficiency non-existent or insignificant for superstars in, say, science and technology or the generation of real knowledge in general. Here, in fact, the superstars earn far less than their marginal contributions because of the global public-good and long-term nature of knowledge (see Section 6.4).

We have ignored the possibility that increasing returns may affect the efficiency–equality relationship (see for example Brown and Heal, 1979, who show that the efficiency of marginal cost pricing may depend on distribution in the presence of increasing returns). However our argument has not dismissed the need to take account of indirect effects, including external effects and those arising from a change in preferences (on preference changes see Bowles, 1998). It may be noted that Congleton (1997) has an interesting argument for equal protection of the law due to its favourable effect in avoiding differential enforcement of the law for the interest of the governing coalition. This argument could be mistakenly regarded as a counterexample of the 'dollar is a dollar' principle. However the equal protection of the law is really a second-best solution to violation of the 'dollar is a dollar' principle (from the viewpoint of the whole population) by a subset of the population, the governing coalition, at a greater cost to the non-governing sections of the population. Hence there is really no violation of the principle.

9.1.6 Summary

The pursuit of equality by means of progressive income taxation is usually limited by the consideration of incentives. Despite this it is not desirable to use distributional weights in cost–benefit analysis, other forms of preferential treatment for the poor, and handicaps or limitations (for example rationing) for the rich. A dollar should be treated as a dollar, no matter to whom it goes. This is because the disincentive effect will also apply to these measures, not just to progressive taxation. In addition such measures incur additional efficiency costs unless they are used (which they are not) as a second-best policy to counteract the disincentive effect of taxation. Even then the information and administrative costs of such a second-best policy are likely to be prohibitive. Hence the third-best policy of a dollar is a dollar prevails. This central argument has been presented in some detail in this appendix and has been shown to be valid, even after considering some complications.

10
Beyond Marginal Analysis: Perspectives from an Inframarginal Analysis of the Division of Labour

10.1 Towards a more complete welfare economics

Traditional welfare economics is incomplete in at least two important respects. First, it is based on an orthodox economic analysis that is largely neoclassical in nature. Neoclassical economics concentrates on resource allocation and largely ignores the important classical economic problems associated with divisions of labour to take advantage of economies of specialisation and the associated evolution of economic organisations. This deficiency is discussed in the present chapter. While attention has recently been paid to the classical problems of specialisation (see for example Yang and Ng, 1993), the related welfare economic issues raised by this new classical framework are only just beginning to be addressed and there is considerable scope for further research.

Second, welfare economics is incomplete because it analyses individual preferences without really going into individual welfare. While the divergences between individual preference and welfare were discussed in Chapter 1, these divergences have been largely ignored in the rest of the book. For cases in which the divergences are either small or could go either way, ignoring them is not a problem. However, as will be argued in Chapter 11, there is at least one case in which the divergences are systematically biased in one direction and combine with other factors to result in excessive consumerism and a related materialistic bias. This requires important adjustments to be made to our welfare economics and cost–benefit analysis, and to other applications and policy measures based on it.

The focus on the above two matters reflects partly their importance and partly my involvement in their development. This focus does not diminish the relevance of other factors that a more complete analysis of welfare needs to take into account, but analysing them all is beyond the capability of a single researcher.

10.2 Marginal versus inframarginal analysis

Economic (and in fact many non-economic) decisions can be classified into marginal decisions about variables, for example how much or how many units one should buy, sell, produce, invest and so on, and inframarginal decisions such as whether to set up a business, and if so, which good to produce; whether to produce a good or input yourself or buy it from the market; and whether to get a job and in which occupation. While marginal decisions on the appropriate value of variables is important, it is often the inframarginal 'whether' and 'which' decisions that are decisive in one's success or failure and welfare. Think of your (or your parents') classmates in high school or university – their fortunes now probably depend much more on which degrees they took at university and on which lines of business or occupation they took up than on how many hours of study or work they allocated to the various activities.

While inframarginal decisions are very important, since the neoclassical marginalism revolution orthodox economic analysis has concentrated on the marginal analysis of resource allocation and has largely ignored the division of labour and specialisation emphasised by classical economists. The economies of specialisation make all-or-nothing choices sensible. A person who specialises in economics does not teach or do research in physics or chemistry. (I violated this principle by spending, when writing my PhD thesis, two weeks on the theory of relativity and understanding it, and two weeks on quantum physics and being mystified by it; and later by publishing a dozen papers on biology, maths, philosophy and psychology; perhaps that is why I am not a better economist! This violation can be explained by a preference for diversity on the consumption side, and the fact that research is both production and consumption, a complication not yet allowed in our analysis.) A farmer does not work in a factory; a factory worker does not grow rice. The value of many variables is zero. The solution point is at a corner. To compare the desirability of corner solutions requires more than just marginal analysis – inframarginal analysis or the comparison of total costs and benefits across different corner solutions is also required. When Marshall (1920) synthesised the contributions of neoclassical economics, the use of differential calculus had already been introduced in economic analysis with great success and was very useful in marginal analyses of resource allocation that involved comparisons of marginal adjustments. However Marshall did not have access to such mathematical techniques as the Kuhn–Tucker conditions for handling corner solutions. Marshall avoided the problems created by corner solutions by adopting a dichotomy between pure consumers and pure producers. The current textbook version of this is the circular flow diagram, with the household or consumer sector in one box and the business or producer sector in another box. This dichotomy takes the pattern and degree of division of labour as given and ignores inframarginal decisions on the 'whether' and 'what' business/occupation problems of individuals.

While inframarginal analyses of various decision problems had been conducted earlier (see Yang and Ng, 1998, and Yang 2001, 2003, for surveys of these developments), the formal inframarginal analysis of the division of labour in a general equilibrium framework with applications to various economic problems to do with trade, growth, industrialisation, urbanisation, economic organisations, property rights and so on was conducted by Yang and Ng (1993). This analysis resurrected the spirit of classical economics in a modern inframarginal analysis, and provided a new framework for the study of many economic problems, as well as new insights. As a *Journal of Economic Literature* reviewer put it: 'This is an ambitious... interesting and original book. Its motivation is sound, and its fundamental insights are compelling... a refreshing new approach to microeconomics, one that has the potential to address many issues that have long resisted formal treatments' (Smythe, 1994, pp. 691–2).

It could be thought that we are already in a fully specialised economy where virtually everyone has only one job or sells only one product, so that the analysis of specialisation is no longer relevant. However even in our era of high specialisation there is still considerable scope for increasing the division of labour. First, things done at home are increasingly being done through the market – think of take-away food and dining out, specialised carpet cleaning and gardening. Second, further specialisation can take place at the level of input usage by producers, with the use of more specialised inputs and more roundabout methods of production. Third, with lower market transaction costs, specialisation between firms could replace specialisation within firms. This is especially characteristic of small and medium-sized firms in Taiwan that specialise in producing a certain input or a particular process, including the final assembly of a product. Thus improvements in transaction efficiency (which are expected to accelerate with the development of e-commerce) could lead to an even greater division of labour and provide benefits through economies of specialisation. Such benefits are better analysed by inframarginal analysis.

10.3   Basic inframarginal analysis of the division of labour

The essence of the Yang–Ng (1993) framework is the trade-off between the economies of specialisation that are made possible by the division of labour and the transaction costs of trade that are necessitated by specialisation. If transaction efficiency is low the economies of specialisation are outweighed by the transaction costs, so that autarky or a small division of labour is efficient and will be chosen. If transaction efficiency is improved, the efficient extent of the division of labour and the related size of the market network will increase.

Figure 10.1 illustrates the evolution of the division of labour (a type of comparative statics of general equilibrium), where the number of goods and the population are assumed to be four in a symmetric version of the model. The lines in the figure denote the flow of goods, the small arrows indicate the direction of the flows, and the numbers beside the lines signify the goods involved. The numbers in the circles denote person i selling good i. Figure 10.1a illustrates autarky, where each person self-provides four goods due to extremely low transaction efficiency. Figure 10.1b illustrates partial specialisation, where each person sells one good, buys one good, trades two goods and self-provides three goods as improvements in transaction efficiency generate a partial division of labour. Figure 10.1c illustrates complete specialisation, where each person sells and self-provides one good, buys three goods and trades four goods due to high transaction efficiency and/or large economies of specialisation.

A simple mathematical model using the Yang–Ng framework and capturing the evolution of the division of labour illustrated above is presented in Appendix 10.1. A comprehensive textbook that covers most major issues in economics using the new framework is Yang (2001). Economies of specialisation have been analysed using modern economic tools and allowing productivity to increase with the number of intermediate goods used (see Ethier, 1979, 1982; see also Francois and Nelson, 2002, for a geometrical illustration). In contrast Yang and Ng (1993) allow for economies of specialisation at the individual level, starting with the very basic individual choices of which goods to produce, trade and so on.

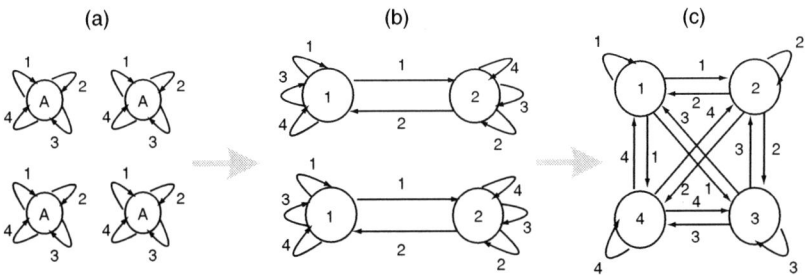

Figure 10.1 Evolution of the division of labour: (a) autarky; (b) partial division of labour; (c) complete division of labour
Source: Yang and Ng (1993).

10.4   The devastating implications of increasing returns on some traditional conclusions

> One clear conclusion is that there are many important areas of economics in which the recognition of increasing returns makes a big difference, and changes the established wisdom significantly.... we have not yet reached the point of diminishing returns in the study of increasing returns: there is a long way to go, and the results of the work yet to be completed will be interesting (Heal, 1999).

Despite the prominent place given to the division of labour in classical economics, it has been left largely unanalysed since the neoclassical revolution. This is related to the difficulty of accommodating the phenomenon of increasing returns in orthodox analysis. However increasing returns are important at the level of the individual, the firm, the industry, the economy and globally. Increasing returns are widespread for a number of reasons. First, there are learning costs in producing virtually any good and in earning better skills through practice. Second, there are usually some degrees of indivisibility, giving rise to sizable fixed costs. A shop has to be of a certain minimum size, office space has to be rented for a certain minimum period and machines come in certain sizes. Arrow (1995) explains how the relevance of information and knowledge in production makes increasing returns prevalent (see also Wilson, 1975; Radner and Stiglitz, 1984; on empirical evidence for increasing returns, see Ades and Glaeser, 1999; Antweiler and Trefler, 2002). A very common situation is for a firm to have a high fixed cost and relatively low and roughly constant (or even decreasing, due, for example, to the economies of bulk purchase) marginal costs, making the average cost curve a sharply decreasing rectangular hyperbola, becoming flatter only at very high levels of output. Such a firm will sell more at any given price above marginal cost (MC). In contrast a perfect competitor will refuse to sell more at the given price (at the profit-maximising equilibrium the MC curve cuts the horizontal price line from below, making the additional cost of producing more greater than the additional revenue generated). If you were to ask 1000 business persons whether they wanted to sell more at the given (prevailing) price, I bet you would receive no fewer than 990 positive answers! Perfect competition prevails in no more than 1 per cent of cases. In addition to increasing returns, product differentiation (including different brands and locations) makes the demand curve for the product of each firm downward sloping. The real economy is characterised more by monopolistic competition with oligopolistic elements than by perfect competition.

Allowing for the presence of increasing returns plays havoc with many of the conclusions of orthodox economics. Some of these are discussed below (numerous others could be added, for example the cost of protection may be much higher in the presence of increasing returns – see Panagariya, 2002).

10.4.1 The possible non-neutrality of money

The problems caused by increasing returns can even be seen using concepts that are familiar to first-year undergraduates. If a firm is a perfect competitor in the factor market, it takes input prices as given. Increasing returns thus makes its average cost curve downward sloping. With a horizontal demand curve for its product it will increase output indefinitely, or at least until increasing returns no longer apply or it is no longer a perfect competitor. The assumption of perfect competition therefore does not allow the continued existence of increasing returns.

With firms that are not perfectly competitive, many of the traditional propositions have to be drastically revised. For example the neutrality of money thesis – that changes in the money supply or other changes in nominal aggregate demand affect only the price level and do not affect real variables – may no longer hold. Even in the absence of time lags, money illusion and other frictions, the relaxation of perfect competition can mean that a change in nominal aggregate demand may affect either the price level (the monetarist case) or real output (the Keynesian case).[1] The crux of the difference is two sided. On the demand side, with a horizontal demand curve under perfect competition, the curve cannot shift to the left or to the right. It can only shift up or down. But an upward shift means an increase in price. In the absence of money illusion, time lags and so on an increase in the price increases the costs proportionately, so there is no real change (this is the crux of the neutrality of money result under perfect competition). In contrast, under non-perfect competition, with a downward-sloping demand curve consistent with a downward-sloping average cost curve due to increasing returns, the demand curve may either shift upward/downward or rightward/leftward, allowing for possible real effects from a change in nominal aggregate demand.

On the supply side, a profit-maximisation equilibrium with a horizontal demand curve implies an upward-sloping MC curve. This associates an expansion in output with a higher MC, which calls for a higher price. But a higher price is contractionary as it reduces real aggregate demand at a given level of nominal aggregate demand. In contrast, in the case of non-perfect competition the MC curve may be horizontal or even downward sloping. The decrease in MC with a higher output, if it is not more than offset by

---

1. Many economists (see Dixon and Rankin, 1994, for a survey) still consider that additional distortions or frictions such as menu costs are necessary, in combination with non-perfect competition, to make money non-neutral. In fact, instead of showing the neutrality of money under non-perfect competition it has only been shown that a real equilibrium can still be an equilibrium even if the money supply changes. However a change in the money supply may also shift the economy from one equilibrium to another, making money not really neutral (Ng, 1998).

an upward shift in the MC curve as aggregate output expands, may make higher output levels possible equilibria. (The full analysis takes into account consistency with the general-equilibrium effects of infinite rounds of feedback between a firm and the rest of the economy, including the effects on its cost and demand functions.) In fact cases of expectation wonderland (where the outcome depends on the expectation of firms, which will then be self-fulfilling) and cumulative expansion/contraction are also possible, which partly explains real-world phenomena such as business cycles, the importance of confidence and the difficulty of economic prediction (Ng, 1980b, 1986a, 1992c, 1998, 1999b). In such non-traditional cases there exists **an interfirm macroeconomic externality**, where the expansion of each firm benefits other firms, **apart from** the familiar income multiplier effects. This is an area in which welfare economics, macroeconomics and its microfoundation intersect, an area that is still not adequately studied. Ng's analysis is based on a representative firm but, using a simplified general-equilibrium method, it takes account of the influence of macro variables and the interaction with the rest of the economy. Moreover a fully general-equilibrium analysis is used to show that (1) for any (exogenous) change in cost or demand, there exists, in a hypothetical sense, a representative firm whose response to the change accurately (no approximation needed) represents the response of the whole economy in terms of aggregate output and average price, and (2) a representative firm defined by a simple method with a weighted average can be used as a good approximation of the response of the whole economy to any economy wide change in demand and/or costs that does not result in drastic interfirm changes (see Ng, 1986a, app. 3A).

10.4.2   Pecuniary external effects may have real efficiency implications

It was mentioned in Chapter 7 that market relationships are not real external effects. Instead they are pecuniary external effects that do not affect the efficiency of a competitive economy. This can be shown by means of a simple supply–demand analysis. The usefulness of this simple method is underrated as it is seen as just a partial equilibrium analysis. However for many analytical purposes it can be viewed as a general equilibrium analysis due to the following consideration a consideration that is so important that it is surprising that it seems to be mentioned nowhere else. The Hicks composite commodity theorem states that if the relative prices between all goods in a given set of commodities remain unchanged, the set may be lumped into a single composite commodity, with the quantity of this composite commodity being the total expenditure on all commodities in this set divided by one of the prices in the set, and with the price of the composite commodity being the price used as the divisor. On the other hand Walras' law states that in an economy with G commodities, equilibrium in any $G - 1$ market implies equilibrium in all markets (as the net demand for any good by any trader has to be financed by a net supply). Thus for the numerous situations in which we can lump all commodities into two composite commodities, we can use the supply–demand analysis on any one of the two commodities and hence the analysis is also a general equilibrium one. It could be thought that relative prices do not usually remain unchanged. This may be true empirically, but in most economic analyses (excluding computable general equilibrium analysis) we seldom consider changes in the relative prices of more than two sets of goods simultaneously.[2] Therefore for analytical purposes such as the present one the supply–demand method can be used for a general equilibrium analysis (even empirically the method can be seen as a good approximation in many cases – see Li and Ng, forthcoming).

First consider the normal case of upward-sloping supply and downward-sloping demand curves. If the demand curve shifts outward, causing the price of the good in question (*X*) to increase, this increase in demand could be coming from new consumers (including foreign demand) or from existing consumers. The increase in price makes the original consumers worse off. However no inefficiency is involved as the loss in consumer surplus is fully offset by the gain in producer surplus (with a curvilinear triangle of additional surplus to spare due to the increase in net surplus that comes from catering to the additional demand).

Next consider the case of a downward-sloping supply curve, as might be caused by increasing returns. The increase in demand causes the price to fall instead of increase. Original consumers gain by having a higher surplus, but, there is no corresponding decrease in real producer surplus as producers are still breaking even at the now lower average costs of production. For the previous case of an upward-sloping supply curve, competitive firms also just break even at the higher price and higher average cost. However the suppliers of inputs to these firms gain by having higher surpluses or rents through the higher prices for these inputs. In the case of a downward-sloping supply curve there is no corresponding decrease in surplus for input suppliers as the decrease in the cost of production is due to real factors that cause increasing returns (for example economies of bulk purchase/usage, specialisation and scale) rather than to decreases in input prices. Thus for the present case of a

---

2. Including cases where only the (set of) price(s) of one (set of) good(s) change (proportionately), with the (relative) prices of all other goods remaining unchanged when the composite commodity theorem may be strictly used and where the possible changes in the prices of other goods are not focused upon when the use of the theorem is similar to the assumption of *ceteris paribus*. The fact that other things do not usually remain unchanged does not prevent us from using *ceteris paribus*. We focus on what will be the case if other things remained unchanged, and what will be the case if other prices do not change.

downward-sloping supply curve from increasing returns, pecuniary external effects may have real efficiency implications.

10.4.3   Market equilibrium is no longer Pareto optimal

In the traditional framework the existence and Pareto optimality of a competitive equilibrium depends on the absence of increasing returns (or at least not global increasing returns). It is well known that increasing returns can give rise to certain efficiency problems in a market economy (see for example Guesnerie, 1975; Arrow, 1987, 2000; Quinzii, 1992; Villar, 1996; Heal, 1999).

The problems caused by increasing returns may be explained simply. The existence of increasing returns causes the average cost curve of a firm to be downward sloping and the marginal cost to be less than the average cost. This makes marginal-cost pricing for efficiency unlikely to be feasible as losses will be involved. Moreover, this means that an increase in demand that causes the average cost of production to fall may benefit others, as will be the case with average-cost pricing, thus explaining the efficiency implication of pecuniary externalities discussed in the previous subsection.

More than eight decades ago Pigou (1920) advocated the taxation (subsidisation) of goods with increasing (decreasing) costs of production or with upward (downward) sloping supply curves to increase the overall surplus. Further discussion (on the costs and returns, reprinted in AEA, 1953) revealed some problems with Pigou's analysis. Pigou used the example of a non-congested, wide but uneven road and a narrow but well-surfaced road to illustrate overuse of the narrow road where usage costs increase with the number of users due to congestion. Knight (1924) correctly pointed out that this was due to the failure of pricing the congested road. With optimal pricing (in the absence of pricing costs, which would be optimal both for the private owner of the road and for social efficiency), no overuse would be involved. This will no come as surprise to modern economists taught with the Pareto optimal nature of a competitive equilibrium in the absence of unaccounted external effects. However more than half a century ago, when environmental consciousness was not high, economists confidently concluded that the 'departure of the economist's *free* competition from the ideal of social costs is in fact negligible for external economies' (Ellis and Fellner, 1943, p. 511). Even if we ignore external costs such as environmental damage (discussed in Chapters 7 and 11), the undisputed and widespread existence of increasing returns still makes a competitive equilibrium non-existent (not in the sense that the economy remains competitive but equilibrium does not exist, but in the sense that the economy cannot remain perfectly competitive), not to mention the question of its Pareto optimality.

Since firms' average cost is downward sloping over all of the relevant range, they will expand output indefinitely as long as they are price takers. However the expansion will eventually render price-taking behaviour irrelevant. These may then be a monopolistic restriction of output, with price above MC (which equals MR). This will lead to underproduction if all other sectors are perfectly competitive. What is the situation if monopolistic competition is prevalent? Dixit and Stiglitz's (1977) analysis (discussed further in Section 10.6.2) shows that no general conclusion can be drawn. The more specific models by Heal (1980, 1999) show that the combination of imperfection competition and increasing returns leads to the overserving of large markets and underserving of small markets (see also Spence, 1976; Lancaster, 1979; Hart, 1985, on optimal product variety). This is consistent with the simple partial equilibrium intuition, which is illustrated by a downward-sloping average cost curve. Now, to abstract away from problems arising from monopolistic power, assume that the market is perfectly contestable (on which see Baumol, 1982) so that price equals average cost. It can be shown, from the viewpoint of Pareto optimality, that industries with increasing returns are underexpanded relative to those without increasing returns, and that those with higher increasing returns are underexpanded relative to those with lower increasing returns (Ng, 2003b). Subsidies on goods produced under conditions of (high) increasing returns financed by taxes on goods produced under non-increasing and lower increasing returns can increase efficiency (ignoring other effects such as second-best and externalities that offset increasing returns).

Pigou's original argument was valid even though it contained incorrect arguments. While the subsequent discussion concentrated on purging these, many economists believed that Pigou's proposal for taxing (subsidising) industries with decreasing (increasing) returns (or increasing/decreasing costs) was based on mistakes and had no substance. Moreover The subsequent influence of the elegant proof of the Pareto optimality of competitive equilibrium and the general inclination of economists to favour the invisible hand and oppose government intervention served to bury Pigou's valid point in a sealed tomb.[3]

Why Pigou's basic point is valid is not difficult to see. With a falling average cost curve, even pricing at average cost (in contrast to a much more restrictive policy of pricing at marginal revenue equals marginal cost) involves pricing above marginal cost (as MC is below AC when AC is decreasing),

---

3. There are studies of the implications of increasing returns in the international economics literature (for example Kemp, 1964; Ethier, 1979, 1982; Panagariya, 1981; Helpman and Krugman, 1985; Chandra *et al.*, 2002) and in the general equilibrium literature (cited in the text above). It should be noted that some of Panagariya's fairly extreme results (including Propositions 1 and 2) are due to the slope of zero for the transformation curve at the point of specialisation (a consequence of the simple modelling of external economies/diseconomies, a slope that is clearly not applicable in the real world.

implying underproduction. This partial equilibrium point is also true in a general equilibrium framework unless it is offset by other considerations, such as the second-best interrelationship of complementarity to (substitutability for) another good of opposite (similar) efficiency considerations. That this is true can be seen by taking all other goods as a composite good, which means that the partial equilibrium analysis also a general equilibrium one. On the other hand, apart from applications to certain areas such as international trade, the more sophisticated analyses of increasing returns in recent decades (for example the papers collected in Heal, 1999) focus more on the existence of general equilibria, particularly the existence and Pareto optimality of marginal cost pricing equilibria.

Nevertheless the inclination of economists to oppose intervention may be correct. First, when increasing returns are prevalent we and the government may not know which industries are subject to higher increasing returns than others. Therefore if we consider a model where all goods have the same degree of increasing returns, the market equilibrium cannot be improved upon by taxes and subsidies, given the infeasibility of taxing leisure (Ng, 2003b; on the encouragement of work see Section 10.6.2 below). Second, imposing taxes (subsidies) on goods with substantially decreasing (increasing) returns would open a floodgate to rent-seeking activities that would probably consume an enormous amount of resources costing much more than the gain from optimal taxes or subsidies. Perhaps it would be optimal to continue to pretend that increasing returns do not exist!

10.5   The Smith dilemma and its resolution

Since the Pareto optimality of competitive equilibria depends on the absence of increasing returns, and since the division of labour gives rise to increasing returns through economies of specialisation, we have the Smith dilemma: 'The inconsistency of the efficiency of the invisible hand (the Smith theory) based on the absence of increasing returns with the facilitation of the economies of specialization (which gives rise to increasing returns) by the extent of the market (the Smith theorem)' (see Stigler, 1951). While Heal (1999) regards this as an inconsistency on the part of Smith, it will be argued below that, interpreted in a practical sense, Smith was in fact correct on both points.

Since the days of Marshall (1920), attempts have been made to save perfect competition from the devastation of increasing returns by confining increasing returns to those resulting from external effects between the production processes of different firms rather than from internal economies within the firm. The unit cost of each firm does not decrease with its own output, though the unit costs of all firms fall as the industry expands. There may then be a competitive equilibrium, although if external economies are not tackled, Pareto optimality will generally be absent (for a formal analysis see Chipman, 1970; Romer, 1986; Suzuki, 1996). More importantly, while external economies capture an important aspect of the real economy, the equally important factors of internal economies and product differentiation are abstracted away.

Buchanan and Yoon (1999) have attempted to resolve the Smith dilemma. Their basic point is as follows. If increasing returns are due to the facilitation of greater economies of specialisation by a larger market, these are generalised increasing returns at the level of the whole economy or the whole network of division of labour. Such increasing returns may be consistent with perfect competition, but will they be Pareto-optimal in the absence of other problems? Buchanan believes that the market equilibrium is suboptimal with respect to the amount of work. This issue is discussed in Section 10.6.2. Here, ignoring the work–leisure choice as well as external economies, we shall consider the implications of increasing returns from internal economies.

Strictly speaking the existence of (perfectly) competitive equilibrium is impossible in practice. The prevalence of increasing returns rules out universal perfect competition and the virtual universality of product differentiation makes perfect competition a rare exception. Marginal cost pricing equilibrium is also impractical as, in the presence of increasing returns, it involves losses. Thus in a sense Heal (1999) is correct to say that the Smith theory on the efficiency of the invisible hand is inconsistent ('strictly an error') with the Smith theorem on the economies of specialisation. However it can be reasonably argued that Smith was correct both on the efficiency of the invisible hand and on the economies of specialisation, or at least to a very large extent. Ignoring external effects (see Chapter 7), ignorance/irrationallty (see Chapter 11) and occasional major failures such as financial crises and depressions (and possibly the inefficiency caused by informational asymmetry, on which see Stiglitz, 2002) as these issues are largely separate from the matter of the consistency between the efficiency of the invisible hand and increasing returns, the real market economy is very efficient (though not 100 per cent efficient) in coordinating the separate activities of individual decision makers in the economy, despite the widespread prevalence of increasing returns and the rarity of perfect competition. The economies of specialisation (especially with the additional power of learning by doing and exogenous technical progress) made possible by the division of labour also lead to increasing returns at the level of the overall economy, as well as propel economic growth and the evolution of economic organisation. Provided that Smith was not suggesting that the invisible hand is 100 per cent efficient (in the same sense as the perfect Pareto efficienty of the Arrow–Debreu model of perfect competition, which has never existed 100 per cent in the real world), he was correct both in his theory and his theorem. The real market economy is characterised by high (even if imperfect) efficiency and increasing returns, so there is really no Smith dilemma.

From this perspective it is misleading to say that 'the fact that a competitive equilibrium has a desirable property is of no significance if such an equilibrium does not exist' (Vohra, 1994, p. 102). Even if a competitive equilibrium does not exist, many of the features that define competitive equilibrium (market coordination, utility and profit maximisation, free enterprise) exist in the real market economy and these features make the real economy largely efficient?

The above common-sense point is very difficult to establish rigorously since it applies only at the 'largely speaking' level, rather than perfectly. Not only may small inefficiencies exist, as noted above, we cannot even rule out occasional large inefficiencies, especially when the dynamic perspective is taken into account. In the presence of increasing returns, 'A technology that improves slowly at first but has enormous long-term potential could easily be shut out, locking an economy into a path that is both inferior and difficult to escape' (Arthur, 1994, p. 10). Here the real case of the elimination of the technically superior Beta video recorders by VHS springs to mind.

It could be thought that, even ignoring occasional large inefficiencies (which may become more frequent in the future with the growing importance of knowledge and increasing returns in the economy), the remaining inefficiencies may still be large. In the case of a firm with a high degree of monopolistic power (or, in the presence of perfect contestability, a firm with high increasing returns), if it were willing to increase its output its efficiency would be significantly improved. So how could the situation $MR = MC < MV = AC$ be said to be highly efficient? The latter is based on comparing an actual situation with some or other infeasible situation. If we confine ourselves to feasible situations, the degree of inefficiency will be much less. It is true that the market solution need not even be (non-negative profit) constrained optimal. But the divergence, if any, of the market solution from the constrained optimum is much less than that from the unconstrained optimum (Ng and Zhang, 2003).

To a large extent Heal is likely to concur with this, as he writes:

> It is puzzling that although economies of scale are undoubtedly important in reality, our belief in the invisible hand, in the efficiency of competition, seems verified by observation and experience, although not supported by current theory. This suggests that our understanding of economies with increasing returns is far from complete: there may be a role for competition and markets in allocating resources in the presence of increasing returns that we have not yet understood (Heal, 1999, p. xvi).

It is true that more research on increasing returns is needed, but the puzzle can be partly explained by the high degree of efficiency of the market economy, as argued above. It may be added that this efficiency is to a large extent due to the more or less free entry/exit of producers. (although free entry/exit contributes to efficiency only in the absence of artificial price maintenance – a combination of price maintenance and free entry could lead to a very inefficient situation). The importance of this can even be seen in traditional analyses.

The Yang–Ng (1993) framework demonstrates the role of the market in coordinating not only resource allocation in an economy with a given division of labour but also in coordinating the division of labour itself, although an important part is also played by entrepreneurs, as discussed in the next section. Thus the increasing returns at the level of the economy due to economies of specialisation at the individual level can be largely realised through a division of labour facilitated by market coordination. However increasing returns at the firm level and the associated efficiency problems have yet to be analysed in the new framework. Other related issues, such as path dependency (and thus the importance of history) due to increasing returns (as ably analysed by Arthur, 1994; see also Arrow, 2000), also require further exploration.

The fact that the real economy is not perfectly efficient means that improvements might be possible. Industries or firms with marked increasing returns (and hence marginal costs that are for below average costs) could be taxed less than others. However the potential advantage of doing this has to be weighed against the costs of administration, rent seeking, mistakes and corruption facilitation. In economies that lack a highly efficient government, a policy of *laissez-faire* would probably be best in this respect. However, this does not mean that an overall *laissez-faire* policy is best. The huge external costs that arise from the environmental damage caused by production and consumption, the prevalence of important relative-consumption effects (a form of external effect) and the widespread existence of imperfect knowledge and imperfect rationality suggest a substantial role for a moderately efficient government, as discussed in Chapter 11.

10.6 The Pareto optimality of general equilibrium in the new framework – the role of entrepreneurs

In Yang and Ng (1993), where individuals are taken as *ex ante* identical and the general equilibrium economic structure is defined as one that maximises the equalised utility level (to ensure equilibrium among identical individuals), the general equilibrium is Pareto optimal by definition. However this concept of general equilibrium is somewhat narrow and does not include the situation in which an economy is in equilibrium in the sense of not changing and the equilibrium applies to the whole economy (hence the 'general'). These narrow versus wider concepts of general equilibrium also apply to general equilibrium in the traditional (perfect competition) framework.

To explain this point, consider Arrow's (1951a, p. 528) example of the non-existence of general equilibrium (a popular discussion of this can be found in Chipman, 1965, which is reprinted in Townsend, 1971/1980). The economy consists only of two farmers and two goods – meat and vegetables:

> Suppose Farmer Jones has some vegetables which he has grown and wishes to market. Assume that if the price of vegetables is high enough in relation to meat, he will sell some of them and buy meat with the proceeds, but below a certain price he will just consume his own vegetables; finally, if vegetables are free, he will want to consume an indefinitely large quantity of them. On the other hand, suppose Farmer Brown has a small and insufficient supply of meat, but a bumper crop of vegetables, more than he could possibly want for himself (Chipman, in Townsend, 1980, p. 448).

Then, at any positive price of vegetables relative to meat, there is a negative excess demand for vegetables as both farmers want to sell vegetables in exchange for meat. At a zero price for vegetables the excess demand for vegetables is infinite. Hence at no price is the excess demand for vegetables equal to zero, so there is no general equilibrium in this sense. However this does not mean that 'the price of vegetables will oscillate indefinitely' (ibid.) Rather there will simply be no transactions. The economy will be at equilibrium, with each farmer consuming his own products. Since this applies to all markets in the economy it should be accepted as a general equilibrium in the wider sense. The narrower concept of equilibrium, in terms of a set of prices that clears all markets, is a Walrasian equilibrium. But not all general equilibria, even if deemed to be perfectly competitive, need be Walrasian. Hence there may be a million identical farmer Joneses and a million identical farmer Browns, none of whom has an appreciable effect on prices. There still does not exist a price at which the excess demand for vegetables is zero. However the economy will still be at equilibrium with no transactions, (with each farmer consuming his own products). Thus we have a non-Walrasian general competitive equilibrium. However, many general equilibrium theorists seem to be for too 'captured' by their abstract theories to see this simple real-world possibility, and they think that the absence of a Walrasian equilibrium set of prices implies that the price will oscillate. The possibility of a no-transaction equilibrium simply does not enter their minds.

Now consider the Yang–Ng (1993) framework. Take the simplest case of two identical individuals, J and K, and two goods, x and y. If the costs of transaction are very high it is efficient for each individual to produce and consume both goods, resulting in an autarkic equilibrium. Now suppose that transaction efficiency has improved to the point where it is efficient for each individual to specialise in the production of one good and to sell part of the product in exchange for another good from the other individual. If transaction efficiency and/or the degree of economy of specialisation are high enough, specialisation will be more efficient than autarky. With the two individuals specialising in the production of one good each, a general equilibrium exists and is Pareto-optimal. However this does not necessarily mean that equilibrium will be attained in the real economy. Some coordination is needed to move from autarkic to specialisation equilibrium. In this simple case of two individuals, coordination is very simple. One of the individuals can just say to the other, 'Why don't you specialise in producing y and I in x and then we can exchange the goods.' If they do not engage in hard bargaining and agree readily on the terms of exchange, the new specialisation equilibrium will be achieved.

It should be noted that the required coordination is over and above that provided by the price system. To understand this, assume the existence of a Walrasian auctioneer who announces the most efficient and fair price of one between x and y (in the simple model where the goods are symmetrical). Each individual (or each of two million individuals) takes the price as given and maximises accordingly. Each will decide to specialise in the production of one good only and will try to exchange it for another good of the same price. However in the absence of extra-price coordination all individuals may produce x, with no one producing y. If y is essential to life, a new equilibrium may be reached in which all individuals are dead!

The fact that some extra-price coordination may be needed does not mean that it would be best done by a central planning board. Consider the more general case of the introduction of a new good in a more realistic setting. Even if transaction efficiency, population size, technology and so on have reached the point at which the marketing of a new good will be efficient, the good may not enjoy instant sales success as people first have to learn of its existence and perhaps make adjustments. For example before the availability of takeaway food, eating out was quite expensive and most people cooked their own dinners and packed their own lunches. Then the introduction of reasonably priced takeaway food significantly reduced the cost of eating purchased meals and people gradually adjusted to this by reducing the extent of their home cooking, thus gaining more time to spend on leisure or specialised activities. Most new goods need some time for consumers to learn of and adjust to before they become profitable, so even the most astute entrepreneurs may have to sustain substantial initial losses. To be able to sustain such losses is one of the requirements of entrepreneurial success. This also highlights the importance of financial institutions in transforming savings into investments. If we compare a centrally planned economy with a free-enterprise market economy in terms of the successful introduction of suitable new goods, the superiority of the latter is even more decisive than in the allocation of resources between existing sets of goods. Thus the need for coordination is largely filled in a market economy by the functioning of entrepreneurial activities (on the importance of entrepreneurs and market entry in transitional economies see McMillan and Woodruff, 2002).

The need for entrepreneurs exists even in the traditional framework as the introduction of lower-cost methods of production and new goods is by definition the function of entrepreneurs. However the need for entrepreneurship is rather slim in the traditional framework of perfect competition with no increasing returns. When the technology/demand/transaction conditions have improved to the point where the demand for and supply of a new good result in the intersection of the downward-sloping demand curve and the upward-sloping supply curve at a positive quantity, the new good will prove to be profitable. Moreover, whoever introduces it will reap supernormal profits as the demand price is initially higher than the supply price. In contrast, in the division of labour framework, someone who shifts to the production of a newly marketed good may not even break even until a sufficient number of individuals stop producing that good at home and purchase it instead, which brings us back to the need to be able to sustain an initial period of losses.

The need for entrepreneurship and perhaps other means of solving the coordination problem is present even before we consider the indirect network externality discussed in the next section, which raises issues in welfare economics that are only just beginning to be addressed.

10.7   Welfare economic issues and the division of labour

There are many welfare economic issues that can be addressed with the help of the new framework, but in this section only two examples will be considered.

10.7.1   Infrastructural improvements and indirect network externalities

Governments have been very active in instigating and encouraging improvements in transaction efficiency, including the provision of legal, social and economic infrastructure. (For the effects of infrastructure on productivity see World Bank, 1994; for a historical perspective and the importance of population size see Boserup, 1981; Chandler, 1990). Even early free-market economists such as Adam Smith found 'the erection and maintenance of the public works which facilitate the commerce of any country, such as good roads, bridges, navigable canals, harbours' desirable, and indeed saw this as 'evident without [the need for] any proof' (Smith, 1776/1976, vol. II, p. 245). Perhaps it was the apparently self-evident nature of this that caused economists to pay little attention to the importance of infrastructure until recently (see Aschauer, 1989; Gramlich, 1994; Bougheas *et al.*, 2000; La Ferrara, 2001).

The need for government involvement can be explained by the public good nature of infrastructure. However if this is the only reason there is little cause to encourage it if the items concerned are excludable and can be priced as applicable to many cases, including communications. Moreover according to traditional analysis, even in the case of non-excludable items there is no reason to provide them beyond the levels indicated by the equation of (aggregate) marginal benefits and marginal costs, evaluated according the existing structure of economic organisations or the degree of specialisation of the whole economy (which is **not** taken as a variable in traditional analysis). If we take the degree of specialisation as endogenous, the provision of infrastructure that decreases transaction costs may produce some indirect network externality. This should be distinguished from the possible network externality of the infrastructure itself, which is well known. For example the usefulness of telephones, fax machines and e-mail facilities increases as more people gain access to them. This is a direct network externality, which we shall abstract away. Rather we shall consider the following more indirect effects.

The improvement of transaction (including communication and transportation) efficiency can generate benefits in excess of direct private benefits by promoting a higher degree of specialisation. If transaction efficiency is very low (that is, transaction costs are very high) it may be optimal for everyone to be autarkic, self-producing all the goods they need. As transaction efficiency improves it becomes optimal to buy some goods from others and to sell a good one specialises in, but to continue to produce other goods for one's own consumption and provide one's own services (home cooking, cleaning, gardening, child minding and so on). As transaction efficiency improves the set of goods bought from others increases. Thus the benefits of improved transaction efficiency consist not only of reducing the costs of transaction but also of promoting the division of labour and the consequent tapping of economies of specialisation. However, even assuming that the cost of exclusion is negligible and that there is no free-rider problem, a private producer of an infrastructural improvement that reduces transaction costs may only be able to capture the direct benefits of lower transaction costs, and not the indirect benefits of promoting specialisation (even in the absence of individual differences that give rise to consumer surpluses). People will just assess the benefits of lower transaction costs given the current degree of specialisation in the economy. Not only that the benefits through a higher degree of specialisation will occur only in the future contingent on the appearance of new marketable goods, but also this development is taken as not affected by the improvement in the transaction efficiency of a single individual herself. It is thus rational, even under conditions of full knowledge, to ignore the indirect benefit that higher transaction efficiency has on the level of specialisation.

In other words there are two public good problems. The improvement of infrastructure to increase transaction efficiency may itself be a public good. However even if this public good problem can be overcome through exclusion, there is another public good problem at the level of the increase in

the degree of specialisation to which the higher transaction efficiency contributes. Even with perfect foresight individuals do not take account of the
benefits of a higher degree of specialisation because that is determined by
the general level of transaction efficiency in the economy as a whole, and is
not appreciably affected by that of the individual. Even if I could correctly
predict that the widespread use of a new communication system would
promote specialisation and result in a number of new products becoming
available in the market, I would not count the benefits of the availability of
the new products when assessing the usefulness to me of the new system
as the products would be available to all even if I did not use the system but
if others do. This second publicness problem is quite impossible to solve
through exclusion as the producers of new products are most likely to be different from the producer of the infrastructure. Thus the indirect externality
of infrastructure may make public provision or encouragement desirable.
The Yang–Ng framework of inframarginal analysis was used by Ng and Ng
(2001) to analyse the case for encouraging the improvement of transaction
efficiency over and above its direct benefits.[4] The results were consistent
with the empirical evidence that public infrastructure capital has positive
long-term effects on output and that 'the short-run rates of return are rather
low while the long-run rates of return tend to be quite high' (Demetriades
and Mamuneas, 2000, p. 689). It takes time for the degree of specialisation
to develop.

Ng and Ng also discovered that the lumpiness in investments to improve
transaction efficiency helps to create a divergence between social and private
benefits. In the case of non-lumpy investments the divergence is negligible.
This may partly explain why large projects are regarded as worthy of encouragement. Of course, like all reasonable justifications, this one could be
misused to justify inefficient projects.

10.7.2   Do economies of specialisation justify the work ethic?

Buchanan (1991, 1994) presents an interesting hypothesis to explain the
prevalence of an ethic that encourages more work. Economies of specialisation mean that a greater division of labour may increase productivity.
If everyone works more, this increases the extent of the market, which in
turn enables a greater division of labour and hence higher productivity.
Individual choice between leisure and work thus results in a suboptimal
level of work. One way to counteract this is to foster a work ethic.

---

4. Chu (1997), Wen (1997) and Wen and King (forthcoming) use the Yang–Ng framework to analyse the part played by infrastructure in economic growth. However
   they concentrate on the positive aspects (such as population density, resource
   endowment and the time path of growth) and do not discuss the possible rationale
   for encouragement.

Economists have paid little attention to this and similar problems, partly – if not mainly – because of the in preoccupation with the sectoral resource allocation problem in neoclassical economics instead of the division of labour problem in classical economics. However even within the traditional framework the problem of increasing returns has not been completely ignored. A well-known analysis is the Dixit–Stiglitz (1977) model of monopolistic competition (the model was later adapted by Ethier, 1979, 1982, to analyse the number of intermediate goods).

In the monopolistic competition sector, each firm produces a product with decreasing average costs (a positive fixed cost plus a constant marginal cost). The rest of the economy is lumped into a composite good. To analyse the question of work ethic we can regard this composite good as leisure – there is nothing in the model to preclude such an interpretation. We can then directly apply the Dixit–Stiglitz result to assess the validity of Buchanan's hypothesis within the monopolistic competition model.

Dixit and Stiglitz compare market equilibrium (with free entry) with the case of the constrained optimum (where each firm must not make a positive loss) and the case of the unconstrained optimum (where lump-sum subsidies to firms are allowed). Due to the difficulties of lump-sum subsidies in the real world and to Buchanan's emphasis on realistic market economies, the case of the constrained optimum is the more relevant one. According to Dixit and Stiglitz (1977, pp. 301–2) then 'results undermine the validity of the folklore of excess capacity, from the point of view of the unconstrained optimum as well as the constrained one... with a constant intra-sector elasticity of substitution, the market equilibrium coincides with the constrained optimum.... It is not possible to have a general result concerning the relative magnitudes of [leisure].' In other words, even if the unconstrained optimum is feasible it may involve more or less leisure than the cases of free market equilibrium and the constrained optimum. This is in contrast to Buchanan's presumption of overconsumption of leisure. However this need not be a fatal blow to Buchanan, who has in mind not so much the traditional economies of scale but the classical economies of specialisation from the division of labour, which is better modelled within the Yang–Ng framework. In fact Buchanan and Yoon (1994) provide a model that gives the result of overconsumption of leisure. The higher productivity that comes from a larger market size is due to the larger supportable number of intermediate goods, which is assumed to increase productivity (the Ethier assumption). Ng and Ng (2003) show this possibility within the Yang–Ng framework without using the Ethier mechanism.[5] They provide some support for

---

5. Leisure has been considered within the Yang–Ng framework by Lio (1996, 2003), who addresses the question of productivity but not the question of welfare or the desirability of encouraging work.

Buchanan's hypothesis by showing that the higher the degree of economies of specialisation, the larger the beneficial effect of a greater work ethic on the trading partner. Buchanan's thesis probably would have had more relevance in bygone times when the work ethic originated, but it is less significant in the current world of global trade where the vast number of individuals involved is largely sufficient to sustain specialisation without artificial encouragement of an additional work effort. (There are some exceptions to this, including industries with huge economies of scale, such as the production of aeroplanes and the production of knowledge, which is a global public good. However the latter consideration favours a larger population more than more work effort – see Ng, 1986b, 2002a.) On the contrary, the competition for relative standing, the materialistic bias caused by advertisements and our instinct to accumulate and the environmental damage caused by production and consumption suggest that discouragement of the long working week may be more conducive to welfare (this is discussed in the next chapter).

10.8 Implications

As mentioned above, the Yang–Ng framework has been used to analyse many economic issues, but the welfare implications are only beginning to be discussed so there is considerable scope for further research. One implication thrown into focus by the new framework is the need to take account of indirect effects on the structure of economic organisation or the division of labour network. This applies to the above discussion of infrastructure investment and work ethic, but it is certainly not confined to them. Rather any changes that affect the organisational structure of the economy can have indirect effects that might be ignored if we only use the traditional framework to model the economy. The new framework not only helps to explain the trade-off between economies of specialisation and transaction costs, but also enables us to focus on the indirect effects of organisational efficiency. The new framework can also make us take a different view of certain issues in the real world. A larger role for entrepreneurs has already been noted above; another point, related to international trade, is outlined next.

According to the traditional Ricardian theory of comparative advantage, international trade and globalisation may make some groups in some countries worse off, but the (monetary) losses are smaller than the gains to others. For example the exportation of high-tech and capital-intensive goods from the United States to China and the importation of labour-intensive goods from China into the United States may lower the US prices of labour-intensive goods and hence the wages of unskilled labour in United States. While the gains to other groups (consumers of labour-intensive goods, producers of capital-intensive goods) more than offset the losses, or at least in monetary terms, unskilled workers in United States are not likely to be happy. The argument in Appendix 9.1 for treating a dollar as a dollar in specific issues suggests that having free trade to maximise the efficiency gains, combined with a general transfer to help the lower income groups, will still achieve a quasi-Pareto improvement (see also Section 3.5). However people may not see the point or may be worried about the lack of corresponding transfer. This is probably the single most important cause of the movement against globalisation. Seen from the US perspective, the opposition to trade appears to have some moral ground as unskilled US workers typically fall into low income groups. However the unskilled workers in China will be made better off by trade, and since they are much poorer than the unskilled workers in United States, seen from the world perspective equality is promoted by trade. (This focuses on the effects of trade as such and ignores the possible effect of globalisation in limiting the pursuit of distributional equality within countries, as discussed towards the end of Chapter 11.) The point here is that, in contrast to the conflict of interest between different groups in the Ricardian theory of trade, according to the analyses by Adam Smith (1776/1976) and Xiaokai Yang (see Yang and Ng, 1993 and Yang, 2001) international trade and globalisation allow the division of labour and specialisation to reach higher levels, making all people in all countries better off. If economists explained this point to the public, the clamour against globalisation might diminish (Buchanan and Yoon, 2002).

Exogenous comparative advantage, economies of scale at the firm level and economies of specialisation at the economy level are present in the real world (not to mention increasing returns at the world level, on which see Ethier, 1979; Chandra *et al.*, 2002). Hence the different types of analysis are all important. However traditional trade theory puts too much emphasis on constant returns and largely ignores economies of specialisation (on the significance of increasing returns at the firm level and of imperfect competition for international trade see Helpman and Krugman, 1985). This bias should be corrected. As for which type of gain from trade is more important in the real world, this depends on the situation in question. During a seminar presented by Buchanan at Monash University in Melbourne in March 2002, Yang stated that according to Ricardian theory trade should be mainly between advanced countries and developing countries as they had different factor endowments, but in fact international trade was mainly between advanced countries with similar technical and factor endowments, which indicated that the gain from specialisation must be more important. Buchanan agreed. In my view this is a *prima facie* case, but further studies are needed as the amount of trade and the gain from trade need not be in constant proportion. This is particularly so since, according to Ricardian theory, trade between countries with very different factor endowments should provide larger gains.

There are wider conceptual implications of the existence of increasing returns. Obviously if a firm has a downward-sloping demand curve for its product, its profits will be increased by any rightward shift in the demand curve at the current (profit-maximising) price. An increase in aggregate demand in the economy as a whole may also increase the profits of most firms if the increase in aggregate output does not push up the in costs significantly, as might well be the case in the presence of excess capacity and unemployed resources (this is true in both the short and the long term, defined by the given/variable number of firms – see Section 10.3.1 above and Ng, 1986a, for details). With full employment, could welfare be improved by increasing aggregate demand through a nominal increase (such as increasing the money supply or an increase in individuals' willingness to spend), an increase in work effort or an increase in population? First consider this question in the absence of real external effects (such as pollution and conspicuous consumption), imperfect knowledge and imperfect rationality. With full employment, an increase in nominal aggregate demand is unlikely to be either profit or welfare improving as firms' costs are likely to increase significantly at higher output levels. However an improvement is not impossible if the response of costs to aggregate output is not large and is offset by the economies of larger output levels, including the greater division of labour and higher economies from knowledge improvements. (An increase in the price elasticity of demand for firms' products, including that caused by more intense competition due to the entry of new firms, may also help to make the improvement possible – see Ng, 1986a, ch. 4.) Just as the presence of increasing returns at the firm and industry level can cause particular firms/industries to be underexpanded, the presence of increasing returns at the economy level can cause the whole economy to be under-expanded. Even if this situation does not apply for an increase in nominal aggregate demand, it can still apply for an increase in real aggregate demand due to a population increase (through immigration or a rise in births, as discussed towards the end of Section 2.3) or a greater work effort (Section 10.6.2). However, while we are likely to benefit from increasing returns that are related to greater specialisation or to the lower average cost of providing infrastructure and obtaining new knowledge, we may suffer from the increasing costs of environmental damage. If we also take account of the relative-income effects and the materialistic bias discussed in the next chapter, discouraging rather encouraging work effort may be desirable.

With regard to population size, there is an additional complication. Even if a population increase results in a fall in per capita income or even in per capita welfare (average welfare), this might not be a bad thing. The question of whether average welfare or total welfare (average welfare multiplied by the number in the population) should be maximised has been debated by economists and philosophers for a long time but no conclusive answer has been reached. My position is that, at the level of ideal morality, total welfare (abstracting away animal welfare) should be maximised but people now may be more concerned about their own welfare than that of people in the far future (Ng, 1989).[6]

When economists ignore the real world and focus on a perfectly competitive equilibrium under simplified assumptions the picture seems consistent, coherent and beautiful. Simplified general-equilibrium analyses have no doubt captured some essential elements of the real economy and are an important achievement in economic analysis, but the simple picture is far removed from the real world in many important respects. The mere recognition of increasing returns has caused havoc with many of the established wisdoms. Competition cannot be perfect; equilibrium may not exist and may not be Pareto-optimal even if it does exist; and so on. The real economy is more likely to mirror the complicated interactions of millions of individual and collective profit and utility-seeking activities that are largely efficient (ignoring certain issues such as environmental damage) but never perfectly so. This is ensured by free exchanges (including employment) free enterprise (including entry/exit) and the rapid advance and utilisation of knowledge in consumption and production. Such a complicated process is very difficult to model precisely. Traditional general equilibrium analysis captures some important elements of it, the Austrian school (see for example Vaughn, 1994; Kirzner, 1997) emphasises a number of important aspects of it (including adjustments out of equilibrium and the importance of entrepreneurial discovery of previously unthought of knowledge), information economics (see Stiglitz, 2002) focuses on complications such as informational asymmetry, and the Yang–Ng (1993) framework captures the classical emphasis on the division of labour, not to mention the more radical departures from rational economic behaviour examined by experimental and behavioural economists and others, as well as studies on the importance of institutional, cultural and historical factors. While a synthesis may be desirable, it could be very difficult to achieve in a formal analysis. Nevertheless we do need to have an overall balanced view, if not a complicated mathematical model.?

10.9 Summary

This chapter started with the differences between marginal decisions (How much?) and inframarginal decisions (Whether? Which?) and introduced an inframarginal analysis of the division of labour. It then discussed some implications of increasing returns, including increasing returns at the firm level and generalised increasing returns at the economy level through economies of specialisation facilitated by the division of labour. Despite the

---

6. If animal welfare (on which see Ng, 1995) is considered, ideal morality dictates the maximisation of total welfare, including animal welfare.

prevalence of increasing returns, Adam Smith (1776/1976) was largely right about the efficiency of the invisible hand. The so-called Smith dilemma between Smith's theory on the efficiency of the market based on the absence of increasing returns and Smith's theorem on the facilitation of economies of specialisation (which gives rise to increasing returns) by the extent of the market does not really exist. While encouraging (discouraging) industries with (without) increasing returns could be efficient, it might not be practically desirable (feasible). Modelling generalised increasing returns at the economy level through the division of labour using a new framework reveals a number of welfare economic issues that have relevance for public policy (including infrastructure, work ethics and other factors affecting the division of labour network). It also gives more emphasis on the importance of entrepreneurship in coordinating economic activities (in particular the introduction of new goods to the market) than the traditional models of competitive equilibrium.

Appendix 10.1: A Simple Model of the Yang–Ng Framework of Specialisation[7]

It is assumed that the economy consists of M *ex-ante* identical consumer-producers and m consumer goods. The self-provided amount of good i is denoted by x_i, the amount purchased from the market of good i by x_i^d, and the amount of good i consumed by $x_i + k\,x_i^d$, where $k\,x_i^d$ is the amount individuals obtain when they purchase x_i^d, $1 - k$ being the transaction cost coefficient and k the transaction efficiency coefficient.

A Cobb–Douglas utility function is adopted to reflect the preference for diverse consumption:

$$u = \prod_{i=1}^{m}(x_i + kx_i^d)^\alpha \tag{A10.1}$$

where $m\alpha = 1$.

Each consumer-producer also has a system of production functions

$$x_i + x_i^s = l_i^a \quad i = 1,\dots.m; \quad a > 1 \tag{A10.2}$$

where x_i^s is the amount of good i sold to the market, $x_i + x_i^s$ is the amount of good i produced and l_i is the amount of labour used to produce good i. The assumption that $a > 1$ captures the economies of specialisation, making labour productivity in the production of each good increase with the individual's level of specialisation in its production, measured by the labour

---

7. This appendix is based on Yang and Ng (1993) and S. Ng (1998).

time used. Apart from the per unit transaction cost, $1 - k$, a fixed cost (measured by labour time) for the purchase of each good, c, is also assumed. With $n - 1$ goods purchased from the market, the endowment constraint of an individual is given by

$$c(n - 1) + \sum_{i=1}^{m} l_i = 1; \quad 0 \le l_i, c(n - 1) \le 1 \tag{A10.3}$$

where the total amount of labour time has been normalised to unity. The budget constraint of the individual is given by

$$p_i x_i^s = \sum_{r \in R} p_r x_r^d \tag{A10.4}$$

where p_i is the price of good i and R is a set of all goods purchased. In Equation A10.4 only one good is supplied to the market by an individual, since $a > 1$ shows that an individual sells only one good at most (see lemma 2.1 in Yang and Ng, 1993). Each individual (effectively) takes the market prices as given, either because the population is large relative to the number of goods and thus the number of individuals producing each good, M_i, is large, and/or because of coincidence with the Walrasian regime in the multilateral bargaining game in the Yang–Ng model (1993, ch. 3; however see Section 10.3 above on some problems of coordination).

Each individual is then allowed to maximise utility by allotting her or his fixed amount of time to the production and purchase of different goods, balancing the trade-off between economies of specialisation ($a > 1$) on the one hand and the costs of market transaction (c, $1 - k > 0$) on the other. Each individual is allowed to choose not only the quantities of the various goods consumed but also which goods to self-provide and sell to the market. If an individual buys a good, she or he does not sell it, and *vice versa*.

Next a market equilibrium in terms of the amount of each good supplied and demanded in the market is imposed:

$$M_i x_i^s = \sum_{r \in R} M_r x_{ri}^d \tag{A10.5}$$

where M_i is the number of individuals selling good i, and x_{ri} is the amount of traded good i purchased by individuals selling good r. It can then be shown that if transaction efficiency and/or the degree of economies of specialisation are very low (proposition 5.1 in Yang and Ng, 1993) the equilibrium is autarky, that is, all individuals self-provide all goods. As transaction efficiency improves (that is, k increases and/or c decreases), each individual sells a good to the market and buys other goods in exchange, (see Figure. 10.1 above). The number of goods purchased from the market, the division of labour and income all increase with transaction efficiency. When the number of goods each person purchases from the market is small, trade occurs within a small local community. When the number of goods purchased from the market becomes larger and larger due to the increase in transaction efficiency and an endogenous increase in comparative advantage through learning by doing (Yang and Borland, 1991; Yang and Ng, 1993, ch. 7), trade expands to unify the national market and then to involve international trade.

This simple analysis has been extended to more complicated issues such as endogenous choice of the number of goods, the use of intermediate inputs or more roundabout methods of production, the emergence of middlemen, firms, urbanisation, industrialisation, money, investment and so on (see Yang and Ng, 1993; Yang, 2001, 2003).

11
From Preference to Happiness[1]

Welfare economics has achieved much, although it still has long-standing weaknesses, such as the inability to make non-Pareto comparisons due to the difficulty of making interpersonal comparisons of cardinal utilities. Ways of overcoming this weakness have been discussed in Chapter 5 and in Ng (1996a, 2000a), but the use of interpersonally comparable cardinal utilities has not been widely accepted by economists. In this chapter it is argued that welfare economics is too narrow in focus and should be expanded to make the analysis more complete, and hence more useful. Important reformulations of welfare economics and cost–benefit analysis are needed. Some of the points discussed below have long been known about but have largely been ignored in welfare economic analysis. Some are less well known or are controversial, but are nevertheless important for welfare.

11.1 Preference economics or welfare economics?

The main reason why welfare economics is incomplete is that it stops at the stage of individual preferences and does not go on to analyse individual welfare or happiness.

Economics started with the analysis of objective variables such as production, consumption and the distribution of income and products between individuals. The analysis of these variables did not go very far or very deep since these variables are really only interesting if they are of value to us. Hence the introduction of utility analysis marked a great leap forward in the history of economic thought. The concept of utility, however, is rather ambiguous and could mean one or a mixture of preference, satisfaction and welfare. Present-day economists attempt to be more precise by using utility as a representation of preference. Moreover, and related to indifference map analysis, preference is confined to ordinal preference only, banishing cardinal

---

1. Much of this chapter is based on Ng (2003a).

utility as old fashioned, useless or even meaningless. With their anticardinal utility and anti-interpersonal comparability bias, most economists are unaware that the Nobel-prize winning research by Mirrlees (discussed in Section 6.3) made use of interpersonal comparisons of cardinal utilities and a fully fledged utilitarian social welfare function (social 'welfare...as the sum of the utilities of individuals' (Mirrlees, 1971, p. 176). It is true that, for the analysis of consumer choice or demand functions, cardinal utility is redundant and therefore should be abstracted away, but denying the use of cardinal utility in other areas – such as social choice, optimum population, valuation of life, and uncertainty – amounts to misplaced abstraction. It is akin to insisting that a person must shave off his moustache as it is not needed for eating, even though he wants to keep it to boost his sex appeal (see Section 1.4 above and Ng, 1997, on the case for cardinal utility and interpersonal comparability).

As noted above, even without purging cardinal utility, welfare economics is incomplete in that the analysis stops at the level of preference and does not go deeper to analyse true welfare. We want to consume products that satisfy our preferences, so going from the analysis of products to the analysis of preferences is going a layer deeper but what we want ultimately is happiness or true welfare (the two are used interchangeably), not just preference satisfaction, as argued below. Some economists regard happiness as a subject to be pursued by psychologists and sociologists, and consider that economists should confine themselves to preferences. In the wake of the utility revolution in economics, many economists probably also thought that economists should confine themselves to the more objective variables of production and consumption. Such self-imposed restrictions stifle interesting analysis of many important issues.

I regard my (net) happiness over any period of time as the excess of my positive affective feelings over my negative affective feelings over that period of time. For most of the time (including dreamless sleep and when I am feeling neutral), my affective feeling is zero. When I am enjoying myself – either bodily, such as when eating delicious food, or mentally/spiritually, such as when I am feeling proud of my achievements – my affective feeling is positive. When I am suffering from pain, sickness, worries and so on my affective feeling is negative. Apart from being positive or negative, there are also different degrees or intensities of affective feelings. If we put this intensity on the vertical axis (with the zero point representing the point of neutrality) and time on the horizontal axis, my affective feelings will be represented by a curve. (This diagram is simple enough to be drawn by the reader in her or his mind. The temporal integration idea had been formulated by the time of Edgeworth in the last decades of the 1800s and has strong support – see Kahneman *et al.*, 1997, Kahneman, 1999, p. 5.) My (net) happiness over any period of time is the excess of the areas above the line of neutrality minus the areas below that line. Affective feelings are those feelings which the individual cares for, either positively or negatively, for their own sake. Individuals may be able to distinguish yellow from green, but if they neither like nor hate either of these colours, their feelings about these colours are not affective.

What about the quality of different affective feelings? Obviously the feelings that arise from beautiful sights are qualitatively different from the feelings that arise from delicious food (the problem of qualia in philosophy). However when the intensity is the same I do not care whether I am enjoying a beautiful sight or delicious food if they do not affect others and my enjoyment in the future. Thus apart from their intensity, different pleasures may have different degrees of desirability in terms of their effect on others and on future happiness, and can thus be analysed accordingly. Therefore we do not need to distinguish between the different qualities of affective feelings for our purpose here (cf. Kahneman, 1999, pp. 9–10, on the possibility of measuring different affective feelings on a common scale and Rozin, 1999, for the argument that, though basic sensory pleasures and aesthetic pleasures are qualitatively different, they both feed into the same subjective and expressive system).

When I prefer an apple to a pear (of the same cost, for simplicity of comparison), it is because I believe that the apple tastes better (gives me more enjoyment) than the pear and/or provides me with more nutrients (an apple a day keeps the doctor away), and therefore will enable me to enjoy better health in the future. Ultimately, it is the degree of happiness that counts, more so than preference. I want money to buy products. I want to consume products to satisfy my preference. I want to satisfy my preference in order to maximise my happiness (subject to ignorance, irrationality and a consideration for the happiness of others). But I want happiness for its own sake, full stop. It is true that being happy can also make one healthier and more successful in social life or work. However being healthier and successful are ultimately valuable because they increase one's and possibly also others' happiness.

From casual observation, conversation, questionnaire surveys, psychological studies and evolutionary biology I know that the above views are not particular to myself but are common to all of us, or at least to a very large extent. Hence we do not need to argue with philosophers as we know in our minds that happiness is valuable in itself because we all gain pleasure from the delicious taste of fresh and nutritious food when hungry and the very rewarding stimulation of sexual intercourse, and hate the pain of injury and sickness. If our parents had not had the genes that give us such feelings but the reverse, they would not have survived to pass on their genes to us. We would not have been born at all!

While humans have gone past the more basic values of sensuous pleasure and pain to embrace higher spiritual and moral feelings, such as a sense of justice, such moral and other principles should ultimately be based on considerations of happiness (Ng, 1981b, 1990, 1999a, 2000a). Ultimately speaking, injustice is the denial of due happiness. (Objections to an exclusive concern with happiness miss the point of ultimateness – see for example Ryff, 1989. Also, while what affect happiness may be culturally dependent, as Christopher, 1999, argues, the ultimate value of happiness as such is culturally independent.) However for the present purpose it is not necessary for readers to go along with my full welfarist view. Even when justice, freedom and so on are not affected or remain unchanged, there is sufficient scope for welfare economics to be extended to analyse the deeper level of happiness (on the importance of subjective indicators for social policy see Veenhoven, 2002).

There are some economists who focus on things other than GNP and preferences. For example Sen (1985) emphasises capabilities and functionings. To the extent that these concepts can be used as surrogates or at least as supplementary indicators for the estimation of welfare in practice, they are very useful. However if they are used to replace considerations of welfare they may be misguided, or at least for those who believe that welfare is the ultimate objective (this is not to deny that, at the non-ultimate level, non-welfare indicators may be important). In any event, since there are other ways of estimating welfare the usefulness of these non-welfare concepts does not preclude the need to be directly concerned with welfare.

Without going into the deeper level of happiness, the analysis of preferences (including intensity of preferences) alone may be adequate if the preference of individuals is always identical to their happiness. They prefer x to y if and only if they are happier at x than at y; they prefer x to y more strongly than they prefer u to v if and only if their happiness at x is greater than their happiness at y by a larger amount than the excess of their happiness at u over v, and so on. Then information on the cardinal utility function (representing their preferences and intensity of preferences) is tantamount to information about their welfare or happiness function and analysis of preferences will be sufficient. (However even then we have to go beyond the ordinal preference framework to analyse preference intensity and find ways to make interpersonal comparisons of utility.) However individual preferences may differ from individual happiness due to ignorance (including imperfect foresight), a pure concern for the welfare of others (non-affective altruism) and imperfect rationality, as discussed in Chapter 1. (In the present chapter we shall largely ignore non-affective altruism – for which see Ng, 1999a – and focus more on imperfect knowledge and imperfect rationality.)

In their analyses economists typically ignore ignorance and assume perfect rationality (exceptions include Simon, 1982; Mullainathan, 2002). Despite the importance of ignorance and imperfect rationality, simplifying assumptions are appropriate and even necessary in most cases to allow a sharper focus on the central relationships in question. Moreover in many cases the effects of ignorance and irrationality may go either way, with largely offsetting or unknown net effects. Considering their effects will not add much. However this may not be true for other cases. In particular, as discussed in the next section, individual preferences are a very poor measure of individual welfare due to a number of factors. Moreover these factors tend to reinforce each other, resulting in a systematic bias in favour of materialism (in the sense of excessive consumerism, excessive accumulation of material wealth and the like – 'excessive' in the sense of placing more importance than can be justified by the real contribution to welfare).

The importance of welfare and the imperfect representation of welfare by preference and similar related problems may have been largely ignored by most economists, but they have not completely escaped their attention. For example Harsanyi (1997) has argued for the replacement of actual preferences by informed preferences in normative issues (I have followed his argument to its logical conclusion and gone for happiness instead of stopping at informed preferences – see Ng, 1999a). Scitovsky (1976/1992) laments joyless economies with abundant wealth but little happiness. Mishan (1969/1993, 1977), Hirsch (1976) and many others are emphatic about the many social costs of economic growth. There have also been calls for the measure of aggregate economic activities to be improved by revising national income accounting to take account of such factors as leisure and pollution (Nordhaus and Tobin, 1972; Brekke, 1997). However, while recognising the need to go beyond goods and services, Mishan (1960) disagrees on the possibility of analysis, especially formal analysis. Gintis (1972, p. 595) emphasises the endogeneity of preferences, but believes that 'the required extended welfare model is *un-operational'*. We emphasise imperfect knowledge and rationality since the endogeneity of preferences does not create problems in the absence of these imperfections. However our argument on the existence of these imperfections does make the endogeneity of preferences and hence Gintis's arguments important. The 'hedonistic paradox' may also suggest that a sensible analysis could be impossible. According to this paradox, those who seek pleasure or happiness for themselves will not find it, but those who help others will find happiness (for supporting evidence see Benson *et al.*, 1980; Switzer *et al.*, 1995; Konow and Earley, 2002). Despite this, some useful analysis is possible (Ng, 2003a). This chapter reports the main arguments in this respect.

11.2   Developments that have prompted a reconsideration

In recent decades, developments in psychological and related studies have suggested that there is a need to reconsider traditional economic analysis in general and welfare economics in particular. These developments include evidence of the failure of happiness and quality-of-life indicators to correlate strongly with per capita income, the importance of relative standing, and the existence of significant ignorant and/or irrational (or 'imperfectly rational' if so preferred) choices, as briefly reviewed below.

11.2.1   Money buys neither happiness nor quality of life

Studies by psychologists and sociologists show that, both within a country and across nations, happiness increases as income rises, but only slightly. For example, classified according to region and culture, the Northern European countries with high incomes score highest on happiness, followed by the United States, the United Kingdom, Australia and Ireland. The Central and South-American countries come next, followed by the Middle East, Central Europe, South-Eastern Europe (Greece, Russia, Turkey and former Yugoslavia), the Indian subcontinent, Africa, and South-Western Europea (France, Italy and Spain), which score significantly lower than Africa. The lowest scoring region is East Asia, including the country that leads in income, Japan. In Singapore per capita income is 82.4 times that in India. Even in terms of purchasing power parity, Singapore ranks 16.4 times higher than India. However the happiness scores of the two countries are exactly the same, significantly higher than that of Japan (see Cummins, 1998; cf. Inglehart *et al.*, 1998, table V18; Diener and Suh, 1999; on the East-Asian happiness gap see Ng, 2002b). While notable cases such as Japan and France are far from the regression line, a statistically significant positive relationship between happiness and income exists cross-nationally. However above a per capita income of US$5000 the correlation disappears (Veenhoven and Timmermans, 1998, fig. 2).

When the above result was presented at a seminar a colleague said that 'the cross-national relationship between income and happiness is affected by cultural differences. The relationship should be stronger within the same country.' In fact the relationship between happiness and income level over time within the same country (or at least for the advanced countries that have such data) is even less encouraging in terms of a positive relationship. For example between the 1940s and 1994 real per capita income in the United States nearly trebled, but the percentage of people who regarded themselves as very happy hovered around 30 per cent and there was no upward trend; average happiness fluctuated around 72 per cent. From 1958 real income in Japan increased more than fivefold, while average happiness stayed around 59 per cent, also without an upward trend (see Veenhoven, 1993; Myers, 1996, p. 445; Diener and Suh, 1997; Frank, 1997; Oswald, 1997. Blanchflower and Oswald, 2000, show that the level of happiness in the United States declined slightly between the early 1970s and the late 1990s while Hagerty and Veenhoven, 1999, found a slight increase. 'Roughly unchanged' seems still to be the best bet). Perhaps we need rising incomes just to sustain happiness at an unchanged level, the so-called 'hedonic treadmill'. However there are studies that show happiness to be *inversely* related to the pace of economic growth (Diener *et al.*, 1993; Diener *et al.*, 1995).

There could be different degrees of cultural bias in reports of happiness levels internationally (Diener *et al.*, 1995). For example people in the United

States are more inclined to profess happiness, as being happy is socially regarded as something positive. The French may have the opposite bias – as Charles de Gaulle was quoted as saying, 'Happy people are idiots', although this assertion has been contradicted by the evidence (Diener, 1984). In Japan the social custom of modesty may make people less ready to describe themselves as very happy. However over time it is likely that, if there have been significant changes in such biases, they are likely to have been towards a greater willingness to profess happiness. Hence cultural bias cannot explain the failure of the happiness measures to increase over time with income. Moreover researchers have used various methods (for example the social desirability scale by Crowne and Marlowe, 1964) to control for the effects of such biases but without changing the conclusions significantly. For example Konow and Earley (2002) report that using the Crowne–Marlowe scale to control for the bias did not significantly affect their finding that people who help others are happier.

On the other hand happiness studies show that a number of factors – including marriage, personality, health, religious belief, social capital and employment – correlate positively and strongly with happiness (e.g. Winkelmann and Winkelmann, 1998; Bjornskov, 2003). Interestingly, age correlates with happiness in an unexpected way. Most people might expect that happiness will increase with age as one gains more independence, income, and knowledge about how to enjoy life, and then to decrease as one grows old and less healthy. At first happiness researchers could find no significant relationship between age and happiness. However when they allowed for the square of age in the regression they found that average happiness decreases with age until people are in their thirties, and then increases monotonically with age until the highest range available in studies, is reached in the seventies. That the minimum point occurs at thirty something could be explained by the pressure of paying off the first mortgage, adjusting to living one's partner and bringing up children. Knowledge of this unexpected U-shaped happiness curve is very important, especially to readers of this book who will soon reach the minimum happiness point. Some of the less happy may think, 'If I am so unhappy at this young age, won't I be even more miserable when I am old? Is it worth going on?' Knowledge of the U-shaped happiness curve may therefore prevent suicide and encourage a more optimistic outlook by showing that a brighter future lies ahead. This knowledge alone is certainly worth many times the opportunity cost of buying and reading this book! Your happiness might also be increased by knowing that your consumer surplus from buying this book is huge.

Many economists may doubt the reliability of happiness studies, which rely heavily on self-assessment of happiness levels that are difficult to compare interpersonally. (Dominitz and Manski, 1999, examine the scientific basis of economists' hostility to subjective data and found it to be 'meager' and 'unfounded'. Rather, 'survey respondents do provide coherent, useful information when queried systematically' – see Manski, 2000, p. 132.) For one thing, these days people may require a larger degree of subjective happiness before describing themselves as very happy. Hence despite a possibly substantial increase in happiness, the percentage of people who describe themselves as very happy may not have increased. To overcome such difficulties I have developed a method that yields happiness measures that are comparable interpersonally, intertemporally and internationally (Ng, 1996a). Stone *et al.* (1999) favour the use of momentary assessment and Larsen and Fredrickson (1999) prefer to use multiple measures. However it has been persuasively argued that the customary measures are reliable. For example various measures of happiness correlate well with one another (Fordyce, 1988) in recollections of positive versus negative life events (Seidlitz *et al.*, 1997), reports by friends and family members (Diener, 1984; Costa and McCrae, 1988; Sandvik *et al.*, 1993), physical measures such as heart rate and blood pressure (Shedler *et al.*, 1993) and EEG measures of prefrontal brain activity (Sutton and Davidson, 1997). Pavot (1991) found that respondents who reported that they were very happy tended to smile more. Di Tella and MacCulloch (2000, pp. 7–8) note that psychologists who study and give advice on happiness for a living use happiness data: 'Presumably, if markets work and there was a better way to study well-being, people who insist on using bad data would be driven out of the market.' Moreover correlations of happiness show remarkable consistency across countries, including developing and transitional countries (Graham and Pettinato, 2001, forthcoming; Namazie and Sanfey, 2001). All this does not rule out the existence of methodological problems (see for example Schwarz and Strack, 1999; Bertrand and Mullainathan, 2001), but reported subjective well-being can still be used as good approximation (Frey and Stutzer, 2002a).

For those economists who are still sceptical or even look down on and deride the happiness measures, they should look to their own back yard. Even the measurement of GNP is subject to all sorts of inaccuracies and an imperfect measure was used for decades. Then came purchasing power parity (ppp) adjustment, which overnight increased China's GNP fourfold! Most happiness measures may not be very accurate but it is doubtful that a fourfold adjustment will ever be necessary for the average figure of any nation. Furthermore the picture is little different if we use more objective indicators of quality of life. Analysing a panel data set of 95 quality of life indicators (including education, health, transport, inequality, pollution, democracy and political stability) for the period 1960–90, Easterly (1999) obtained some remarkable results.

While virtually all of these indicators showed that quality of life across nations was positively associated with per capita income, when country effects were removed, using either fixed effects or an estimator in first differences, the effects of economic growth on the quality of life were uneven and often nonexistent. It was found that 'quality of life is about equally likely to improve or worsen with rising income.... In the sample of 69 indicators available for the First Differences indicator, 62 percent of the indicators had time shifts improve the indicator more than growth did' (Easterly, ibid., pp. 17–18). Even for the 20 indicators with a significantly positive relationship with income under fixed effects, time improved 10 of the 20 indicators more than income did.

These surprising results were not due to a worsening of income distribution (there is some evidence that the share of the poor becomes larger with growth). Rather it seems that quality of life in any country depends less on its economic growth or income level and more on scientific, technological and other breakthroughs at the world level, which in turn depend more on public spending than on private consumption. Many studies show that measures of social progress strongly correlate with income level for low incomes (up to about US$3000 at 1981 prices) but the correlation disappears after that (see for example Estes, 1988; Slottje, 1991; see Offer, 2000, for a review). Others show a similar relationship between happiness and income (for example Veenhoven, 1991; Diener and Suh, 1999).

Higher income and consumption may lead to a preference for even higher levels, but they could reduce the happiness level if the consumption level remains unchanged. In other words people adapt to higher consumption and then need even higher consumption to remain at the same welfare level. As illustrated in Figure 11.1, when a customary consumption level is indicated by point A the (total) welfare curve is X. When the customary level increases to B, the curve moves to Y. Hence the welfare level does not increase to BB'' but only marginally to BB'. However the marginal welfare of consumption (originally measured by the slope of the curve X at point A') may increase (to the slope of curve Y at B'). This causes individuals to feel that it is important to have more money to spend. However the long-term welfare curve passes through $A'B'C'$, which has a much lower marginal welfare of consumption. According to Kapteyn *et al.* (1976), up to 80 per cent of the welfare increase expected from additional income disappears with an actual increase in income. In Fuentes *et al.*'s (2001, p. 289) view, income does not have a strong influence on either wellbeing or on the probability of happiness, and that 'people tend to overstress the impact that additional income would have on their subjective well-being'.

If we take into account the costs of adjustment, the long-term welfare curve is also a function of individuals' accustomed level of consumption, a higher level of which lowers the long-term welfare curve. To maximise happiness in the long term it is better to start with a not too high consumption level and gradually increase the level over time. From this perspective, children of the rich may suffer a great disadvantage. (this is supported by evidence on adolescents in Csikszentmihalyi and Schneider, 2000). From birth such children are accustomed to very high levels of consumption that they may find difficult to surpass and therefore suffer in happiness terms. Hence wise rich people will not shower their children with money and/or consumer goods. But peer-group pressure (for both parents and children) may make it difficult for the rich to limit their consumption levels. This may partly explain why there is little difference in happiness terms between rich and poor.

Reich (2000–1) argues in favour of devoting more time to one's family than to long working hours, and therefore is in agreement with the theme here. But his proposal of providing US$60 000 to everyone when they turn 18 contrary to the principle of starting from a low consumption level, as well as to the principle of self-reliance. However, for certain items of consumption, especially those which are important for health, too low a level could impair individuals' future happiness. This is especially so in childhood and adolescence, when adequate nutrients (material and spiritual) are vital for healthy bodily growth, the development of a healthy personality and the continuing acquisition of knowledge (Glewwe *et al.*, 2001). If individuals are handicapped by serious deficiencies in early life they might never catch up later. However this consideration is more important than the adaptation effect only at very low consumption levels. It could be thought that an informed and rational individual will be aware of the long-term effects and take them into account, and therefore the problem will not arise. However the evidence discussed in Section 3.3 below suggests that most individuals are not rational and/or informed in this sense, and thus are guided more by short-term considerations

11.2.2   The importance of relative standing

The importance of relative standing, such as relative income and relative consumption, has long been recognised by economists (most economists refer to Veblen, 1899, and Duesenberry, 1949, in this respect, but Rae, 1834, discussed the problem of relative income much earlier). However recent studies have revealed that the magnitude, scope and importance of relative standing (relative to absolute income) are beyond the imagination of most people. For example Clark and Oswald (1996) have found that while income has little effect on happiness, comparitive income has a significant effect (see also Neumark and Postlewaite, 1998; Woittiez and Kapteyn, 1998). Likewise one might expect that the importance of relative standing is least in the area of health care, where the absolute effects can be expected to dominate. However Wilkinson (1997) shows that even in health care, relative standing is more important than absolute standards. The relatively poor, even with higher absolute incomes and health care, can have a much lower level of health than those who are absolutely poor but relatively well-off. Hence mortality is more a function of relative than of absolute income and health care. (For a survey of the relationships of health, inequality and economic development, see Deaton 2003.) Ball *et al.* (2001) show that even purely artificial and randomly awarded status bestows an advantage in market transactions. (On the motivation for competition for relative income, see Pingle and Mitchell, 2002. On relative-income concerns between sisters, see Neumark and Postlewaite, 1998, who found that a woman was 16 to 25 **times** more likely to seek paid employment if her sister's husband earned more than her own husband. For psychological evidence see Smith *et al.*, 1989; Tversky and Griffin, 1991. For direct neurological evidence of the relativity of preference, see Tremblay and Schultz, 1999; Watanabe, 1999. See also Kockesen, *et al.*, 2000, on the strategic advantage of relative versus. absolute fitness maximisation.)

Other unexpected results have been obtained when using panel data. For example Clark (2000) shows that a measure of individual well-being (1) rises with own income, (2) falls with others' average income and (3) is significantly correlated with variables that reflect the distribution of others' income. A wider distribution of others' income often *increases* individual well-being. This finding runs counter both to the perceived public dislike of inequality and to risk-aversion (if individuals have a probability of both dropping down and climbing up the income distribution in their reference group). Do the very poor produce external benefits (by making others feel relatively well-off and lucky) that are larger than the external costs produced by the very rich? Alesina *et al.* (2001) have found that inequality negatively affects happiness in Europe but not in the United States due to greater mobility in the latter. Obviously a lot more research is needed. (Interestingly, even ignoring such problems as identification and implementation, we may not be able to use the Pigovian subsidy to generate more external benefits from the very poor, because when they receive subsidies they become less poor. This is related to the paradox of redistribution discussed in Section 8.4 and Appendix 8.1.)

While the existence of wasteful conspicuous consumption in the West is well known (Frank, 1999), the new rich in East Asia are quickly catching up and even surpassing those in the West. For example, as reported on the front page of *Lianhe Zaobao* (*United Morning Daily*, Singapore) on 27 September 2002, in an auction in China someone paid RMB$400 000 (more than US$48 000) for a mud crab weighing 1.37 kg. It could be thought that this was just a transfer of purchasing power from the super-rich individual to the lucky crab farmer. However additional resources would have been diverted to cater to this person's fancy. In this respect it is desirable to have public auctions of things that are not intrinsically costly (such as car number plates bearing the owner's initials, special lucky numbers and so on) and give the proceeds to charity or public facilities. The rich should be encouraged to compete in their ability to pay for things that are beneficial to society, rather than engage in wasteful conspicuous consumption. The practice of burning cash in public, as reported some time ago in China, is seen as wasteful by the public but is actually a 99 per cent donation to the government.

Nevertheless it is still a symbolic and wasteful demonstration of wealth, while donating to charity is more symbolic of public spirited expenditure. In part the importance of relative standing may have a biological explanation. Having reviewed biological and non-biological evidence, Frank (1999, p. 145) concludes that 'concern about relative position is a deep-rooted and ineradicable element of human nature'. Individuals compete for survival and reproductive fitness. For an individual (and natural selection works mainly at the level of the individual), once beyond the absolute minimum requirement for survival, reproductive fitness is determined largely by relative standing, especially for males. In many species the dominant male has almost exclusive access to a whole harem of females. The (mainly male) fetishism for sporting competition may also be partly due to this biological 'winner takes all' factor in male competition (Dekel and Scotchmer, 1999). The dominance of males in spheres where aggressive competition to get to the top is important (such as the battle for top executive positions in the world of business) may also be partly explained by the same factor. Of course biological inclinations can be reinforced by nurture, especially in a society that values competition and materialistic achievements (on the biological basis of behaviour see Wilson, 1975; Dawkins, 1989; Robson, 1999). The nurture-influenced nature to do better than others is also a factor in imperfect rationality (discussed in the next subsection), although it can also foster advances in knowledge that are externally beneficial.

The importance of relative income has been used to explain the failure of economic growth to increase happiness at the societal level on the one hand, and the rat race to make more money at the individual level on the other (Easterlin, 1974; Ng and Wang, 1993; Frank, 1999; Ng and Ng, 2001; Kapur, 2002). Higher incomes contribute more to the individual as both the absolute and relative levels are increased. At the societal level, relative incomes cannot be increased on average. Where absolute consumption is no longer very important for welfare, economic growth can make the whole of society worse off through its detrimental effects on the environment. We may then have to rely on advances in knowledge to keep the happiness level from falling.

11.2.3   Individual irrational choices, including the rat race to make more money

At the individual level, higher incomes increase not only absolute but also relative income and consumption levels, and hence are perceived to be very important. However, once past a certain level, higher incomes seem not to make individuals significantly happier. For example, studies (such as Diener *et al.*, 1985) suggest that millionaires are only slightly happier than the average person. Moreover the direction of causation need not just be from money to happiness. In fact 'if there is any causal relationship in rich countries, it appears to run from happiness to growth, not vice-versa'

(Kenny, 1999, p. 19). Happier people may be more able to win and keep better paid jobs. Taken as a whole the evidence suggests that income may matter more for happiness at very low levels of income but it still accounts for less than 2 per cent of the overall variance in individual happiness (Diener *et al.*, 1993; Diener, 2002). In fact all objective factors combined seem to contribute little to happiness. For example Campbell *et al.* (1976) have found that demographic factors (including income, age, gender, race, education and marital status) explain less than 20 per cent of the variance in happiness, while Andrews and Withey (1976) find that these factors account for only 8 per cent of the variance in happiness or well-being. If we take away marital status (which correlates significantly with happiness – on the correlates of happiness see Argyle, 1999, for a survey), other objective factors are very unimportant indeed. This is consistent with the finding of studies of identical twins that objective factors, including of social and economic status, education, family income and marital status, account for no more than 3 per cent of the variance in happiness (Stones *et al.*, 1995; Lykken and Tellegen, 1996).

There is evidence that the more materialistically inclined are less happy. People whose goals are intrinsic (oriented towards self-acceptance, affiliation and community feeling) are happier than those whose goals are extrinsic (oriented towards external rewards such as financial success and popularity – see Richins *et al.*, 1992; Kasser and Ryan, 1993, 1996, 1998; Wright and Larsen, 1993; Ryan *et al.*, 1999; Ryan and Dziurawiec, 2001; Diener, 2002). 'Materialism, a preoccupation with economic well-being, is negatively correlated with SWB [subjective well-being], and especially so in those that believe that more money would make one happier'(Offer, 2000, p. 20, reviewing Ahuvia and Friedman, 1998, pp. 154, 161). Yet people continue to be or even become more materialistically inclined.

If money is not very important for happiness but many people still sacrifice their health and leisure and jeopardise their relationships with friends and family, and even violate moral principles and the law (thus threatening their own freedom and even their lives) to make more money, is that not irrational? Why sacrifice things that are important for happiness in order to make more money, which is not very important for happiness? This can be at least partly explained by the irrational materialistic bias that emanates from nature and nurture. Apart from the competition for relative standing discussed above, there is instinctive accumulation. Even without studying biology, most people are aware of the instinctive storage of food by animals such as mice, squirrels, ants and bees. Many animals also exhibit instinctive behaviour in respect of territorial guarding and resource grabbing. Obviously the storage of food can enhance survival and reproductive fitness as it reduces the probability of death from starvation. While *Homo sapiens* is probably the most rational species, it is still not perfectly rational. (the word 'rational' here refers to the special meaning of rationality defined in Ng,

1996b, p. 304 – A more rational species is one whose behaviour is controlled more by the reward–penalty system than by automatic, inflexible responses). In other words our behaviour is still influenced by our genetic programming (on the biological basis of social behaviour see Wilson, 1975; Crawford and Kreps, 1998). Like other species we still have an animal urge to accumulate.[2] Our instinctive inclinations and drives are programmed to maximise our reproductive fitness and therefore may not be consistent with welfare maximisation (Ng, 1995, 1999a). Also, 'Given the cumulative character of biological change – that is, its tendency to build opportunistically on pre-existing structures – the evolutionary approach leads us to expect that the mind is most unlikely to be a perfect reasoning machine' (Ben-Ner and Putterman, 2000, p. 95, reviewing Damasio, 1994, Goleman, 1995, and Elster, 1998).

It has been shown that 'wanting' (preference) and 'liking' (welfare) are mediated by different neural systems in the brain and are psychologically dissociable from each other. In other words an individual can want something without liking it, and *vice versa*. For example sensitisation of the brain's dopamine system by addictive drugs can create an intense 'wanting' that goes far beyond that which can be explained by 'liking' and the need to relieve withdrawal symptoms (see Berridge, 1999, for a review; cf. Fehr and Zych, 1998). Gamblers also are well known to have all sorts of irrationalities (see Rubinstein, 2002).

We are brought up in a consumption-oriented society with omnipresent advertisements encouraging us to consume more goods and services (on the effects of advertising see Galbraith, 1958; Dixit and Norman, 1978; Wilkie, 1994, ch. 16 and appendices; Tremblay and Tremblay, 1995). Worse than just creating a consumption bias, some advertisements set out to create unhappiness – as a top executive of a large merchandising chain admitted, 'It is our job to make women unhappy with what they have' (quoted in Walsh and Gillespie, 1990, p. 5). The bias in favour of consuming goods and services is because people can only profit by selling goods and services, not by selling leisure or happiness as such.

The animal spirit and the influence of materialistic society interact to cause an insatiable demand for higher incomes. For example it seems that no income group is content with its income level, as judged by Americans' answers to the question 'What would be the smallest income... your family

---

2. Keynes dubbed as 'animal spirits' the spontaneous urge of the entrepreneur to act not on grounds of rational and careful calculation but from 'habit, instinct, preference, desire, will, etc.'. Thus at one stage I thought Keynes had in mind something similar to my concept of the instinct to accumulate. However Marchionatti (1999) has shown that Keynes did not invoke the biological connection, or at least not in terms of the instinct to accumulate.

would need to make ends meet?' (US Bureau of Labor Statistics, 1986): 'Families with incomes below $5,000 felt that $7,822 would suffice. Families with incomes from 5,000 to $10,000 felt $10,139 was needed. Those who averaged $44,837 knew that almost three times that sum was absolutely necessary' (Lebergott, 1993, p. 71).

There are also psychological studies that show that most people are not perfectly rational. We are not speaking here in terms of certain violations of transitive preference or expected utility maximisation, as shown by Allais (1979), Kahneman and Tversky (1982) and others, interesting as these paradoxes are. Rather we have in mind an even more significant violation of rationality. Psychological studies show that most people ignore or underestimate the negative effects of current consumption/enjoyment on future happiness and the positive effects of current abstinence/suffering on future happiness (Headey and Wearing, 1991). Most people believe that it would be better to be killed in an accident than to become disabled. I have asked for shows of hands in classes and public lectures, and the response has consistently been about 3–5: 1 in favour of being killed (that is about four times more people would prefer to be killed than disabled). However studies show that quadriplegics are only slightly less happy than healthy people (for example Brickman *et al.*, 1978). After a period of adjustment the happiness of seriously disabled accident victims is more or less restored to the pre-accident level (but still less than the pre-accident level, so it is not recommended that readers cut off their legs), and they are glad that they were not killed in the accident.

Many people spend a lot of money on lottery tickets, but there is evidence that lottery winners are no happier than non-winners (Brickman *et al.*, 1978). While they are delighted about winning, within weeks their happiness fall back to the original level (Frederick and Loewenstein, 1999, found a quick decline to a level slightly above that of a control group). Hence their expectation that they will have a much happier life is not fulfilled. With regard to those who never win, or occasionally win only a small amount, it is therefore not really worthwhile wasting their money each week unless they get a big kick out of daydreaming about what to buy when the big win happens. (Even then the welfare-rational preference is based on epistemological irrationality, as there is no basis for daydreaming about unbounded happiness.) Obviously we are subject to big adaptation effect, making our welfare depend considerably on our reference position, not just our actual position. However 'individuals seem unable to anticipate changes in their reference position' (Frijters, 1999, p. 8; on the related but quite different 'endowment effect', see Kahneman *et al.*, 1991). On the other hand people fail to purchase flood insurance even when it is offered at less than its actuarial value (and hence the expected welfare is increasing – Kunreuther *et al.*, 1978). The failure to take adequate account of the adaptation effect and the influence of the 'market culture' are also used by Lane (1993, 2000) to explain why people think that money is more important than it really is. Kahneman *et al.* (1999, p. x) conclude that the *'evidence available suggests that people may not have the ability to predict their future tastes and hedonic experiences with the accuracy that the economic model requires'* (on the problem of predicting future feelings see also Loewenstein and Schkade, 1999). When I decided to shift from white to wholemeal and multigrain breads on health grounds I almost decided to change back on grounds of taste. However after persisting for a few more weeks I came to like wholemeal bread even more than white. Now I find that white bread tastes like flour, which is unacceptable on any grounds! I told myself never to become a dictator, because if I did I might ban white bread!

There are many studies to show that individuals' decisions are considerably affected by their current emotional state (Elster, 1999; Isen, 2000; see Loewenstein, 2000, for a survey of the part that passions play in decisions). Hermalin and Isen (1999) analyse this within a rational choice framework by allowing emotions or utility at the beginning of a period (or rather at the end of the previous period) to influence preferences. While this is a useful way of looking at certain aspects of the problem, it hides the point of imperfect information/rationality. One could explain the effect of mood on individuals' willingness to help others by the fact that *'an increase in mood either increases an individual's pleasure from helping or lowers the psychic cost of helping'* (ibid., p. 2). However it is difficult not to impute imperfect information/rationality when an irrelevant current emotion influences a choice that will affect one's long-term opportunity. (On the effects of emotional states on cognitive ability see Kaufman, 1999; Ashby *et al.*, 1999. Also, the existence of self-deception is not in doubt. The focus is on explaining the cause of such irrationalities. See for example Elster, 1986; Lazar, 1999. cf. Benabou and Tirole, 2002.)

Even without the findings of psychological studies, one would be convinced of the existence of widespread imperfect rationality just by casual observation. For example many people, especially those with problems such as excess weight and high cholesterol, tend to overeat. They may agree that it is in their own interest to resist temptation and would prefer not to have to face that temptation, but when they do they tend to give in. An economist might argue that, given the cost of resisting temptation, it would be rational to give in when presented with a temptation. While this is true to some extent and for some cases, some degree of imperfect rationality is most certainly present in most cases. Otherwise there would be little ground for such measures as the prohibition of hard drugs. In fact most people will admit to being not perfectly rational. I regard myself as a particularly rational person, and certainly among the top 1 per cent rationality scale (this may seem arrogant, but it is my sincere belief). However I cannot say that I am perfectly rational. I can think of actual cases and hypothetical situations in which I have made or would make irrational choices. For readers who think that they are immune from imperfect rationality, let them consider the following situation. You and a person who is attractive beyond your dreams are alone in a locked room. That person makes advances towards you. Assuming there will be no legal or family complications, the only negative side of having sex with this person will be the danger of contracting Aids. When faced with such a choice, rationality dictates that the right choice is to maximise expected welfare (Ng, 1984b). If the odds of contracting Aids are such that your expected welfare will be lower than the cost of giving in to temptation, rationally you should refuse the advance. However as the person is so attractive most people would gladly choose not to resist. Some might even swallow the key.

An other example of imperfect rationality is allowing inertia and laziness to prevent one from exercising. It is generally agreed that exercise is good for one's health and long-term welfare (excessive exercise, however, can be unhealthy). Nonetheless most people whose jobs do not involve physical exertion do not have enough exercise. Moreover most of them would agree that they should exercise more. However the combination of an excessive pursuit of higher income (as discussed above), inertia, procrastination, myopia and so on result in most people not having sufficient exercise.

There is a particular source of potentially incorrect choice: imperfect memory. As noted earlier, a natural and generally agreed measure of total enjoyment or suffering over a period of time is the integral of the intensity of enjoyment (positive) or pain (negative) over that period. However, probably due to the difficulty of estimating such an integral, human subjects appear to extract only two key values from the temporal profile: the peak intensity and the intensity at the end of the period. Some intermediate value, such as the average of the peak and the end value, becomes the 'remembered utility' (Kahneman *et al.*, 1993). Such a peak-end heuristic is insensitive to the duration of the experience, as confirmed in experiments on human subjects. For example in retrospective evaluations of colonoscopy procedures that varied in duration from four to 67 minutes, aversiveness was not correlated with duration but was strongly correlated with the rating of peak pain and pain at the end (Redelmeier and Kahneman, 1996). Obviously this 'duration neglect' can result in incorrect choices from the viewpoint of net welfare maximisation.

Intertemporal choices (see for example Loewenstein and Elster, 1992) are known to be riddled with impulsiveness, inconsistencies, hyperbolic discounting and excessive discounting (discussed in Section 1.3). Excessive discounting or inadequate concern for the future is the opposite of the instinct to accumulate, yet the two may exist simultaneously in the same individual. The instinct to accumulate causes individuals to engage excessively (from the viewpoint of welfare) in the rat race to make more money, while the faulty telescopic faculty causes them to save insufficient amounts for the future. In addition there are the omnipresent advertisements for goods and services, and the demonstration effects and so on of the materialistic society. In combination these lead to excessive current consumption. The faulty telescopic faculty also has a biological explanation: the faculty is costly to program, (see Ng, 1999a, for details. However some discounting may be fitness-maximising – see Rogers, 1994).

Just as perfect intelligence is impossible to program, perfect rationality is too costly. It is therefore not surprising that there is some degree of ignorance (or imperfect information) and imperfect rationality in most individuals, the present writer included. Denying the existence of irrationality is not only inconsistent with common sense and the findings of psychological studies (particularly on the effects of biological drives on behaviour), it also violates the basic principles of evolutionary biology (Ng, 1999a). Moreover since mad people must have some irrational preferences, it would be ridiculous to assume that people are either perfectly rational or completely mad; it is more realistic to accept that most people fall between the two extremes.

Our analysis of imperfect rationality in general complements other research on specific issues. For example Lane (1992, 2000) emphasises the 'basic market error' of taking work as 'disutility' and money as 'happiness', while (Juster, 1985, p. 340) finds that 'the intrinsic rewards from work are, on average, higher than the intrinsic rewards from leisure'. Lane (1992, p. 46) calls for a change from the consumption-dominated economy to a 'producer economy [that] gives work satisfaction priority over consumer satisfaction, because, under most conditions, work satisfaction contributes more to satisfaction with life-as-a-whole, happiness, and subjective well being'. In our analysis this is probably due to imperfect knowledge, imperfect rationality and their interaction with certain external effects. In the absence of such factors, employers who give due emphasis to work satisfaction will be able to obtain more work at lower pay and the desired producer economy will be the result of the free market. However the analyses by Lane and others provide specific details of the various manifestations of imperfect knowledge, imperfect rationality and external effects in different areas.[3]

On the other hand, many apparent irrationalities may not really be irrational and only appear to be so because of the narrow framework used by economists for simplicity. I attended an AEA conference where a speaker

---

3. Similarly studies of transaction costs, asymmetric information, endogenous preferences and the like are important complements to simple Walrasian general-equilibrium analyses that abstract from these complications. Although Walrasian analyses might have served largely as 'their competition' (Bowles and Gintis, 2000, p. 1430) than as complements or preconditions, they should really be regarded complementary explanations of the complicated real world. As Bowles and Gintis (ibid., p. 1433) recognise, 'The inadequacy of *Walrasian* general equilibrium in no way diminishes the importance of general equilibrium thinking.'

made the point that a low rate of inflation was desirable as it made it easier to make intersectoral adjustments. Real wages in some contracting sectors might have to be reduced, but with a zero rate of inflation this could only be done by cutting nominal wages, which people hated more than the same cut in real wages through inflation, with nominal wages remaining unchanged. Another commentator argued that this was not possible as the real consumption possibility was the same for both alternatives. After a further defence from the speaker, the commentator said that it was irrational (and hence impossible). This commentator assumed not only rationality but also that utility depended only on goods and services and therefore an aversion to cuts in nominal wages was not possible. In the real world such an aversion applies to most people, including one of the most rational persons, the present writer! One loses real purchasing power if nominal wages fail to increase with the rate of inflation, let alone when nominal wages are cut. Cuts in nominal wages also impose more loss of face and/or self esteem than cuts in real wages through inflation. The fact that the simple models used by economists do not capture this only means that their models are not complete, not that people are irrational. (See Loewenstein and Prelec, 1991, for other apparent violations of the narrow concept of economic rationality that are not really irrational in the wider sense. The subtle distinction between 'non-irrationality' and real irrationality is a good topic to ponder.)

11.3 A simplified analysis of welfare**

To capture the effects of inadequate recognition of the adaptation effect, excessive materialism, relativity in income, environmental quality and so on, Ng (2003a) uses a simplified model of a representative individual who maximises her overall utility. The utility level in each period depends on consumption, leisure, relative income, environmental quality and the provision of public goods. In addition it is assumed that the true marginal contribution of additional consumption to her welfare may be less than the perceived marginal utility of consumption to reflect inadequate recognition of the adaptation effect, excessive discounting and excessive materialism/ consumerism. Using this simple model, and making some compelling assumptions, it is shown that:

- An increase in income or earning ability is perceived to be very important by virtually all individuals, rich and poor alike, as the intrinsic consumption effect is very important for the poor and the relative-income/ consumption effect is very important for the rich.
- Excessive consumerism not only makes people overvalue the contribution of consumption, it also makes them overvalue the contribution of higher earning rates.

- Despite the rat race to make more money, economic growth can be welfare-reducing due to relative-income effects and environmental damage, even though growth finances public goods and pollution abatement.
- Excessive consumerism increases the possibility and degree of welfare-reducing growth if higher earning rates reduce leisure.
- Excessive consumerism causes people to overvalue the contribution made by economic growth.
- Despite an optimal choice of the income tax rate and the proportion of tax revenue on environmental damage abatement, economic growth may still be welfare-reducing if environmental damage is not taxed (or otherwise controlled) directly at low cost.

The last point came as a surprise. I had thought that growth could not be welfare-reducing if the tax rate and abatement ratio were optimised by a benevolent and omniscient government (while this assumption was clearly unrealistic, it nevertheless strengthens our conclusion about the possibility of welfare-reducing growth). The explanation of the unexpected result is that taxation only transfers resources from private production to public goods, which also have environmental effects. If these effects are large and abatement is difficult, growth may be welfare-reducing, unless it is not too costly to tax or otherwise directly reduce environmentally damaging activities.

With welfare economics extending to the level of real welfare, other areas of economic analysis related to welfare evaluation are similarly affected. Thus further useful analysis could be conducted. Here we shall consider how a cost–benefit analysis aimed at welfare maximisation differs from the traditional one.

- In the presence of excessive materialism (defined by the positive excess of the marginal utility over marginal welfare of consumption), a cost–benefit analysis aimed at welfare maximisation should adjust the marginal consumption benefits of public projects upward by a proportion determined by the proportionate excess of marginal utility over the marginal welfare of consumption; the productive contributions of public projects should not be so adjusted.

The asymmetrical treatment of consumption benefits (the direct contribution of public goods to individual welfare) and productive benefits (contributions to raising the output or reducing the costs of production) again came as a surprise. However this asymmetry can be explained intuitively. The consumption benefits of public projects should be adjusted upward since excessive materialism creates a bias among individuals towards private consumption. Productive benefits need not be so adjusted because higher productivity increases both private consumption and public revenue (through income tax).

Even in the absence of excessive materialism, additional results are obtained from the broader model, which allows for relative-income effects. For example:

- Even in the absence of excessive materialism, a cost–benefit analysis aimed at either preference or welfare maximisation should offset the excess burden effect due to the disincentive effect of a public project and its financing by the indirect effect through the relative-income effect. Irrespective of whether the indirect effect through the relative-income effect is positive or negative (this depends on whether the disincentive effect is positive or negative), it always offsets the excess burden effect through the disincentive effect (see Ng, 2003a, for details).

11.4 Implications and concluding remarks

While this game [of models based on perfect rationality and self-interest] will go on for many years into the future, we think that in the long-run, the economics discipline as a whole will recognize that the old assumption of rational, strictly self-interested individuals is not only an inexact and special approximation, but also inconsistent with a scientific view of human nature as the product of an evolutionary process (Ben-Ner and Putterman, 2000, p. 97).

All economists are familiar with the following simple point: as production or income is not the ultimate thing we value, an increase in GNP (even in real and per capita terms with no deterioration in equality) may not be desirable as a high enough decrease in leisure and/or increase in environmental damage may offset the benefits of the increase in GNP. Hence modern economists are willing to go beyond production to the level of preference. However preference is also not what we ultimately value. As argued above and elsewhere (Ng, 1999a), what we ultimately want is real welfare or happiness. Thus a Pareto improvement in terms of preference may be undesirable if happiness decreases. Individuals with inadequate knowledge, a faulty telescopic faculty and imperfect rationality (including the instinct to accumulate), amplified by the influence of our competitive and commercial society, may eagerly engage in the rat race to make more money without really increasing their happiness (this deplorable fact is also related to external effects on each other). Thus the questions of whether economic growth increases happiness and what types of public policy increase happiness are the most important questions that economists should try to answer.

If it can be reliably established that increases in private consumption do not increase social happiness, it will be clear that funding for public projects may be costly in monetary terms but not in happiness terms. Since happiness is more fundamental, this has profound implications for public policy. Among others, projects or measures (public or private) that will increase happiness (such as environmental protection, education, research and improvements in safety and working conditions) may be worthwhile even at a very high monetary cost. Di Tella and MacCulloch (2000) have found positive correlations between government consumption and happiness, but Veenhoven (2000b) could find no correlation between government spending on social security benefits and happiness. Putting the two pieces of evidence together, it seems that government spending on public goods (which accounts for the bulk of the difference between government consumption and social security benefits) should correlate even more positively with happiness (I was tempted to regress this but feel that I should leave it to unbiased researchers). If we take into account the global public good and long-term nature of spending on such items, we can see that a concerted international increase in spending on these items may well be highly welfare-improving, which is consistent with the results by Easterly (1999) mentioned above.

This does not negate the possibility of gross inefficiency in public spending, including that arising from the excessive influence of interest groups. (See Tanzi and Schuknecht, 2000, for the argument that public spending in most large countries could be significantly reduced without reducing social wellbeing; Wagner and Sobel, 2000, for the part played by interest groups in increased public spending; and Milesi *et al.*, 2002, on the role of the electoral system. On the US experience see Holsey and Borcherding, 1997; Bradburya and Crain, 2001. See also Appendix 12.1.1.) However, inefficient public spending can in fact increase the optimum size of public spending (Ng, 2000a, ch. 8). Moreover the almost exclusive emphasis on the inefficiency of public spending while ignoring the arguably greater inefficiency of private consumption (mutually cancelling competition, environmental damage, materialistic bias) is certainly one-sided. In fact, as argued by Kaplow (1996) and Ng (2000b), even just in dollar terms the true costs of public spending have been considerably overestimated by economists (see Chapter 8). For example economists emphasise the excess burden of taxation (including disincentive effects) but ignore the largely offsetting benefits on the spending side in the form of increased incentives, as well as the corrective nature of taxation due to the increasingly important relative-income effects (even though this was discussed as early as 1834 by Rae), the diamond goods effect (Ng, 1987a) and the environmental damage caused by most production and consumption.

While agreeing with the significance of excessive materialism, relative-income effects and environmental damage effects, one commentator suggests that all that is needed is 'a corrective income tax...with the proceeds distributed in lump-sum form'. (It has in fact been proposed that higher taxes on income or consumption be used to tackle the problem of relative status; see Akerlof, 1976; Frank, 1999; Ireland, 1998, 2001). To understand why this may be insufficient, consider a case in which the elasticity of substitution between income/consumption and leisure is very low. (This is realistic as many people are willing to work six to eight hours a day for a wide range of pay rates, even abstracting away the income effect. Such hours of work may be the 'necessity of life', as Karl Marx believed, and happiness studies have shown that the unemployed are far more unhappy than can be accounted for by the loss of income.) In such a case the higher tax rate plus the lump-sum transfer will only marginally reduce work/income/(private) consumption. If we continue to use the traditional CBA rules based on preferences (which are distorted by the instinct to accumulate, relative-income effects and advertisements), we shall continue to believe that most public projects are not worth the money. Then private consumption, production and environmental damage will remain high, but welfare will remain low. However, higher public spending may yet increase welfare. Secondly, using only a higher tax rate (as proposed by the commentator) misses out the distinction between the consumption benefits of public projects, which should be adjusted upward by the current degree of excessive materialism, the productive benefits, which should not be so adjusted, and intricate interrelationships between relative-income effects, environmental damage effects and abatement effects in both the presence and the absence of excessive materialism (for details see Ng, 2003a). In fact, given the substantial divergence of individual preference from welfare, an extensive reformulation of the welfare foundation of public policy is needed, and not just in cost–benefit analyses.

Due to the prohibitive costs of paternalism, governments should not interfere in the day-to-day activities of individuals, despite the existence of substantial ignorance and irrationality. That would be disastrous to my free society, on which individual welfare depend so much (Veenhoven, 2000a, has found a positive correlation between freedom and happiness; Frey and Stutzer, 2000, have found a positive correlation between democracy and happiness). Also, when government spending is typically very inefficient or is used in a way that is welfare-reducing, higher public spending may not be appropriate. However this does not mean that research on the divergence of welfare from preference cannot make a positive practical contribution. First, if individuals become aware of this divergence as a result of such research, they might adjust their preferences accordingly. For example they might put more emphasis on things that are really important for welfare and spend less time and resources on competitive (both interpersonally through the relative-income effect and intertemporally through the habituation, aspiration formation and myopia effects) and largely fruitless consumption. Instead, competition in activities that have external benefits, such as the discovery of new knowledge, should be encouraged. Second, our analysis suggests that some adjustments have to be made with respect to cost–benefit analysis in general and on the need to take account of environmental protection in particular. These adjustments could be made without directly interfering with individual free choice. Public policies could be adjusted in the light of better understanding of the divergence of preference from welfare in areas where such an adjustment would not impose significant costs in terms of paternalism, including increased spending on environmental protection, research, education and health. However, much more study is needed, and the measurement of happiness needs to be made more accurate (Kahneman, 1999) and more interpersonally and intertemporally comparable (Ng, 1996a). Also, recognition of imperfect rationality may help to explain widely implemented measures that go against free choice, such as fluoridation and the prohibition of hard drugs and gambling (this does not rule out the possibility that a reduction of prohibition may be welfare-increasing in certain cases).

As it adopts a representative individual approach, our analysis does not address the issues of income distribution and individual differences. Elsewhere I have argued that, for any specific issue in economic policy and cost–benefit analysis, we should follow the principle of 'a dollar is a dollar', that is, concentrate on efficiency only, without regard to distributional effects and leaving the objective of equality to be achieved more efficiently through the general tax/transfer system (see Ng, 1979/1983, 1984a, and Chapter 9 above). While the latter may have disincentive effects, trying to achieve equality with each specific policy has similar disincentive effects (this point is usually ignored) and also imposes additional distortions. This conclusion assumes rational individual choice, so in the presence of significantly imperfect information and irrationality, some adjustments may be needed. However such adjustments are intended to achieve efficiency from the welfare viewpoint, and not equality as such. Nevertheless if additional income is not very important in increasing welfare, it may be desirable to move more in the direction of equality in the general tax/transfer system. But this should not affect the applicability of the 'a dollar is a dollar' principle for specific issues unless imperfect information and irrationality cause biases in specific areas, possibly calling for adjustments for the purpose of welfare efficiency (but see the next paragraph).

Analysing welfare also allows us to address problems created by changes in preference (which are frequent and omnipresent – see Bowles, 1998. In fact preferences may be changed by conscious choices by individuals – see Ng and Wang, 2001). Economists know how to compare different situations in terms of a given preference ordering by an individual. In the presence of preference changes, alternative situations cannot be compared by using the standard tools of economic analysis. Examples are the effects of advertisements, education, social influences, and so on that necessarily change preferences. Since advertisements change preferences, standard methods cannot satisfactorily evaluate the desirability of advertisements (see, however, alternative analyses by Pollak and Wales, 1992; Becker and Murphy,

1993; Brester and Schroeder, 1995). When there are changes in preference a satisfactory analysis of the desirability of applicable alternatives may still be possible if we can compare the levels of happiness or welfare before and after the change. Gintis (1974) points to the endogeneity of preferences and the havoc it plays with traditional welfare analysis. However he acknowledges that traditional analysis 'will not loosen its grasp on the minds of economists until a replacement is found' (ibid., p. 429). Analysing alternative sets of preferences and other factors that relate to happiness is that replacement, as happiness is our ultimate objective. With the recent interest in the study of happiness (as shown, for example, by the recent appearance of the *Journal of Happiness Studies* and the conference on 'Economics and the pursuit of happiness' at Nuffield College in 2000 – the current chapter is a revised version of the invited keynote paper presented at that conference) and more interdisciplinary studies, some useful advances in this direction may be possible.

Our analysis throws light on the differing views between most economists and the general public. For example many economists (myself included before I formulated the ideas in this chapter) fail to understand why people are so preoccupied with issues such as unemployment and inequality (on the importance of equality, rather than absolute income, for health and happiness see Wilkinson, 1997; Eckersley, 1998, p. 15). In many instances the efficiency costs of measures such as protective tariffs or quotas are many times the combined incomes of all protected employees. Even if it is true that the removal of protection would cause some transitory unemployment, it would clearly be inefficient to maintain protection when we figure in terms of monetary gains and losses, with or without distributional weights. However if we reckon in terms of happiness the picture is less clear. As summarised by Winkelmann and Winkelmann (1998), the unhappiness of the unemployed goes far beyond the degree that can be explained by reduced income. In fact '*joblessness depressed well-being more than any other single characteristic including important negative ones such as divorce and separation*' (Clark and Oswald, 1994, p. 655; see also Frey and Stutzer, 1999). The frustration caused by failing to get a job and the resulting loss of confidence and self-esteem inflict a toll on happiness that is greater than any gain from having more leisure time. In a society where higher income/consumption levels have little effect on social happiness, sacrificing an amount (shared by the entire society) that is several times the combined income of the affected workers need not necessarily be a bad choice. It must be added that the validity of this observation does not mean that the public may not be misguided; ignoring the secondary costs of protection and the efficiency gains of liberalisation in the longer term. Thus despite the validity of this observation, economists still have an important role to play in clarifying these costs and gains. However in some situations the choice may not be as clear-cut as most economists believe, reckoning as they do in terms of monetary costs and benefits only. When we go to the deeper level of welfare, on which we have less information, the picture becomes less clear. Conclusions such as 'On benefit-cost grounds alone, a proposed ban [on the use of cellular phones by drivers] and a mandate to use hands-free devices are not likely to be justified in the United States' (Hahn *et al.*, 2000, p. 53) would have to be changed if they were reckoned in happiness terms.

Our analysis also suggests the need for more international cooperation in the case of global public goods such as research and environmental protection. Without sufficient cooperation there may be immiserising growth. The higher productivity brought by technological advances and globalisation may reduce welfare if appropriate environmental measures are not taken. The international competition for higher GNP and foreign investment can also result in much lower environmental protection standards than is globally desirable. Similarly the level of tax rates, help for the poor and public spending chosen by individual countries may be much lower than is globally optimal. Hence international cooperation is needed to tackle not only global problems such as the environment but also domestic problems with equality and other public goods. The United Nations and the United States (as the world's dominant power) should take the lead here (in this respect the refusal of the United States to sign the Kyoto Protocol was most discouraging).

Due to their familiarity with the traditional narrow analysis and to the comparative lack of information on welfare, economists have a vested interest in denying the significant divergence of preference from welfare and the normative relevance of welfare. Working with just income or even preference is much easier for them, but welfare is ultimately the most important thing. Economists should face up to the challenge despite the difficulties – they were not born to live an easy life! (See Frey and Stutzer, 2002a, 2002b, for further evidence and the implications of happiness research.)

11.5   Summary

Traditional welfare economics is incomplete as it analyses preference without going on to analyse welfare (or happiness), which is the ultimate objective. Preference and welfare may differ due to imperfect knowledge, imperfect rationality and/or a concern for the welfare of others (non-affective altruism). Imperfect knowledge and irrationality have a biological basis, and the instinct to accumulate combines with advertising-fostered consumerism to produce a systematic materialistic bias, as evidenced by recent studies on happiness and quality of life. This bias, in combination with relative-income effects, environmental degradation and overestimation of the excess burden of taxation, results in overspending on private consumption and the underprovision of public goods, and can make economic growth welfare-reducing. A cost–benefit analysis aiming even just at preference maximisation should offset the excess burden of financing for public projects by the indirect effect through the relative-income effect and by the environmental damage effect. Cost–benefit analyses aimed at welfare maximisation should also adjust the marginal consumption benefits of public projects upward by a proportion determined by the proportionate excess of marginal utility over marginal welfare of consumption. The environmental damage effect should be similarly adjusted upward. However the productive contributions of public projects should not be so adjusted.

12
Conclusion: Towards an Interdisciplinary Study of Welfare?[1]

We started off by defining welfare economics as a branch of study that endeavours to formulate propositions that enable us to state that social welfare in one economic situation is greater or lesser than in another. Is the welfare economics presented in this book useful in this respect?

As noted in Chapter 1, whether welfare economics is a positive or a normative study depends on the definition of social welfare. Defined in a positive way, such as a vector, a sum or some other function of individual welfare or preferences, welfare economics is a positive study (on the differences between welfare and preference see Section 1.3). If social welfare is defined normatively, as something that we ought to pursue or maximise, then welfare economics must have a normative aspect. But even with the latter interpretation we can leave the normative aspect (determination of the objective function) aside and concentrate on the positive aspect. As long as it is agreed that social welfare depends (positively) on individual welfare, the discussion of the conditions for and attainment of Pareto optimality in Chapter 2 can provide a useful guide to the pursuit of social welfare. If some persons are made worse off and some better off, can we still say something about the change in social welfare? The answer is positive if the change satisfies certain welfare criteria that are regarded as acceptable.

In Chapter 3, Little's criterion is defended against the criticism that it is inconsistent and/or redundant. But Little's criterion requires satisfaction of both the efficiency condition (the Kaldor criterion and/or Scitovsky's reversal test) and the distributional condition. When the two conflict, presumably one has to be weighed against the other. The numerical measurement of surpluses (Chapter 4) may then be of some assistance. Despite some ambiguities (such as path dependency) at the theoretical level, the surplus measurement can be accepted as an approximate measure of welfare change in most cases. (For special cases where this is not so, I propose the use of

---

1. Parts of this chapter are based on Ng (1978).

284

a 'marginal dollar' equivalent and suggest an appropriate adjustment when the diamond effect is significant.)

A more tricky problem is how to decide whether we have a distributional improvement and how to weigh distributional against efficiency considerations. Different people may have different opinions. Can their differences be resolved by a suitable democratic procedure? Can social preferences be based on individual preferences? The impossibility theorems by Arrow, Kemp–Ng, Parks and so on show that social choice cannot be satisfactorily based on individual ordinal preferences. Subject to practical difficulties, it is possible to reveal the intensity of individual preferences. With the concept of infinite sensibility, marginal indifference can be used as a unit in cardinal utility measurement. Using a reasonable criterion of weak majority preference, in Section 5.4.1 it is shown that a social welfare function (SWF) must be the unweighted sum of individual utilities.

With a specific SWF the optimal distribution of income can be determined if the utility feasibility frontier is also known (Section 6.1). Income distribution considerations are relevant in such issues as the degree of progressiveness in income taxation. An important factor here is the degree of the disincentive effect. Mirrlees' (1971) rigorous analysis of optimal income taxation (discussed in Section 6.3) produces the somewhat surprising result of a tax schedule that is regressive in marginal tax rates but progressive in average rates. This conclusion must be qualified by the fact that the analysis ignores external effects (utility interdependency).

External effects are analysed in Chapter 7. In particular, the existence of the conscience effect means that the welfare significance of the problem of externalities may be much larger than suggested by traditional analysis. In Chapter 8 the discussion of public goods gives some emphasis to the recent controversy over whether economists overestimate the costs of public spending, and to the proposed incentive-compatible mechanism for preference revelation, which opens up exciting possibilities for tackling the free-rider problem.

In light of the above, it seems reasonable to say that we have learned something useful. Even if we cannot jump right to the summit of social welfare, at least we have gained some insights that can help us to make improvements. However according to the theory of second best (Section 9.1), if we cannot jump to the summit it will be quite impossible to make a definite improvement. If some of the first-best optimality conditions cannot be satisfied, satisfaction of other first-best conditions may make matters worse. The second-best conditions are so complicated that they are practically impossible to define, let alone to satisfy. This seems to be a deadly blow to the practical usefulness of welfare economics. However Section 9.3 presents the theory of third best, which shows that in the absence of relevant information it is best to stick to the first-best rules even in the presence of second-best constraints. This provides a powerful case for the usefulness of welfare economics in general and analyses based on first-best assumptions in particular.

In Appendix 9.1 the third-best argument is extended to cover the question of the equality–efficiency trade-off. It is concluded that a (marginal) dollar should be treated as a dollar irrespective of whether it goes to the rich or the poor. Instead of using such measures as income weighting, rationing and so on to achieve equality, it is better to use income taxation. It is true that taxation has disincentive effects, but income weighting and so on have efficiency costs in addition to their disincentive effects (which are not usually recognised). So unless they are used as a second-best policy or are based on other efficiency considerations, these measures are inferior to taxation. The conclusion that 'a dollar is a dollar' offers a powerful simplification for the formulation of economic policies in general and for cost–benefit analysis in particular.[2]

Chapter 10 discusses the extension of welfare economics to include increasing returns, especially those arising from the economies of specialisation made possible by the division of labour. This central area of classical economics was largely neglected after the neoclassical marginalism revolution. However the Yang–Ng (1993) framework has enabled easy analysis and others many insights into growth, trade, development, the evolution of economic organisations and many other areas. The welfare economic issues raised by this have only just begun to be analysed and many fruitful lines of study await younger talent.

Chapter 11 attempts to push welfare economics from its preoccupation with preferences towards a deeper analysis of welfare or happiness. It discusses recent evidence on the failure of higher incomes – once past a basic survival/comfort level of around US$5000 per capita per annum – to be significantly associated with higher levels of happiness or with quality-of-life indicators. Also discussed are the importance of relative standing and the prevalence of imperfect knowledge and imperfect rationality (including the excessive

---

2. It may appear that our argument that a dollar is a dollar is inconsistent with Little's (1949, 1957) criterion (defended in Chapter 3), which takes distributional considerations into account. However in fact there is no conflict. 'A dollar is a dollar' is evaluated prior to the introduction of disincentive effects while Little's criterion should be applied to the final outcome, including the presence of disincentive effects. See the discussion of Figure A9.2, in which the utility possibility curve moves inward due to disincentive effects. If a change satisfies Little's criterion even when disincentive effects and so on are taken into account, then it should be adopted. It will also be sanctioned by 'a dollar is a dollar', except perhaps when the distributional effects are not marginal (see the subsection on redistributive effects in Section A9.1.2). Little's criterion and the concept of marginal dollar equivalent may then be useful. (I expect that it will take some reflection to assimilate the argument in this footnote.)

materialism caused by the instinct to accumulate and fostered by omnipresent commercial advertisements and peer pressure). In combination these factors suggest that it may be desirable to make important revisions to, if not to reformulate, welfare economics and cost–benefit analysis.

12.1 Further considerations

While we have covered many areas of welfare economics we have omitted a number of relevant issues that are not necessarily less important. They have mainly been left out because of space limitations, but also because some would have required more complicated treatment. One first has to master the basic elements of welfare economics before taking account of the complications. For those who wish to pursue the matter further, Appendix 12.1 provides a very brief and incomplete guide to the literature on changes in taste, price-dependent preferences, merit goods, X-efficiency, rent-seeking activities, informational asymmetry, the process of public choice and so on. Even if we had extended our analysis to take account of these complications (some of which are very tricky), some people might still have been sceptical of the relevance (or at least the adequacy) of welfare economics to problems of social welfare due to the in belief that a market economy concentrates too narrowly on purely economic objectives to the disregard of broader social objectives, that decision making by separate economic units may not conform to overall interests, that economic abundance may not improve happiness and so on. We have considered some of these and related issues in Chapters 10 and 11. Here we shall consider some others.

It is shown in Section 2.3 and Appendix 2.1 that a perfectly competitive equilibrium is Pareto-optimal under the assumptions of rational choice absence of externalities, plus some minor assumptions. Thus the main factors that can account for the imperfection of a market economy are: (1) externalities, (2) imperfect rationality and imperfect knowledge of individuals, (3) an undesirable distribution of income and (4) that the economy is not in perfectly competitive equilibrium. Externalities are discussed in Chapter 7. Irrational choice and knowledge imperfection are briefly discussed in Chapter 1 and more fully with respect to materialistic bias in Chapter 11. The concept of merit and demerit goods is considered in Section A12.1.3. (We shall return to these subjects later.) Chapter 6 is devoted to problems relating to distribution. It should be emphasised that what many people regard as a desirable distribution of income is usually based on ignoring the costs of arriving at that distribution (such as the disincentive effects of all practicable forms of redistribution and the loss of efficiency, freedom of choice and liberty in general if more bureaucratic methods are used to achieve equality). Here we shall briefly examine the possibility that a market economy may be undesirable due to the fact that it is not in perfectly competitive equilibrium.

An actual economy is unlikely to be in equilibrium since changes occur all the time. But if it is moving towards an equilibrium (even a changing one), equilibrium analyses may not be far off the mark. A more important difficulty arises if we do not have stable equilibria. But such difficulties fade into insignificance when compared with the fact that the economy is not perfectly competitive. The presence of monopolistic (including oligopolistic) elements may be the result of knowledge imperfection, institutional factors such as cartel-like associations, including trade unions, or the presence of product differentiation/decreasing costs/indivisibilities (these are related factors). The presence of monopolistic elements makes the attainment of Pareto optimality impossible in practice. In principle, if the government knows the cost and demand conditions it can design a system of taxes/ subsidies to achieve optimality. But this possibility exists only in utopia. It could be argued that, if we take account of such complications as imperfect knowledge, administrative costs and political and institutional constraints, the very concept of Pareto optimality, which ignores such complications (admitting only the technological constraint on production), is itself utopian. On the other hand, if the concept of Pareto optimality were to take account of all relevant constraints, costs, knowledge imperfection and so on it could be argued that any given situation must be Pareto optimal, or at least is in the process of moving towards a Pareto optimum. If it is possible to make everyone better off, net of all relevant costs and satisfying all relevant constraints and so on, the improvement must already have been made or is being made unless it is hampered by such factors as failure to recognise the possible improvement or to agree on the division of the gain, for example a stalemate due to strategic bargaining. The last factor is very difficult to analyse objectively (see however Nash, 1950), but the degree of knowledge imperfection can be reduced by economic analysis, including analysis of various types of cost. If the costs of a certain institutional constraint can be shown to be very high there may be grounds for its removal. In other words, in a wider perspective the constraint need not be taken as absolute. Analyses that ignore certain constraints or complications may also be useful if they study the relevant central relationships in depth. But when applying the conclusions thus arrived at to the real world, it is important to bring back the complications and assess (it may be necessary to be content with very rough estimates) their effects on the theoretical conclusions. As the study, progresses more and more factors could be brought into the formal analysis (on the relevance of informational asymmetry see Section A12.1.7).

We shall now return to the problem of the absence of perfect competition. When attempting to prove the Pareto optimality of perfect competition, profit maximisation by firms can be built into the definition of perfect competition. Alternatively it can be used as an independent assumption. No matter what the case, its absence would cause some difficulty. However if profit is defined as being net of the cost of management and so on, it can be argued that utility maximisation implies profit maximisation for an owner-managed firm (Koplin, 1963; Ng, 1969a, 1974b). Thus the assumption of utility maximisation or rational choice on the part of owner-managers is sufficient (together with other assumptions) for proving the Pareto optimality of a competitive equilibrium. With the separation of ownership from control, the utility-maximising choices made by managers need not conform completely to the interests of owners. However if there is a competitive market for managers they will be induced by the forces of competition to maximise profits for owners.[3] Hence one can say that non-optimality is due to the presence of monopolistic power (of the manager).

Even abstracting away the problems of market imperfection (due to monopoly and so on) and market failure (due to externality and so on – see Bator, 1958, for an 'anatomy'), many people still believe that the functioning of a market economy and economic progress do not necessarily contribute to social welfare. Among the numerous factors that are alleged to make the functioning of a market economy and/or economic growth undesirable, many are actually familiar factors (market imperfection, externality and so on) discussed under other names. For example, when discussing the 'tyranny of small decisions' Kahn (1966) explicitly notes that the undesirable results of 'small decisions' are associated with the presence of externalities, decreasing costs and so on. Similarly the market failure due to the problem of 'option demand' discussed by Weisbrod (1964) can actually be attributed to decreasing costs. The so-called option demand refers to the fact that (present) non-consumers of a product may suffer a loss from the disappearance of the product as they might want to consume it in the future. But the revenues of a private producer come only from consumers. 'It follows that the inability of the operator to make a profit does not necessarily imply the economic inefficiency of the firm' (ibid., p. 476). This can only be true (assuming that no externality, decreasing costs and so on are involved) if the firm can expect to earn more than normal profits in the future. It can then sustain a temporary loss in anticipation of eventual profits (abstracting from capital market imperfection, uncertainty and so on). In such a case there is no valid ground for a government subsidy. However the closure of the enterprise may constitute a social loss if there are

---

3. In the presence of uncertainty, maximisation of expected profits may not be the best policy. With owners having different attitudes towards risk, a general objective function does not exist (Diamond, 1967; Ekern and Wilson, 1974). However when there is a large number of firms, prospective owners could segregate themselves by their degree of risk aversion, that is, risk-averse individuals could buy shares of 'safe' firms. In any case, the problem of the existence of an objective function is not important in comparison with the problem of the conflict between managers and owners.

increasing returns. It can then be analysed by traditional analysis. Similarly, many of the alleged costs of economic growth can be seen as no more than external diseconomies and can be treated as such.

However there are aspects where the traditional analysis of Pareto optimality is inadequate. For example the analysis is with respect to the allocation of resources and the consumption of goods; no analysis is made with respect to other activities. Extending the analysis to these possibly extra-economic activities need not necessarily show that choices are non-Pareto optimal. But it may for some choices. For example, as discussed towards the end of Section 2.3, contrary to the usual argument to restrict immigration and introduce population control, traditional economic analysis actually presents a case for subsidising births. However if we allow for the existence of an irrational urge to procreate, there may be a bias towards excessive family size. This is especially so if combined with the existence of 'untreated' distortions such as congestion, pollution and unemployment, which are typical of underdeveloped economies. (Clarke and Ng, 1993, show that if these external effects are properly priced through taxes/subsidies, immigration makes the existing population better off even if it increases the levels of pollution and congestion.)

As another example, consider the Harrod–Hirsch concept of positional goods. Harrod (1958) used the concept of oligarchic wealth in connection with the problem of satiety; Hirsch (1976) developed this into the concept of positional goods and used it to question the desirability of economic growth (see also Ancil and Hakes, 1991; Huberman *et al.*, 1999). Positional goods are those goods or aspects of goods, services, work positions and other social relationships that are (1) scarce in some absolute or socially imposed sense, and (2) subject to congestion or crowding through more extensive use.[4] Positional goods include goods whose supply is more or less fixed, such as natural landscapes, old masterpieces and personal services on a per capita basis, and goods valued mainly for their relative scarcity or status. For example if a higher level of awards is created the existing awards become less venerable. As more people obtain a bachelor degree one may need a PhD to feel distinguished.

To examine the contrast between positional goods and non-positional goods, let us assume that the relative prices of different positional goods do not change with respect to each other so that we can lump them into a single composite good, X. Similarly all non-positional goods are lumped

---

4. Both conditions were mentioned by Hirsch (1976, p. 27), who regarded either condition as sufficient to denote a good as positional. But it fits his argument better to make both conditions necessary. If a good is subject to congestion (as most goods are) but can be expanded in supply to relieve the congestion, then obviously it cannot be classified as a positional good.

together as Y. This permits us to work with the two-dimensional Figure 12.1. Ignoring for the moment the possibility of differences and changes in tastes, we shall operate with the same set of indifference curves. Consider individuals with an average income facing the budget line AA'. They may consume an average amount of both positional goods (X^O) and non-positional goods (Y^O). (Individuals with an average income may have an above average consumption of Y and a below average consumption of X, or *vice versa*, depending on the consumption pattern of society as a whole. This divergence does not affect the main contention below.) Since positional goods are likely to be income elastic, their rich contemporaries are likely to consume a disproportionately larger amount of X, for example at point E^3. In other words the income consumption curve, OC, is likely to be concave. However this is not an essential assumption for the central argument here. With economic growth our average individuals can expect their income to increase, eventually catching up with or even surpassing the original income of the rich. Does this mean that they can eventually consume at E^3 on indifference curve K_3? The answer is no. Because positional goods cannot increase in number with economic growth, their prices will increase relative to those of non-positional goods as the latter become abundant.

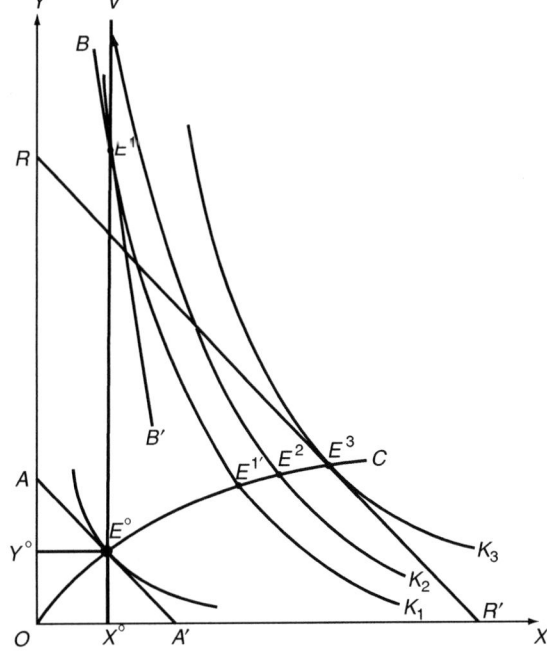

Figure 12.1

Hence the budget line of average individuals will not move from AA' towards RR'. Rather it will move outwards and rotate in a clockwise direction to a position such as BB'. Therefore they can never reach point E^3, although they may reach point E^1 or even some point vertically above E^1 with further growth. While E^1 is beyond the reach of even rich individuals before economic growth, it may lie below indifference curve K_3. It is even likely that, no matter how far one moves up the vertical line X^OV, one will never be able to reach, say, indifference curve K_2, which could approach X^OV asymptotically or eventually become vertical and/or turn rightward. Nevertheless, as we move upward on X^OV we hit successively higher indifference curves before they become vertical and turn rightward. This seems to suggest that economic growth will improve the welfare of average individuals even though it cannot make them as well off as the rich. However this will not necessarily be true if we take account of the likelihood that economic growth will increase their aspirations. With economic growth they may aspire to reach consumption point E^3 but find that this aspiration is repeatedly frustrated. For example an individual may work hard to earn enough to give his or her children a good education in the hope that this will enable them to get good jobs. However, since other people will be doing the same thing, his or her children may have a better education than he or she had but so will many others of their generation and they are likely to end up with no better than average jobs. The aspiration for good jobs will therefore be frustrated.

Moving upward along X^OV the successively higher indifference curves become closer and closer to each other, as measured along the income-consumption curve OC. An increase in Y from E^0 to E^3 is equivalent to a move from E^0 to $E^{3'}$. But no matter how many times Y is increased above E^1 the indifference curve will not lie above E^2. Thus even if we do not assume that the marginal utility of income diminishes but remains constant as we move along OC, the marginal utility of Y must still be diminishing rapidly as we move along X^OV. A small gain in utility can therefore be easily outweighed by the loss from frustrated aspirations. Hence economic growth, to the extent that it causes socially unrealisable aspirations, can actually reduce social welfare.

It can, however, be argued that the cause of the reduction in welfare is unrealistic aspirations rather than growth as such. What is needed is not to stop growth but to recognise that growth can make average individuals better off along X^OV but not along DC, that is, they can enjoy more non-positional goods but not more positional goods. If they can stick to this realistic path, no frustration need arise. Whether this is possible in practice cannot be answered here as it involves the psychological and sociological aspects of the formation of aspirations. In any event it seems clear that the problem of aspiration is as important if not more important than economic abundance, or at least in economically advanced countries (cf. the discussion in Section 11.2 above).

It can also be argued that if a change in aspiration or something else leads to a reduction in happiness, then the external factor that causes this change should be seen as producing an external diseconomy. On the other hand, if the factor is internal (that is, under the control of the individual concerned) its effect will be taken into account by the individual unless imperfect foresight or irrational preference is involved. Following on from this, it might be thought that problems such as changes in aspiration and so on could be handled by the traditional concepts of externality, imperfect foresight and so on. In a formal sense this is so, but it somewhat over-stretches the concept of external economy. Certainly no court in the world would grant compensation for damages caused by a change in aspiration. Moreover the individuals affected may not know of the existence of the effects, or whether the effects are beneficial or harmful. One could then say that this is a problem of imperfect foresight. Quite so. But when we take account of long-term effects, including changes in aspiration, the assumption of perfect foresight becomes very dubious. Just by lumping everything together as an externality and/or imperfect foresight is not going to solve the problems. Rather we have to begin analysing them.

12.2 Towards an interdisciplinary study of welfare

Whether a certain measure (to promote economic growth or any other objective) will increase or reduce social welfare depends both on its effects on the objective world (a change in distribution, increased production and/or pollution, or a change in the output mix) and its effects on the subjective world (changes in individuals' knowledge, beliefs, aspirations and so on). However it is also useful to think in terms of a third group of factors that have both subjective and objective elements and are products of the interaction of these elements. These are the institutional factors, including governments, laws, religions, families, customs, organisations and so on. Institutions are formed by the interactions of individuals between themselves and with the objective environment. Once formed, they serve to regulate and constrain these interactions and hence affect the future course of the subjective and objective worlds (see the arrows on the right-hand side of Figure 12.2). All measures originate from the subjective world (all initiatives are taken by some individuals) and work through the institutional setting to affect the objective world, the institutional setting and/or the subjective world itself (see the arrows on the left-hand side of Figure 12.2). In the process it is almost certain that not only will the objective world be affected but the institutional setting and the subjective world will change as well. Therefore a complete analysis of any significant policy or event has to take account of all its effects on the objective world, the institutional setting and the subjective world.

Economic analysis (including cost–benefit analysis – an application of welfare economics) is mostly confined to the study of objective effects.

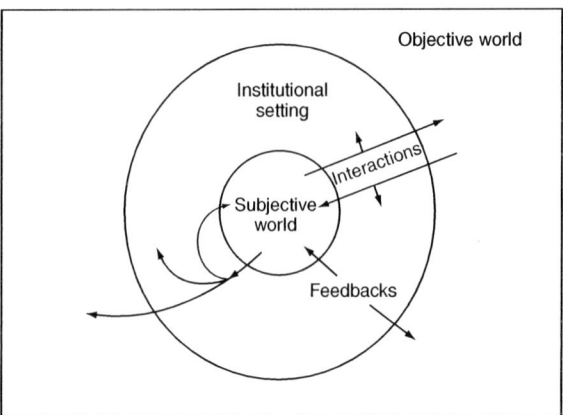

Figure 12.2

While this may include a consideration of how these effects are evaluated by individuals, in effect on the institutional setting and on the psychology of individuals are usually excluded. This is due partly to the fact that these effects are very difficult to identify (not to mention quantify) and partly to the fact that the various fields of study are largely isolated from one another. The confinement of the analysis to objective effects means that it is mainly useful for relatively small changes whose institutional and subjective effects are negligible. For example if the problem is to choose between two alternative routes for a motorway, both of which will have similar social and environmental effects, a study of the direct costs and benefits will be sufficient. However if the problem is whether the motorway should be built at all, the effects on the environment and so on will also have to be taken into account. For even larger problems such as the desirability of economic growth, a more complete analysis will be needed and all significant objective, institutional and subjective effects will have to be taken into account.

Because of the increasing complexity and interrelatedness of modern society, it is likely that more and more problems will involve all the objective, institutional and subjective effects. For example in the motorway example above it is likely that each of the two alternative routes will have different social and environmental effects, in which case a more complete analysis will be required even for this seemingly straightforward choice of alternative routes. However since institutional and subjective effects are very tricky to analyse we have a dilemma. We know that the effects are there but they are very difficult to study. One way out of this is to say that, since the institutional and subjective effects will be almost impossible to identify and may be either beneficial or harmful, in the absence of better information we should disregard them and concentrate on the objective effects (this is a generalisation of the theory of third best discussed in Section 9.3). This may be a valid approach for some problems at the moment but it does not mean that we should not devote more attention and resources to the study of institutional and subjective effects in the hope of achieving a more complete analysis in the future ('indirect externality' could serve as a useful analytical concept in this more complete analysis – see Ng, 1975d).

To this end it seems that interdisciplinary studies are required. A relevant discipline in this respect is psychology. Easterlin (1974, 2002) has brought together the findings of various psychological studies of human happiness and concludes that while there is a clear and positive correlation between income and (self-reported) happiness within a country at a particular time, it is uncertain whether such a positive association exists across countries and over time. Easterlin also discusses some of the conceptual and measurement problems involved in using self-reports of happiness and concludes with a qualified approval of their usage (see also Section 11.2.1 above). One basic difficulty is the problem of comparability. For example the same degree of happiness may be described as 'very happy' in a poor country but only as 'fairly happy' in a rich country. The same applies to comparisons over time there is a simple way of reducing this difficulty that does not seem to have been used, as discussed below.

In most happiness questionnaires the respondents are asked to tick one of the following: very happy, fairly (or pretty) happy, not very (or not too) happy. This has the advantage of being very simple but it causes problems with comparability. Cantril (1965) has devised a so-called 'self-anchoring striving scale'. The respondents register a number from 0 to 10, with 0 representing the worst possible life and 10 representing the best, as defined by the respondents themselves. This method may be useful for certain comparative studies but it does not overcome the comparability problem since the same number may represent different degrees of happiness for different people. While this is very difficult to overcome completely (see however Section 5.4.1 and Ng, 1996a) it can be reduced by employing the following simple method. Although different people will select different adjectives or numbers to describe the same degree of happiness, there is one level of happiness that is more objectively identifiable, that is, zero (net) happiness. No matter how large or small the gross degree of happiness, if in the opinion of the individual it is roughly equal to the degree of pain or suffering, net happiness is zero and has an interpersonal significance in comparability. Hence an intertemporally and interregionally comparable piece of information is the proportion of people who have zero, positive or negative net happiness. Such descriptions as 'not too happy' can subsume negative, zero and relatively small degrees of positive happiness. Moreover this relatively small degree is determined by the subjective judgement of the respondent and therefore is not interpersonally comparable. Hence a simple way of reducing the difficulty of comparability is to pin down the dividing line of zero happiness.

Different people obtain happiness from different thing. Some obtain it from serving God, some from having a good family life, some from being adventurous and so on. But virtually everyone wants happiness for themselves, for their family and perhaps for others. According to a major school of moral philosophy, happiness is the only acceptable ultimate objective in life. Yet the study of happiness is still at a primitive stage and therefore more attention and more resources should be devoted to the interdisciplinary study of happiness, taking account of all relevant objective, subjective and institutional factors.

It could happen that, when studies on desirable and undesirable institutional and subjective effects have been completed, these studies, instead of being used to guide policies to improve welfare, will be used by unscrupulous politicians or bureaucrats to further their ambitions and power, to the detriment of freedom and welfare. But this is true of almost all developments, including electricity, explosives, nuclear power and so on. Are institutional and subjective factors so delicate that a dividing line ought to be drawn here? Is happiness something that is less likely to be obtained the more one tries to obtain it? Should we have a meta-study of the desirability of pursuing different studies? Would this present a danger to freedom? The more I ponder on these questions the less certain I become of their answers. The only thing that is certain is that I now have a better understanding of how Socrates felt.

12.3   Summary

The analyses in the previous chapters were summarised at the start of this chapter. Wider questions relating to social welfare were briefly considered, such as 'Does economic growth increase social welfare?' The answers to such questions can only be provided by means of interdisciplinary analysis (eudaimonology) of all the relevant objective, subjective and institutional effects. All measures originate from the subjective world, working through the institutional setting to affect the objective world, the institutional setting and/or the subjective world. Due to the increasing complexity of modern society it is likely that more problems will involve significant institutional and subjective effects, making comprehensive multidisciplinary studies even more necessary (Section 12.2). As an introduction to this argument, the Harrod–Hirsch concept of positional goods and its implications for the desirability of economic growth were analysed geometrically and extended. Finally, section 12.2 suggested a simple way of reducing the problem of comparability in happiness surveys, that is, to pin down the dividing line of zero net happiness.

Appendix 12.1: Notes and References on Some Advanced and Applied Topics

This book has covered only the basic topics in welfare economics. Readers who wish to pursue the subject further may find this appendix useful as a guide to more advanced and applied topics. These topics could also be assigned to students for essays or practice in writing seminar papers. The topics in Sections A12.1.2, A12.1.3 and A12.1.8 are easier to handle. Several considerations have influenced the selection of topics and references below. First, practical relevance and conceptual interest rank higher than technical complication. Hence the question of Pareto optimality when infinity is involved, complicated extensions of proofs of existence, the optimality of competitive equilibrium and so on are not included. Second, obviously relevant topics such as cost–benefit analysis are excluded because they are likely to be covered by separate courses in the university curriculum. Third, my personal interests and knowledge limitations have exerted some influence.

A12.1.1 Some institutional factors

Like most studies in welfare economics, this book has concentrated on analysing what is socially optimal in some sense or other while presuming that governments will pursue social optimality. Over a century ago Wicksell (1896) admonished economists for their failure to recognise the fact that governments do not behave like benevolent despots. Collective decisions are made by ordinary people – voters, politicians, bureaucrats – who usually base their decisions more on their own interests. For a long time this point has been repeatedly emphasised by Buchanan (see for example Buchanan, 1975; Buchanan *et al.*, 1978; see also the interesting debate in Buchanan and Musgrave, 1999). Despite substantial early works in this area their impact on orthodox economic writings still has some way to go (see Downs, 1957; Olson, 1965; Tullock, 1965, 1967b, 1976; Niskanen, 1971; Breton, 1974; Brennan and Buchanan, 1977, 1980; Fiorina and Noll, 1978; Buchanan *et al.*, 1980; see also the surveys and collected volumes by Ferejohn and Fiorina, 1975; Mueller, 1976, 1979, 1989, 1997, 2001; Rowley, 1993; Pardo and Schneider, 1996; Kimenyi and Mbaku, 1999; see also Breton, 1996; Dixit, 1998; Ahmed and Greene, 2000; Glazer and Rothenberg, 2001; Besley and Coates, 2003). This is due partly to the complicated nature of actual public choice processes and partly to the fact that the simple social optimality approach can still usefully serve as an ideal to aim at, a standard to compare with and a foundation on which to base further analysis.

A very important aspect of actual democratic public choice processes is minority pressure or interest groups. Governments typically succumb to the pressure of particular interest groups even if this involves a greater cost to society. Since the cost of, say, higher tariffs, subsidies and so on is usually thinly spread across society as a whole, it does not usually arouse strong protest. No satisfactory solution (within the democratic framework) to this widely recognised problem has been found. It might not be optimal to ban pressure group activities, even if this were feasible, as they also perform useful functions, such as revealing the intensity of preferences, as remarked in Section 5.3. (On the efficiency loss caused by pressure groups see for example Mahler, 1994; Becker, 1985; Besley and Coate, 2001; Kirchsteigera and Prat, 2001; cf. Weingast *et al.*, 1981; Sheffrin, 2000; Tollison, 2001. See also Gerber, 1999, and Grossman and Helpman, 2001, for the role of interest groups; Bortolotti and Fiorentini, 1999, on interest groups in relation to regulation; van Winden, 1999, on the perspective of social groups; Parker, 1996, on the US Congress. See also Wittman, 1995, for the provocative argument that many governmental institutions and rules are really efficient; and the critical review by Rowley, 1997. cf. Caplan, 2001b.)

Preventing the government or government officials from abusing their power may be much more important for safeguarding welfare. Therefore a crucial issue is the design of a good constitution, which is a special and arguably the most important case of mechanism design – see Brennan and Buchanan (1980), Brennan and Hamlin (2000) and Laffont (2000). (For a graduate textbook introduction to the general problems of mechanism design see Mas-Colell *et al.*, 1995, ch. 23. See Groves *et al.*, 1987, for an exposition of information, incentives and mechanism design. For mechanisms, implementation and other related issues see Corchon, 1996; Goodin, 1996; Arrow *et al.*, 1997, vol. 2. See also Maskin *et al.*, 2000.)

Parallel to the study of public choice processes, institutional factors in the private sector have been analysed in the literature on property rights, including the emergence and functions of private property rights, their relation to externalities, the theory and regulation of modern corporations and so on. This literature has been surveyed by Furubotn and Pejovich (1972), Schmid (1976) and Randall (1978). (On the role of regional competition in fostering private property rights in China, see Li *et al.*, 2000.) Related to the problems of property rights, pressure groups and public choice processes is the issue of rent seeking. Individuals and groups spend considerable resources (including time) on trying to secure rights that will yield surpluses (or rents). A privileged position such as tariff protection may then only generate transitory gains at a permanent cost (Tullock, 1967c, 1975; Krueger, 1974; Posner, 1975; Buchanan *et al.*, 1980; Tollison and Congleton, 1995; Sobel, 2002). On the implications of rent-seeking for cost–benefit analysis see Ng (1983).

A12.1.2   X-efficiency

Welfare economics has mainly been concerned with allocative efficiency. The concept of X-efficiency was advanced by Leibenstein (1966). X-inefficient producers allow their cost of production to rise higher than is necessary.

For example a monopolist, not being subject to strong competition, may opt to pursue a quiet life instead of taking the trouble to achieve the lowest cost curve. Welfare losses due to X-inefficiency are said to be much more important than those due to allocative inefficiency (Comanor and Leibenstein, 1969). However this argument ignores the gain to the producer by being X-inefficient (ease, leisure and so on). Taking account of this, Parish and Ng (1972) show that X-inefficiency as such gives rise to no welfare loss. However when it is coupled with some form of allocative inefficiency, such as monopoly, the amount of welfare loss involved differs from both the Comanor–Leibenstein measure and the traditional measure that ignores X-inefficiency. For a review of this debate see Crew (1975, pp. 154–64). Perhaps partly in response to Parish and Ng, Leibenstein (1976, 1978) has extended his critique of traditional theory by questioning the assumption of rational, maximising individuals and by providing an analysis of group interactions, 'selectively rational man', 'inert area' and so on. On X-efficiency in the production of public goods see Olson (1974). For estimates of monopolistic losses see Harberger (1954), Cowling and Mueller (1978, 1981), Sawyer (1980), Littlechild (1981), Yarrow (1985), Aiginger and Pfaffermayr (1997) and Neumann (1999) (the latter emphasises the long-term or dynamic effects on growth). For a survey of the literature and an argument allowing for X-inefficient behaviour in a generalised neoclassical theory with transaction and adjustment costs see de Alessi (1983). For more recent discussions of X-inefficiency see Frantz (1992, 1997), Button and Weyman (1994) and Stennek (2000).

A12.1.3 Merit goods

If the voluntary consumption of a good by individuals, given their incomes, is deemed deficient (excessive) not due to the existence of externalities or pricing inefficiency, it is a merit (demerit) good. The most widely accepted example of a demerit good is an addictive drug with severe harmful effects. Examples of merit goods (exercise, health care, the arts, education) are more debatable. Given that the social objective should be a function of individual welfare, the only acceptable ground for recognising merit (hereafter taken as subsuming demerit) goods is the divergence of individual preference from individual welfare. In Chapter 1 we identified three factors that account for this divergence: concern for others, ignorance and imperfect foresight, and irrationality. Since the first factor generally serves to increase social welfare when the other two factors are not involved, the main justifications for merit goods are ignorance and irrationality. Liberals might hesitate to accept this and argue that if ignorance is the problem, what should be done is to provide more information or education. Moreover even if some individuals are too slow to learn or are irrational, it may still be undesirable to tinker with their consumer sovereignty. If one believes that this tinkering is undesirable, one is a fundamental liberal. If one believes that it is undesirable because of the undesirable effects on social welfare of, say, greater government control, one is an instrumental liberal.

Many writers include in the concept of merit goods such factors as externality, distributional consideration and so on (for example McMaster and Mackay, 1998), but since these factors can be and have been analysed independently of the concept of merit goods, it is best not to include them. For discussions of merit goods see Head (1966, 1969), McLure (1968), Pulsipher (1971), Pazner (1972). Pazner's formal analysis (similarly that of Roskamp, 1975) consists in the inclusion of the quantities of consumption of merit goods directly into a social welfare function independent of individual welfares. But why should society care (does it have an independent mind?) if no individual welfare is involved? A more satisfactory formalisation of the merit good problem is outlined below (a similar formulation in terms of the 'pathological choice' of individuals can be found in Racionero, 2001).

The social objective is to maximise social welfare as a function of individual welfares, $W = W(W^1, \ldots, W^I)$, where, abstracting from externality, $Wi = Wi(x_1^i, \ldots, x_G^i)$. Each individual maximises $Ui = Ui(x_1^i, \ldots, x_G^i)$. A merit good is defined as one in which $W_g^i > U_g^i$ ($W_g^i \equiv aW^i/a\, x_G^i$, and so on), and conversely for a demerit good. If $W_g^i \neq U_g^i$ over the relevant range, one can clearly see that taxes/subsidies may be desirable. As formulated these taxes/subsidies may differ among individuals, so for administrative simplicity a uniform measure may be more practicable. But the basic problem is how do we know that $W_g^i > U_g^i$ or the reverse? (cf. Baigent, 1981. See also Hutchinson and Schumacher, 1997, who report that spending on merit goods has a positive effect on economic growth. See Chapter 11 on excessive consumerism and an analysis that distinguishes utility from welfare.) In the terminology used here, private consumption in general may have some demerit aspect (on the taxation of specific demerit 'internalities' such as cigarettes see Gruber and Koszegi, 2001).

A12.1.4　Price-dependent preferences and changes in taste

Simple analyses take individual preferences as given and independent of the prices of goods. Considerable complications are introduced when these assumptions are relaxed. Prices may affect preferences because of the intention to demonstrate one's wealth (Veblen, 1899) or because of the habit of judging quality by price (Scitovsky, 1944–5). Kalman (1968) provides an analysis of consumer demand (deriving the Slutsky equation), where prices enter utility functions, and Pollak (1977) remarks on the sparse literature on the topic, the welfare significance and the distinction between 'conditional' interpretation (where prices affect preference ordering) and 'unconditional' interpretations (where the objects of choice are quantity–price situations). (See Basmann *et al.*, 1987, on the importance of price-dependent preferences. The special case of price-dependent preferences in the form of diamond effects is discussed in Section 4.6 above.)

Evaluating welfare when there are changes in taste is a tricky task. For example Rothenberg (1953) takes welfare to be a function of the ratio of satisfaction over desire, such that if both change by the same proportion, welfare stays constant. But this clearly conflicts with the common-sense observation that a person who has strong desires (for example appetite for food, sexual libido) and is well satisfied is likely to be much happier than a person with few desires even if they are fully satisfied. Gintis (1974) postulates a long-term utility or welfare function that determines, with the consumption history, changes in the short-term function (see also Gorman, 1967;) for other discussions see Harsanyi, 1953–4; Weizsacker, 1971; Pollak, 1976, Bowles (1998, 2000). Stigler and Becker (1977) use the household production function approach (expounded in Michael and Becker, 1973) to analyse problems associated with changing tastes (for example addiction, advertising, fashion) while assuming constant tastes. This approach seems to be more suitable for analysing the positive rather than the welfare aspects of the problem. For a survey of both the positive and the welfare aspects of changing tastes see Pollak (1978). For a comparison of the radical and traditional approaches see Burns (1980). For the use of the generalised Fechner–Thurstone direct utility function see Basmann *et al.* (1987). On the need to use cardinal utility and the non-arbitrariness of commodity units see Ng and Wang (1995).

A12.1.5 Optimal taxation and public pricing

Essentially optimal taxation is to do with assessing which structure of taxes on commodities will minimise the total cost imposed on the economy for any given amount of revenue raised, while public pricing is to do with establishing the best prices to charge for the products of public enterprises (usually public utilities). Although these may seem to be two separate issues, in fact both relate to government revenue and the price of commodities, though one is mainly concerned with the private sector and the other with the public sector. In line with the theory of second best the problem has to be considered in the setting of the economy as a whole. Commodity taxation and public utility pricing then become two components of the general problem. This is also true for welfare economics considerations. On a more practical level the two issues may be subject to different considerations. For example the motivation and accountability of managers is an important consideration in public utility pricing but not in taxation. Partly because of this the two issues are usually discussed separately (another reason is the difference in the assumptions used – see Green, 1975).

Although the rigorous analysis of optimal taxation dates from the 1920s (Ramsey, 1927), further developments in this mathematical approach did not take place until about 1970, apart from a few exceptions such as the work by Boiteux in the 1950s (see Boiteux, 1971). Since then the literature has burgeoned. For an introduction to this literature see Sandmo (1976, 1999) and Atkinson and Stiglitz (1980, pp. 366–93). For a synthesis of optimal commodity and income tax theories see Mirrlees (1976, 1986). For a recent collection of authoritarian reviews of various topics see Quigley and Smolensky (1994/2000). For optimal taxation in the presence of home production and externalities, see Kleven *et al.* (2000) and Cremer *et al.* (1998) respectively. On the part played by uncertainty see Cremer and Gahvari (1995). For optimal income taxation in the presence of international human mobility see Wilson (1992).

The celebrated Ramsey rule states that taxes should induce equal percentage reductions in the compensated demand for all commodities. This and similar rules are usually based on a one-consumer economy or some or other distributional neutrality assumption (Wildasin, 1977). In view of our argument in Appendix 9.1, distributional neutrality is not an unduly restrictive assumption. In the 1940s and 1950s discussions on the welfare economics of taxation tended to concentrate on the relative 'excess burden' of direct versus indirect taxes, using mainly geometrical analysis. A survey of this literature is provided by Walker (1955; Atkinson, 1977, compares this older literature with the newer optimal tax literature). Further contributions were made by Harberger (1964). The expenditure function technique can also be used to analyse the excess burden of taxation and other types of welfare cost (Diamond and McFadden, 1974).

Early discussions of public utility pricing centred on the desirability of marginal cost pricing, as surveyed by Ruggles (1949–50). A discussion of pricing policies for public enterprises at the undergraduate level is contained in Webb (1976). The analysis has been extended in many directions (Auerbach and Feldstein, 1985–2000; Bos, 1986), including to the issues of peak load (surveyed by Greene, 1970) and two-part tariff (theoretical analyses by Mayston, 1975; Ng and Weisser, 1974; Schmalensee, 1981; Brown *et al.*, 1992; applications by Cicchetti *et al.*, 1977; Mitchell, 1978; see also Trebing, 1971, 1976; Marchand *et al.*, 1984; Bousquet and Ivaldi, 1997; DeBorger, 2001.)

A12.1.6   Optimal saving/growth and resource exhaustion

As with optimal taxation, the theory of optimal saving was pioneered by Ramsey (1928). (Had he not died young, one wonders whether there would be any interesting major topics left for us to discover.) In this case the Ramsey rule states that the amount of saving multiplied by the marginal utility of consumption equals the amount by which total utility falls short of bliss. Assuming constant elasticity of marginal utility, this gives the simple rule that the rate of saving equals the inverse of this (absolute) elasticity. The rule is derived by maximising a utility function over time without a time discount rate. Since the integral does not converge, the shortfall from bliss is minimised. Alternatively the overtaking criterion (Weizsacker, 1965) may be used (if the cumulated utility value, – that is, instantaneous utility integrated to any given time – of stream A overtakes that of stream B at any finite time and remains higher than that of B forever thereafter, stream A is to be preferred to stream B). But the ranking may be incomplete (Chichilnisky, 1996). While many writers are against the discounting of future utility (not consumption), to me it seems quite justifiable because we cannot be absolutely sure of perpetual human existence. (Mendel Weisser regards this as an understatement due to the second law of thermo-dynamics. Fortunately this law applies only to a closed system. But is the universe an open system?) Ramsey's analysis has been extended in many directions – see Shell (1967) and Mirrlees and Stern (1973, part 5). The less mathematically inclined could start with Sen (1961), who expresses doubts about the practical usefulness of the intertemporal utility maximisation approach. For a more practical solution see Ng (1973c).

With the sharp increases in oil prices in the early 1970s, and in response to the concerns of environmentalists and conservationists, economists have become more interested in the specific problem of optimal resource exhaustion instead of optimal growth in general; see for example the 1974 symposium issue of the *Review of Economic Studies* and Solow (1974). However the pioneering analysis was conducted by Hotelling (1931). The basic message is that scarcity rent (the market price of the resource minus the extraction costs) should increase at the rate of interest and this will tend to be achieved by the market mechanism, given the available information. When the market rate of interest cannot be accepted as the social rate of time preference, some complications arise (Hanson, 1977). For complications arising from uncertainty about the amount of deposits see Gilbert (1979) and Kemp and Long (1978, 1980). On resource utilisation with technical progress see Kamien and Schwartz (1978) and the references therein. On the effect of the industrial structure see Aivazian and Callen (1979). On the counterproductiveness of subsidising energy production see Baumol and Wolff (1981). For a survey see Devarajan and Fisher (1981). On sustainability versus optimal growth see Quiggin (1997). On optimal growth in connection with environmental and sustainability issues see Islam (2001). On optimal greenhouse taxes see Lewis and Seidman (1996). On a possible poverty trap with high time preference see Askenazy and Le Van (1999). In my view the problem of environmental damage is caused more by disregard of the harmful effects on others rather than disregard of future generations (Ng and Wills, 2002).

A12.1.7 Informational asymmetry

While imperfect information applies both to individuals and to the government most economists focus on the lack of information about individual abilities and preferences (but individuals themselves are taken to have no informational imperfection) and the implications, including policy implications, of this asymmetry. (Informational asymmetry between buyers and sellers and between principals and agents have also been analysed – see for example Akerlof, 1970; Holmstrom, 1979; Mas-Colell *et al.*, 1995, chs 13, 14 – but asymmetrical information involving the government has more direct welfare policy implications.) The Nobel-prize winning contribution by Mirrlees (1971), discussed in Section 6.3, is an important example.

The presence of informational asymmetry gives rise to moral hazards, adverse selection and incomplete markets. An important issue is whether the market economy is constrained Pareto-efficient given these imperfections, such that no government intervention could improve efficiency. Arnott *et al.* (1994; see also the references therein) argue that inefficiency and improvements are possible. See also Rothschild and Stiglitz (1976, 1997), Groves *et al.* (1987), Archibald (1992), Vines and Stevenson (1997), Riley (2001) and Stiglitz (2002). See also the references on mechanism design in Section A12.1.1.

A12.1.8   Some specific topics

The following more specific topics offer good scope for essays or seminar papers.

Price stability

Do consumers and/or producers benefit from price stability (of specific products)? Consult Massell (1969), Samuelson (1972), Hueth and Schmitz (1972). The analytical tool used is mainly geometrical measurement of changes in consumer/producer surplus. For more advanced analyses see Turnovsky *et al.* (1980) and Newberry and Stiglitz (1982). For a small country facing foreign price instability see Choi and Johnson (1991). For an empirical analysis of the Australian wool and lamb industry see O'Donnell (1993). See also Stennek (1999) on the problem of using the expected values of consumer surplus. However Stennek's negative conclusions are somewhat extreme – the lack of perfect reliability does not imply zero reliability; cf. our comment on Boadway at the end of Section 4.5.

Brain drain

What should be done about the international emigration of highly skilled and educated people, especially from less developed countries to developed countries? Consult Bhagwati (1976, especially ch. 5, vol. II), Kwok and Leland (1982), Iqbal (2000) and Beine et al. (2001). (When I was conducting a seminar on this topic for students I had to declare that I was not a representative of the brain drain since I had in a sense been 'pushed away' by failing to receive an offer from any home university upon completing my PhD.)

Road congestion

One application of the theory of externality is that of road congestion. On charging for road usage to account for congestion costs see Walters (1961).

On the wider problem of transport economics see Sharp (1973). For a geometrical survey of the general congestion problem see Porter (1978). For the case of Singapore see Toh (1992). For a recent collection of writings see Button and Verhoef (1998). On the unwillingness of the public to report road pricing, see Oberholzergee and Weck-Hannemann (2002).

Market structure and innovation

The static efficiency of competition may be relatively trivial if the Schumpeterian thesis on the dynamic efficiency of monopoly with respect to innovation is correct. Arrow (1962) argues that the incentive to innovate is greater under competition than under monopoly. Demsetz (1969) argues that the reverse is true. Using a different argument that meets Demsetz's objection, Ng (1971d, 1977b) re-establishes Arrow's conclusion. see Boone (2001) on the non-monotonic relationship between the intensity of competition and the incentive to innovate; cf. Denicolo and Delbono (1999), Sah and Stiglitz (1987) and Spulber (2002). For a review see Needham (1975). See also Kamien and Schwartz (1975) for a survey on more general issues related to market structure and innovation. However most writers have only considered the amount or degree of incentive instead of the optimal incentive. The latter seems to be a fruitful avenue for further research as it is not true that the larger the incentive to invent the better, because obviously we do not want to spend the whole national product on invention. Arrow has briefly considered the social benefit of innovation within his framework, but no one seems to have considered this cost–benefit problem in Demsetz's or Ng's framework. It should not be difficult to undertake such an analysis (see however Dasgupta and Stiglitz, 1980).

Uncertainty

I am uncertain whether I should add a topic on uncertainty, but am certain that I must stop now as the publisher is certain to refuse to publish an overlength book with an uncertain demand.

References and Author Index*

Acemoglu, Daron and Ventura, Jaume (2002) 'The world income distribution', *Quarterly Journal of Economics*, 7(2): 659–94. *136*

Ackerman, Frank (ed.) (1997) 'Human well-being and economic goals', *Frontier Issues in Economic Thought*, vol. 3, Washington, DC: Island Press. *13*

Ades, Alberto F. and Glaeser, Edward L. (1999) 'Evidence on growth, increasing returns, and the extent of the market', *Quarterly Journal of Economics*, 114(3): 1025–45. *234*

Aghion, Philippe and Williamson, Jeffrey (1999) *Growth, Inequality and Globalization: Theory, History and Policy*, Cambridge: Cambridge University Press. *142, 228*

Ahmed, Sultan and Greene, Kenneth V. (2000) 'Is the median voter a clear-cut winner?: comparing the median voter theory and competing theories in explaining local government spending', *Public Choice*, 105(3–4): 207–30. *297*

Ahuvia, Aaron C. and Friedman, Douglas C. (1998) 'Income, consumption, and subjective well-being: toward a composite macromarketing model', *Journal of Macromarketing*, 18(2): 153–68. *269*

Aiginger, Karl and Pfaffermayr, Michael (1997) 'Looking at the cost side of "monopoly"', *Journal of Industrial Economics*, 45(3): 245–67. *299*

Aivazian, Varoiy A. and Callen, Jeffrey L. (1979) 'A note on the economics of exhaustible resources', *Canadian Journal of Economics*, 12: 83–9. *303*

Akerlof, George (1970) 'The market for lemons: quality uncertainty and the market mechanism', *Quarterly Journal of Economics*, 89: 488–500. *304*

Akerlof, George (1976) 'The economics of caste and of the rat race and other woeful tales', *Quarterly Journal of Economics*, 95: 599–617. *278*

Alchian, Armen A. and Demsetz, Harold (1972) 'Production, information costs and economic organisation', *American Economic Review*, 62: 777–95. *153*

Aldrich, John (1977) 'The dilemma of a Paretian liberal', *Public Choice*, 30: 1–22. *120*

Alesina, Alberto, Di Tella, Rafael and Macculloch, Robert (2001) 'Inequality and happiness: are Europeans and Americans different?', *NBER Working Paper* No. W8198, available from the SSRN Electronic Paper Collection: http://papers.ssrn.com/ paper.taf?abstract_id=293781. *267*

Allais, Maurice (1979) *Expected Utility and The Allais Paradox*, Dordrecht: Reidel. *271*

Allingham, Michael and Archibald, G. C. (1975) 'Second best and decentralisation',* *Journal of Economic Theory*, 10: 157–73. *188, 194*

American Economic Association (AEA) (1953) *Readings in Price Theory*, London: Allen & Unwin. *238*

Ancil, Ralph E. and Hakes, David R. (1991) 'Antecedents and implications of Hirsch's positional goods', *History of Political Economy*: 23(2): 263–78. *290*

Andrews, F. M. and Withey, S. B. (1976) *Social Indicators of Well-being*, New York: Plenum. *269*

Antweiler, Werner and Trefler, Daniel (2002) 'Increasing returns and all that: a view from trade', *American Economic Review*, 92: 93–119. *234*

Apps, Patricia and Rees, Ray (1999) 'Household production, human capital and optimal linear income taxation', in D. Sami, A. Philip and J. Grahl (eds), *Essays in*

---

* Index page numbers to author can be found at the end of references 1–1 in italics.

Honour of Bernard Corry and Maurice Peston. Vol 3: Regulation Strategies and Economic Policies, Cheltenham, UK and Northampton, Mass.: Edward Elgar. *136*

Archibald, G. C. (1992) *Information, Incentives and the Economics of Control*, Cambridge, New York and Melbourne: Cambridge University Press. *304*

Argyle, Michael (1999) 'Causes and correlates of happiness', in Kahneman, Diener and Schwarz (1999) pp. 353–73. *269*

Armstrong, W. E. (1951) 'Utility and the theory of welfare', *Oxford Economic Papers*, 3: 257–71. *17, 108*

Arnott, Richard J., Greenwald, Bruce and Stiglitz, Joseph E. (1994) 'Information and economic efficiency', *Information Economics and Policy*, 6(1): 77–88. *304*

Arrow, Kenneth J. (1950) 'A difficulty in the concept of social welfare', *Journal of Political Economy*, 58: 328–46. *94, 102*

Arrow, Kenneth J. (1951a) 'An extension of the basic theorems of classical welfare economics',* in J. Neyman (ed.), *Proceedings of the Second Berkeley Symposium on Mathematical Statistics and Probability*, Berkeley, CA: University of California Press. *243*

Arrow, Kenneth J. (1951b/1963) *Social Choice and Individual Values*, New York: Wiley. *92–7, 105, 115*

Arrow, Kenneth J. (1962) 'Economic welfare and the allocation of resources for invention', in National Bureau of Economic Research, *The Rate and Direction of Inventive Activity*, Princeton: Princeton University Press. *305*

Arrow, Kenneth J. (1970) 'Political and economic evaluation of social effects and externalities', in J. Margolis (ed.), *The Analysis of Public Output*, London: Cambridge University Press. *106*

Arrow, Kenneth J. (1971a) 'The firm in general equilibrium theory',* in R. Marris and A. Wood (eds), *The Corporate Economy*, Cambridge, Mass.: Harvard University Press.

Arrow, Kenneth J. (1971b) 'The utilitarian approach to the concept of equality in public expenditure', *Quarterly Journal of Economics*, 85: 409–15. *139*

Arrow, Kenneth J. (1973) 'Higher education as a filter', *Journal of Public Economics*, 2: 193–216. *139*

Arrow, Kenneth J. (1984) 'The property rights doctrine and demand revelation under incomplete information', in *Collected Papers of Kenneth J. Arrow, Vol. 4: The Economics of Information*, Cambridge, Mass.: Belknap Press, pp. 216–32. *112*

Arrow, Kenneth J. (1987) 'Technical information, returns to scale, and the existence of competitive equilibrium', in Groves, Radner and Reiter (1987), pp. 243–55. *238*

Arrow, Kenneth J. (1995) 'Returns to scale, information and economic growth', in Koo and Perkins (1995). *234*

Arrow, Kenneth J. (2000) 'Increasing returns: historiographic issues and path dependence', *European Journal of the History of Economic Thought*, 7(2): 171–80. *238, 243*

Arrow, Kenneth J. and Debreu, Gerard (1954) 'Existence of an equilibrium for a competitive economy',* *Econometrica*, 22: 256–90.

Arrow, Kenneth J. and Hahn, F. H. (1971) *General Competitive Equilibrium*,* San Francisco: Holden-Day.

Arrow, Kenneth J. and Intriligator, Michael D. (1981–91) *Handbook of Mathematical Economics, Vol. III: Mathematical Approaches to Welfare Economics*, Amsterdam: North-Holland.

Arrow, Kenneth J., Ng, Yew-Kwang and Yang, Xiaokai (eds) (1998) *Increasing Returns and Economic Analysis*, London, Macmillan.

Arrow, Kenneth J. and Scitovsky, Tibor (eds) (1969) *Readings in Welfare Economics*, London: Allen & Unwin.

Arrow, Kenneth J., Sen, Amartya and Suzumura, Kotaro (eds) (1997) *Social Choice Re-examined*, New York and London: St. Martin's Press and Macmillan. *106, 298*

Arthur, W. B. (1994) *Increasing Returns and Path Dependence in the Economy*, Ann Arbor, Mich.: University of Michigan Press. *242, 243*

Aschauer, David A. (1989) 'Is public expenditure productive?', *Journal of Monetary Economics*, 23: 177–200. *246*

Ashby, F. Gregory, Isen, Alice M. and Turken, U. (1999) 'A neuropsychological theory of positive affect and its influence on cognition', *Psychological Review*, 106(3). *272*

Askenazy, Philippe and Le Van, Cuong (1999) 'A model of optimal growth strategy', *Journal of Economic Theory*, 85(1): 24–51. *303*

Assaf, Razin., Sadka, Efrain and Swagel, Phillip (2002) 'Tax burden and migration: a political economy theory and evidence', *Journal of Public Economics*, 85(2): 167–90.

Athanasiou, L. (1966) 'Some notes on the theory of second best', *Oxford Economic Papers*, 18: 83–7. *207*

Atkinson, Anthony B. (1973) 'How progressive should income tax be?', in M. Parkin (ed.), *Essays on Modern Economics*, London: Longman. *134, 138*

Atkinson, Anthony B. (1975) *The Economics of Inequality*, Oxford: Clarendon Press. *136*

Atkinson, Anthony B. (ed.) (1976) *The Personal Distribution of Income*, London: Allen & Unwin. *136*

Atkinson, Anthony B. (1977) 'Optimal taxation and the direct versus indirect tax controversy', *Canadian Journal of Economics*, 10: 590–605. *302*

Atkinson, Anthony B. (1995) 'Public economics in action: The basic income/flat tax proposal', *Lindahl Lectures Series*, Oxford and New York: Oxford University Press and Clarendon Press. *134, 136*

Atkinson, Anthony B. and Harrison, A. J. (1978) *Distribution of Personal Wealth in Britain*, London: Cambridge University Press. *136*

Atkinson, Anthony B. and Stiglitz, Joseph E. (1972) 'The structure of indirect taxation and economic efficiency',* *Journal of Public Economics*, 1: 97–119. *205, 210*

Atkinson, Anthony B. and Stiglitz, Joseph E. (1980) *Lectures on Public Economics*, New York: McGraw-Hill. *170, 212, 302*

Atoda, Naosumi and Tachibanaki, Toshiaki (2001) 'Optimal nonlinear income taxation and heterogeneous preferences', *Japanese Economic Review*, 52(2): 198–207. *136*

Auerbach, Alan J. and Feldstein, Martin (1985–2000) *Handbook of Public Economics*, Amsterdam and New York: North-Holland. *302*

Aumann, Robert J. (1964) 'Market with a continuum of traders',* *Econometrica*, 32: 39–50. *30*

Auster, Richard D. (1977) 'Private markets in public goods (or qualities)', *Quarterly Journal of Economics*, 91: 417–30. *183*

Baigent, Nick (1981) 'Social choice and merit goods', *Economic Letters*, 7: 301–5. *300*

Bailey, Martin J. (1979). 'The possibility of rational social choice in an economy', *Journal of Political Economy*, 87: 37–56. *98*

Baland, Jean M. and Platteau, Jean P. (1997) 'Wealth inequality and efficiency in the commons', Part I, *Oxford Economic Papers*, 49: 451–482. *142, 228*

Ball, S., Eckel, C., Grossman, P. J. and Zame, W. (2001) 'Status in markets', *Quarterly Journal of Economics*, 116: 161–88. *266*

Barbera, Salvador (1977) 'Manipulation of social decision functions',* *Journal of Economic Theory*, 15: 266–78. *113*

Barbera, Salvador, Masso, Jordi and Neme, Alejandro (1999) 'Maximal domains of preferences preserving strategy-proofness for generalized median voter schemes', *Social Choice and Welfare*, 16(2): 321–36. *113*

Barone, Enrico (1908) 'Il ministerio della produzione nello stato collectivist a', *Giornale degli Economisti*, 37: 267–93, 391–414. English translation: 'The ministry of production in the collectivist state', in F. A. Hayek (ed.), *Collectivist Economic Planning*, London: Routledge and Kegan Paul, 1935. *48*

Basmann, Robert L., Molina, David J. and Slottje, Daniel J. (1987) 'Price-dependent preferences and the Fechner–Thurstone direct utility function: an exposition', *Journal of Institutional and Theoretical Economics*, 143(4): 568–94. *300, 301*

Batina, Raymond G. (1990) 'On the interpretation of the modified Samuelson rule for public goods in static models with heterogeneity', *Journal of Public Economics*, 42: 125–133. *170*

Bator, Francis M. (1957) 'The simple analytics of welfare maximisation', *American Economic Review*, 47: 22–59. *28, 33*

Bator, Francis M. (1958) 'The anatomy of market failure', *Quarterly Journal of Economics*, 72: 351–79. *289*

Battalio, Raymond C., Kagel, John H. and Reynolds, Morgan O. (1977) 'Income distributions in two experimental economies', *Journal of Political Economy*, 85: 1259–71. *139*

Bauer, P. T. (1976) 'Equal shares, unequal earnings', *Times Literary Supplement*, July: 23. *141*

Baumol, William J. (1965) *Welfare Economics and The Theory of The State*, 2nd edn, London: Bell. *156*

Baumol, William J. (1977) 'The public-good attribute as independent justification for subsidy', *Intermountain Economic Review*, 8: 1–10. *165*

Baumol, William J. (1982) 'Contestable markets: an uprising in the theory of industry structure', *American Economic Review*, 72: 1–15. *40, 239*

Baumol, William J. and Bradford, David F. (1970) 'Optimal departures from marginal cost pricing', *American Economic Review*, 60: 265–83. *205*

Baumol, William J. and Bradford, David F. (1972) 'Detrimental externalities and non-convexity of the production set', *Economica*, 39: 160–76. *148*

Baumol, William J. and Oates, W. E. (1975) *The Theory of Environmental Policy: Externalities, Public Outlays, and the Quality of Life*, Englewood Cliffs, NJ: Prentice-Hall. *153*

Baumol, William J., Panzar, John C. and Willig, Robert D. (1982) *Contestable Markets and the Theory of Industry Structure*, San Diego, CA: Harcourt Brace Jovanovich. *40*

Baumol, William J. and Wolff, Edward N. (1981) 'Subsidies to new energy sources: Do they add to energy stocks?', *Journal of Political Economy*, 89: 891–913. *303*

Becker, Gary (1985) 'Public policies, pressure groups, and deadweight costs', *Journal of Public Economics*, 28: 329–47. *298*

Beine, Michel, Docquier, Frederic and Rapoport, Hillel (2001) 'Brain drain and economic growth: theory and evidence', *Journal of Development Economics*, 64(1): 275–89. *304*

Becker, G. S. and Murphy, K. M. (1993) 'A simple theory of advertising as a good or bad', *Quarterly Journal of Economics*, 108: 941–64. *280, 281*

Benabou, Roland (1996) 'Inequality and growth', *NBER Macroeconomics Annual*, Cambridge, Mass.: NBER, pp. 11–92. *142, 228*

Benabou, Roland and Ok, Efe (2001) 'Social mobility and the demand for redistribution', *Quarterly Journal of Economics*, 116(2): 447–87. *136*

Benabou, Roland and Tirole, Jean (2002) 'Self-confidence and personal motivation', *Quarterly Journal of Economics*, 117(3): 871–915. *272*

Ben-Ner, Avner and Putterman, Louis (2000) 'On some implications of evolutionary psychology for the study of preferences and institutions', *Journal of Economic Behavior and Organization*, 43: 91–9. *11, 270, 277*

Bennett, John (1981) 'A variable-production generalization of Lerner's theorem', *Journal of Public Economics*, 16: 371–6. *131*

Bennet, T. L. (1920) 'The theory of measurement of changes in cost of living', *Journal of the Royal Statistical Society*, 83: 445–62. *75*

Benson, Peter L. *et al.* (1980) 'Intrapersonal correlates of nonspontaneous helping behavior', *Journal of Social Psychology*, 110: 87–95. *261*

Berglas, Eitan (1976) 'On the theory of clubs', *AER/Papers and Proceedings*, 66: 116–21. *183*

Bergson (Burk), Abram (1938) 'A reformulation of certain aspects of welfare economics', *Quarterly Journal of Economics*, 52: 310–34. *3, 47*

Bergstrom, Theodore C. (1996) 'Economics in a family way', *Journal of Economic Literature*, 34: 1903–34. *7*

Bergstrom, Theodore C. and Cornes, Richard C. (1981) 'Gorman and Musgrave are dual: an antipodean theorem on public goods',* *Economic Letters*, 7: 371–8. *167*

Bergstrom, Theodore C. and Cornes, Richard C. (1983) 'Independence of allocative efficiency from distribution in the theory of public goods', *Econometrica*, 51(6): 1753–65. *212*

Bernholz, Peter (1997) 'Property rights, contracts, cyclical social preferences and the Coase Theorem: a synthesis', *European Journal of Political Economics*, 13(3): 419–42. *159*

Berridge, Kent C. (1999) 'Pleasure, pain, desire, and dread: hidden core processes of emotion', in Kahneman, Diener and Schwartz (1999), pp. 525–57. *12, 270*

Berry, R. Albert (1969) 'A note on welfare comparisons between monopoly and pure competition', *Manchester School*, 1: 39–59. *73*

Berry, R. Albert (1972) 'A review of problems in the interpretation of producers' surplus', *Southern Economic Journal*, 36: 79–92. *82*

Berry, R. A. and Soligo, R. (1969) 'Some welfare aspects of international migration', *Journal of Political Economy*, 77: 195–221. *42, 73*

Bertrand, Marianne and Mullainathan, Sendhil (2001) 'Do people mean what they say? Implications for subjective survey data', *American Economic Review*, 91(2): 67–72. *264*

Besley, Timothy and Coate, Stephen (1991) 'Public provision of private goods and the redistribution of income', *American Economic Review*, 81: 979–84. *221*

Besley, Timothy and Coate, Stephen. (2001) 'Lobbying and welfare in a representative democracy', *Review of Economic Studies*, 68(234): 67–82. *298*

Besley, Timothy and Coate, Stephen (2003) 'On the public choice critique of welfare economics', *Public Choice*, 114(3–4): 253–73. *297*

Bhagwati, Jagdish N. (ed.) (1976) *The Brain Drain and Taxation*, Amsterdam: North-Holland. *304*

Binswanger, Hans P., Deininger, Klaus and Feder, Gershon (1995) 'Power, distortions, revolt and reform in agricultural land relations', *Handbooks in Economics, vol. 9: Handbook of Development Economics*, Vol. 3B: 1659–2772, Amsterdam, New York and Oxford: Elsevier Science, North-Holland. *142, 228*

Birdsall, Nancy, Ross, David and Sabot, Richard (1995) 'Inequality and growth reconsidered', *World Bank Economic Review*, 9: 477–508. *142, 228*

Bjornskov, Christian (2003) 'The happy few: cross-country evidence on social capital and life satisfaction', *Kyklos*, 56(1): 3–16. *263*

Black, Duncan (1948) 'On the rationale of group decision making', *Journal of Political Economy*, 56: 23–34. *102*

Blackorby, Charles (1999) 'Partial-equilibrium welfare analysis', *Journal of Public Economy Theory*, 1(3): 359–74.

Blackorby, Charles and Donaldson, David (1990) 'A review article: the case against the use of the sum of compensating variations in cost–benefit analysis', *Canadian Journal of Economics*, 23(3): 471–94. *117*

Blackorby, Charles, Donaldson, David and Weymark, John A. (1984) 'Social choice with interpersonal utility comparisons: A diagrammatic introduction', *International Economic Review*, 25(2): 327–56. *82, 120*

Blanchflower, David G. and Oswald, Andrew J. (2000) 'Well-being over time in Britain and the USA', paper presented at the Economics and Happiness Conference, Nuffield College, Oxford, 11–12 February. *142, 262*

Blank, Rebecca, M. (2002) 'Can equity and efficiency complement each other?', *Labour Economics*, 9(4): 451–68. *142*

Blau, Julian H. (1957) 'The existence of social welfare functions', *Econometrica*, 25: 302–13. *97*

Blin, Jean-Marie and Satterthwaite, Mark A. (1978) 'Individual decisions and group decisions: the fundamental differences', *Journal of Public Economics*, 10: 247–68. *113*

Boadway, Robin W. (1974) 'The welfare foundations of cost–benefit analysis', *Economic Journal*, 84: 926–39. *76, 78, 117*

Boadway, Robin and Bruce, Neil (eds) (1984) *Welfare Economics*, Oxford and New York: Blackwell. *28*

Boadway, Robin W. and Harris, Richard (1977) 'A characterisation of piecemeal second best policy', *Journal of Public Economics*, 8: 169–90.

Boadway, Robin W. and Keen, Michael (1993) 'Public goods, self-selection and optimal income taxation', *International Economic Review*, 34 (3): 463–78. *170*

Bohm, Peter (1979) 'Estimating willingness to pay: Why and how?', *Scandinavian Journal of Economics*, 81: 142–53. *179*

Bohm, Peter (1984) 'Revealing demand for an actual public good'. *Journal of Public Economics*, 24(2): 135–51. *177*

Boiteux, M. (1971) 'On the management of public monopolies subject to budgetary constraints', *Journal of Economic Theory*, 3: 219–40. *205, 301*

Boone, Jan (2001) 'Intensity of competition and the incentive to innovate', *International Journal of Industrial Organization*, 19(5): 705–26. *305*

Boone, Jan and Bovenberg, Lans (2002) 'Optimal Labour Taxation and Search', *Journal of Public Economics*, 85(1): 53–97. *135*

Borda, J. C. de (1781) 'Memoire sur les elections au scrutin', *Memoires de l'Academie Royale des Sciences*. English translation by A. De Grazia, *Isis* 44 (1953). *107*

Borghans, Lex and Groot, Loek (1998) 'Superstardom and monopolistic power: why media stars earn more than their marginal contribution to welfare', *Journal of Institutional and Theoretical Economics*, 154(3): 546–71. *137, 228*

Bortolotti, Bernardo and Florentini, Gianluca (eds) (1999) *Organized Interests and Self-Regulation: An Economic Approach*, Oxford and New York: Oxford University Press. *298*

Bos, Dieter (1986) *Public Enterprise Economics: Theory and Application*, Amsterdam and New York: North-Holland. *302*

Bos, Dieter and Seidl, Christian (eds) (1986) *Welfare Economics of the Second Best*, Vienna and New York: Springer-Verlag. *208*

Boserup, Ester (1981) *Population and Technological Change*, Chicago, Ill.: University of Chicago Press. *246*

Boskin, Michael J. and Sheshinski, Eytan (1978) 'Optimal redistribution taxation when individual welfare depends upon relative income', *Quarterly Journal of Economics*, 92: 589–601. *135*

Bougheas, Spiros, Demetriades, Panicos O. and Mamuneas, Theofanis P. (2000) 'Infrastructure, specialization, and economic growth', *Canadian Journal of Economics*, 33: 506–22. *246*

Bousquet, Alain and Ivaldi, Marc (1997) 'Optimal pricing of telephone usage: an econometric implementation', *Information Economics and Policy*, 9(3): 219–39. *204, 302*

Bowles, Samuel (1998) 'Endogenous preferences: the cultural consequences of markets and other economic institutions', *Journal of Economic Literature*, 36: 75–111. *229, 280, 301*

Bowles, Samuel (2000) 'Group conflicts, individual interactions, and the evolution of preferences', in S. Durlouf and P. Young (eds), *Social Dynamics*, Cambridge, Mass.: MIT Press. *7, 301*

Bowles, Samuel and Gintis, Herbert (1996) 'Efficient redistribution: new rules for markets, states and communities', *Politics and Society*, 24: 307–42. *142, 228*

Bowles, Samuel and Gintis, Herbert (2000) 'Walrasian economics in retrospect', *Quarterly Journal of Economics*, 115: 1411–39. *7, 274*

Bowley, A. L. (1928) 'Notes on index numbers', *Economic Journal*, 38: 216–37. *75*

Boyd, Robert and Richerson, Peter J. (1985) *Culture and The Evolutionary Process*, Chicago, Ill.: Chicago University Press. *7*

Boyer, M. and Kihlstrom, R. E. (eds) (1984) *Bayesian Models in Economic Theory*, Amsterdam: Elsevier Science.

Bradburya, John Charles and Crain, W. Mark (2001) 'Legislative organization and government spending: cross-country evidence', *Journal of Public Economics*, 82(3): 309–25. *278*

Bradford, David F. and Rosen, Harvey S. (1976) 'The optimal taxation of commodities and income', *AER/Papers and Proceedings*, 66: 94–101. *205*

Breen, Richard (1997) 'Inequality, economic growth and social mobility', *British Journal of Sociology*, 48: 429–49. *142, 228*

Brekke, Kjell A. (1997) *Economic Growth and the Environment: On the Measurement of Income and Welfare*, Cheltenham and Brookfield: Edward Elgar. *261*

Brennan, Geoffrey and Buchanan, James M. (1977) 'Towards a tax constitution for Leviathan', *Journal of Public Economics*, 8: 255–73. *297*

Brennan, Geoffrey and Buchanan, James M. (1980) *The Power to Tax: The Analytical Foundations of a Fiscal Constitution*, Cambridge: Cambridge University Press. *297, 298*

Brennan, Geoffrey and Flowers, Marilyn (1980) 'All "Ng" up on clubs? Some notes on the current status of club theory', *Public Finance Quarterly*, 8: 153–69. *183*

Brennan, Geoffrey and Hamlin, Alan (2000) *Democratic Devices and Desires*, Cambridge, New York and Melbourne: Cambridge University Press. *298*

Brennan, Geoffrey and McGuire, Thomas (1975) 'Optimal policy choice under uncertainty', *Journal of Public Economics*, 4: 205–9. *202*

Bresnahan, Timothy F. and Gordon, Robert J. (eds) (1997) 'The economics of new goods. National', in National Bureau of Economic Research, *Studies in Income and Wealth*, vol. 58, Chicago and London: University of Chicago Press. *72*

Brester, G. W. and Schroeder, T. C. (1995) 'The impacts of brand and generic advertising on meat demand', *American Journal of Agricultural Economics*, 77: 969–79. *281*

Breton, Albert (1974) *The Economic Theory of Representative Government*, Chicago, Ill.: Aldine. *297*

Breton, Albert (1996) *Competitive Governments: An Economic Theory of Politics and Public Finance*, Cambridge: Cambridge University Press. *169, 297*

Brickman, Phillip, Coates, Dan and Janoff-Bulman, Ronnie (1978) 'Lottery winners and accident victims: is happiness relative?', *Journal of Personality and Social Psychology*, 36: 917–27. *271*

Brookshire, David S., Thayer, Mark A., Schulze, William D. and D'Arge, Ralph C. (1982) 'Valuing public goods: a comparison of survey and hedonic approaches', *American Economic Review*, 72: 165–77. *179*

Brown, Donald J. and Heal, Geoffrey (1979) 'Equity, efficiency and increasing returns', *Review of Economic Studies*, XLVI(4): 571–85. *217, 229*

Brown, Donald J., Heller, Walter P. and Starr, Ross M. (1992) 'Two-part marginal cost pricing equilibria: existence and efficiency', *Journal of Economic Theory*, 57(1): 52–72. *302*

Bruno, Michael (1972) 'Market distortions and gradual reform',* *Review of Economic Studies*, 39: 373–83. *196*

Buchanan, James M. (1965) 'An economic theory of clubs', *Economica*, 32: 1–14. *182*

Buchanan, James M. (1975) 'Public finance and public choice', *National Tax Journal*, 28: 383–94. *297*

Buchanan, James M. (1978) 'Markets, states, and the extent of morals', *AER/Papers and Proceedings*, 68: 364–8.

Buchanan, James M. (1991) 'Economic interdependence and the work ethics', in *The Economics and the Ethics of Constitutional Order*, Ann Arbor, Mich.: University of Michigan Press, pp. 159–78. *248*

Buchanan, James M. (1994) 'The supply of labor and the extent of the market', in Buchanan and Yoon (1994), pp. 331–42. *248*

Buchanan, James M. *et al.* (1978) *The Economics of Politics*, London: Institute of Economic Affairs. *297*

Buchanan, James M. and Kafoglis, M. Z. (1963) 'A note on public good supply', *American Economic Review*, 53: 403–14. *156*

Buchanan, James M. and Musgrave, Richard A. (1999) *Public Finance and Public Choice: Two Contrasting Visions of the State*, Cambridge, Mass.: MIT Press. *297*

Buchanan, James M. and Stubblebine, W. C. (1962) 'Externality', *Economica*, 29: 371–84. *149*

Buchanan, James M., Tollison, Robert and Tullock, Gordon (1980) *Towards a Theory of the Rent-Seeking Society*, College Station: Texas A & M University Press. *297, 298*

Buchanan, James M. and Tullock, Gordon (1962) *The Calculus of Consent*, Ann Arbor, Mich.: University of Michigan Press. *104*

Buchanan, James M. and Yoon, Yong J. (eds) (1994) *The Returns to Increasing Returns*, Ann Arbor, Mich.: University of Michigan Press. *249*

Buchanan, James M. and Yoon, Yong J. (1999) 'Generalized increasing returns, Euler's theorem, and competitive equilibrium', *History of Political Economy*, 31(3): 511–23. *241*

Buchanan, James M. and Yoon, Yong J. (2002) 'Globalization as framed by the two logics of trade', *Independent Review*, 6(3): 399–405. *251*

Burns, Michael E. (1973) 'A note on the concept and measure of consumer's surplus', *American Economic Review*, 63: 335–44. *82*

Burns, Michael E. (1977) 'On the uniqueness of consumer's surplus and the invariance of economic index numbers', *Manchester School*, 45: 41–61. *74*

Burns, Michael E. (1980) 'Consumer theory and individual welfare: a radical approach re-examined', *Australian Economic Papers*, 19: 233–47. *301*

Button, Kenneth J. and Verhoef, Erik T. (eds) (1998) *Road Pricing, Traffic Congestion and The Environment: Issues of Efficiency and Social Feasibility*, Cheltenham, UK, and Northampton, Mass.: Edward Elgar. *305*

Button, Kenneth, Weyman, Jones X. and Thomas, G. (1994) 'Efficiency and technical efficiency', *Public Choice*, 80(1–2): 83–104. *299*

Calabresi, Guido (1968) 'Transaction costs, resource allocation and liability rules – a comment', *Journal of Law and Economics*, 11: 67–73. *159*

Campbell, A., Converse, P. E. and Rodgers, W. L. (1976) *The Quality of American Life*, New York: Sage. *269*

Campbell, Donald E. and Kelly, Jerry S. (1997) 'Sen's theorem and externalities', *Economica*, 64(255): 375–86. *120*

Cantor, G. (1895) 'Beitrage zur begriindrung der transfiniten mengenlehre',* *Mathematical Annals*, 46: 481–512.

Cantril, H. (1965) *The Pattern of Human Concerns*, New Brunswick, NJ: Rutgers University Press. *295*

Caplan, Bryan (2001a) 'Standing Tiebout on his head: tax capitalization and the monopoly power of local governments', *Public Choice*, 108(1–2): 101–22. *183*

314   *References and Author Index*

Caplan, Bryan (2001b) 'Rational irrationality and the microfoundations of political failure', *Public Choice*, 107(3–4): 311–31. *298*

Castello, Amparo and Domenech, Rafael (2002) 'Human capital inequality and economic growth: Some new evidence', *Economic Journal*, 112: C187–200. *136*

Chambers, Robert G. (2001) 'Consumers' surplus as an exact and superlative cardinal welfare indicator', *International Economic Review*, 42(1): 105–19. *75*

Chander, Parkash and Wilde, Louis L. (1998) 'A general characterization of optimal income tax enforcement', *Review of Economic Studies*, 65(1): 165–83. *135*

Chandler, Alfred D. (1990) *Scale and Scope: The Dynamics of Industrial Capitalism*, Cambridge, Mass.: Belknap Press. *246*

Chandra, V., Franck, D. and Naqvi, N. (2002) 'World increasing returns and production subsidies', *Economica*, 69: 223–7. *239, 251*

Chang, Ming Chung (2000) 'Rules and levels in the provision of public goods: the role of complementarities between the public good and the taxed commodities', *International Tax and Public Finance*, 7: 83–91. *170*

Chao, Chi Chur and Yu, Eden S. H. (2002) 'Immigration and welfare for the host economy with imperfect competition', *Journal of Regional Science*, 42(2): 327–38.

Charness, Gary and Rabin, Matthew (2002) 'Understanding social preferences with simple tests', *Quarterly Journal of Economics*, 117(3): 817–69. *7*

Chen, Yan (forthcoming) 'Incentive-compatible mechanisms for pure public goods: a survey of experimental research', in Plott and Smith.

Chichilnisky, Graciela (1996) 'An axiomatic approach to sustainable development', *Social Choice and Welfare*, 13: 231–57. *303*

Chipman, John S. (1960) 'The foundation of utility',* *Econometrica*, 28: 193–224.

Chipman, J. S. (1965) 'The nature and meaning of equilibrium in economic theory', in D. Martindale (ed.), *Functionalism in Social Sciences*, American Academy of Political and Social Sciences. Reprinted in Townsend. *244*

Chipman, John S. (1970) 'External economies of scale and competitive equilibrium', *Quarterly Journal of Economics*, 84: 347–85. *241*

Chipman, John S. (1976) 'The Paretian heritage', *Revue Europenne des sciences sociales et Cahiers Vilfredo Pareto*, 14: 65–171. *48*

Chipman, John S. and Moore, James C. (1976) 'The scope of consumer's surplus arguments', in M. Tang (ed.) *Evolution, Welfare, and Time in Economics: Essays in Honor of Nicholas Georgescu-Roegan*, Toronto: Lexington. *48, 72*

Chipman, John S. and Moore, James C. (1978) 'The new welfare economics 1939–1974', *International Economic Review*, 19: 547–84. *53*

Choi, E. Kwan and Johnson, Stanley R. (1991) 'Uncertainty, price stabilization and welfare', *Southern Economics Journal*, 57(3): 789–97. *304*

Christiansen, Vidar (1981) 'Evaluation of public projects under optimal taxation', *Review of Economic Studies*, XLVIII: 447–57. *170*

Christopher, John C. (1999) 'Situating psychological well-being: exploring the cultural roots of its theory and research, *Journal of Counseling and Development*, 77(2): 141–52. *260*

Chu, Cyrus C. Y. (1997) 'Population density and infrastructure development', *Review of Development Economics*, 1(3): 294–304. *248*

Chu, Cyrus C. Y. and Wang, C. (1998) 'Economy of specialization and diseconomy of externalities', *Journal of Public Economics*, 69: 249–61. *153*

Cicchetti, Charles J., Gillen, William J. and Smolensky, Paul (1977) *The Marginal Cost and Pricing of Electricity*, Cambridge, Mass.: Ballinger. *302*

Clark, Andrew E. (2000) 'Inequality-aversion or inequality-loving?: Some surprising findings', paper presented at the Economics and Happiness Conference, Nuffield College, Oxford, 11–12 February. *267*

Clark, A. E. and Oswald, A. J. (1994) 'Unhappiness and unemployment', *Economic Journal*, 104: 648–59. *281*

Clark, A. E. and Oswald, A. J. (1996) 'Satisfaction and comparison income', Discussion paper 419, Department of Economics, Essex University. *266*

Clark, Colin (1973) 'The marginal utility of income', *Oxford Economic Papers*, 25: 145–59. *142*

Clarke, Edward H. (1971) 'Multipart pricing of public goods', *Public Choice*, 11:17–33. *112, 174*

Clarke, Edward H. (1972) 'Multipart pricing of public goods: an example', in Mushkin (1972) *174*

Clarke, Edward H. (1980) *Demand Revelation and the Provision of Public Goods*, Cambridge, Mass.: Harper & Row, Ballinger.

Clarke, Harry and Ng, Yew-Kwang (1993) 'Immigration and economic welfare: resource and environmental aspects', *Economic Record*, 69(206): 259–73. *290*

Coase, R. H. (1960) 'The problem of social cost', *Journal of Law and Economics*, 3: 1–44. *158*

Coate, Stephen (2000) 'An efficiency approach to the evaluation of policy changes', *Economic Journal*, 110(463): 437–55. *61*

Cohen, L. J. (1983) 'The controversy about irrationality', *Behavioral and Brain Sciences*, 6: 510–17. *10*

Cohn, Elchanan and Johnes, Geraint (eds) (1994) *Recent Developments in the Economics of Education*, Aldershot: Edward Elgar. *139*

Coleman, James S. (1966) 'The possibility of a social welfare function', *American Economic Review*, 56: 1105–22. *104*

Collard, David, Lecomber, Richard, and Slater, Martin (eds) (1980) *Income Distribution: The Limits to Redistribution*, Bristol: John Wright.

Comanor, W. S. and Leibenstein, Harvey (1969) 'Allocative efficiency, X-efficiency, and the measurement of welfare losses', *Economica*, 36: 304–9. *299*

Congleton, R. D. (1997) 'Political efficiency and equal protection of the law', *Kyklos*, 50, 405–505. *229*

Corchon, Luis C. (1996) *The Theory of Implementation of Socially Optimal Decisions in Economics*, New York and Basingstoke: St. Martin's Press and Macmillan. *298*

Corden, W. M. (1974) *Trade Policy and Economic Welfare*, Oxford: Oxford University Press. *220*

Corlett, W. J. and Hague, D. C. (1953) 'Complementarity and the excess burden of taxation', *Review of Economic Studies*, 21: 21–30. *188, 210*

Corneo, Giacomo (2002) 'The efficient side of progressive income taxation', *European Economics*, 46(7): 1359–68. *138*

Corneo, Giacomo and Grüner, Hans Peter (2002) 'Individual preferences for political redistribution', *Journal of Public Economics*, 83(1): 83–107. *136*

Cornes, R. and Sandler, T. (1996) *The Theory of Externalities, Public Goods, and Club Goods*, 2nd edn, Cambridge, New York and Melbourne: Cambridge University Press. *183*

Costa, Paul T. and McCrae, Robert R. (1988) 'Personality in adulthood: a six-year longitudinal study of self-reports and spouse ratings on the NEO personality inventory', *Journal of Personality and Social Psychology*, 54(5): 853–63. *264*

Cowling, Keith and Mueller, Dennis C. (1978) 'The social costs of monopoly power', *Economic Journal*, 88: 727–48. *299*

Cowling, Keith and Mueller, Dennis C. (1981) 'The social costs of monopoly power revisited', *Economic Journal*, 91: 721–5. *299*

Craven, John (1996) 'Best fit social choices: an alternative to Arrow', *Economic Journal*, 106(438): 1161–74. *120*

Crawford, Charles and Kreps, Dennis L. (1998) *Handbook of Evolutionary Psychology*, Mahwah, NJ: Lawrence Erlbaum. *10, 270*

Creedy, John (ed.) (1999) *Economic Welfare: Concepts and Measurement*, Cheltenham, UK, and Northampton, Mass.: Edward Elgar. *82*

Creedy, John and Mcdonald, Ian M. (1990) 'A tax package to reduce the marginal rate of income tax and wage demands of trade unions', *Economic Record*, 66: 195–202. *142, 228*

Cremer, Helmuth and Gahvari, Firouz (1995) 'Uncertainty, optimal taxation and the direct versus indirect tax controversy', *Economic Journal*, 105(432): 1165–79. *205, 302*

Cremer, Helmuth, Gahvari, Firouz and Ladoux, Norbert (1998) 'Externalities and optimal taxation', *Journal of Political Economy*, 70(3): 343–64. *205, 302*

Crew, M. A. (1975) *Theory of the Firm*, London: Longman. *299*

Crowne, Douglas P. and Marlowe, David A. (1964) *The Approval Motive: Studies in Evaluative Dependence*, New York: Wiley. *263*

Csikszentmihalyi, Mihaly and Schneider, Barbara (2000) *Becoming Adult: How Teenagers Prepare for the World of Work*, New York: Basic Books. *265*

Cummins, Robert A. (1998) 'The second approximation to an international standard for life satisfaction', *Social Indicators Research*, 43: 307–44. *142, 262*

Currie, David A. and Peters, William (eds) (1980) *Contemporary Economic Analysis, Vol. II: Proceedings of the 1978 A UTE Conference*, London: Croom Helm.

Currie, John M., Murphy, John A. and Schmitz, Andrew (1971) 'The concept of economic surplus and its use in economic analysis', *Economic Journal*, 81: 741–99. *72, 82, 83*

Damasio, A. (1994) *Descartes' Error: Emotion, Reason, and the Human Brain*, New York: Putnam. *270*

Danziger, Sheldon, Haveman, Robert, and Plotnick, Robert (1981) 'How income transfer programs affect work, savings, and the income distribution: a critical review', *Journal of Economic Literature*, 9: 957–1028.

Dasgupta, Partha and Stiglitz, Joseph (1980) 'Industrial structure and the nature of innovative activity', *Economic Journal*, 90: 266–93. *305*

D'Aspremont, C. and Gevers, L. (1977) 'Equity and the informational basis of collective choice', *Review of Economic Studies*, 44: 199–209. *94*

David, Paul and Reder, Melvin W. (eds) (1974) *Nations and Households in Economic Growth, Essays in Honor of Moses Abramovitz*, New York: Academic Press.

Davies, James B. and Hoy, Michael (2002) 'Flat rate taxes and inequality measurement', *Journal of Public Economics*, 84(1): 33–46. *138*

Davis, Otto A. and Hinich, M. (1966) 'A mathematical model of policy formation in a democratic society', in J. L. Berad (ed.), *Mathematical Applications in Political Science*, vol. II, Dallas, Texas: Southern Methodist University Press. *106*

Davis, Otto A. and Whinston, Andrew B. (1965) 'Welfare economics and the theory of second best', *Review of Economic Studies*, 32: 1–14. *195, 196*

Dawkins, Richard (1989) *The Selfish Gene*, Oxford: Oxford University Press. *268*

De Alessi, Louis (1983) 'Property rights, transaction costs, and x-efficiency: an essay in economic theory', *American Economic Review*, 73 (1): 64–81. *299*

Deaton, Angus (2003) 'Health, inequality, and economic development', *Journal of Economic Literature*, 41(1): 113–58. *266*

Deb, Rajat, Pattanaik, Prasanta K. and Razzolini, Laura (1997) 'Game forms, rights, and the efficiency of social outcomes',* *Journal of Economic Theory*, 72(1): 74–95. *120*

DeBartolome, Charles A. M. (1995) 'Which tax rate do people use: average or marginal?', *Journal of Public Economics*, 56(1): 79–96. *218*

DeBorger, Bruno (2001) 'Discrete choice models and optimal two-part tariffs in the presence of externalities: optimal taxation of cars', *Regional Science and Urban Economics*, 31(4): 471–504. *204, 302*

Debreu, Gerard (ed.) (1996) *General Equilibrium Theory*, Cheltenham: Edward Elgar. *38*

Debreu, Gerard and Scarf, H. (1963) 'A limit theorem on the core of an economy',* *International Economic Review*, 4: 235–46. *30*

Dekel, Eddie and Scotchmer, Suzanne (1999) 'On the evolution of attitudes towards risk in winner-take-all games', *Journal of Economic Theory*, 87: 125–43. *268*

Demetriades, Panicos O. and Mamuneas, Theofanis P. (2000) 'Intertemporal output and employment effects of public infrastructure capital: Evidence from 12 OECD countries', *Economic Journal*, 110: 687–712. *248*

DeMeyer, Frank and Plott, Charles R. (1971) 'A welfare function using "relative intensity" of preference', *Quarterly Journal of Economics*, 85: 179–86. *101*

Demsetz, Harold (1969) 'Information and efficiency: another viewpoint', *Journal of Law and Economics*, 12: 1–22. *305*

Denicolo, Vincenzo and Delbono, Flavio (1999) 'Monopoly, competition, and the speed of R&D', *International Review of Economics and Business*, 46(1): 35–43. *305*

De Serpa, Alan C (1977) 'A theory of discriminatory clubs', *Scottish Journal of Political Economy*, 21: 33–41. *183*

De Serpa, Alan C. (1978) 'Congestion, pollution, and impure public goods', *Public Finance/Finances Publiques*, 33: 68–83. *182*

Devarajan, Shantayanan, and Fisher, Anthony C. (1981) 'Hotelling's "economics of exhaustible resources": fifty years later', *Journal of Economic Literature*, 19: 65–73. *303*

Devins, Neal and Douglas, Davison M. (1998) *Redefining Equality*, New York and Oxford: Oxford University Press. *142, 228*

Diamond, Peter A. (1967) 'The role of the stock market in a general equilibrium model with technological uncertainty',* *American Economic Review*, 57: 759–76. *289*

Diamond, Peter A. and McFadden, D. L. (1974) 'Some uses of the expenditure function in public finance', *Journal of Public Economics*, 3: 3–21. *302*

Diamond, Peter A. and Mirrlees, James A. (1971) 'Optimal taxation and public production',* *American Economic Review*, 61: 8–27, 261–78. *205*

Diener, Ed (1984) 'Subjective well-being', *Psychological Bulletin*, 95: 542–75. *263, 264*

Diener, Ed (2002) 'Will money increase subjective well-being?', *Social Indicators Research*, 57(2): 119–69. *269*

Diener, Ed, Diener, Marissa and Diener, Carol (1995) 'Factors predicting the subjective well-being of nations', *Journal of Personality and Social Psychology*, 69(5): 851–64. *262*

Diener, Ed, Horowitz, J. and Emmons, R. A. (1985) 'Happiness of the very wealthy', *Social Indicators Research*, 16: 263–74. *268*

Diener, Ed, Sandvik, E., Seidlitz L. and Diener, M. (1993) 'The relationship between income and subjective well-being: relative or absolute?', *Social Indicators Research*, 28: 195–223. *262, 269*

Diener, Ed and Suh, Eunkook (1997) 'Measuring quality of life: economic, social and subjective indicators', *Social Indicators Research*, 40: 189–216. *142, 262*

Diener, Ed and Suh, Eunkook (1999) 'National differences in subjective well-being', in Kahneman, Diener and Schwartz (1999) pp. 434–50. *262, 265*

Diener, Ed and Suh, Eunkook (eds) (2000) *Culture and Subjective Well-Being*, Cambridge, Mass.: MIT Press.

Di Tella, Rafael and MaCculloch, Robert (2000) 'Partisan social happiness', paper presented at the Economics and Happiness Conference, Nuffield College, Oxford, 11–12 February. *264, 278*

Dixit, Avinash K. (1970) 'On the optimum structure of commodity taxes', *American Economic Review*, 60: 295–301. *205*

Dixit, Avinash K. (1998) *The Making of Economic Policy: A Transaction-Cost Politics Perspective*, Cambridge, Mass.: MIT Press. *297*

Dixit, A. and Norman, V. (1978) 'Advertising and welfare', *The Bell Journal of Economics*, 9: 1–17. *270*

Dixit, Avinash and Olson, Mancur (2000) 'Does voluntary participation undermine the Coase theorem?', *Journal of Public Economics*, 76(3): 309–35. *159*

Dixit, Avinash K. and Stiglitz, Joseph E. (1977) 'Monopolistic competition and optimum product diversity', *American Economic Review*, 67(3): 297–308. *239, 249*

Dixon, Huw and Rankin, Neil (1994) 'Imperfect competition and macroeconomics: a survey', *Oxford Economic Papers*, 46: 171–99. *235*

Dodsworth, J. R. (1975) 'Reserve pooling: an application of the theory of clubs', *Economica Internazionale*, 28: 103–18. *183*

Dominitz, Jeff and Manski, Charles F. (1999) 'The several cultures of research on subjective expectations', in Smith, James P. and Willis, Robert J. (eds), *Wealth, Work, and Health: Innovations in Measurement in the Social Sciences – Essays in Honor of F. Thomas Juster*, Ann Arbor: University of Michigan Press: 15–33. *263*

Downs, Anthony (1957) *An Economic Theory of Democracy*, New York: Harper. *297*

Duesenberry, James S. (1949) *Income, Saving and the Theory of Consumer Behavior*, Cambridge, Mass.: Harvard University Press. *266*

Dummett, Michall and Farquharson, Robin (1961) 'Stability in voting', *Econometrica*, 29: 33–43. *113*

Dupuit, Jules (1944) 'De la mesure de l'utilite des travaus publics', *Annales des Ponts et Chaussées*, translated by R. H. Barback in *International Economic Papers*, 2(1952): 83–110.

Dusansky, Richard and Walsh, John (1976) 'Separability, welfare economics, and the theory of second best', *Review of Economic Studies*, 43: 49–51.

Dutta, Bhaskar (1994) *Welfare Economics*, Delhi: Oxford University Press.

Easterlin, Richard A. (1974) 'Does economic growth improve the human lot? Some empirical evidence', in David and Reder (1974). *268, 295*

Easterlin, Richard A. (ed.) (2002) *Happiness in Economics*, Cheltenham: Edward Elgar. *295*

Easterly, William (1999) 'Life during growth', World Bank Working Paper, available at http://www.worldbank.org/html/prdmg/grthweb/growth_t.htm. *264, 265, 278*

Eaton, B. Curtis and White, William (1991) 'The distribution of wealth and the efficiency of institutions', *Economic Inquiry*, 29: 336–50. *142, 228*

Eckersley, Richard (ed.) (1998) *Measuring Progress: Is Life Getting Better?*, Australia: CSIRO. *281*

Edgeworth, F. Y. (1881) *Mathematical Psychics*, London: Kegan Paul. *30, 107, 108*

Ekern, Steiner and Wilson, Robert (1974) 'On the theory of the firm in an economy with incomplete markets', *Bell Journal of Economics and Management Science*, S5: 171–80. *289*

Ellis, Howard S. and Fellner, William (1943) 'External economies and diseconomies', *American Economic Review*, 33: 493–511. *238*

Elster, Jon (ed.) (1986) *The Multiple Self*, Cambridge: Cambridge University Press. *272*

Elster, Jon (1998) 'Emotions and economic theory', *Journal of Economic Literature*, 36(1): 47–74. *270*

Elster, Jon (1999) *Alchemies of the Mind: Rationality and the Emotions*, Cambridge: Cambridge University Press. *272*

Estes, Richard J. (1988) *Trends in World Social Development: The Social Progress of Nations, 1970–1987*, New York: Praeger. *265*

Ethier, Wilfred (1979) 'Internationally decreasing costs and world trade', *Journal of International Economics*, 9: 1–24. *233, 239, 249, 251*

Ethier, Wilfred (1982) 'National and international returns to scale in the modern theory of international trade', *American Economic Review*, 72: 388–405. *233, 239, 249*

Evans, Jonathan St. B. T. and Over, D. E. (1996) *Rationality and Reasoning*, Hove: Psychology Press. *10*

Facchini, Giovanni, Hammond, Peter J. and Nakata, Hiroyuki (2001) 'Spurious deadweight gains', *Economic Letters*, 72(1): 33–37. *72*

Fair, Ray C. (1971) 'The optimal distribution of income', *Quarterly Journal of Economics*, 85: 551–79. *128*

Faith, Roger L. and Thompson, Earl A. (1981) 'A paradox in the theory of second best', *Economic Inquiry*, 19: 235–44.

Farquharson, Robin (1969) *Theory of Voting*, New Haven, CT: Yale University Press. *113*

Farrell, M. J. (1958) 'In defence of public-utility price theory', *Oxford Economic Papers*, 10: 109–23. *204*

Farrell, M. J. (1976) 'Liberalism in the theory of social choice', *Review of Economic Studies*, 3: 3–10. *120*

Fehr, Ernst and Zych, Peter K. (1998) 'Do addicts behave rationally?', *Scandinavian Journal of Economics*, 100(3): 643–62. *270*

Feldstein, Martin S. (1974) 'Distributional preferences in public expenditure analysis', in H. M. Hochman and G. E. Peterson (eds), *Redistribution Through Public Choice*, New York: Columbia University Press. *218*

Feldstein, Martin (1997) 'How big should government be?', *National Tax Journal*, 50(2): 197–213. *169, 171, 172*

Ferejohn, John A. and Fiorina, Morris P. (1975) 'Purposive models of legislative behavior', *AER/Papers and Proceedings*, 65: 407–14. *297*

Ferejohn, John A. and Grether, David M. (1977a) 'Weak path independence',* *Journal of Economic Theory*, 14: 19–31. *112*

Ferejohn, John A. and Grether, David M. (1977b) 'Some new impossibility theorems',* *Public Choice*, 30: 34–43. *106*

Fernandez, Raquel and Rogerson, Richard (2001) 'Sorting and long-run inequality', *Quarterly Journal of Economics*, 116(1): 1305–41. *136*

Fiorina, Morris P. and Noll, Roger G. (1978) 'Voters, bureaucrats and legislators: a rational choice perspective on the growth of bureaucracy', *Journal of Public Economics*, 9: 239–54. *297*

Fishburn, Peter C. (1970) 'Intransitive indifference in preference theory: a survey', *Operations Research*, 18: 207–28. *97, 108*

Fishburn, Peter C. (1973) 'Interval representations for interval orders and semiorders', *Journal of Mathematical Psychology* 10: 91–105. *108*

Fishburn, Peter C. (1974) 'On collective rationality and a generalised impossibility theorem', *Review of Economic Studies*, 41: 445–57.

Fisher, Irving (1927) 'A statistical measure for measuring "marginal utility" and testing the justice of a progressive income tax', in G. Hollander (ed.), *Economic Essays Contributed in Honour of J. B. Clark*, London: Macmillan. *142*

Fleming, Marcus (1952) 'A cardinal concept of welfare', *Quarterly Journal of Economics*, 66: 366–84. *108*

Fleurbaeya, Marc, Gary-Bobo, Robert J. and Maguain, Denis (2002) 'Education, distributive justice, and adverse selection', *Journal of Public Economics*, 84(1): 113–50.

Forbes, K. J. (2000), 'A reassessment of the relationship between inequality and growth', *American Economic Review*, 90: 869–87. *136, 142*

Fordyce, M. (1988) 'A review of research on happiness measures: a sixty second index of happiness and mental health', *Social Indicators Research*, 20: 355–81. *264*

Foster, C. D. and Neuburger, H. L. (1974) 'The ambiguity of the consumer's surplus measure of welfare change', *Oxford Economic Papers*, 26: 66–77. *82*

Foster, E. and Sonnenschein, H. (1970) 'Price distortion and economic welfare',*
Econometrica, 38: 281–97. *196*
Francois, Joseph F. and Nelson, Douglas (2002) 'A geometry of specialisation',
Economic Journal, 112: 649–78. *233*
Frank, Robert H. (1984) 'Are workers paid their marginal products?', *American
Economic Review*, 74(4): 549–71. *138*
Frank, Robert H. (1987) 'If *Homo Economicus* could choose his own utility function,
would he want one with a conscience?', *American Economic Review*, 77(4):
593–604. *14*
Frank, Robert H. (1997) 'Conspicuous consumption: money well spent?', *Economic
Journal*, 107: 1832–47. *262*
Frank, Robert H. (1999) *Luxury Fever: Why Money Fails to Satisfy in an Era of Excess*,
New York: Free Press. *267, 268, 278*
Frank, Robert H. (2000) 'Does growing inequality harm the middle class?', *Eastern
Economic Journal*, 26(3): 253–64.
Frank, Robert H. and Cook, Philip J. (1995) *The Winner-Take-All Society*, New York,
London and Toronto: Simon and Schuster, Free Press, Martin Kessler. *137*
Frantz, Roger (1992) 'X-efficiency and allocative efficiency: what have we learned?,
American Economic Review, 82(2): 434–38. *299*
Frantz, Roger (1997) *X-efficiency: Theory, Evidence and Applications* 2nd edn, Boston,
Kluwer Academic Publishers. *262, 299*
Frederick, Shane and Loewenstein, George (1999) 'Hedonic adaptation', in Kahneman
et al. (1999). *271*
Frey, Bruno S. and Stutzer, Alois (1999) 'Measuring preferences by subjective well-
being', *Journal of Institutional and Theoretical Economics*, 155: 755–78. *281*
Frey, Bruno S. and Stutzer, Alois (2000) 'Happiness, economy and institutions',
Economic Journal, 110(446): 918–38. *279*
Frey, Bruno S. and Stutzer, Alois (2002a) 'What can economists learn from happiness
research?' *Journal of Economic Literature*, XL: 402–35. *264, 282*
Frey, Bruno S. and Stutzer, Alois (2002b) *Happiness and Economics: How the Economy
and Institutions Affect Well-Being*, Princeton, NJ: Princeton University Press. *282*
Friedman, David (1980) 'Many, few, one: social harmony and the shrunken choice
set', *American Economic Review*, 70: 225–32. *34*
Friedman, Milton (1947) 'Lerner on the economics of control', *Journal of Political
Economy*, 55: 405–16. *131*
Friedman, Milton (1953) 'Choice, chance, and the personal distribution of income',
Journal of Political Economy, 61: 277–90. *138*
Frijters, Paul (1999) 'Do individuals try to maximize general satisfaction?', unpublished
manuscript. *271*
Frisch, Ragnar A. K. (1932) *New Methods of Measuring Marginal Utility*, Tübingen:
Mohr. *142*
Fuentes, Nicole and Rojas, Mariano (2001) 'Economic theory and subjective well-
being: Mexico', *Social Indicators Research*, 53(3): 289–314. *265*
Furubotn, Eirik B. and Pejovich, Svetozar (1972) 'Property rights and economic
theory: a survey of recent literature', *Journal of Economic Literature*, 10: 1137–2. *298*
Gaertner, Wulf, Pattanaik, Prasanta K. and Suzumura, Kotaro (1992) 'Individual rights
revisited', *Economica*, 59(234): 161–77. *120*
Galbraith, J. K. (1958) *The Affluent Society*, Boston: Houghton Mifflin. *270*
Gerber, Elisabeth R. (1999) *The Populist Paradox: Interest Group Influence and the Promise
of Direct Legislation*, Princeton, NJ: Princeton University Press. *298*

Gibbard, A. (1973) 'Manipulation of voting schemes: a general result',* *Econometrica*, 41: 587–601. *113*

Gibbard, A. (1974) 'A Pareto-consistent libertarian claim', *Journal of Economic Theory*, 7: 388–410. *120*

Gifford, Adam Jr and Stone, Courtenay C. (1975) 'Externalities, liability, separability, and resource allocation: comment', *American Economic Review*, 65: 724–7.

Gilbert, Richard J. (1979) 'Optimal depletion of an uncertain stock',* *Review of Economic Studies*, 46: 47–57. *303*

Gintis, Herbert (1972) 'A radical analysis of welfare economics and individual development', *Quarterly Journal of Economics*, 86: 572–99. *261*

Gintis, Herbert (1974) 'Welfare criteria with endogenous preferences: the economics of education', *International Economic Review*, 15(2): 415–30. *281, 301*

Glaister, S. (1974) 'Generalised consumer surplus and public transport pricing', *Economic Journal*, 84: 849–67.

Glazer, Amihai and Rothenberg, Lawrence S. (2001) *Why Government Succeeds and Why it Fails*, Cambridge, Mass.: Harvard University Press. *297*

Glewwe, Paul, Jacoby, Hanan G. and King, Elizabeth (2001) 'Early childhood nutrition and academic achievement: a longitudinal analysis', *Journal of Public Economics*, 81(3): 345–68. *266*

Goldfarb, Robert S. and Woglom, Geoffrey (1974) 'Government investment decisions and institutional constraints on income redistribution', *Journal of Public Economics*, 3: 171–80.

Goleman, D. (1995) *Emotional Intelligence*, New York: Bantam Books. *270*

Good, I. J. (1977) 'Justice in voting by demand revelation', *Public Choice*, 9: 65–70 (supplement). *114*

Goodin, Robert E. (ed.) (1996) *The Theory of Institutional Design*, Cambridge and New York: Cambridge University Press. *298*

Goodin, Robert E. (2000) 'Preference failures', paper presented at the 'Fairness and Goodness' Conference (sponsored by the World Health Organization), Trivandrum, India, 11–15 March.

Goodman, Leo A. and Markowitz, Harry (1952) 'Social welfare functions based on individual rankings', *American Journal of Sociology*, 58: 257–62. *108, 125*

Gorman, W. M. (1953) 'Community preference fields',* *Econometrica*, 21: 63–80.

Gorman, W. M. (1967) 'Tastes, habits, and choices', *International Economic Review*, 8: 218–22. *301*

Gould, J. R. (1977) 'Total conditions in the analysis of external effects', *Economic Journal*, 87: 558–64. *148*

Graaff, J. de V. (1957) *Theoretical Welfare Economics*, London: Cambridge University Press. *49*

Graham, Carol and Pettinato, Stefano (2001) 'Happiness, markets, and democracy: Latin America in comparative perspective', *Journal of Happiness Studies*, 2: 237–68. *264*

Graham, Carol and Pettinato, Stefano (2002) 'Frustrated achievers: winners, losers, and subjective well being in new market economies', *Journal of Development Studies*, 38(4): 100–40.

Gramlich, Edward M. (1994) 'Infrastructure investment: a review essay', *Journal of Economic Literature*, 32: 1176–96. *246*

Grandmont, Jean-Michel (1977) 'Temporary general equilibrium theory',* *Econometrica*, 45: 535–72.

Grandmont, Jean-Michel (1978) 'Intermediate preferences and the majority rule',* *Econometrica*, 46: 317–30. *102, 103*

Gratton, Chris and Holliday, Simon (1996) 'The economics of pleasure choices', in David M. Warburton and Neil Sherwood (eds), *Pleasure and Quality of Life*, New York: John Wiley, pp. 209–41.

Green, H. A. John (1961) 'The social optimum in the presence of monopoly and taxation', *Review of Economic Studies*, 29: 66–77. *196, 204*

Green, H. A. John (1975) 'Two models of optimal pricing and taxation', *Oxford Economic Papers*, 27: 352–82. *301*

Green, H. A. John (1976) *Consumer Theory*, rev. edn, London: Macmillan. *73, 74*

Green, Jerry, Kohlberg, Elon and Laffont, Jean-Jacques (1976) 'Partial equilibrium approach to the free-rider problem',* *Journal of Public Economics*, 6: 373–94. *177*

Green, Jerry and Laffont, Jean-Jacques (1977a) 'Characterisation of satisfactory mechanisms for revelation of preferences for public goods',* *Econometrica*, 45: 427–38. *174*

Green, Jerry and Laffont, Jean-Jacques (1977b) 'Imperfect personal information and the demand-revealing process: a sampling approach', *Public Choice*, 29: 79–94. *179*

Green, Jerry and Laffont, Jean-Jacques (1978a) 'An incentive compatible planning procedure for public good production',* *Swedish Journal of Economics*, 80: 20–33. *174*

Green, Jerry and Laffont, Jean-Jacques (1978b) *Incentives in Public Decision Making*, Amsterdam: North-Holland. *174*

Greene, Robert L. (1970) *Welfare Economics and Peak-Load Pricing*, Gainesville, Fla: University of Florida Press; Melbourne: Cambridge University Press. *302*

Griliches, Zvi, W. Krelle, H. J. Krupp and O. Kyn (eds) (1978) *Income Distribution and Economic Inequality*, Somerset, NJ: Halsted. *136*

Grossman, Gene M. and Helpman, Elhanan (2001) *Special Interest Politics*, Cambridge, Mass., and London: MIT Press. *298*

Grossman, Herschel (1994) 'Production, appropriation and land reform', *American Economic Review*, 84(3): 705–12. *142, 228*

Groves, Theodore (1970) 'The allocation of resources under uncertainty: the inform ational and incentive roles of prices and demands in a team', unpublished PhD dissertation, University of California, Berkeley. *112, 174*

Groves, Theodore (1973) 'Incentives in teams', *Econometrica*, 41: 617–33. *112, 174*

Groves, Theodore (1976) 'Information, incentives and the internalisation of production externalities', in Lin (1976). *174*

Groves, Theodore (1979) 'Efficient collective choice when compensation is possible',* *Review of Economic Studies*, 46: 227–41. *115*

Groves, Theodore and Ledyard, John (1977a) 'Optimal allocation of public goods: a solution to the "free rider problem" ',* *Econometrica*, 45: 783–809. *114, 174*

Groves, Theodore and Ledyard, John (1977b) 'Some limitations of demand-revealing processes', *Public Choice*, 29: 107–24 (spring supplement). *179*

Groves, Theodore and Ledyard, John (1980) 'The existence of efficient and incentive compatible equilibria with public goods',* *Econometrica*, 48: 1487–506.

Groves, Theodore and Loeb, Martin (1975) 'Incentives and public input', *Journal of Public Economics*, 4: 211–26. *174*

Groves, Theodore, Radner, Roy and Reiter, Stanley (eds) (1987) *Information, Incentives, and Economic Mechanisms: Essays in Honor of Leonid Hurwicz*; Oxford: Basil Blackwell. *174, 298, 304*

Gruber, Jon and Saez, Emmanuel (2002) 'The elasticity of taxable income: evidence and implications', *Journal of Public Economics*, 84(1): 1–32. *134*

Gruber, Jonathan and Koszegi, Botond (2001) 'Is addiction "rational"? Theory and evidence', *Quarterly Journal of Economics*, 116(4): 1261–303. *300*

Guesnerie, Roger (1975) 'Pareto optimality in non-convex economies', *Econometrica*, 43: 1–29. *238*

Guesnerie, Roger (1977) 'On the direction of tax reform', *Journal of Public Economics*, 7: 179–202.

Guesnerie, Roger (1995) *A Contribution to the Pure Theory of Taxation*, Cambridge, New York and Melbourne: Cambridge University Press. *38*

Gwilliam, K. M. and Nash, C. A. (1972) 'Evaluation of urban road investment: a comment', *Applied Economics*, 4: 307–15. *73*

Hagerty, Michael R. and Veenhoven, Ruut (1999) 'Wealth and happiness revisited: growing wealth of nations does go with greater happiness', unpublished manuscript. *262*

Hahn, Robert W., Tetlock, Paul C. and Burnett, Jason K. (2000) 'Should you be allowed to use your cellular phone while driving?', *Regulation*, 3: 46–55. *282*

Hahnel, Robin and Abert, Michael (1990) *Quiet Revolution in Welfare Economics*, Princeton, NJ: Princeton University Press.

Hamilton, William D. (1964) 'The genetical evolution of social behavior, I and II', *Journal of Theoretical Biology*, 7(1): 1–52. *7*

Hammond, Peter J. (1977) 'Dynamic restrictions on metastatic choice', *Economica*, 44: 337–50. *103*

Hammond, Peter J. and Myles, Gareth D. (eds) (2000) *Incentives, Organization, and Public Economics: Papers in Honour of Sir James Mirrlees*, Oxford and New York: Oxford University Press. *135*

Hanson, Donald A. (1977) 'Second best pricing policies for an exhaustible resource', *AER/Papers and Proceedings*, 67: 351–4. *303*

Hansson, B. (1969) 'Group preferences', *Econometrica*, 67: 50–4. *103*

Hansson, B. (1976) 'The existence of group preference functions',* *Public Choice*, 28: 89–98. *97*

Harberger, A. C. (1954) 'Monopoly and resource allocation', *American Economic Review*, 45: 77–87. *299*

Harberger, A. C. (1964) 'Taxation, resource allocation, and welfare', in NBER and Brookings Institution, *The Role of Direct and Indirect Taxes in the Federal Revenue System*, Princeton, NJ: Princeton University Press. *302*

Harberger, A. C. (1971) 'The three basic postulates for applied welfare economics: an interpretive essay', *Journal of Economic Literature*, 9: 785–97. *75, 82, 208*

Harberger, A. C. (1978) 'On the use of distributional weights in social cost–benefit analysis', *Journal of Political Economy*, 86: S87–120. *208*

Hardy, J. D., H. G. Wolfe, H. Goodell, and E. G. Boring (1952, 1967) *Pain Sensations and Reactions*, Baltimore and New York: *111*

Harrod, Roy F. (1948) *Towards a Dynamic Economics*, London: Macmillan. *10*

Harrod, Roy F. (1958) 'The possibility of economic satiety', in *Problems of United States Economic Development*, vol. I, New York: Committee for Economic Development. *290*

Harsanyi, John C. (1953) 'Cardinal utility in welfare economics and in the theory of risk-taking', *Journal of Political Economy*, 61: 434–5. *105*

Harsanyi, John C. (1953–4) 'Welfare economics of variable tastes', *Review of Economic Studies*, 21: 204–13. *105, 301*

Harsanyi, John C. (1955) 'Cardinal welfare, individualistic ethics, and interpersonal comparisons of utility', *Journal of Political Economy*, 63: 309–21. *105, 108*

Harsanyi, John C. (1997) 'Utilities, preferences, and substantive goods', *Social Choice and Welfare*, 14: 129–45. *6, 261*

Hart, Oliver D. (1985), 'Monopolistic competition in the spirit of Chamberlin: special results', *Economic Journal*, 95 (380): 889–908. *239*

Hatta, Tatsuo (1977) 'A theory of piecemeal policy recommendations',* *Review of Economic Studies*, 44: 1–21. *196*

Hau, Timothy D. (1998) 'Congestion pricing and road investment' in Button and Verhoef, pp. 39–78.

Hause, John C. (1975) 'The theory of welfare cost measurement', *Journal of Political Economy*, 83: 1145–82. *70, 78, 82*

Hausman, Jerry A. (1981) 'Exact consumer's surplus and deadweight loss',* *American Economic Review*, 71: 662–76. *70*

Haveman, Robert H. (1988) *Starting Even: An Equal Opportunity Program to Combat the Nation's New Poverty*, New York: Simon & Schuster. *142, 228*

Hayek, F. A. von (1945) 'The use of knowledge in society', *American Economic Review*, 35: 519–30. *39*

Hayes, Kathy J., Lambert, Peter J. and Slottje, Daniel J. (1995) 'Evaluating effective income tax progression', *Journal of Public Economics*, 56(3): 461–74. *117, 210*

He, Ying (2000) 'Who is really wrong?', *Economic Highlights*, 380: 4. *161*

Head, John (1966) 'On merit goods', *Finanzarchiv*, 25: 1–29. *300*

Head, John (1969) 'Merit goods revisited', *Finanzarchiv*, 28: 214–25. *300*

Head, John (1974) *Public Goods and Public Welfare*, Durham, NC: Duke University Press.

Head, John (1977) 'Misleading analogies in public goods analysis', *Finanzarchiv*, 36(1): 1–18.

Headey, Bruce and Wearing, Alexander (1991) 'Subjective well-being: a stocks and flows framework', in F. Strack, M. Argyle and N. Schwarz (eds), *Subjective Well-Being*, Oxford: Pergamon, pp. 49–73. *271*

Heal, Geoffrey (1980) 'Spatial structure in the retail trade: a study in product differentiation with increasing returns', *Bell Journal of Economics*, 11(2): 545–83. *239*

Heal, Geoffrey (1999) *The Economics of Increasing Returns*, Cheltenham: Edward Elgar. *234, 238, 239, 240, 241, 242*

Heller, Walter P. and Starrett, David A. (1976) 'On the nature of externalities', in Lin,

Helpman, Robert. C. E. (1974) 'Optimal income taxation for transfer payments under different social welfare criteria', *Quarterly Journal of Economics*, 88: 656–70. *134*

Helpman, Robert C. E. and Hillman, A. L. (1977) 'Two remarks on optimal club size', *Economica*, 44: 293–6. *183*

Helpman, Elhanan and Krugman, Paul R. (1985) *Market Structure and Foreign Trade: Increasing Returns, Imperfect Competition, and the International Economy*, Cambridge, Mass.: MIT Press. *239, 251*

Henderson, A. (1941) 'Consumer's surplus and the compensating variation', *Review of Economic Studies*, 8: 117–21. *66*

Hennipman, Pieter (1995) *Welfare Economics and The Theory of Economic Policy*, Aldershot: Edward Elgar. *5*

Herberg, H. and Kemp, M. C. (1969) 'Some implications of variable returns to scale', *Canadian Journal of Economics*, 2: 403–15. *35*

Hermalin, Benjamin E. and Isen, Alice M. (1999) 'The effects of affect on economic and strategic decision making', unpublished manuscript. *272*

Hersoug, Tor (1984) 'Union wage responses to tax changes', *Oxford Economic Papers*, 36: 37–51. *142, 228*

Hewitt, Daniel P. (1987) 'Market vote trading and efficient public choice', *Public Finance*, 42(1): 85–104. *105*

Hicks, John R. (1939) 'Foundations of welfare economics', *Economic Journal*, 49: 696–712. *36, 48*

Hicks, John R. (1940) 'The valuation of social income', *Economica*, 7: 105–24. *48, 66*

Hicks, John R. (1941) 'The rehabilitation of consumer's surplus', *Review of Economic Studies*, 8: 108–16. *48, 66*

Hicks, John R. (1943) 'The four consumers' surplus', *Review of Economic Studies*, 11: 31–41. *66*

Hildenbrand, Werner (1977) 'Limit theorems on the case of an economy',* in Intriligator (1977). *30*

Hildenbrand, Werner and Kirman, A. P. (1976) *Introduction to Equilibrium Analysis*, Amsterdam: North-Holland.

Hildock, C. (1953) 'Alternative conditions for social orderings', *Econometrica*, 51: 21–81. *104*

Hirsch, Fred (1976) *Social Limits to Growth*, Cambridge, Mass.: Harvard University Press. *261, 290*

Ho, Lok Sang (2001) *Principles of Public Policy Practice*, Boston, Mass.: Kluwer. *136*

Hochman, Harold M. and Peterson, George E. (eds) (1974) *Redistribution Through Public Choice*, New York: Columbia University Press. *136*

Hochman, Harold M. and Rodgers, J. D. (1969) 'Pareto-optimal redistribution', *American Economic Review*, 59: 542–57. *181*

Hoff, Karla (1996) 'Market failures and the distribution of wealth: a perspective from the economics of information', *Politics & Society*, 24: 411–432. *142, 228*

Hoff, Karla and Lyon, Andrew (1995), 'Non-leaky buckets: optimal redistributive taxation and agency costs', *Journal of Public Economics*, 58: 365–90. *142, 228*

Hoffman, Martin L. (1981) 'Is altruism part of human nature?', *Journal of Personality and Social Psychology*, 40: 121–37. *7*

Holmstrom, B. (1979) 'Moral hazard and Observability', *Bell Journal of Economics*, 10(1): 74–91. *304*

Holsey, Cheryl M. and Borcherding, Thomas E. (1997) 'Why does government's share of national income grow? An assessment of the recent literature on the U.S. experience', in Mueller (1997). *278*

Hook, S. (ed.) (1967) *Human Values and Economic Policy: A Symposium*, New York: New York University Press.

Horvat, Branko (1972) 'A model of maximal economic growth', *Kyklos*, 25, fasc. 2: 215–28.

Hotelling, Harold (1931) 'The economics of exhaustible resources', *Journal of Political Economy*, 39: 137–75. *303*

Hotelling, Harold (1938) 'The general welfare in relation to problems of taxation and of railway and utility rates', *Econometrica*, 6: 242–69. *74, 75*

Huberman, Bernardo A., Loch, Christoph H. and Onculer, Ayse (1999) 'Status as a valued resource', INSEAD Working Paper no. 99/83/TM. *290*

Hueth, Darrall and Schmitz, Andrew (1972) 'International trade in intermediate and final goods: some welfare implications of destabilising prices', *Quarterly Journal of Economics*, 86: 351–65. *304*

Hurwicz, Leonid (1960) 'Optimality and informational efficiency in resource allocation processes',* in K. J. Arrow, S. Karlin and P. Suppe (eds), *Mathematical Methods in the Social Sciences*, Stanford, CA: Stanford University Press. *39*

Hurwicz, Leonid (1972) 'On informationally decentralised systems',* in R. Radner and B. McGuire (eds), *Decision and Organisation*, Amsterdam: North-Holland. *176*

Hurwicz, Leonid (1981–91) 'Incentive aspects of decentralization',* in Arrow and Intriligator (1981–91).

Hurwicz, Leonid (1999) 'Revisiting externalities', *Journal of Public Economic Theory*, 1(2): 225–45. *148*

Hutchinson, Gladstone A. and Schumacher, Ute (1997) 'Fiscal expenditure policy and economic growth: evidence from Latin America and the Caribbean', *Social and Economic Studies*, 46(4): 1–16. *300*

Inada, Ken-Ichi (1970) 'Majority rule and rationality', *Journal of Economic Theory*, 2: 27–40. *103*

Inglehart, Ronald, Basnez, Miguel and Moreno, Alejandro (1998) *Human Values and Beliefs: A Cross-Cultural Sourcebook: Political, Religious, Sexual, and Economic Norms in 43 Societies; Findings from the 1990–1993 World Value Survey*, Ann Arbor, Mich.: University of Michigan Press. *262*

Intriligator, Michael D. (ed.) (1977) *Frontiers of Quantitative Economics*, vol. III, Amsterdam: North-Holland.

Iqbal, Mahmood (2000) 'Brain drain: empirical evidence of emigration of Canadian professionals to the United States', *Canadian Tax Journal*, 48(3): 674–88. *304*

Ireland, Norman J. (1998) 'Status-seeking, income taxation and efficiency', *Journal of Public Economics*, 70: 99–113. *278*

Ireland, Norman J. (2001) 'Optimal income tax in the presence of status effects', *Journal of Public Economics*, 81: 193–212. *278*

Isen, Alice M. (2000) 'Positive affect and decision making', in M. Lewis and J. Haviland (eds), *Handbook of Emotions*, 2nd edn, New York: Guilford Press. *272*

Islam, Sardar M. N. (2001) 'Optimal growth economics: an investigation of the contemporary issues and the prospect for sustainable growth', in *Contributions to Economic Analysis*, vol. 252, Amsterdam, London and New York: Elsevier Science, North-Holland. *303*

Jencks, C., *et al.* (1972) *Inequality: A Reassessment of the Effect of Family and Schooling in America*, New York: Basic Books. *139*

Jerison, Michael (1994) 'Optimal income distribution rules and representative consumers', *Review of Economic Studies*, 61(4): 739–71. *50*

Jewitt, Ian (1981) 'Preference structure and piecemeal second best policy',* *Journal of Public Economics*, 16: 215–31.

Johansen, Leif (1963) 'Some notes on the Lindahl theory of determination of public expenditures', *International Economic Review*, 4: 346–58. *169*

Juster, F. T. (1978) *The Distribution of Economic Well-Being*, New York: Wiley. *136*

Juster, F. T. (1985) 'Preferences for work and leisure', in J. Stafford and F. P. Stafford (eds), *Time, Goods, and Well-being*, Ann Arbor, Mich.: Institute for Social Research. *274*

Kagel, John, H. and Roth, Alvin E. (eds) (1995) *Handbook of Experimental Economics*, Princeton, NJ: Princeton University Press.

Kahn, Alfred E. (1966). 'The tyranny of small decisions: market failures, imperfections, and the limits of economics', *Kyklos*, 19(1): 23–47. *289*

Kahn, R. F. (1935) 'Some notes on ideal output', *Economic Journal*, 45: 1–35. *194*

Kahneman, Daniel (1999) 'Objective happiness', in Kahneman, Diener and Schwarz (1999). *253, 254, 280*

Kahneman, Daniel, Diener, Ed and Schwarz, Norbert (eds) (1999) *Well-Being: The Foundations of Hedonic Psychology*, New York: Russell Sage Foundation. *142, 272*

Kahneman, D., Fredrickson, B. L., Schreiber, C. A. and Redelmeier, D. A. (1993) 'When more pain is preferred to less: adding a better end', *Psychological Science*, 4(6): 401–5. *273*

Kahneman, Daniel, Knetsch, D. and Thaler, R. (1991) 'The endowment effect, loss aversion, and status quo bias', *Journal of Economic Perspectives*, 5: 193–206. *79, 271*

Kahneman, Daniel and Tversky, Amos (1982) *Judgment under Uncertainty: Heuristics and Biases*, Cambridge: Cambridge University Press. *271*

Kahneman, Daniel and Tversky, Amos (1996) 'On the reality of cognitive illusions', *Psychological Review*, 103: 582–91. *10*

Kahneman, Daniel, Wakker, Peter P. and Sarin, Rakesh (1997) 'Back to Bentham? Explorations of experienced utility', *Quarterly Journal Economics*, 112(2): 375–405. *6, 253*

Kalai, Ehud and Schmeidler, David (1977) 'Aggregation procedure for cardinal preferences: a formulation and proof of Samuelson's impossibility conjecture',
Econometrica, 45: 1431–8. *101*

Kaldor, N. (1939), 'Welfare propositions of economics and interpersonal comparisons
of utility', *Economic Journal*, 49: 549–52. *48*

Kaldor, N. (1947) 'A comment', *Review of Economic Studies*, 14: 49. *48*

Kalman, Peter J. (1968) 'Theory of consumer behavior when prices enter the utility
function',* *Econometrica*, 36: 497–510. *80, 300*

Kamien, Morton and Schwartz, Nancy L. (1975) 'Market structure and innovation:
a survey', *Journal of Economic Literature*, 13: 1–37. *305*

Kamien, Morton and Schwartz, Nancy L. (1978) 'Optimal exhaustible resource
depletion with endogenous technical change', *Review of Economic Studies*, 45:
179–96. *303*

Kaneko, Mamoru and Nakamura, Kenjiro (1979) 'The Nash social welfare function',
Econometrica, 47: 423–35. *129*

Kaplow, Louis (1996) 'The optimal supply of public goods and the distortionary cost
of taxation', *National Tax Journal*, 49(4): 513–33. *170, 171, 172, 278*

Kaplow, Louis and Shavell, Steven (2002) *Fairness versus Welfare*, Cambridge, Mass.:
Harvard University Press. *119, 120*

Kapteyn, A., Van Praag, B. M. S. and van Herwaarden, F. G. (1976) 'Individual welfare
functions and social reference spaces', *Economic Letters*, 1: 173–8. *265*

Kapteyn, Arie and van Herwaarden, Floor G. (1980) 'Interdependent welfare
functions and optimal income distribution', *Journal of Public Economics*, 14:
375–97.

Kapteyn, A. and Wansbeek, T. J. (1985) 'The individual welfare function', *Journal of
Economic Psychology*, 6: 333–63.

Kapur, Basant (2002) 'Can faster income growth reduce well-being?', Working Paper,
Department of Economics, National University of Singapore. *268*

Kasser, Tim and Ryan, Richard M. (1993) 'A dark side of the American Dream:
correlates of financial success as a central life aspiration', *Journal of Personality
and Social Psychology*, 65(2): 410–22. *269*

Kasser, Tim and Ryan, Richard M. (1996) 'Further examining the American Dream:
differential correlates of intrinsic and extrinsic goals', *Journal of Personality and Social
Psychology*, 22(3): 280–7. *269*

Kasser, Tim and Ryan, Richard M. (1998) 'Be careful what you wish for: optimal functioning and the relative attainment of intrinsic and extrinsic goals', unpublished
manuscript. *269*

Kaufman, Bruce E. (1999) 'Emotional arousal as a source of bounded rationality',
Journal of Economic Behavior & Organization, 38: 135–44. *272*

Kaul, I., Grunberg, I. and Stern, M. A. (eds) (1999) *Global Public Goods: International
Cooperation in the 21ˢᵗ Century*, Oxford: Oxford University Press. *164*

Kawamata, Kunio (1977) 'Price distortion and the second best optimum',* *Review of
Economic Studies*, 44: 23–9. *196*

Kearl, J. R., Pope, Clayne L., Whiting, Gordon C. and Wimmer, Larry T. (1979) 'A confusion of economists?', *AER/Papers and Proceedings*, 69: 28–37. *23*

Keefer, Philip and Knack, Stephen (2002) 'Polarization, politics and property rights:
links between inequality and growth', *Public Choice*, 11(1–2): 127–54. *142*

Kelly, Jerry S. (1977) *Arrow Impossibility Theorems*, New York: Academic Press. *120*

Kemp, Murray C. (1964) *The Pure Theory of International Trade*, Englewood Cliffs,
NJ: Prentice-Hall. *239*

Kemp, Murray C. (1968) 'Some issues in the analysis of trade gains', *Oxford Economic
Papers*, 20: 129–61. *196*

Kemp, Murray C. and Asimakopulos, A. (1952) 'A note on "social welfare functions" and cardinal utility', *Canadian Journal of Economics*, 18: 195–200. *104*

Kemp, Murray C. and Long, Ngo Van (1978) 'The optimal consumption of depletable resources: comment', *Quarterly Journal of Economics*, 92: 345–53. *303*

Kemp, Murray C. and Long, Ngo Van (1980) 'Eating a cake of unknown size: pure competition versus social planning', in *Essay 5 of Exhaustible Resources, Optimality, and Trade*, Amsterdam: North-Holland. *303*

Kemp, Murray C. and Ng, Yew-Kwang (1976) 'On the existence of social welfare functions, social orderings and social decision functions', *Economica*, 43: 59–66. *99, 115, 120, 121*

Kemp, Murray C. and Ng, Yew-Kwang (1977) 'More on social welfare functions: the incompatibility of individualism and ordinalism', *Economica*, 44: 89–90. *101*

Kennedy, C. (1953) 'The economic welfare function and Dr. Little's criterion', *Review of Economic Studies*, 20: 137–42. *53*

Kennedy, C. (1963a) 'Welfare criteria – a further note', *Economic Journal*, 73: 338–41. *53*

Kennedy, C. (1963b) 'Two comments (II)', *Economic Journal*, 73: 780–1. *53*

Kenny, Charles (1999) 'Does growth cause happiness, or does happiness cause growth?', *Kyklos*, 52: 3–26. *142, 269*

Khanna, Jyoti (1993) 'Cooperative versus noncooperative behavior: The case of agricultural research', *Review of Economics and Statistics*, 75(2): 346–52. *169*

Kimenyi, Mwangi S. and Mbaku, John Mukum (eds) (1999) *Institutions and Collective Choice in Developing Countries: Applications of the Theory of Public Choice*, Aldershot, UK, and Brookfield, VT: Ashgate. *297*

King, Mervyn A. (1986) 'A Pigovian rule for the optimum provision of public goods', *Journal of Public Economics*, 30: 273–91. *170*

Kirchsteigera, Georg and Prat, Andrea (2001) 'Inefficient equilibria in lobbying', *Journal of Public Economics*, 82(3): 349–75. *298*

Kirman, Alan, and Sondermann, Dieter (1972), 'Arrow's theorem, many agents and invisible dictators',* *Journal of Economic Theory*, 5: 267–77. *97*

Kirzner, Israel M. (1997) 'Entrepreneurial discovery and the competitive market process: An Austrian approach', *Journal of Economic Literature*, 35(1): 60–85. *253*

Klappholz, K. (1964) 'Value judgments and economies', *British Journal for the Philosophy of Science*, 15(58): 97. *23*

Kleven, Henrik J., Richter, Wolfram F. and Sorensen, Peter B. (2000) 'Optimal taxation with household production', *Oxford Economic Papers*, 52(3): 584–94. *205, 302*

Klibanoff, Peter and Morduch, Jonathan (1995) 'Decentralization, externalities, and efficiency', *Review of Economic Studies*, 62(2): 223–47. *152*

Kling, Catherine L. (1989) 'A note on the welfare effects of omitting substitute prices and qualities from travel cost models', *Land Economics*, 65(3): 290–6. *73*

Knight, F. H. (1924) 'Some fallacies in the interpretation of social cost', *Quarterly Journal of Economics*, 38: 582–606. *238*

Kockesen, Levent, Ok, Efe and Sethi, Rajiv (2000) 'On the strategic advantage of negatively interdependent preferences', *Journal of Economic Theory*, 92: 274–99. *267*

Kolm, Serge Christopher (1993) 'The impossibility of utilitarianism', in P. Koslowski and Y. Shionoya (eds), *The Good and The Economical: Ethical Choices in Economics and Management*, Berlin and New York: Springer-Verlag. *115*

Kolm, Serge C. (1996a) 'The theory of justice', *Social Choice and Welfare*, 13(2): 151–82. *135*

Kolm, Serge C. (1996b) *Modern Theories of Justice*, Cambridge and London: MIT Press. *136*

Konishi, Hideo (1995) 'A Pareto-improving commodity tax reform under a smooth nonlinear income tax', *Journal of Public Economics*, 56: 413–46. *170*

Konow, James and Earley, Joseph (2002) 'The hedonistic paradox: is homo economicus happier?', unpublished manuscript. *261*

Koo, Bon H. and Perkins, Dwight H. (1995) *Social Capability and Long-Term Economic Growth*, London: Macmillan.

Koplin, H. T. (1963) 'The profit maximisation assumption', *Oxford Economic Papers*, 15: 130–9. *41, 289*

Kramer, G. (1973) 'On a class of equilibrium conditions for majority rule',* *Econometrica*, 41: 285–97. *99*

Krelle, Wilhelm and Shorrocks, Anthony F. (eds) (1978) *Personal Income Distribution*, Amsterdam: North-Holland. *136*

Krueger, Anne O. (1974) 'The political economy of the rent-seeking society', *American Economic Review*, 64: 291–303. *243*

Kunreuther, H., Ginsberg, R., Miller, R., Sagi, P., Borkan, B. and Katz, N. (1978) *Disaster Insurance Protection*, New York: Wiley. *271*

Kwok, Viem and Leland, Hayne (1982) 'An economic model of the brain drain', *American Economic Review*, 72: 91–100. *304*

La Ferrara, Eliana (2001) 'TFP, costs, and public infrastructure: An equivocal relationship', SSRN Electronic Paper Collection: http://papers.ssrn.com/paper.taf?abstract_id=262511. *246*

Laffont, Jean J. (ed.) (1979) *Aggregation and Revelation of Preferences*, Amsterdam: North-Holland. *113*

Laffont, Jean J. (2000) *Incentives and Political Economy*, Oxford and New York: Oxford University Press. *298*

Lancaster, Kelvin (1968) *Mathematical Economics*, London: Collier-Macmillan. *36*

Lancaster, Kelvin (1979) *Variety, Equity, and Efficiency*, New York: Columbia University Press. *239*

Lane, Robert E. (1992) 'Work as "disutility" and money as "happiness": cultural origins of a basic market error', *Journal of Socio Economics*, 21(1): 43–64. *274*

Lane, Robert E. (1993) 'Does money buy happiness?', *Public Interest.*, 113: 56–65. *271*

Lane, Robert F. (2000) *The Loss of Happiness in Market Democracies*, New York: Yale University Press. *271, 274*

Larsen, Randy J. and Fredrickson, Barbara L. (1999) 'Measurement issues in emotion research', in Kahneman, Diener and Schwarz (1999), pp. 40–60. *264*

Lazar, Ariela (1999) 'Deceiving oneself or self-deceived? On the formation of beliefs "under the influence" ', *Mind*, 108(430): 265–90. *272*

Lebergott, Stanley (1993) *Pursuing Happiness: American Consumers in the Twentieth Century*, Princeton, NJ: Princeton University Press. *271*

Ledyard, John (1995) 'Public goods: a survey of experimental research', in Kagel and Roth.

Lee, Woojin and Roemer, John E. (1999) 'Income distribution, redistributive politics, and economic growth', *Jounal of Economic Growth*, 3: 217–40. *142, 228*

Le Grand, Julian (1997) 'Knights, knaves or pawns? Human behaviour and social policy', *Journal of Social Policy*, 26: 149–69. *142, 273*

Leibenstein, Harvey (1966) 'Allocative efficiency vs. X-efficiency', *American Economic Review*, 56: 392–415. *298*

Leibenstein, Harvey (1976) *Beyond Economic Man – A New Foundation for Microeconomics*, Cambridge, Mass.: Harvard University Press. *299*

Leibenstein, Harvey (1978) 'On the basic proposition of X-efficiency theory', *AER/Papers and Proceedings*, 68: 328–32. *299*

Lerner, Abba P. (1944) *The Economics of Control*, New York: Macmillan. *131*

Lerner, Abba P. (1970) 'On optimal taxes with an untaxable sector', *American Economic Review*, 60: 284–94. *205*

Lewis, Kenneth A. and Seidman, Laurence S. (1996) 'An optimal greenhouse tax in an optimal growth model', *Southern Economic Journal*, 63(2): 418–28. *303*

Li, Hongyi and Zou, Heng-fu (1998) 'Income inequality is not harmful for growth: theory and evidence', *Review of Development Economics*, 2(3): 318–34. *142*

Li, Michael Z. and Ng, Yew-Kwang (forthcoming) 'Using the partial-equilibrium method to do general-equilibrium analysis: A combined use of Walras' law and Hicks' composite commodity theorem', unpublished manuscript under preparation. *237*

Li, Shaomin, Li, Shuhe and Zhang, Weiying (2000) 'The road to capitalism: competition and institutional change in China', *Journal of Comparative Economics*, 28(2): 269–92. *298*

Lin, Steven A. (ed.) (1976) *Theory and Measurement of Economic Externalities*, New York: Academic Press.

Lindbeck, Assar, Nyberg, Sten and Weibull, Jorgen W (1999) 'Social norms and economic incentives in the welfare state', *Quarterly Journal of Economics*, 114(1): 1–35. *220*

Lio, Monchi (1996) 'Three essays on increasing returns and specialization: a contribution to new classical microeconomic approach', Unpublished PhD dissertation, Department of Economics, National Taiwan University. *249*

Lio, Monchi (2003) 'The division of labor and the allocation of time', in Ng, Shi and Sun (2003). *249*

Lipsey, Richard G. and Lancaster, Kelvin (1956) 'The general theory of second best', *Review of Economic Studies*, 24: 11–32. *188*

Lipsey, Richard G. and Lancaster, Kelvin (1959) 'McManus on second best', *Review of Economic Studies*, 26:225–6. *194*

Little, Ian M. D. (1949) 'The foundations of welfare economics', *Oxford Economic Papers*, 1 (NS): 227–46. *52, 286*

Little, Ian M. D. (1951) 'Direct versus indirect taxes', *Economic Journal*, 61: 577–84. *188*

Little, Ian M. D. (1952) 'Social choice and individual values', *Journal of Political Economy*, 60: 422–32. *98*

Little, Ian M. D. (1957) *A Critique of Welfare Economics*, 2nd edn, London: Oxford University Press. *28, 49, 52, 53, 286*

Little, Ian M. D. and Mirrlees, James A. (1974) *Project Appraisal and Planning for Developing Countries*, London: Heinemann.

Littlechild, S. C. (1981) 'Misleading calculations of the social costs of monopoly power', *Economic Journal*, 91: 348–63. *299*

Liu, Pak-Wai and Wong, Yue-Chin (1982) 'Educational screening by certificates: an empirical test', *Economic Inquiry*, 20: 72–83. *139*

Ljungqvist, Lars and Uhlig, Harald (2000) 'Tax policy and aggregate demand management under catching up with the Jones', *American Economic Review*, 90(3): 356–66.

Lloyd, Peter J. (1974) 'A more general theory of price distortions in open economies', *Journal of International Economics*, 4: 365–86. *196*

Lockwood, Ben and Manning, Alan (1993) 'Wage setting and the tax system: theory and evidence for the United Kingdom values', *Journal of Public Economics*, 52: 1–29. *142, 228*

Loeb, Martin (1977) 'Alternative versions of the demand-revealing process', *Public Choice*, 29: 15–26 (supplement). *174*

Loewenstein, George (2000) 'Emotions in economic theory and economic behavior', *American Economic Review*, 90 (2): 426–32. *272*

Loewenstein, George and Elster, Jon (eds) (1992) *Choice Over Time*, New York: Russell Sage Foundation. *273*

Loewenstein, George, O'Donoghue, Ted and Rabin, Matthew (2000) 'Projection bias in predicting future utility', U. C. Berkeley Economics Working Paper E00–284, available from the SSRN Electronic Paper Collection at http://papers.ssrn.com/ paper.taf?abstract_id = 239901.

Loewenstein, George and Prelec, D. (1991) 'Preferences over outcome sequences', *AER/Papers and Proceedings*, 81: 247–351. *275*

Loewenstein, George and Schkade, David (1999) 'Wouldn't it be nice? Predicting future feelings', in Kahneman, Diener and Schwarz (1999), pp. 85–105. *272*

Luce, R. D. (1956) 'Semi-orders and a theory of utility discrimination', *Econometrica*, 24: 178–91. *108*

Luce, R. D. and Edwards, W. (1958), 'The derivations of subjective scales from just noticeable differences',* *Psychological Review*, 65: 222–37. *141*

Luce, R. D. and Suppes, P. (1965) 'Preference, utility, and subjective probability',* in R. D. Luce, R. R. Bush and E. Galanter (eds), *Handbook of Mathematical Psychology*, vol. III, New York: Wiley.

Lundberg, Mattias and Squire, Lyn (2003) 'The simultaneous evolution of growth and inequality', *Economic Journal*, 113: 326–44. *136*

Lykken, David and Tellegen, Auke (1996) 'Happiness is a stochastic phenomenon', *Psychological Science*, 7(3): 186–9. *269*

Macdougall, Donald (1977) 'Economic growth and social welfare', *Scottish Journal of Political Economy*, 24: 193–206.

Machlup, Fritz (1940) 'Professor Hicks' statics', *Quarterly Journal of Economics*, 54: 280–2. *70*

Machlup, Fritz (1957) 'Professor Hicks' revision of demand theory', *American Economic Review*, 47: 119–35. *70*

Mackenzie, W. J. M. (1967) *Politics and Social Science*, Harmondsworth: Penguin. *106*

Mahler, Peter (1994) 'Efficiency losses as a result of insufficient structural adjustments due to the EC sugar regime: the case of Germany', *European Review of Agricultural Economics*, 21(2): 199–218. *298*

Malinvaud, E. (1972) *Lectures on Microeconomic Theory*, Amsterdam: North-Holland. *71*

Manski, Charles F. (2000) 'Economic analysis of social interactions', *Journal of Economic Perspectives*, 14(3): 115–36. *264*

Marchand, Maurice, Pestieau, Pierre and Tulkens, Henry (eds) (1984), *The Performance of Public Enterprises: Concepts and Measurement*, Amsterdam and New York: North-Holland and Elsevier Science. *204, 302*

Marchionatti, Roberto (1999) 'On Keynes' animal spirits', *Kyklos*, 52: 415–39. *270*

Margolis, J. and Guitton, H. (eds) (1969) *Public Economics*, London: Macmillan.

Marschak, Thomas A. (1981–91) 'Organization design',* in Arrow and Intriligator (1981–91).

Marshall, Alfred (1920) *Principles of Economics*, 8th edn, London: Macmillan. *65, 231, 240*

Mas-Colell, Andreu and Sonnenschein, Hugo (1972) 'General impossibility theorems for group decisions',* *Review of Economic Studies*, 39: 185–92. *106*

Mas-Colell, Andreu, Whinston, Michael D. and Green, Jerry R. (1995) *Microeconomic Theory*, New York: Oxford University Press. *298, 304*

Maskin, Eric (1978) 'A theorem on utilitarianism', *Review of Economic Studies*, 45: 93–6. *108*

Maskin, Eric, Qian, Yingyi and Xu, Chenggang (2000) 'Incentives, information, and organizational form', *Review of Economic Studies*, 67(2): 359–78. *298*

Massell, Benton F. (1969) 'Price stabilisation and welfare', *Quarterly Journal of Economics*, 83: 284–98. *304*

Mathur, Vijay K. (1991) 'How well do we know Pareto optimality?', *Journal of Economic Education*, 22(2): 172–8. *33*

Mayston, David J. (1975) 'Optimal licensing in public sector: tariff structures',* in Parkin and Nobay (1975). *125, 204, 302*

Mayston, David J. (1980) 'Ordinalism and quasi-ordinalism in the theory of social choice', in Currie and Peters (1980). *121, 125*

McConnell, K. E. (1995) 'Consumer surplus from discrete choice models', *Journal of Environmental Economics and Management*, 29(3): 263–70. *82*

McFadden, Daniel L. (1969) 'A simple remark on the second best Pareto optimality of market equilibria', *Journal of Economic Theory*, 1: 26–38. *196*

McGuire, Martin (1974), 'Group segregation and optimal jurisdiction', *Journal of Political Economy*, 82: 112–32. *182*

McGuire, Martin C. and Aaron, Henry (1969) 'Efficiency and equity in the optimal supply of a public good', *Review of Economics and Statistics*, 51: 31–9. *167*

McKenzie, Lionel W. (1951) 'Ideal output and the interdependence of firms', *Economic Journal*, 61: 785–803. *194*

McLure, Charles E. (1968) 'Merit wants: a normatively empty box', *Finanzarchiv*, 27: 474–83. *300*

McManus, Maurice (1959) 'Comments on "the general theory of second best"',* *Review of Economic Studies*, 26: 209–24. *190, 194*

McManus, Maurice (1975) 'Inter-tastes consistency in social welfare functions', in Parkin and Nobay (1975). *99*

McManus, Maurice (1978) 'Social welfare optimisation with tastes as variables',* *Weltwirtschaftliches*, 114: 101–23. *99*

McManus, Maurice, Walton, Gary M. and Coffman, Richard B. (1972) 'Distributional equality and aggregate utility: further comment', *American Economic Review*, 2: 489–96. *131*

McMaster, Robert and Mackay, Daniel F. (1998) 'Distribution, equity and domestic water charging regimes: The case of Scotland', *Annuals of Public & Cooperative Economics*, 69(1): 85–105. *300*

McMillan, John and Woodruff, Christopher (2002) 'The central role of entrepreneurs in transition economies', *Journal of Economic Perspectives*, 16(3): 153–70. *245*

Meade, James E. (1955a) *The Theory of Customs Unions*, Amsterdam: North-Holland. *188*

Meade, James E. (1955b) *Trade and Welfare*, London: Oxford University Press. *188*

Meade, James E. (1964) *Efficiency, Equality, and the Ownership of Property*, London: Allen and Unwin. *141*

Meade, James E. (1976) *The Just Economy*, London: Allen and Unwin. *136*

Michael, Robert T. and Becker, Gary S. (1973) 'On the new theory of consumer behavior', *Swedish Journal of Economics*, 75: 378–96. *301*

Milesi Ferretti, Gian, Maria, Perotti, Roberto and Rostagno, Massimo (2002) 'Electoral systems and public spending', *Quarterly Journal of Economics* 117(2): 609–57. *278*

Milgrom, Paul (1993) 'Is sympathy an economic value? Philosophy, economics, and the contingent valuation method', in J. A. Hausman (ed.), *Contingent Valuation: A Critical Assessment*, Amsterdam: North-Holland. *79*

Mill, J. S. (1844) *Essays on Some Unsettled Questions of Political Economy*, 5

Miller, Nicholas R. (1977) 'Logrolling, vote trading, and the paradox in of voting', *Public Choice*, 30: 51–76. *104*

Mirrlees, James A. (1971) 'An exploration in the theory of optimum income taxation',* *Review of Economic Studies*, 38: 175–208. *132, 133, 134, 135, 140, 143, 213, 222, 258, 285, 304*

Mirrlees, James A. (1976) 'Optimal tax theory: a synthesis',* *Journal of Public Economics*, 6: 372–58. *205, 212, 302*

Mirrlees, James A. (1986) 'The theory of optimal taxation',* in Arrow and Intriligator (1981–91). *212, 302*

Mirrlees, James A. (1990) 'Taxing uncertain incomes', *Oxford Economic Papers*, 42(1): 34–45. *134*

Mirrlees, James A. (1997) 'Information and incentives: the economics of carrot and sticks', *Economic Journal*, 107: 1311–29. *132, 134*

Mirrlees, James A. and Stern, N. H. (eds) (1973) *Models of Economic Growth,** London: Macmillan. *303*

Mishan, Ezra J. (1952) 'The principle of compensation reconsidered', *Journal of Political Economy*, 60: 312–22.

Mishan, Ezra J. (1960) 'A survey of welfare economics 1939–1959', *Economic Journal*, 70: 197–256. *261*

Mishan, Ezra J. (1962a) 'Welfare criteria: an exchange of notes', *Economic Journal*, 72: 234–44. *49*

Mishan, Ezra J. (1962b) 'Second thoughts on second best', *Oxford Economic Papers*, 14: 205–17. *193, 204*

Mishan, Ezra J. (1963) 'Welfare criteria: are compensation tests necessary?', *Economic Journal*, 73: 342–50. *61*

Mishan, Ezra J. (1969/1993) *The Costs of Economic Growth*, London: Weidenfeld & Nicolson. *261*

Mishan, Ezra J. (1969a) *Welfare Economics: An Assessment*, Amsterdam: North-Holland. *49*

Mishan, Ezra J. (1969b) *Welfare Economics: Ten Introductory Essays*, New York: Random House. *2*

Mishan, Ezra J. (1971) 'The postwar literature on externalities: an interpretative essay', *Journal of Economic Literature*, 9: 1–28. *86, 145*

Mishan, Ezra J. (1973) 'Welfare criteria: resolution of a paradox', *Economic Journal*, 83: 747–67. *57, 58, 59*

Mishan, Ezra J. (1976) 'The new welfare criteria and the social welfare function', *Economisch en Sociaal Tijdschrift*, 30(5): 775–83. *57*

Mishan, Ezra J. (1977) *The Economic Growth Debate: An Assessment*, London: Allen & Unwin. *261*

Mishan, Ezra J. (1980) 'The new welfare economics: an alternative view', *International Economic Review*, 21: 691–705.

Mitchell, Bridger M. (1978) 'Optimal pricing of local telephone service', *American Economic Review*, 68: 517–37. *302*

Mitchell, Robert C. and Carson, Richard T. (1989) 'Using surveys to value public goods: The contingent valuation method', *Washington, D.C.: Resources for the Future*, Baltimore, MD: Johns Hopkins University Press. *79*

Mohring, Herbert (1971) 'Alternative welfare gain and loss measurement', *Western Economic Journal*, 9: 349–68. *82*

Monroe, Kristen R. (1996) *The Heart of Altruism*, Princeton, NJ: Princeton University Press. *7*

Morawetz, David (1977) 'Income distribution and self-rated happiness: some empirical evidence', *Economic Journal*, 87: 511–22. *180*

Morrison, Clarence C. (1968) 'Generalisation on the methodology of second best', *Western Economic Journal*, 6: 112–20.

Moulin, Herve (1996) 'Cost sharing under increasing returns: a comparison of simple mechanisms', *Games and Economic Behavior*, 13: 225–51. *217*

Mueller, Dennis C. (1967) 'The possibility of a social welfare function: comment', *American Economic Review*, 57: 1304–11. *105*

Mueller, Dennis C. (1976) 'Public choice: a survey', *Journal of Economic Literature*, 14: 395–433. *120, 297*

Mueller, Dennis C. (1979) *Public Choice*, Cambridge: Cambridge University Press. *297*

Mueller, Dennis C. (1989) *Public Choice II*, Cambridge and New York: Cambridge University Press. *101, 110, 120, 297*

Mueller, Dennis C. (ed.) (1997) *Perspectives on Public Choice: A Handbook*, Cambridge, New York and Melbourne: Cambridge University Press. *297*

Mueller, Dennis C. (ed.) (2001) 'The economics of politics, 2 vols', *Elgar Reference Collection. International Library of Critical Writings in Economics*, vol. 131, Cheltenham: Edward Elgar (distributed in the US by the American International Distribution Corporation, Williston, Vt). *297*

Mullainathan, Sendhil (2002) 'A memory-based model of bounded rationality', *Quarterly Journal of Economics*, 117(3): 735–74. *260*

Murakami, Y. (1961) 'A note on the general possibility theorem of the social welfare function', *Econometrica*, 29: 244–6. *98*

Murphy, K., Shleifer, A. and Vishny, R. (1989) 'Income distribution, market size, and industrialization', *Quarterly Journal of Economics*, 537–64. *142, 228*

Musgrave, Richard A. (1959) *The Theory of Public Finance*, New York: McGraw-Hill. *166*

Musgrave, Richard A. (1969a) 'Provision for social goods', in Margolis and Guitton (1969). *166*

Musgrave, Richard A. (1969b) 'Cost–benefit analysis and the theory of public finance', *Journal of Economic Literature*, 7: 797–806. *211*

Mushkin, S. (ed.) (1972) *Public Prices for Public Products*, Washington, DC: Urban Institute.

Myers, David (1996) *Social Psychology*, New York: Macmillan. *262*

Nagel, Stuart S. (ed.) (1998) 'Applications of super-optimizing policy analysis', *Research in Public Policy Analysis and Management*, vol. 8, Greenwich, CT, and London: JAI Press. *142, 228*

Namazie, Ceema and Sanfey, Peter (2001) 'Happiness and transition: The case of Kyrgyzstan', *Review of Development Economics*, 5(3): 392–405. *264*

Nash, John F. Jr (1950) 'The bargaining problem', *Econometrica*, 18: 155–62. *128, 288*

Nath, S. K. (1969) *A Reappraisal of Welfare Economics*, London: Routledge & Kegan Paul. *27*

Needham, D. (1975) 'Market structure and firms' R & D behavior', *Journal of Industrial Economics*, 23: 241–55. *305*

Neumann, Manfred (1999) 'Monopoly welfare losses in the long run', *Empirica*, 26(1): 1–9. *299*

Neumark, David and Postlewaite, Andrew (1998) 'Relative income concerns and the rise in married women's employment', *Journal of Public Economics*, 70(1): 157–83. *266, 267*

Newberry David M. G. and Stiglitz, Joseph E. (1982) 'Risk aversion, supply response, and the optimality of random prices: a diagrammatic analysis', *Quarterly Journal of Economics*, 97: 1–26. *304*

Ng, Siang (1998) 'Economics of specialization and trade', in Arrow, Ng and Yang (1998). *254*

Ng, Siang and Ng, Yew-Kwang (2001) 'Welfare-reducing growth despite individual and government optimization', *Social Choice and Welfare*, 18: 497–506. *173, 268*

Ng, Yew-Kwang (1969a) 'A note on profit maximisation', *Australian Economic Papers*, 8: 106–10. *41, 289*

Ng, Yew-Kwang (1969b) 'A study of the interrelationships between efficient resource allocation, economic growth, and welfare and the solution of these problems in market socialism', unpublished PhD thesis, University of Sydney. *7*

Ng, Yew-Kwang (1971a) 'Recent developments in the theory of externality and the Pigovian solution', *Economic Record*, 47: 169–85. *149, 156, 159, 160*

Ng, Yew-Kwang (1971b) 'The possibility of a Paretian liberal: impossibility theorems and cardinal utility', *Journal of Political Economy*, 79: 1397–402. *120*

Ng, Yew-Kwang (1971c) 'Little's welfare criterion under the equality assumptions', *Economic Record*, 47: 579–83. *56, 61*

Ng, Yew-Kwang (1971d) 'Competition, monopoly, and the incentive to invent', *Australian Economic Papers*, 10: 45–9. *305*

Ng, Yew-Kwang (1972a) 'Pareto conditions, behavioural rules, and the theory of second best', *Australian Economic Papers*, 2: 124–5. *195*

Ng, Yew-Kwang (1972b) 'Value judgments and economists' role in policy recommendation', *Economic Journal*, 82: 1014–18. *18, 23, 115, 206*

Ng, Yew-Kwang (1973a) 'Income distribution as a peculiar public good: the paradox of redistribution and the paradox of universal externality', *Public Finance/Finances Publiques*, 28(1): 1–10. *181, 182*

Ng, Yew-Kwang (1973b) 'The economic theory of clubs: Pareto optimality conditions', *Economica*, 40: 291–8. *182, 183*

Ng, Yew-Kwang (1973c) 'Optimum saving: a practicable solution', *Indian Journal of Economics*, 53: 285–94. *303*

Ng, Yew-Kwang (1974a) 'The economic theory of clubs: optimal tax/subsidy', *Economica*, 41: 308–21. *182*

Ng, Yew-Kwang (1974b) 'Utility and profit maximisation by an owner-manager: towards a general analysis', *Journal of Industrial Economics*, 23: 97–108. *289*

Ng, Yew-Kwang (1975a) 'Bentham or Bergson? Finite sensibility, utility functions, and social welfare functions', *Review of Economic Studies*, 42: 545–70. *107, 108, 110, 113, 116, 130*

Ng, Yew-Kwang (1975b) 'Coase's theorem and first party priority rule: Reply', *Economic Record*, 51: 272–4. *159*

Ng, Yew-Kwang (1975c) 'The paradox of universal externality', *Journal of Economic Theory*, 10: 258–64. *186*

Ng, Yew-Kwang (1975d) 'Non-economic activities, indirect externalities, and third best policies', *Kyklos*, 29(3): 507–25. *154, 187, 204, 205, 295*

Ng, Yew-Kwang (1977a) 'Towards a theory of third best', *Public Finance/Finances Publiques*, 32: 1–15. *196*

Ng, Yew-Kwang (1977b) 'Competition, monopoly, and the incentive to invent: a reply', *Australian Economic Papers*, 16: 154–6. *305*

Ng, Yew-Kwang (1978) 'Economic growth and social welfare: the need for a complete study of happiness', *Kyklos*, 31(4): 575–87. *284*

Ng, Yew-Kwang (1979/1983) *Welfare Economics: Introduction and Development of Basic Concepts*, London: Macmillan. *2, 8, 17, 38, 51, 116, 118, 182, 280*

Ng, Yew-Kwang (1980a) 'Optimal corrective taxes/subsidies when revenue raising imposes excess burden', *American Economic Review*, 70: 744–51. *147*

Ng, Yew-Kwang (1980b) 'Macroeconomics with non-perfect competition', *Economic Journal*, 90, 598–610. *236*

Ng, Yew-Kwang (1981a) 'Bentham or Nash? On the acceptable form of social welfare functions', *Economic Record*, 57: 238–50. *129*

Ng, Yew-Kwang (1981b) 'Welfarism: a defence against Sen's attack', *Economic Journal*, 91: 527–30. *260*

Ng, Yew-Kwang (1982) 'The necessity of interpersonal cardinal utilities in distributional judgments and social choice', *Zeitschrift fur National Ökonomie*, 42: 207–33. *101, 116, 120*

Ng, Yew-Kwang (1983) 'Rents and pecuniary externalities in cost–benefit analysis', *American Economic Review*, 73: 1163–70. *298*

Ng, Yew-Kwang (1984a) 'Quasi-Pareto social improvements', *American Economic Review*, 74(5): 1033–50. *62, 63, 118, 226, 280*

Ng, Yew-Kwang (1984b) 'Expected subjective utility: Is the Neumann–Morgenstern utility the same as the neoclassical's?', *Social Choice and Welfare*, 1: 177–86. *273*

Ng, Yew-Kwang (1984c) 'Interpersonal level comparability implies comparability of utility differences', *Theory and Decision*, 17: 141–7. *18*

Ng, Yew-Kwang (1985) 'Equity and efficiency versus freedom and fairness: An inherent conflict', *Kyklos*, 38(4): 495–516. *139*

Ng, Yew-Kwang (1986a) *Mesoeconomics: A Micro-Macro Analysis*, London: Harvester. *236, 252*

Ng, Yew-Kwang (1986b) 'On the welfare economics of population control', *Population and Development Review*, 12: 247–66. *250*

Ng, Yew-Kwang (1987a) 'Diamonds are a government's best friend: Burden-free taxes on goods valued for their values', *American Economic Review*, 77: 186–191. *80, 278*

Ng, Yew-Kwang (1987b) 'Relative-income effects and the appropriate level of public expenditure', *Oxford Economic Papers*, 39: 293–300. *172*

Ng, Yew-Kwang (1988) 'Economic efficiency versus egalitarian rights', *Kyklos*, 41(2): 215–37. *119, 221, 227*

Ng, Yew-Kwang (1989) 'What should we do about future generations? The impossibility of Parfit's theory X', *Economics and Philosophy*, 5: 135–253. *253*

Ng, Yew-Kwang (1990) 'Welfarism and utilitarianism: A rehabilitation', *Utilitas*, 2(2): 171–93. *260*

Ng, Yew-Kwang (1992a) 'Do individuals optimize in inter-temporal consumption/saving decisions? A liberal method to encourage savings', *Journal of Economic Behavior and Organization*, 17: 101–14. *11*

Ng, Yew-Kwang (1992b) 'Utilitarianism and interpersonal comparison: Some implications of a materialist solution to the world knot', *Social Choice and Welfare*, 9(1): 1–15. *115*

Ng, Yew-Kwang (1992c) 'Business confidence and depression prevention: A meso-economic perspective', *American Economic Review*, 82(2): 365–71. *236*

Ng, Yew-Kwang (1993) 'Mixed diamond goods and anomalies in consumer theory: Upward-sloping compensated demand curves with unchanged diamondness', *Mathematical Social Sciences*, 25: 287–93. *81, 232*

Ng, Yew-Kwang (1995) 'Towards welfare biology: Evolutionary economics of animal consciousness and suffering', *Biology and Philosophy*, 10: 255–85. *12, 253, 270*

Ng, Yew-Kwang (1996a) 'Happiness surveys: Some comparability issues and an exploratory survey based on just perceivable increments', *Social Indicators Research*, 38(1): 1–29. *48, 112, 116, 257, 264, 280, 295*

Ng, Yew-Kwang (1996b) 'Complex niches favour rational species', *Journal of Theoretical Biology*, 179: 303–11. *11, 270*

Ng, Yew-Kwang (1996c) 'The enrichment of a sector (individual/region/country) benefits others: the third welfare theorem?', *Pacific Economic Review*, 1(2): 93–115. *38*

Ng, Yew-Kwang (1997), 'A case for happiness, cardinal utility, and interpersonal comparability', *Economic Journal*, 107(445): 1848–1858. *18, 258*

Ng, Yew-Kwang (1998) 'Non-neutrality of money under non-perfect competition: why do economists fail to see the possibility?', in Arrow, Ng and Yang (1998). *235, 236*

Ng, Yew-Kwang (1999a) 'Utility, informed preference, or happiness?', *Social Choice and Welfare*, 16(2): 197–216. *7, 260, 261, 270, 274, 277*

Ng, Yew-Kwang (1999b) 'On estimating the effects of events like the Asian financial crisis: a mesoeconomic approach', *Taiwan Economic Review*, 27(4): 393–412. *236*

Ng, Yew-Kwang (2000a) *Efficiency, Equality, and Public Policy: With a Case for Higher Public Spending*, Basingstoke: Macmillan. *10, 101, 115, 120, 257, 260, 278*

Ng, Yew-Kwang (2000b) 'The optimal size of public spending and the distortionary costs of taxation', *National Tax Journal*, 52(2): 253–72. *171, 278*

Ng, Yew-Kwang (2001a) 'Optimal environmental charges/taxes: Easy to estimate and surplus-yielding', Monash University Economics Discussion Paper no. 13–01, Melbourne: Monash University. *148*

Ng, Yew-Kwang (2001b) 'Externality, Pigou and Coase: a case for bilateral taxation and amenity rights', Monash University Economics Discussion Paper no. 11–01, Melbourne: Monash University. *161, 162*

Ng, Y. K. and Liu, P. T. (2002) Global environmental protection: Solving the international public goods problem by empowering the United Nations through co-operation with WTO, unpublished manuscript. *148*

Ng, Yew-Kwang (2002a) 'The welfare economics of encouraging more births', in A. E. Woodland (ed.), *Economic Theory and International Trade: Essays in Honour of Murray C. Kemp*, Cheltenham: Edward Elgar. *41, 108, 250*

Ng, Yew-Kwang (2002b) 'The East-Asian happiness gap: speculating on causes and implications', *Pacific Economic Review*, 7: 51–63. *262*

Ng, Yew-Kwang (2003a) 'From preference to happiness: towards a more complete welfare economics', *Social Choice and Welfare*, forthcoming 20: 307–50. *257, 261, 279*

Ng, Yew-Kwang (2003b) 'Increasing returns and economic efficiency', Monash University Economics Working Paper, Melbourne: Monash University. *239, 240*

Ng, Yew-Kwang and Ng, Siang (2001) 'Why do governments encourage improvements in infrastructure? Indirect network externality of transaction efficiency', paper presented at the International Symposium on the Economics of E-commerce and Networking Decisions, July, 2001, Monash University, Melbourne. *248*

Ng, Yew-Kwang, Shi, Heling and Sun, Guangzhen (2003) *E-Commerce and Economic Organization: Inframarginal Analysis of Networking Decisions*, London: Macmillan.

Ng, Yew-Kwang and Ng, Siang (2003) 'Do the economies of specialization justify the work ethics? An examination of Buchanan's hypothesis', *Journal of Economic Behavior and Organization*, 50: 339–53. *249*

Ng, Yew-Kwang and Singer, Peter (1981) 'An argument for utilitarianism', *Canadian Journal of Philosophy*, 11: 229–39. *109*

Ng, Yew-Kwang and Wang, Jianguo (1993) 'Relative income, aspiration, environmental quality, individual and political myopia: Why may the rat-race for material growth be welfare-reducing?', *Mathematical Social Sciences*, 26: 3–23. *268*

Ng, Yew Kwang and Wang, Jianguo (1995) 'A case for cardinal utility and non-arbitrary choice of commodity units', *Social Choice and Welfare*, 12(3): 255–66. *301*

Ng, Yew Kwang and Wang, Jianguo (2001) 'Attitude choice, economic change, and welfare', *Journal of Economic Behavior and Organization*, 45: 279–91. *280*

Ng, Yew-Kwang and Weisser, Mendel (1974) 'Optimal pricing with a budget constraint – the case of the two-part tariff',* *Review of Economic Studies* 41: 337–45. *204, 302*

Ng, Yew-Kwang and Wills, Ian (2002) 'Welfare economics and sustainable development', in UNESCO, *Knowledge for Sustainable Development – An Insight into the*

Encyclopedia of Life Support Systems, vol. 3, Paris and Oxford: UNESCO/Eolss, pp. 485–506. *303*

Ng, Yew-Kwang and Zhang, Dingsheng (2003) 'The Smith dilemma: towards a resolution', typescript. *242*

Ng, Yew-Kwang (2003a) 'From preference to happiness: Towards a more complete welfare economics', *Social Choice and Welfare*, 20: 307–50. *275, 277*

Niskanen, William (1971) *Bureaucracy and Representative Government*, Chicago, Ill.: Aldine. *297*

Nordhaus, William and Tobin, James (1972) 'Is growth absolute?', in National Bureau of Economic Research, *Economic Growth*, New York: Columbia University Press. *261*

Oakland, William H. (1972) 'Congestion, public goods and welfare', *Journal of Public Economics*, 1: 339–57. *182*

Oberholzer-Gee, Felix and Weck-Hannemann, Hannelore (2002) 'Pricing road use: politico-economic and fairness considerations', *Transportation Research, Part D: Transport & Environment*, 7(5): 357–71. *305*

O'Donnell, Christopher (1993) *Commodity Price Stabilisation: An empirical analysis*, Aldershot: Avebury. *304*

Offer, Avner (2000) 'Economic welfare measurements and human well-being', *University of Oxford Discussion Papers in Economic and Social History*, no. 34. *265, 269*

Okun, Arthur M. (1975) *Equality and Efficiency: The Big Tradeoff*, Washington, DC: Brookings Institution. *136*

Olson, Mancur (1965) *The Logic of Collective Action: Public Goods and the Theory of Groups*, Cambridge, Mass.: Harvard University Press. *297*

Olson, Mancur (1974) 'On the priority of public problems', in R. Marris, *The Corporate Society*, New York: Wiley. *299*

Orr, Larry L. (1976) 'Income transfers as a public good: an application to AFDC', *American Economic Review*, 66: 359–71. *180*

Osborne, D. K. (1976) 'Irrelevant alternatives and social welfare',* *Econometrica*, 44: 1001–15. *95, 101*

Oswald, Andrew J. (1997) 'Happiness and economic performance', *Economic Journal*, 107: 1815–31. *262*

Otani, Yoshihiko and Sicilian, Joseph (1977) 'Externalities and problems of non convexity and overhead costs in welfare economics',* *Journal of Economic Theory*, 14: 239–51. *148*

Ozga, S. A. (1955) 'An essay in the theory of tariffs', *Journal of Political Economy*, 63: 489–99. *188*

Page, Talbot (1988) 'Pivot mechanisms as a link between probability and preference revelation',* *Journal of Economic Theory*, 44(1): 43–62. *174*

Panagariya, Arvind (1981) 'Variable returns to scale in production and patterns of specialization', *American Economic Review*, 71(1): 221–30. *239*

Panagariya, Arvind (2002) 'Cost of protection: Where do we stand?', *AER/Papers and Proceedings*, 92: 175–9. *234*

Papandreou, Andreas A. (1994) *Externality and Institutions*, Oxford and New York: Oxford University Press, Clarendon Press. *144*

Pardo, Jose C. and Schneider, Friedrich (eds) (1996) *Current Issues in Public Choice*, Cheltenham: Edward Elgar. *297*

Pareto, V. (1909) *Manuel d'Economie politique*, Paris: Girard & Briere.

Pareto, V. (1935) *The Mind and Society*, vol. 4, ed. Arthur Livingston, trans. Arthur Livingston and Andrew Borgiorno, London: Cape. *27*

Parish, Ross M. (1972) 'Economic aspects of pollution control', *Australian Economic Papers*, 11: 32–43. *153*

Parish, Ross M. (1976) 'The scope of benefit–cost analysis', *Economic Record*, 52: 302–14. *208*

Parish, Ross M. and Ng, Yew-Kwang (1972) 'Monopoly, X-efficiency, and the measurement of welfare loss', *Economica*, 39: 301–8. *299*

Park, Robert E. (1967) 'The possibility of a social welfare function: comment', *American Economic Review*, 57: 1300–4. *104*

Parker, Glenn R. (1996) *Congress and the Rent-Seeking Society*, Ann Arbor, Mich.: University of Michigan Press. *298*

Parker, Simon C. (1999) 'The optimal linear taxation of employment and self-employment incomes', *Journal of Public Economics*, 73(1): 107–23.

Parkin, Michael and Nobay, A. R. (eds) (1975) *Current Economic Problems*, Cambridge: Cambridge University Press.

Parks, Robert P. (1976) 'An impossibility theorem for fixed preferences: a dictatorial Bergson–Samuelson welfare function', *Review of Economic Studies*, 43: 447–50. *99, 115, 120*

Patinkin, Don (1963) 'Demand curves and consumer's surplus', in C. Christ *et al.*, *Measurement in Economics: Studies in Mathematical Economics and Econometrics in Memory of Yehula Grundfeld*, Stanford, CA: Stanford University Press. *72*

Pattanaik, Prasanta K. (1971) *Voting and Collective Choice*, Cambridge: Cambridge University Press. *103*

Pattanaik, Prasanta K. (1978) *Strategy and Group Choice*, Amsterdam: North-Holland. *113*

Pauly, M. (1970) 'Cores and clubs', *Public Choice*, 9: 53–65. *182*

Pavot, W. (1991) 'Further validation of the satisfaction with life scale: evidence for the convergence of well-being measures', *Journal of Personality Assessment*, 57: 149–61. *264*

Pazner, Elisha A. (1972) 'Merit wants and the theory of taxation', *Public Finance/ Finances Publiques*, 27(4): 460–72. *300*

Peacock, Alan T. and Wiseman, Jack (1979) 'Approaches to the analysis of government expenditure growth', *Public Finance Quarterly*, 7: 3–23.

Pen, Jan (1971) *Income Distribution*, trans. T. S. Preston, London: Allen Lane, Penguin. *136*

Pencavel, John (1986) 'Labor supply of man: a survey', in O. C. Ashenfelter and R. Layard (eds), *Handbook of Labor Economics*, vol. 1, Amsterdam: North-Holland, pp. 3–102.

Perotti, Roberto (1996) 'Growth, income distribution, and democracy: What the data say', *Journal of Economic Growth*, 1: 149–87. *142, 228*

Persson, Torsten and Tabellini, Guido (1994) 'Is inequality harmful for growth?', *American Economic Review*, 84: 600–21. *142, 228*

Pethig, Rudiger (1979) 'Environmental management in general equilibrium: a new incentive compatible approach', *International Economic Review*, 20: 1–27. *174*

Pfouts, R. W. (1953), 'A critique of some recent contributions to the theory of consumers' surplus', *Southern Economic Journal*, 19: 315–33. *65*

Phelps, Edmund S. (ed.) (1973) *Economic Justice: Selected Readings*, Harmondsworth: Penguin. *136*

Piderit, John J. (1993) *The Ethical Foundations of Economics*, Washington, DC: Georgetown University Press. *24*

Pigou, Arthur C. (1912/1929/1932) *Wealth and Welfare*, London: Macmillan later editions – 1920, 1924, 1929 and 1932 – assume the title *The Economics of Welfare*. *10, 39, 47, 238*

Pigou, Arthur C. (1922) 'Empty economic boxes: a reply', *Economic Journal*, 32: 458–65. *1*

Pigou, Arthur C. (1928) *Public Finance*, London: Macmillan. *170*

Pigou, Arthur C. (1932) *The Economics of Welfare*, 4th edn, London: Macmillan. *39*

Pingle, Mark and Mitchell, Mike (2002) 'What motivates positional concerns for income?', *Journal of Economic Psychology*, 23(1): 127–48. *267*

Plott, Charles R. (1972) 'Ethics, social choice, and the theory of economic policy', *Journal of Mathematical Sociology*, 2: 181–208. *95, 123*

Plott, Charles R. (1973) 'Path dependence, rationality and social choice',* *Econometrica*, 41: 1075–91. *112*

Plott, Charles, R. and Smith, Vernon, L. (eds) (forthcoming) *Handbook of Experimental Economics Results*, Amsterdam: North-Holland.

Polinsky, A. M. (1972) 'Probabilistic compensation criteria', *Quarterly Journal of Economics*, 86: 407–25. *57*

Pollak, Robert A. (1976) 'Habit formation and long-run utility functions',* *Journal of Economic Theory*, 13: 72–97. *301*

Pollak, Robert A. (1977) 'Price dependent preferences', *American Economic Review*, 67: 64–75. *300*

Pollak, Robert A. (1978) 'Endogenous tastes in demand and welfare analysis', *AER/Papers and Proceedings*, 68: 374–9. *301*

Pollak, Robert A. (1979) 'Bergson–Samuelson social welfare functions and the theory of social choice', *Quarterly Journal of Economics*, 93: 73–90. *99*

Pollak, R. A. and Wales, T. J. (1992) *Demand System Specification and Estimation*, Oxford: Oxford University Press. *230*

Porter, Richard C. (1978) 'The economics of congestion: a geometric review', *Public Finance Quarterly*, 6: 23–52. *182, 305*

Posner, Richard (1975) 'The social cost of monopoly and regulation', *Journal of Political Economy*, 83: 807–27. *293*

Posner, Richard (1981) *The Economics of Justice*, Cambridge, Mass.: Harvard University Press. *227*

Pulsipher, Allan G. (1971) 'The properties and relevancy of merit goods', *Finanzarchiv*, 30: 266–86. *300*

Putterman, Louis, Roemer, John E. and Silvestre, Joaquim (1998) 'Does egalitarianism have a future?', *Journal of Economic Literature*, 36: 861–902. *142, 223*

Quah, Euston and Tan, K. C. (2002) *Siting Environmentally Unwanted Facilities*, Cheltenham, UK, and Northampton, Mass.: Edward Elgar. *153*

Quesada, Antonio (2002) 'More on independent decisiveness and Arrow's theorem', *Social Choice Welfare*, 19(2): 449–54. *95*

Quiggin, John (1997) 'Discount rates and sustainability', *International Journal of Social Economics*, 24(1–3): 65–90. *303*

Quigley, John M. and Smolensky, Eugene (eds) (1994/2000) *Modern Public Finance*, Cambridge, Mass., and London: Harvard University Press. *212, 301*

Quinzii, Martine (1992) *Increasing Returns and Efficiency*, New York and Oxford: Oxford University Press. *238*

Quirk, James and Saposnik, Rubin (1968) *Introduction to General Equilibrium Theory and Welfare Economics*, New York: McGraw-Hill. *50, 95*

Racionero, Maria del Mar (2001) 'Optimal tax mix with merit goods', *Oxford Economic Papers*, 53(4): 628–41. *300*

Radner, Roy and Stiglitz, Joseph (1984) 'A non-concavity in the value of information', in Boyer and Kihlstrom (1984). *234*

Rae, John (1834) *New Principles of Political Economy*, reprinted as *The Sociological Theory of Capital*, ed. C. W. Mixter, New York: Macmillan, 1990. *172, 266, 278*

Ramsey, F. P. (1927) 'A contribution to the theory of taxation', *Economic Journal*, 37: 47–61. *301*

Ramsey, F. P. (1928) 'A mathematical theory of saving', *Economic Journal*, 38: 543–59. *10, 302*

Randall, Alan (1978) 'Property institutions and economic behavior', *Journal of Economic Issues*, 12: 1–21. *298*

Redelmeier, D. A. and Kahneman, D. (1996) 'Patients' memories of painful medical procedures: real-time and retrospective evaluations of two minimally invasive treatments', *Pain*, 66: 3–8. *273*

Reich, Robert (2000–1) *The Future of Success*, [pub. details unknown]. *266*

Reiter, Michael (2000) 'Relative preferences and public goods', *European Economic Review*, 44(3): 565–85.

Richins, Marsha L., McKeage, Kim K. R. and Najjar, Debbie (1992) 'An exploration of materialism and consumption-related affect', *Advances in Consumer Research*, 19: 229–36. *269*

Riley, John G. (1979) 'Testing the educational screening hypothesis', *Journal of Political Economy*, 87: S225–52. *139*

Riley, John G. (2001) 'Silver signals: twenty-five years of screening and signalling', *Journal of Economic Literature*, 39(2): 432–78. *304*

Riley, Jonathan (1988) *Liberal utilitarianism: Social Choice Theory and J. S Mill's Philosophy*, Cambridge, New York and Sydney: Cambridge University Press. *120*

Rivlin, Alice M. (1975) 'Income distribution – can economists help?', *AER/Papers and Proceedings*, 65: 1–IS. *136*

Robbins, Lionel (1932) *An Essay on the Nature and Significance of Economic Science*, London: Macmillan. *18, 47*

Robbins, Lionel (1938) 'Interpersonal comparison of utility: a comment', *Economic Journal*, 48: 635–41. *18, 47, 115*

Roberts, Kevin W. S. (1980a) 'Possibility theorems with interpersonally comparable welfare levels',* *Review of Economic Studies*, 47: 409–20. *101, 120*

Roberts, Kevin W. S. (1980b) 'Interpersonal comparability and social choice theory',* *Review of Economic Studies*, 47: 421–39. *94, 120*

Roberts, Kevin W. S. (1980c) 'Social choice theory: the single-profile and multi profile approaches',* *Review of Economic Studies*, 47: 441–50. *99, 120*

Robertson, D. (1962) 'Welfare criteria: an exchange of notes', *Economic Journal*, 72: 226–9. *49*

Robson, Arthur J. (1999) 'The biological basis of economic behavior', unpublished manuscript, University of Western Ontario. *268*

Rogers, Alan (1994) 'Evolution of time preference by natural selection', *American Economic Review*, 84: 460–81. *274*

Romer, P. (1986) 'Increasing returns and long-run growth', *Journal of Political Economy*, 94: 1002–37. *241*

Roskamp, Karl W. (1975) 'Public goods, merit goods, private goods', *Public Finance/Finances Publiques*, 30(1): 61–9. *300*

Rothenberg, Jerome (1953) 'Welfare comparisons and changes in tastes', *American Economic Review*, 43: 885–90. *301*

Rothenberg, Jerome (1961) *The Measurement of Social Welfare*, Englewood Cliffs, NJ: Prentice-Hall. *108*

Rothschild, Michael and Stiglitz, Joseph (1976) 'Equilibrium in competitive insurance markets: An essay on the economics of imperfect information', *Quarterly Journal of Economics*, 90(4): 629–49. *304*

Rothschild, Michael and Stiglitz, Joseph (1997) 'Competition and insurance twenty years later', *Geneva Papers on Risk and Insurance Theory*, 22(2): 73–9. *304*

Rowley, Charles K. (ed.) (1972) *Readings in Industrial Economics*, vol. II, London: Macmillan.

Rowley, Charles K. (1978) 'Liberalism and collective choice: a return to reality?', *Manchester School*, 46: 224–51. *120*

Rowley, Charles K. (ed.) (1993) *Public Choice Theory*, vols 1–3, Aldershot: Edward Elgar. *106, 297*

Rowley, Charles K. (1997) 'Donald Wittman's the myth of democratic failure', *Public Choice*, 92: 15–26. *298*

Rozin, Paul (1999) 'Preadaptation and the puzzles and properties of pleasure', in Kahneman, Diener and Schwarz (1999), pp. 109–33. *259*

Rubinstein, Ariel (2002) 'Irrational diversification in multiple decision problems', *European Economic Review*, 46(8): 1369–78. *270*

Ruggles, Nancy (1949–50) 'Recent developments in the theory of marginal cost pricing', *Review of Economic Studies*, 17: 107–26. *204, 302*

Ryan, Lisa and Dziurawiec, Suzanne (2001) 'Materialism and its relationship to life satisfaction', *Social Indicators Research*, 55(2): 185–97. *269*

Ryan, Richard M., Chirkov, Valery I., Little, Todd D., Sheldon, Kennon M., Timoshina, Elena and Deci, Edward L. (1999) 'The American dream in Russia: aspirations and well being in two cultures', *Personality and Social Psychology Bulletin*, 25(12): 1509–24. *269*

Ryff, C. D. (1989) 'Happiness is everything or is it? Explorations on the meaning of psychological well-being', *Journal of Personality and Social Psychology*, 57: 1069–81. *260*

Sadka, Efrain (1976) 'On income distribution, incentive effects, and optimal income taxation', *Review of Economic Studies*, 43: 261–7. *134*

Saez, Emmanuel (2002) 'Optimal income transfer programs: intensive versus extensive labor supply responses', *Quarterly Journal of Economics*, 117(3): 1039–73. *135*

Sah, Raaj Kumar and Stiglitz, Joseph E. (1987) 'The invariance of market innovation to the number of firms', *Rand Journal of Economics*, 18(1): 98–108. *305*

Samuelson, Paul A. (1942) 'Constancy of the marginal utility of income', in O. Lange, *Studies in Mathematical Economics and Econometrics in Memory of Henry Schultz*, Chicago, Ill.: Chicago University Press. *72*

Samuelson, Paul A. (1947) *Foundations of Economic Analysis*, Cambridge, Mass.: Harvard University Press. *83, 100, 188*

Samuelson, Paul A. (1950) 'Evaluation of real national income', *Oxford Economic Papers*, 2(1): 1–29. *51*

Samuelson, Paul A. (1954) 'The pure theory of public expenditure', *Review of Economics and Statistics*, 36: 387–9. *167*

Samuelson, Paul A. (1955) 'Diagrammatic exposition of a theory of public expenditure', *Review of Economics and Statistics*, 37: 350–6. *167*

Samuelson, Paul A. (1967) 'Arrow's mathematical politics', in Hook (1967). *98, 100*

Samuelson, Paul A. (1969) 'Pure theory of public expenditure and taxation', in Margolis and Guitton (1969). *167*

Samuelson, Paul A. (1972) 'The consumer does benefit from feasible price stability', *Quarterly Journal of Economics*, 86: 476–98. *304*

Samuelson, Paul A. (1977) 'Reaffirming the existence of reasonable Bergson–Samuelson social welfare functions', *Economica*, 44: 81–8. *100, 101, 121*

Sandler, Todd (1977) 'Impurity of defence: an application to the economics of alliances', *Kyklos*, 30(3): 443–60. *183*

Sandler, Todd (1997) 'Club theory: thirty years later', *Public Choice*, 93(3–4): 335–55. *183*

Sandler, Todd and Tschirhart, John T. (1980) 'The economic theory of clubs: an evaluative survey', *Journal of Economic Literature*, 18: 1481–521.

Sandmo, Agnar (1976) 'Optimal taxation: an introduction to the literature', *Journal of Public Economics*, 6: 37–54. *205, 212, 301*

Sandmo, Agnar (1999) 'Asymmetric information and public economics: the Mirrlees–Vickrey Nobel Prize', *Journal of Economic Perspectives*, 13(1): 165–80. *212, 301*

Sandvik, Ed, Diener, Ed and Seidlitz, Larry (1993) 'Subjective well-being: the convergence and stability of self-report and non-self report measures', *Journal of Personality*, 61(3): 317–42. *264*

Satterthwaite, M. A. (1975) 'Strategy-proofness and Arrow's conditions',* *Journal of Economic Theory*, 10: 187–217. *113*

Sawyer, Malcolm (1980) 'Monopoly welfare loss in the United Kingdom', *Manchester School*, 48: 331–54. *299*

Schmalensee, Richard (1976) 'Another look at the social valuation of input price changes', *American Economic Review*, 66: 239–43. *82*

Schmalensee, Richard (1981) 'Monopolistic two-part pricing arrangements',* *Bell Journal of Economics*, 12: 445–66. *302*

Schmid, A. Allan (1976) 'The economics of property rights: a review article', *Journal of Economic Issues*, 10: 159–68. *298*

Schmid, G. (1993) 'Equality and efficiency in the labor market', *Journal of Socio-Economics*, 22: 31–67. *142, 228*

Schwarz, Norbert and Strack, Fritz (1999) 'Reports of subjective well-being: Judgmental processes and their methodological implications', in Kahneman, Diener and Schwarz (1999). *264*

Schyns, Peggy (1998) 'Cross-national differences in happiness', *Social Indicators Research*, 43: 3–26.

Scitovsky, Tibor (1941) 'A note on welfare propositions in economics', *Review of Economic Studies*, 9: 77–88. *48, 51*

Scitovsky, Tibor (1944–5) 'Some consequences of the habit of judging quality of price', *Review of Economic Studies*, 11: 100–5. *80, 300*

Scitovsky, Tibor (1976/1992) *The Joyless Economy*, New York: Oxford University Press. *261*

Scully, Gerald M. (2002), 'Economic freedom, government policy and the trade-off between equity and economic growth', *Public Choice* 113(1–2): 77–96. *141, 142*

Seade, Jesus K. (1977) 'On the shape of optimal tax schedules', *Journal of Public Economics*, 7: 203–35. *222*

Seade, Jesus K. (1978) 'Consumer's surplus and linearity of Engel curves', *Economic Journal*, 88: 511–23. *70*

Seidl, Christian (1990) 'On the impossibility of a generalization of the libertarian resolution of the liberal paradox', *Journal of Economics (Zeitschrift-fur-Nationalokonomie)*, 51(1): 71–88. *120*

Seidlitz, Larry, Wyer, Robert S. Jr. and Diener, Ed (1997) 'Cognitive correlates of subjective well-being: the processing of valenced life events by happy and unhappy persons', *Journal of Research in Personality*, 31(2): 240–56. *264*

Sen, Amartya K. (1961) 'On optimising the rate of saving', *Economic Journal*, 71: 479–96. *303*

Sen, Amartya K. (1963) 'Distribution, transitivity, and Little's welfare criteria', *Economic Journal*, 73: 771–8. *53*

Sen, Amartya K. (1967) 'The nature and classes of prescriptive judgments', *Philosophical Quarterly*, 17: 46–62.

Sen, Amartya K. (1969a) 'Planners' preferences: optimality, distribution, and social welfare', in Margolis and Guitton (1969). *131*

Sen, Amartya K. (1969b) 'Quasi-transitivity, rational choice, and collective decisions', *Review Economic Studies*, 36: 381–93. *106, 115*

Sen, Amartya K. (1970a) *Collective Choice and Social Welfare*, Amsterdam: North-Holland. *17, 20, 23, 94, 95, 101, 106, 115, 123*

Sen, Amartya K. (1970b) 'Interpersonal aggregation and partial comparability', *Econometrica*, 38: 393–409. *4, 17*

Sen, Amartya K. (1970c) 'The impossibility of a Paretian liberal', *Journal of Political Economy*, 78: 152–7. *119*

Sen, Amartya K. (1973a) *On Economic Inequality*, Oxford: Clarendon Press. *136*

Sen, Amartya K. (1973b) 'On ignorance and equal distribution', *American Economic Review*, 63: 1022–4. *131*

Sen, Amartya K. (1973c) 'Behaviour and the concept of preference', *Economica*, 40: 241–59. *7*

Sen, Amartya K. (1974) 'Informational bases of alternative welfare approaches: aggregation and income distribution', *Journal of Public Economics*, 3: 387–404. *18*

Sen, Amartya K. (1976) 'Liberty, unanimity, and rights', *Economica*, 43: 217–45. *120*

Sen, Amartya K. (1977a) 'Social choice theory: a re-examination', *Econometrica*, 45: 53–89. *120*

Sen, Amartya K. (1977b) 'On weights and measures', *Econometrica*, 44: 1539–72. *18, 94*

Sen, Amartya K. (1985) *Commodities and Capabilities*, Amsterdam: North-Holland. *260*

Sen, Amartya K. (1987) *On Ethics and Economics*, Oxford: Blackwell. *8*

Sen, Amartya K. (1992) 'Minimal liberty', *Economica*, 59(234): 139–59. *120*

Sen, Amartya K. and Pattanaik, P. K. (1969), 'Necessary and sufficient conditions for rational choice under majority decision', *Journal of Economic Theory*, I: 128–202.

Sengupta, Manimay (1978) 'On a difficulty in the analysis on strategic voting',* *Econometrica*, 46: 331–43. *113*

Sharp, C. H. (1973) *Transport Economics*, London: Macmillan. *305*

Shavell, Steven, see Kaplous and Shavell.

Shedler, J., Mayman, M. and Manis, M. (1993) 'The illusion of mental health', *American Psychologist*, 48(11): 1117–31. *264*

Sheffrin, Steven M. (2000) 'Regulation, politics, and interest groups: what do we learn from an historical approach?', *Critical Review*, 14(2–3): 259–69. *298*

Shell, Karl (ed.) (1967) *Essays on the Theory of Optimal Economic Growth*,* Cambridge, Mass.: MIT Press. *303*

Shibata, Hirofumi (1971) 'A bargaining model of the pure theory of public expenditure', *Journal of Political Economy*, 79: 1–29. *149, 152*

Shubik, M. (1959) 'Edgeworth market games', in R. D. Luce and A. W. Tucker (eds), *Contributions to the Theory of Games, IV, Annals of Mathematical Studies*, vol. 40, Princeton: Princeton University Press, 276–78. *30*

Sichelstiel, Gerhard and Sollner, Fritz (1996) 'Finite sensibility and utility functions', *Social Choice and Welfare*, 13(1): 25–41. *108*

Silber, Jacques (ed.) (1999) *Handbook of Income Inequality Measurement*, Boston, Dordrecht and London: Kluwer. *136*

Silberberg, Eugene (1972) 'Duality and the many consumer's surplus', *American Economic Review*, 55: 942–52. *74*

Sillamaa, M. A. (1999) 'How work effort responds to wage taxation: an experimental test of a zero top marginal tax rate, *Journal of Public Economics*, 73(1): 125–34. *134*

Simon, Herbert A. (1982) *Models of Bounded Rationality*, Cambridge, Mass.: MIT Press. *260*

Skolnik, M. L. (1970) 'A comment on Professor Musgrave's separation of distribution from allocation', *Journal of Economic Literature*, 8: 440–42. *220*

Slesnick, Daniel T. (1998) 'Empirical approaches to the measurement of welfare', *Journal of Economic Literature*, 36(4): 2108–65. *97*

Slottje, Daniel (1991) *Measuring the Quality of Life Across Countries: A Multidimensional Analysis*, Boulder, CO: Westview. *265*

Slutsky, Steven (1977) 'A characterisation of societies with consistent majority decision', *Review of Economic Studies*, 44: 211–25. *103*

Smith, Adam (1776/1976) *The Wealth of Nations*, reprint edited by E. Cannan, Chicago, Ill.: University of Chicago Press. *246, 251, 254*

Smith, Richard, Diener, Ed and Wedell, Douglas H. (1989) 'Intrapersonal and social comparison determinants of happiness: a range-frequency analysis', *Journal of Personality and Social Psychology*, 56(3): 317–25. *267*

Smith, Vernon L. (1977) 'The principle of unanimity and voluntary consent in social choice', *Journal of Political Economy*, 85: 1125–40. *177*

Smith, Vernon L. (ed.) (1979) *Research in Experimental Economics*, New York: Greenwich. *177*

Smith, Vernon L. (1980) 'Experiments with a decentralized mechanism for public good decisions', *American Economic Review*, 70: 584–99. *177*

Smith, V. Kerry (1993) 'Welfare effects, omitted variables, and the extent of the market', *Land Economics*, 69(2): 121–31. *73*

Smythe, Donald (1994) 'Review of Yang and Ng's *Specialization and Economic Organization*', *Journal of Economic Literature*, 32: 691–2. *232*

Sobel, Russell S. (2002) 'On the measurement of rent seeking and its social opportunity cost', *Public Choice*, 112(1): 115–36. *298*

Sober, Elliot and Wilson, David S. (1998) *Unto Others: The Evolution and Psychology of Unselfish Behavior*, Cambridge, Mass.: Harvard University Press. *7*

Solow, Robert M. (1974) 'The economics of resources or the resources of economics', *AER/Papers and Proceedings*, 64: 1–14. *303*

Sosnow, Neil D. (1974) 'Optimal policies for income redistribution', *Journal of Public Economics*, 3: 159–69.

Spence, Michael (1973) 'Job market signalling', *Quarterly Journal of Economics*, 87: 355–74. *139*

Spence, Michael (1976) 'Product selection, fixed costs and monopolistic competition', *Review of Economic Studies*, 43(2): 217–35. *239*

Spulber, Daniel, F. (2002) 'Market microstructure and incentives to invest', *Journal of Political Economy*, 110(2): 352–81. *305*

Stanovich, Keith E. and West, Richard F. (2000) 'Individual differences in reasoning: Implications for the rationality debate', *Behavioral and Brain Sciences*, 22(5). *10*

Starrett, D. A. (1972) 'Fundamental non-convexities in the theory of externalities',* *Journal of Economic Theory*, 4: 180–99. *148*

Stavins, R. N. (2000) *Economics of the Environment: Selected Readings*, 4th edn, New York: Norton. *144*

Stein, Edward (1996) *Without Good Reason: The Rationality Debate in Philosophy and Cognitive Science*, Oxford: Oxford University Press. *10*

Stennek, Johan (1999) 'The expected consumer's surplus as a welfare measure', *Journal of Public Economics*, 73(2): 265–88. *304*

Stennek, Johan (2000). 'Competition increases X-efficiency: A limited liability mechanism', *European Economic Review*, 44(9): 1727–44. *299*

Sternbach, Richard A. and Tversky, Bernard (1964) 'On the psychophysical power function in electric shock', *Psychonomic Science*, 1: 217–18.

Stigler, George J. (1951) 'The division of labor is limited by the extent of the market', *Journal of Political Economy*, 59(3): 185–93. *240*

Stigler, George J. and Becker, Gary S. (1977) 'De gustibus non est disputandum', *American Economic Review*, 67: 76–90. *301*

Stiglitz, Joseph E. (1975) 'The theory of "screening", education, and the distribution of income', *American Economic Review*, 65: 283–300. *139*

Stiglitz, Joseph E. (1982) 'Utilitarianism and horizontal equity: the case for random taxation', *Journal of Public Economics*, 18(1): 1–33. *140*

Stiglitz, Joseph E. (1988) *Economics of the Public Sector*, New York: Norton. *170*

Stiglitz, Joseph E. (1994) *Whither Socialism?*, Cambridge, Mass., and London: MIT Press. *39*

Stiglitz, Joseph E. (2002) 'Information and the change in the paradigm in economics', *American Economic Review*, 92(3): 460–501. *241, 253, 304*

Stiglitz, Joseph E. and Dasgupta, P. (1971) 'Differential taxation, public goods, and economic efficiency', *Review of Economic Studies*, 38: 151–74. *205*

Stone, Arthur A., Shiffman, Saul S. and DeVries, Marten W. (1999) 'Ecological momentary assessment', in Kahneman *et al.* (1999), pp. 26–39. *264*

Stones, M. J., Hadjistavropoulos, Thomas, Tuuko, Holly, and Kozma, Albert (1995) 'Happiness has trait like and state like properties: a reply to Veenhoven', *Social Indicators Research*, 36(2): 129–144. *269*

Stratmann, Thomas (1995) 'Logrolling in the U.S. Congress', *Economic Inquiry*, 33(3): 441–56. *104*

Strauss, John and Thomas, Duncan (1995) 'Health and labour productivity: sorting out the relationships', in *Agricultural Competitiveness: Market Forces and Policy Choice: Proceedings of the Twenty-Second International Conference of Agricultural Economists*, (held in Harare, Zimbabwe, 22–29 August), Aldershot: Dartmouth, pp. 570–90. *142, 228*

Strotz, R. (1958) 'Two propositions related to public goods', *Review of Economics and Statistics*, 40: 329–31. *167*

Sugden, Robert and Weale, Albert (1979) 'A contractual reformulation of certain aspects of welfare economics', *Economica*, 46: 111–23. *108*

Sutton, S. and Davidson, R. (1997) 'Prefrontal brain symmetry: a biological substrate of the behavioral approach and inhibition systems', *Psychological Science*, 8(3): 204–10. *264*

Suzuki, Takashi (1996) 'Intertemporal general equilibrium model with external increasing returns', *Journal of Economic Theory*, 69: 117–33. *241*

Swan, Peter L. (1975) 'The Coase theorem and "sequential" Pareto optimality', *Economic Record*, 51: 269–71. *159*

Switzer, Galen E. *et al.* (1995) 'The effect of a school-based helper program on adolescent self-image, attitudes, and behavior', *Journal of Early Adolescence*, 15(4): 429–55. *261*

Tanzi, Vito and Schuknecht, Ludger (2000) *Global Perspective*, Cambridge: Cambridge University Press. *278*

Tarascio, V. J. (1968) *Pareto's Methodological Approach to Economics*, Chapel Hill, NC: University of North Carolina Press. *47*

Taubman, Paul (1975) *Sources of Inequality in Earnings*, Amsterdam: North-Holland. *136, 138, 139*

Taubman, Paul (1976) 'Earnings, education, genetics, and environment', *Journal of Human Resources*, 11: 447–61. *139*

Taylor, M. J. (1968) 'Graph theoretical approaches to the theory of social choice', *Public Choice*, 4: 35–48. *106*

Thompson, Earl A. (1974) 'Taxation and national defence', *Journal of Political Economy*, 82: 755–82. *206*

Thompson, Earl A. (1979) 'An economic basis for the "national defence argument" for protecting certain industries', *Journal of Political Economy*, 87: 1–36. *206*

Thurow, Lester C. (1971) 'The income distribution as a pure public good', *Quarterly Journal of Economics*, 85: 327–36. *181*

Thurow, Lester C. (1987) *The Zero-sum Society: Distribution and the Possibilities for Economic Change*, London: Penguin.

Tian, Guoqiang (2000) 'Double implementation of Lindahl allocations by a pure mechanism', *Social Choice and Welfare*, 17(1): 125–41. *169*

Tideman, T. Nicolaus and Tullock, Gordon (1976) 'A new and superior process for making social choices', *Journal of Political Economy*, 84: 1145–59. *112, 174, 177*

Tideman, T. Nicolaus and Tullock, Gordon (1977) 'Some limitations of demand revealing process: comment', *Public Choice*, 29: 125–8 (supplement). *179*

Tideman, T. Nicolaus and Tullock, Gordon (1981) 'Coalitions under demand revealing', *Public Choice*, 36: 323–8. *114, 174*

Tiebout, C. M. (1956) 'A pure theory of public expenditures', *Journal of Political Economy*, 64: 416–24. *182*

Tinbergen, Jan (1972) 'Some features of the optimum regime', in Jan Tinbergen *et al.*, *Optimum Social Welfare and Productivity*, New York: New York University Press. *140*

Tinbergen, Jan (1975) *Income Distribution: Analysis and Policies*, Amsterdam: North-Holland. *136*

Toh, Rex S. (1992) 'Experimental measures to curb road congestion in Singapore: pricing and quotas', *Logistics and Transportation Review*, 28(3): 289–317. *305*

Tollison, Robert D. (2001) 'Public spending in the 20th century: the interest-group theory of government: problems and prospects', *Kyklos*, 54(2–3): 465–72. *298*

Tollison, Robert D. and Congleton, Roger D. (eds) (1995) 'The economic analysis of rent seeking', *Elgar Reference Collection. International Library of Critical Writings in Economics*, 49: 371–79, Aldershot: Elgar. *298*

Townsend, H. (ed.) (1971/1980) *Price Theory*, London: Penguin. *244*

Trebing, Harry M. (ed.) (1971) *Essays on Public Utility Pricing and Regulation*, East Lansing, Mich.: Institute of Public Utilities, Michigan State University. *302*

Trebing, Harry M. (ed.) (1976) *New Dimensions in Public Utility Pricing*, East Lansing, Mich.: Institute of Public Utilities, Michigan State University. *302*

Tremblay, C. H. and Tremblay, V. J. (1995), 'Advertising, price, and welfare: evidence from the U.S. brewing industry', *Southern Economic Journal*, 6: 367–381. *270*

Tremblay, Leon and Schultz, Wolfram (1999) 'Relative reward preference in primate orbitofrontal cortex', *Nature*, 398: 704–8. *267*

Tullock, Gordon (1965) *The Politics of Bureaucracy*, Washington, DC: Public Affairs Press. *297*

Tullock, Gordon (1967a) 'The general irrelevance of the general impossibility theorem', *Quarterly Journal of Economics*, 81: 256–70. *106*

Tullock, Gordon (1967b) *Toward a Mathematics of Politics*, Ann Arbor, Mich.: University of Michigan Press. *106, 297*

Tullock, Gordon (1967c) 'The welfare costs of tariffs, monopolies and theft', *Western Economic Journal*, 5: 224–32. *298*

Tullock, Gordon (1975) 'The transitional gains trap', *Bell Journal of Economics*, 6: 671–8. *298*

Tullock, Gordon (1976) *The Vote Motive*, London: Institute of Economic Affairs. *297*

Tullock, Gordon (1977) 'Demand-revealing process, coalitions, and public goods', *Public Choice*, 29: 103–5 (supplement). *180*

Tullock, Gordon (1998) *On Voting: A Public Choice Approach*, Cheltenham, UK and Northampton, Mass.: Edward Elgar. *104*

Tullock, Gordon and Campbell, C. B. (1970) 'Computer simulation of a small voting system', *Economic Journal*, 80: 97–104. *106*

Tuomala, Matti (1990) *Optimal Income Tax and Redistribution*, Oxford, New York, Toronto and Melbourne: Oxford University Press, Clarendon Press. *134*

Turnovsky, Stephen I., Shalit, Haim and Schmitz, Andrew (1980) 'Consumer's surplus, price instability, and consumer welfare',* *Econometrica*, 48: 135–52. *304*

348   *References and Author Index*

Turvey, Ralph (ed.) (1968) *Public Enterprise, Selected Readings*, Harmondsworth: Penguin.

Tversky, Amos and Griffin, Dale (1991) 'Endowment and contrast in judgement of well-being', in R. J. Zecjhauser (ed.), *Strategy and Choice*, Cambridge, Mass.: MIT Press. *79, 287*

Ulph, David (1977) 'On the optimal distribution of income and educational expenditure', *Journal of Public Economics*, 8: 341–56. *139*

US Bureau of Labor Statistics (1986) *Consumer Expenditure Survey: Interview Survey, 1984*, Bulletin 2267, Washington, DC: US Bureau of Labor Statistics. *271*

Van Herwaarden, Floor, Kapteyn, Arie and van Praag, Bernard (1977) 'Twelve thousand individual welfare functions', *European Economic Review*, 9: 283–300. *142*

Van Praag, Bernard M. S. (1968) *Individual Welfare Functions and Consumer Behavior,** Amsterdam: North-Holland. *142*

Van Praag, Bernard M. S. and Frijters, Paul (1999) 'The measurement of welfare and well-being: the Leyden approach', in Kahneman *et al.* (1999), pp. 413–33. *142*

Van Winden, Frans (1999) 'On the economic theory of interest groups: Towards a group frame of reference in political economics', *Public Choice*, 100(1–2): 1–29. *293*

Vaughn, Karen I. (1994) *Austrian Economics in America*, Cambridge: Cambridge University Press. *253*

Veblen, Theodor (1899) *The Theory of the Leisure Class*, New York: Macmillan. *266, 300*

Veenhoven, Ruut (1984) *Conditions of Happiness*, Dordrecht: Kluwer.

Veenhoven, Ruut (1991) 'Is happiness relative?', *Social Indicators Research*, 24: 1–34. *265*

Veenhoven, Ruut (1993) *Happiness in Nations: Subjective Appreciation of Life in 56 Nations 1946–1992*, Rotterdam: RISBO. *142, 262*

Veenhoven, Ruut (2000a) 'Freedom and happiness: a comparative study in 44 nations in the early 1990s', in Diener and Suh. *279*

Veenhoven, Ruut (2000b) 'Well-being in the welfare state: level not higher, distribution not more equitable', *Journal of Comparative Policy Analysis*, 2(1): 91–125.

Veenhoven, Ruut (2002) 'Why social policy needs subjective indicators', *Social Indicators Research*, 58(1–3): 33–45.

Veenhoven, Ruut and Timmermans, D. (1998) *Welvaart en geluk*, ESB. *262*

Vega, Redondo Fernando (1987) 'Efficiency and nonlinear pricing in nonconvex environments with externalities: a generalization of the Lindahl equilibrium concept', *Journal of Economic Theory*, 41(1): 54–67. *169*

Viard, Alan D. (2001) 'Optimal categorical transfer payments: the welfare economics of limited lump-sum redistribution', *Journal of Public Economic Theory*, 3(4): 483–500. *220*

Vickers, Douglas (1997) *Economics and Ethics: An Introduction to Theory, Institutions, and Policy*, Westport, Conn.: Praeger. *5*

Vickrey, William (1945) 'Measuring marginal utilities by reactions to risk', *Econometrica*, 13: 319–33. *105*

Vickrey, William (1961) 'Counterspeculation, auctions and competitive sealed tenders', *Journal of Finance*, 16: 8–37. *174*

Villar, Antonio (1996) *General Equilibrium with Increasing Returns*, Berlin: Springer. *238*

Viner, Jacob (1950) *The Customs Unions Issue*, New York: Carnegie Endowment for International Peace. *133*

Vines, David and Stevenson, Andrew A. (eds) (1997) *Information, Strategy and Public Policy*, Westport, Conn., and London: Greenwood, Praeger. *304*

Vohra, Rajiv (1992) 'Equity and efficiency in non-convex economies', *Social Choice and Welfare*, 9: 185–202. *217*

Vohra, Rajiv (1994) 'Efficient resource allocation under increasing returns', in Dutta (1994). *242*

Wagner, Gary A. (2000) 'New empirical evidence of the role of interest groups in influencing the growth of government', *Journal of Public Finance and Public Choice/ Economia-DelleScelte-Pubbliche*, 18(2–3): 89–99.

Wagner, Gary A. and Sobel, Russell S. (2000) 'New empirical evidence of the role of interest groups in influencing the growth of government', *Journal of Public Finance and Public Choice*, 18(2–3): 83–99. *278*

Walker, David (1955) 'The direct–indirect tax problem: fifteen years of controversy', *Public Finance*, 10: 153–77. *302*

Walsh, Cliff (1975) 'First-party-priority revisited', *Economic Record*, 51: 275–7. *159*

Walsh, David and Gillespie, Austin (1990) *Designer Kids: Consumerism and Competition: When is it all too much?*, Minneapolis, MN: Deaconess Press. *270*

Walters, A. A. (1961) 'The theory measurement of private and social cost of highway congestion', *Econometrica*, 29: 676–97. *304*

Wane, Waly (2001) 'The optimal income tax when poverty is a public "bad" ', *Journal of Public Economics*, 82(2): 271–99. *135*

Warr, Peter (1979) 'Tariff compensation without omniscience', *Economic Record*, 55: 20–32. *207*

Watanabe, Masataka (1999) 'Neurobiology: attraction is relative not absolute', *Nature*, 398: 661–3. *267*

Webb, Michael G. (1976) *Pricing Policies for Public Enterprise*, London: Macmillan. *302*

Weingast, Barry R., Shepsle, Kenneth A. and Johnsen, Christopher (1981) 'The political economy of benefits and costs: a neoclassical approach to distributive politics', *Journal of Political Economy*, 89: 642–64. *298*

Weisbrod, Burton A. (1964) 'Collective-consumption services of individual-consumption goods', *Quarterly Journal of Economics*, 78: 471–7. *289*

Weitzman, Martin L. (2001) 'A contribution to the theory of welfare accounting', *Scandinavian Journal of Economics*, 103(1): 1–23. *82*

Weizsacker, Carl C. von (1965) 'Existence of optimal programs of accumulation for an infinite time horizon',* *Review of Economic Studies*, 32: 85–104, *302*

Weizsacker, Carl C. von (1971) 'Notes on endogenous change of tastes',* *Journal of Economic Theory*, 3: 345–72. *301*

Weldon, J. C. (1952) 'On the problem of social welfare functions', *Canadian Journal of Economics*, 18: 452–63. *104*

Wen, Mei (1997) 'Infrastructure and evolution in division of labor', *Review of Development Economics*, 1(2): 191–206. *248*

Wen, Mei and King, Stephen P. (forthcoming) 'Push or pull? The relationship between development, trade and primary resource endowment'. *Journal of Economic Behavior and Organization. 248*

Wicksell, Knut (1896) *Finanzthearetische Untersuchungen*, Jena: Gustav Fischer. *297*

Wicksteed, Philip H. (1933) *The Common Sense of Political Economy*, in L. Robbins (ed.), London: Routledge. *18, 115*

Widmalm, Frida (2001) 'Tax structure and growth: are some taxes better than others?', *Public Choice*, 107(3–4): 199–219. *135*

Wildasin, David E. (1977) 'Distributional neutrality and optimal commodity taxation', *American Economic Review*, 67: 889–98. *302*

Wiles, P. J. D. (1964) *The Political Economy of Communism*, Cambridge, Mass.: Harvard University Press. *39*

Wilkie, William L. (1994) *Consumer Behavior*, 3rd edn, New York: John Wiley. *270*

Wilkinson, Richard G. (1997) 'Health inequalities: relative or absolute material standards?', *British Medical Journal*, 314: 591–5. *266, 281*

Willig, Robert D. (1976) 'Consumer's surplus without apology', *American Economic Review*, 66: 589–97. *82*

Wilson, E. O. (1975) *Sociobiology: The New Synthesis*, Cambridge, Mass.: Harvard University Press. *10, 268, 270*

Wilson, John D. (1991) 'Optimal public good provision with limited lump-sum taxation', *American Economic Review*, 81(1): 153–66. *170*

Wilson, John D. (1992) 'Optimal income taxation and international personal mobility', *American Economic Review*, 82(2): 191–6. *205, 302*

Wilson, Robert (1969) 'An axiomatic model of logrolling', *American Economic Review*, 59: 331–41. *105*

Wilson, Robert (1975) 'Informational economies of scale', *Bell Journal of Economics and Management Science*, 6(1): 184–95. *234*

Winch, David M. (1965) 'Consumer's surplus and the compensation principle', *American Economic Review*, 55: 395–423. *71, 72, 85*

Winch, David M. (1971) *Analytical Welfare Economics*, Harmondsworth: Penguin. *28, 190*

Winkelmann, Liliana and Winkelmann, Rainer (1998) 'Why are the unemployed so unhappy?', *Economica*, 65: 1–15. *263, 281*

Wittman, Donald (1995) *The Myth of Democratic Failure: Why Political Institutions Are Efficient*, Chicago, Ill: University of Chicago Press. *298*

Woittiez, I. and Kapteyn, A. (1998) 'Social interactions and habit formation in a model of female labour supply' *Journal of Public Economics*, 70: 185–205. *266*

Wolpin, Kenneth I. (1977) 'Education and screening', *American Economic Review*, 67: 949–58.

World Bank (1994) *World Development Report: Infrastructure for Development*, Oxford: Oxford University Press. *246*

Wright, Newell and Larsen, Val (1993) 'Materialism and life satisfaction: a meta-analysis', *Journal of Consumer Satisfaction, Dissatisfaction, and Complaining Behavior*, 6: 158–65. *269*

Yang, Xiaokai (2001) *Economics: New Classical versus Neoclassical Frameworks*, Malden, Mass.: Blackwell. *232, 233, 251, 265*

Yang, Xiaokai (2003) 'Where do we stand: a review of the literature of infra-marginal analysis of network of division of labour', in Ng et al. (2003). *232, 256*

Yang, Xiaokai and Borland, J. (1991) 'A microeconomic mechanism for economic growth', *Journal of Political Economy*, 99: 460–82. *256*

Yang, Xiaokai and Ng, Siang (1998) 'Specialization and division of labor: a survey', in K. Arrow, Y.-K. Ng and Xiaokai Yang (eds), *Increasing Returns and Economic Analysis*, London, Macmillan. *232*

Yang, Xiaokai and Ng, Yew-Kwang (1993) *Specialization and Economic Organization*, Amsterdam: North-Holland. *230, 232, 233, 243, 244, 251, 253, 254, 255, 256, 286*

Yarrow, G. K. (1985) 'Welfare losses in oligopoly and monopolistic competition', *Journal of Industrial Economics*, 33(4): 515–29. *299*

Yeh, Y. (1972) 'On the situation utility possibility curve', *Kyklos*, 38: 413–20. *33*

Subject Index